P9-CDF-377

READY TO GO ³

Language • Lifeskills • Civics

Joan Saslow

Regional Consultant Board

Ann Belletire	Sandra Bergman	Sherie Burnette	Michael Feher	Susan B. Kanter
Illinois	*New York*	*Texas*	*Massachusetts*	*Texas*
Brigitte Marshall	Monica Oliva	Mary E. O'Neill	Grace Tanaka	Marcia L. Taylor
California	*Florida*	*Virginia*	*California*	*Indiana*

Edwina Hoffman
Dade County Public Schools
Series Advisor

Grace Tanaka
Santa Ana College
Pedagogical Advisor

Kristin Sherman
Teacher's Edition
Writer

Longman

Ready to Go: Language, Lifeskills, Civics 3
Teacher's Edition

Pearson Education, 10 Bank Street, White Plains, NY 10606

Vice president, instructional design: Allen Ascher
Senior acquisitions editor: Marian Wassner
Senior development editor: Marcia Schonzeit
Development editors: Julie Rouse, Peter Benson
Vice president, director of design and production: Rhea Banker
Executive managing editor: Linda Moser
Production editor: Kathleen Silloway
Ready to Go production editor: Marc Oliver
Production supervisor: Liza Pleva
Ready to Go production supervisor: Ray Keating
Director of manufacturing: Patrice Fraccio
Senior manufacturing buyer: Dave Dickey
Cover design: Ann France
Text design: Ann France
Text composition and art direction: Word and Image Design Studio Inc.
Ready to Go text composition: Lehigh Press
Illustrations: Craig Attebery, pp. 1, 3, 6, 7, 19, 20, 34, 44, 48, 58, 60, 61, 62, 74, 86, 87, 88, 89, 90, 105, 118, 119; Brian Hughes, pp. 16, 17, 18, 25, 29, 30, 31, 39, 43, 46, 47, 72, 73, 83, 99, 100, 101, 115; Dave McKay, pp. 57, 67, 102, 109, 127, 128, 137; Suzanne Mogensen, pp. 21, 37, 39, 53, 66, 75, 85, 87, 95, 111; NSV Productions, pp. 4, 15, 16, 28, 33, 44, 45, 71, 75, 77, 78, 79, 80, 81, 84, 102, 103, 113, 114, 117, 122, 123; Dusan Petricic, pp. 2, 31, 32, 108; Meryl Treatner, pp. 5, 8, 22, 23, 36, 50, 64, 76, 92, 106, 120, 134; Anna Veltfort, pp. 5, 12, 26, 40, 54, 68, 82, 89, 96, 105, 124, 129, 138; Word & Image Design, pp. 11, 14, 17, 32, 35, 39, 42, 53, 59, 62, 70, 95, 98, 108, 110, 116, 123, 126, 128, 133, 137, 139, 152, 153, 154, 155, 156, 157, 158, 160, 161, 162, 163
p. 159: Reprinted by permission of New York City Department of Sanitation, Bureau of Waste Prevention, Reuse and Recycling.
Photography: Gilbert Duclos, pp. 2, 3, 4, 5, 9, 10, 16, 17, 18, 19, 23, 30, 31, 32, 33, 35, 37, 39, 43, 44, 45, 46, 47, 48, 49, 51, 58, 59, 60, 61, 65, 72, 75, 77, 86, 87, 88, 89, 93, 95, 100, 101, 102, 103, 107, 114, 115, 116, 117, 121, 128, 129, 130, 131, 133, 135

This book was set in 10/12 Palatino.

ISBN: 0-13-183466-5

1 2 3 4 5 6 7 8 9 10—WC— 08 07 06 05 04 03

Contents

Introduction to the *Ready to Go* Teacher's Edition

What Is the *Ready to Go* Course?

Ready to Go: Language, Lifeskills, Civics is a four-level, standards-based course in English as a second language. *Ready to Go* prepares adults for self-sufficiency in the three principal areas of their lives: the community, the home, and the workplace.

Communicative competence in English is of critical importance in achieving self-sufficiency. *Ready to Go* applies the best of current second language acquisition research to ensure immediate success, rapidly enabling learners to

➤ understand the spoken and written language of daily life.

➤ communicate orally and in writing.

➤ understand the culture and civic expectations of their new environment.

➤ master lifeskills necessary to survive and thrive in the American community and workplace.

To achieve these goals with efficiency and speed, *Ready to Go* weaves together three integrated strands: language, lifeskills, and civics*, tightly correlating the major state and federal standards with a complete language syllabus and relevant social language.

Ready to Go is designed to be used in a period of 60 to 90 classroom hours. This period can be shortened or lengthened, based on the needs of the group or the program.

Who Is the *Ready to Go* Student?

The adult intermediate learner: *Ready to Go 3* is designed for the adult learner who understands much spoken and written English but often communicates with difficulty and many errors. *Ready to Go 3* is appropriate for multilevel intermediate classes, or for students who have completed *Ready to Go 2*. A placement test is available for accurately placing students in the *Ready to Go* series. The *Ready*

to Go student is an adult immigrant to the United States whose goal is to be able to communicate orally and in writing in all aspects of life.

What Is the *Ready to Go* Approach?

Controlled introduction of language: To build confidence and ensure success, the *Ready to Go* Student's Book controls the introduction and practice of language. All new words and grammatical structures are carefully and completely presented so that students acquire them with ease and speed. All language tasks and activities can be successfully accomplished by students of all ability levels, using the language learned in *Ready to Go*.

Practical conversational models: Conversational models in *Ready to Go* have been thoughtfully created to be practical in the life and work of all students in the class. Some models take place in the world of work. It should be noted, though, that none of the conversations that take place in a workplace are job- or work-specific. Moreover, the language in such conversations is social and usable in the life of every student in the class. This universality makes *Ready to Go* broadly usable and effective for all students, those who work and those who don't, and it speeds their arrival at self-sufficiency in any life or work path.

Authentic practice: In addition to the controlled productive tasks and activities in each Student's Book unit, a unique set of activities labeled *Authentic practice* exposes students to comprehensible language <u>above</u> their own productive levels and provides a rehearsal in dealing with it. This real-life rehearsal prepares students to meet their urgent need to function outside an English class and gives them practice responding to real spoken and written language they will encounter, at home, in their communities, and on the job if they work.

Activities for students of diverse levels within the same classroom: Every task and activity in *Ready to Go* can be successfully completed by all students in the class. In addition, each two-page spread pro-

---

*In *Ready to Go*, the term "civics" refers to concepts that introduce learners to expected social behavior in this culture, an understanding of which is essential *before* students can participate fully or truly understand their rights and responsibilities as citizens. The term does not refer to citizenship education.

vides a closing activity labeled *Do it yourself!* in which students of diverse language abilities and levels can move ahead at their own pace.

A communicative ESL course with an integrated and enriched focus: *Ready to Go* employs the most up-to-date language teaching methodology, emphasizing

➤ acquisition of vocabulary and social language.

➤ presentation and practice of essential grammatical structures.

➤ continual opportunities for controlled and free communicative practice in all four language skills of listening, speaking, reading, and writing.

➤ frequent recycling and review.

Classroom Methodology

The following information has been provided to help you understand the underlying philosophy behind *Ready to Go* and to offer some general suggestions for using the material. Specific suggestions for teaching every exercise in every unit are given in the interleaved *Teacher's Notes* pages of this Teacher's Edition. The extent to which you use these recommendations is up to you; all suggestions may not be appropriate for all groups, and you should tailor the lesson to reflect your own background, personal approach, and training, as well as the specific needs of your students.

Pair work and collaborative activities: On every page of *Ready to Go*, opportunities for pair work, group work, and collaborative activities encourage students to take a more active and creative role in learning and allow the maximum number of students to participate. These activities encourage students to use their own language resources, making the lesson more personalized and meaningful. They also ensure that students have opportunities to initiate, as well as to respond to, conversation in English. Furthermore, in working together to solve problems, students get to know each other faster and become more independent, relying less on the teacher for guidance and ultimately taking more responsibility for their own learning. We recommend the following approaches for pair and group work activities:

➤ A student-centered approach: Some students, particularly those accustomed to teacher-centered lessons, may not immediately see the benefits of working in pairs or groups. The first time you use pair and group work, point out to students that working together allows them more time to practice English and allows you to listen to more students at once.

➤ Cooperative learning: Encourage students to help and learn from each other. Whenever possible, try to elicit answers from other students before answering a question yourself. If a student asks a question that was previously asked by another student, direct the question to the student who first asked the question. In restating information they have recently obtained in their own words, students internalize the language, increasing the likelihood that it will be retained.

➤ Seating arrangement: To ensure that students interact with a variety of partners, have students sit in a different location for each class. In multicultural classes, when dividing the class into pairs or groups, try to match students from different nationalities and backgrounds. One method of forming groups is to have students count off according to the number of groups needed. (The 1s work together, the 2s work together, and so on.)

➤ Teacher monitoring: Circulate during pair and group work activities, keeping students on task and offering help as needed. When dividing the class into pairs, avoid playing a partner role yourself, as this will limit your ability to monitor and offer assistance to the class. If faced with an odd number of students, create a group of three students, with a third role added as a helper to encourage eye contact and to correct mistakes.

➤ Building student confidence: Before asking students to speak in front of the class, build their confidence by having them rehearse language in pairs, in small groups, or as a class. Also, allowing students to collaborate on writing exercises, either by comparing their answers with a partner or by completing the activity in pairs, helps avoid the potential embarrassment of giving an incorrect answer when reviewing as a class.

➤ Time management: To keep students on task, set time limits for each activity. End activities before most of the class is finished to avoid dead time. Prepare additional activities for students who finish early. For example, have students who have finished practicing a *Pair work* conversation write the conversation that they created.

Correction: Most students of languages, particularly adult learners, like feedback and expect to be corrected when they make a mistake. However, studies have shown that it is repeated exposure to correct usage, rather than constant correction, that results in the internalization of new speech. In addition, excessive correction can embarrass and discourage students, making them reluctant to attempt the experimentation and practice that lead to language acquisition. We recommend the following approaches for providing effective positive feedback:

➤ Accuracy: For activities in which accuracy is the focus, such as in the *Practical conversations*, correct mistakes shortly after they occur. Immediate correction is important for controlled activities in which students need guidance in using the new language.

➤ Fluency: For activities in which fluency is the focus, such as the *Do it yourself!* activities, refrain from stopping the flow of student conversation with corrections. In these activities, accuracy is less important than the ability to improvise with known language. Developing improvisation skills is critical if students are to convert the English they have learned in the classroom into the English they need to function in their own lives. Interrupting students with corrections discourages this experimentation. Instead, take notes on common student mistakes and then review these errors as a class at the end of the activity.

➤ Self-correction: Students are often able to correct their own mistakes. First, allow the student to finish the thought; then show by sound or gesture that there has been a mistake. Try to indicate where the mistake was and give the student an opportunity to self-correct. Some techniques for eliciting self-correction include counting off each word of the phrase on fingers and pausing at the mistake, repeating the student sentence and pausing at the mistake, or prompting the student with a missing word. A less intrusive method is to correct the student's mistake by reformulating what the student said without stopping the flow of conversation. For example: *S: He have a car. T: Oh, he has a car? S: Yes, he has a car.* Note that this technique often prompts the student to self-correct.

➤ Selectivity: Don't discourage or overwhelm students by correcting every mistake. Focus corrections on the skills that are being taught or mistakes that prevent comprehension.

➤ Supportiveness: Above all, avoid making students feel pressured; give students enough time to think. Be careful not to stigmatize or embarrass students. Be aware that students from some cultural backgrounds may be sensitive to criticism in front of their peers and may prefer more private feedback.

Checking answers: For exercises or homework requiring a written response, have students check their answers with a partner. This encourages students to correct their own mistakes and also helps them avoid the possible embarrassment of giving incorrect answers in front of the entire class. When the class has finished comparing answers, review the correct answers as a class, either by eliciting the answers from individual students or by having volunteers write their answers on the board. In classes with time constraints, write answers on the board and have the class self-correct.

Repetition: Repetition of conversational models and new vocabulary within the *Practical conversations* sections helps students internalize correct word order, stress, and pronunciation. Note that the language that students repeat in these activities has been recorded twice on the cassette. After each recorded utterance, there is space for student repetition, followed by the recorded utterance again to confirm and reinforce pronunciation. Students listen to each utterance, repeat, and then listen again to the confirmation. Here are some tips for using repetition to facilitate learning:

➤ Open or closed books: For activities requiring students to listen and repeat, have students first listen while looking at the written form in their textbooks. This allows students to link the written form in the book to the sound they hear. In the next step, when students are asked to listen and repeat, have them listen and repeat with their books closed. This serves to reduce distractions and allows students to focus exclusively on listening and repeating rather than reading.

➤ Practice drills: Periodically, introduce short, fast-paced repetition drills to offer the class more pronunciation practice, reinforce word order or grammatical structures, and provide a change of pace. Start by modeling the new language and having the class repeat after you. Say the new language again and elicit further repetition from the class. Continue in this manner several times. Then say the language again, point to an individual student, and have that student repeat. Continue the drill by saying the language again and pointing to another student. Modeling the new language before and after each student's response helps students build auditory memory while providing students with a correct model for repetition.

➤ Pace: Keeping the pace of repetition drills lively gives the maximum number of students a chance to speak and maximizes their exposure to the language. If a student cannot respond or makes a mistake, move on quickly to another student and then return to the student who made a mistake. Maintaining the pace gives weaker students the time that they need to internalize and ultimately access new language.

Realia—bringing the outside in: Research has demonstrated that language is easier to comprehend and retain if presented in conjunction with sensory input such as pictures, sounds, props, and authentic documents. In addition, bringing real material into the classroom serves to motivate students and help them understand the relevance of their language study to their own lives.

The *Do it yourself!* and *Authentic practice* sections of *Ready to Go* build students' understanding and competence with authentic documents by including near-authentic documents within the text itself. The *Teacher's Notes* include suggestions for enhancing this material with other realia, such as job applications, maps, building diagrams, and product warranties.

In addition, a *Supplementary authentic documents* section on pages 151 through 162 provides more real-life documents—such as applications, maps, forms, and letters—that students can use for role-plays and more writing practice.

Elicitation: Asking questions keeps the class active and involved and helps you to identify what students understand and what they do not. An effective method for eliciting language from the class is first to provide a model that students understand and then to have them create language using the model. For example, before eliciting a list of weather adjectives from the class, provide examples by writing on the board several weather adjectives that students have learned. Some additional elicitation techniques to consider include the following:

➤ Warming up: Direct questions to the entire class before eliciting answers from individual students. This reduces the pressure on individual students to produce a response before they are ready and provides the class with a model of a correct response.

➤ Allowing one-word answers: It is not always necessary for students to answer in full sentences; often a one-word answer is sufficient to demonstrate understanding of the question and to respond appropriately. This encourages students to communicate using any relevant productive English they have previously acquired. Moreover, it allows students to speak "real" language from the start, as one-word responses are often more authentic in informal contexts than full-sentence responses.

➤ Pairing or grouping students: To maximize students' oral productivity, it is often helpful to provide opportunities for students to practice with a partner or in a small group before asking them to respond in open class.

Teaching multilevel classes: The adult education ESL class is generally made up of students at different levels of ability and achievement. To accommodate students of diverse levels within the same classroom, we recommend the following approaches:

➤ Modeling: Use more advanced students to model activities. Advanced students, with their quicker comprehension time, are more likely to respond quickly and correctly. This will allow weaker students, who need longer exposure time to new language, to use the stronger students' responses as a model and respond successfully.

➤ Grouping: In pair and group work activities, varying your approach to grouping students keeps the activities fresh. Partnering more advanced students with weaker students encourages the class to help and learn from each other. Partnering students with similar ability levels also has advantages, as this allows pairs to speak at their own pace and level of production.

➤ Differentiating instruction: Optional and *Challenge* activities with varying levels of difficulty are suggested throughout the interleaved *Teacher's Notes* pages of this Teacher's Edition. Pairs or groups of students can be engaged in different activities at the same time, according to their levels of proficiency or learning styles.

The *Ready to Go* Unit: General Teaching Suggestions

The following information has been provided to describe the features and offer general suggestions for getting the most out of each section of a *Ready to Go* unit. More detailed procedures for teaching each exercise in each unit, as well as ideas for optional expansion activities and relevant notes on language and culture, are suggested in the interleaved *Teacher's Notes* pages of this Teacher's Edition.

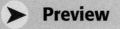 **Preview**

The *Preview* page provides an introduction to each unit's content and is designed to activate students' prior knowledge and experience. Previous exposure to English enables the *Ready to Go 3* student to discuss and make predictions about the content of a unit before it is fully presented. The *Preview* page consists of a *Warm up* activity and the *Unit objectives*.

Warm up: A picture, near-authentic document, or other illustration helps focus students on the content of the unit and provides them with an opportunity to relate what they already know. The interleaved *Teacher's Notes* pages of this Teacher's Edition contain numerous concrete suggestions for presenting the *Warm up* activity. Some general suggestions follow:

➤ Focus students' attention on the illustration in the *Warm up*. Ask questions that prompt students to look closely at the illustration and to speculate about the information represented.

➤ Ask questions that encourage students to relate the content represented in the illustration to their own lives and prior experiences.

➤ Summarize and check comprehension by eliciting answers to the question that precedes the illustration.

➤ Note that the illustration presented in the *Warm up* often reappears later in the unit. In-depth discussions of near-authentic documents with extensive text are more appropriate when the same or a similar document is presented the second time, as the purpose of the *Warm up* is more to generate interest than to master new material.

Unit objectives: Making students aware of unit objectives helps them to assess their needs, set learning goals, and evaluate their own progress. Being cognizant of what they should know and be able to do by the end of the unit may encourage students to take greater responsibility for their own learning and increase retention. Discussing the objectives also creates an opportunity to provide students with additional comprehensible input. The interleaved *Teacher's Notes* pages of this Teacher's Edition contain numerous concrete suggestions for presenting the *Unit objectives*. Some general suggestions follow:

➤ Read each objective out loud. Check comprehension by eliciting the meaning of words or phrases that might be difficult or unfamiliar to students. If necessary, use simple definitions to explain new vocabulary.

➤ For each objective, elicit from the class examples of how to do what is described. If after prompts or hints the class is unable to provide any examples, move on to the next objective.

➤ Note that the objectives appear again at the end of the unit, where students are asked to check what they are then able to do.

➤ Practical conversations

This section provides natural, memorable conversation models that can be used in diverse, out-of-class situations. They show students the purposeful use of essential vocabulary and social language. Active vocabulary introduced on the *Practical conversations* page supports and reinforces the topics of the conversation and of the unit. In the controlled *Pair work* activities that follow each conversation, students use the words they know to manipulate the conversational model. In this way, students gain confidence and take ownership of the language, transferring the language to their own lives.

The interleaved *Teacher's Notes* pages of this Teacher's Edition contain numerous concrete suggestions for presenting the model conversations, *Vocabulary*, and *Pair work* activities on the *Practical conversations* pages. Some general suggestions follow:

Conversational model:

➤ Focus students' attention on the photo and any related illustration. Set the scene for the conversation by asking questions about the people, actions, setting, and content of the illustration. When asking questions, be mindful of what students are capable of answering; don't elicit information or language that students would not know prior to reading the conversation.

➤ For Exercise A, read the model conversation out loud or play the cassette. Have students listen and read with books open. If you read the conversation yourself, attempt to distinguish the two speakers by changing your voice or position for each role. Alternatively, have a student who reads clearly and comprehensibly play one of the roles. If possible, choose a student at the back of the room so that the class will be able to hear.

➤ Check that students understand the model conversation. One method is to ask the class comprehension questions about the conversation. For each model conversation, the *Teacher's Notes* offer concrete suggestions on how to check comprehension and convey the meaning of any new language that is introduced.

➤ For Exercise B, read the conversation again or play the cassette. With books open or closed—depending on students' needs or your preference, or alternating for variety—have students listen and repeat after each line. Encourage students to imitate the rhythm, stress, and intonation of the conversation as closely as possible. Correct where necessary, helping students to pronounce the language clearly.

Vocabulary:

➤ Focus students' attention on the illustrations in the *Vocabulary* box.

➤ Read each vocabulary word or phrase out loud or play the cassette. When pronouncing vocabulary, say each word clearly, but do not slow down to the point of sounding unnatural. You may wish to first say each word a little more slowly first and then at a natural speed.

➤ Note that singular count nouns are preceded by the indefinite article *a / an* in the *Vocabulary* box. Use the article when reading the words out loud to contrast singular count nouns from non-count nouns. For students of certain language backgrounds, the concept of count and non-count nouns provides a great challenge, even at this level; internalizing it is a lengthy process and the use of the indefinite article is an important first step.

➤ If necessary, clarify or reinforce the meaning of any words students have difficulty understanding. The *Teacher's Notes* offer suggestions on how to effectively convey ideas physically through the use of mime, gestures, tone of voice, pictures, flash cards, props, or other realia.

➤ You may wish to say some or all of the words in a sentence using known vocabulary to demonstrate usage, make them more memorable, and put them into the context of the unit. It may also be helpful to elicit from the class synonyms, antonyms, examples, and simple definitions of the words.

➤ Brainstorm and write on the board other similar words and phrases that students already know. List students' ideas in the same way that the *Vocabulary* is presented, for example, using the indefinite article or in gerund form. This provides students with more language to use in the *Pair work* activity and increases students' confidence by helping them realize how much English they have already acquired.

Pair work:

➤ For the *Pair work* activity (Exercise C), read the instructions out loud. Then model the conversa-

tion with a more advanced student to demonstrate that students should substitute their own words or the words provided.

➤ Note that for many *Practical conversations* models, a list of relevant language has been surprinted on the Student's Book page in the Teacher's Edition. This list has been provided as a summary of the productive-level language that students have learned in prior *Ready to Go 3* activities and that could be substituted in the model. Actual student responses will vary, depending on each student's ability or ideas.

➤ Have students practice the *Pair work* conversation in pairs. The importance of this activity cannot be overstated, for it is in producing their own language in this controlled activity that students take their first steps toward truly free language.

➤ Circulate and offer help as needed. Be sure that students make eye contact during conversations to encourage natural pronunciation and tone. To review, have several volunteer pairs act out their conversations in front of the class.

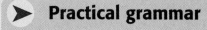

➤ Practical grammar

Each new grammar structure is clearly presented through examples followed by concise, controlled exercises to help students begin to use that structure. Grammar boxes generally offer examples rather than rules, except where necessary avoiding the use of terminology and concepts that might not be familiar to many students. Exercises provide written practice of the structures just taught while also offering further models of authentic language. For more thorough practice, many additional exercises appear in the accompanying workbook.

While grammar structures are formally presented in the *Practical grammar* section, exposure to the structures is integrated into the entire unit so that students have multiple opportunities to see and use them. For example, the *Practical conversations* section shows the grammar structure in action without requiring students to manipulate it. The grammar structures are also reinforced and practiced in the *Do it yourself!* and *Authentic practice* sections.

The interleaved *Teacher's Notes* pages of this Teacher's Edition contain numerous concrete suggestions for presenting the grammar structure and exercises. Some general suggestions follow:

➤ Inductive presentation: To present grammar with an inductive approach, start by providing numerous examples of the new structure in a natural context. Then encourage students to infer how to form or use the structure from the examples.

➤ Deductive presentation: Begin by presenting the concept and then follow it with examples from the grammar box. Involve students while you write these examples on the board.

➤ Exercises: Read the instructions out loud. If necessary, model how to do the first item in each task. Have students complete the exercises individually, in pairs, or in small groups. Circulate and offer help as needed. Before reviewing answers as a class, have students check answers with a partner.

➤ Authentic practice

Because adult immigrants must function in the world outside class immediately, even with the limited language they know, the *Authentic practice* sections provide opportunities for students to respond to language that they will encounter outside class.

This practice boosts students' confidence and decreases their potential panic when confronted with unknown language. In addition, these activities build the essential skill of improvisation: accessing known language in a spontaneous way to respond appropriately in the uncontrolled environment outside an English class.

Picture story: Students are presented with an illustrated conversation containing a mixture of known ("productive-level") language and not-yet-known ("receptive-level") language. The receptive-level language has been carefully chosen and extensively classroom tested for comprehensibility. Although students are encouraged to comprehend this new language through context—aided by carefully drawn illustrations—and through its similarity to language they know, it is not essential for students to know what every word means.

Three exercises follow the picture story. The purpose of Exercise A is to check students' comprehension of the conversation. In Exercises B and C, students listen to receptive-level language models and select or read an appropriate response. The student's role (titled (YOU)) consists entirely of language students have already learned and is meant to serve as an example of what they can do with this language. These exercises further suggest to stu-

dents how much language they already know and prepare them for success with the free-response *Do it yourself!* activities on the facing page.

The interleaved *Teacher's Notes* pages of this Teacher's Edition contain numerous concrete suggestions for presenting the picture stories and accompanying exercises. Some general suggestions follow:

➤ Set the scene for the conversation. One method is to focus students' attention on the illustrations. For example, point to a picture and ask questions about the people, actions, and setting. When asking questions, however, be mindful of what students are capable of saying; don't elicit information or language that students would not know prior to reading the conversation.

➤ Read the conversation out loud or play the cassette. Have students listen and read with books open. If you read the conversation yourself, attempt to distinguish between or among the speakers by changing your voice or position for each role. Alternatively, have more advanced students read the other roles.

➤ Check that students understand the picture story. One method is to ask the class comprehension questions about the conversation. For each picture story, the *Teacher's Notes* offer concrete suggestions on how to check comprehension and encourage students to relate the content of the conversation to their own lives and prior experiences.

➤ For Exercise A, read the instructions out loud, and have students read the items individually. Then play the cassette or read the conversation a second time. Students complete the activity, referring to the picture story as necessary, and then compare answers with a partner. Review as a class.

➤ For Exercise B, model the task by completing item 1 as a class. Copy the two answer choices from item 1 on the board. Read item 1 from the tapescript or play the cassette. Elicit the correct response from the class. Demonstrate on the board that students should underline the correct response. Then read items 2 and 3 from the tapescript or play the cassette. Working individually, students listen to the items and underline the correct response.

➤ Have students compare their answers to Exercise B with at least one classmate before having them read their responses out loud as a class in Exercise C. If necessary, help students to pronounce their responses correctly by reading each answer and having students repeat.

Listening comprehension: By further exposing students to authentic models of both already learned ("productive-level") and comprehensible unknown ("receptive-level") language, these exercises reinforce students' confidence and skill in dealing with "real-world" encounters. Great care has been taken to ensure the comprehensibility of the receptive-level language. By encouraging students to use the pictures, context clues, intonation, and language they already know to understand new language, these activities demonstrate to students that it's not necessary to know every word in order to understand what is being said. As students increase their listening confidence, potential panic with unknown language outside of class will decrease.

The interleaved *Teacher's Notes* pages of this Teacher's Edition contain numerous concrete suggestions for presenting the *Listening comprehension* activities. Some general suggestions follow:

➤ Before class, read the tapescript to anticipate its content and language. Keep in mind—and point out to students—that a major cause of lack of comprehension is the natural panic that occurs when learners hear unknown words and that it is not necessary for students to understand every word to understand the selection. Again, if a student specifically asks for the meaning of a new word, give the meaning but avoid spending a lot of time on it.

➤ Before students listen to the selection, you may wish to tell them what they are about to hear by identifying the speakers, setting, or situation.

➤ To give students an idea of the "big picture," read the selection on the tapescript out loud or play the cassette while students listen with books closed.

➤ If you read the conversation yourself, attempt to distinguish the two speakers by changing your voice or position for each role. Be sure to read in a clear, natural voice. Avoid slowing down your speech so much that it becomes unnatural. Instead, read the selection with a natural voice as many times as necessary for students to understand.

➤ Read the instructions out loud. Before having students listen again and complete the exercise, focus their attention on the specific listening task, such as listening for do's and don'ts.

➤ Read the selection on the tapescript out loud or play the cassette as many times as necessary for students to complete the activity. Do not approach these exercises as "tests." Repeated exposure to each listening sample has substantial instructional value; increasing students' exposure to challenging language enhances their comprehension and confidence.

➤ Have students check their answers to the exercises with a partner before reviewing as a class.

➤ In *True story* activities, students have an opportunity to relate the content of the *Listening comprehension* selection to their own lives or prior experiences. Read the instructions for the *True story* activity out loud. Then model the activity by describing your own experience. Ask the class comprehension questions about your story to reinforce what information students should include when they talk about their own experiences in small groups. Circulate and listen as students discuss.

Ask Joan: In *Ask Joan*— an advice column that provides culture tips for newcomers—a humorous and personalized set of questions and answers prepares students to understand their rights and responsibilities and the civic and behavioral expectations of the North American community and workplace. Each column is followed by activities that build students' ability to function in the community and workplace with confidence. Again, the goal of this practice is to boost students' level of comfort and decrease their potential panic when confronted with unfamiliar situations.

The interleaved *Teacher's Notes* pages of this Teacher's Edition contain numerous concrete suggestions for presenting the *Ask Joan* feature. Some general suggestions follow:

➤ Play the cassette or read the letters. Pause after each letter and ask the class to identify the problem or suggested solution. To foster students' ability to capture the main idea, discourage the use of dictionaries. Point out that students do not need to understand every word to understand the question the newcomer has and the advice Joan offers in response.

➤ Encourage students to guess at the meaning of new words as much as possible. In this way, you will be preparing students to cope with readings outside class while also developing their ability to function independently without the aid of an instructor.

➤ You may wish to ask additional comprehension questions about what was read. Note that a single word or phrase is often sufficient to demonstrate understanding of the question and respond appropriately. Suggested comprehension questions are offered in the *Teacher's Notes*.

➤ Have students read the directions for each exercise, or read the directions out loud. If necessary, model the task on the board. Allow students a set period of time to refer to the reading as necessary and complete the exercises individually, in pairs, or in a small group.

➤ Have students check their work with a partner and then review answers as a class.

➤ You may wish to use the *Ask Joan* readings to point out in context the use of structures presented in the *Practical grammar* section or patterns of stress and intonation that can be heard on the cassette.

Authentic documents: Adult immigrants are called on daily to interact with written documents containing unknown language. For this reason, *Ready to Go 3* provides practice with documents and other text types (including information from Web sites) similar to the ones they will encounter within the safe environment of the English class. These documents have been carefully constructed to be comprehensible yet challenging and authentic. The focus is on purposefulness; students practice dealing with such essential documents as employment applications, public transportation maps, product warranties and proof-of-purchase cards, consumer complaint letters and responses, and classified job ads. In addition, the exercises that follow each document help students to develop critical thinking skills such as reasoning, problem solving, and decision making.

The interleaved *Teacher's Notes* pages of this Teacher's Edition contain numerous concrete suggestions for presenting activities based on near-authentic documents. Some general suggestions follow:

➤ Before formally presenting each document, allow students a set period of time to explore the document silently.

➤ Have students read without dictionaries to encourage them to read for general meaning rather than word for word. Again, encourage students to guess at the meaning of new words as much as possible.

➤ Read the document out loud or have students take turns reading it out loud.

➤ To check comprehension, you may wish to ask questions about the document. Suggested comprehension questions are offered in the *Teacher's Notes*.

➤ To prepare students for the task, read the directions to the exercise out loud. If necessary, model the task on the board.

➤ Allow students a set period of time to read the document again and then complete the exercise individually, in pairs, or in a small group.

➤ Have students check their work with a partner and then review answers on the board as a class.

➤ Review

Following each unit is a three-page, four-skill review that offers students an opportunity to check their progress. It also allows the teacher to identify any areas of particular difficulty that may require additional practice.

Exercise A (full-page illustration): A special feature of the *Ready to Go* series is the full-page illustration located at the end of each unit. This open-ended activity is designed to elicit from students all the language they know—vocabulary, social language, and grammar. The picture provides a clear visual context for practice and helps students bridge the gap between language practice and authentic language use.

The picture can be used a number of ways for extensive oral practice. Working in pairs, in small groups, or as a class, students can find and name items in the picture, ask and answer questions about the picture, create conversations between the people in the picture, or take turns telling stories about people or situations in the picture. More specific suggestions for getting the most out of each illustration are given in the interleaved *Teacher's Notes* pages of this Teacher's Edition. Some general suggestions follow:

➤ Begin by allowing students time to look at the illustration. Note that, for some illustrations, students will have already practiced talking about a portion of the illustration in the *Do it yourself!* exercises earlier in the unit.

➤ In pairs, small groups, or as a class, students practice asking and answering questions, creating their own conversations for the people in the picture, and making up stories based on the illustration. For each illustration, several *Options* provide specific ideas for prompting students to tell stories and use essential content from the unit to say as much as they can about the picture.

➤ Circulate and offer help as needed. To encourage the risk taking and improvisation that are the major goals of these activities, avoid interrupting students with corrections. Instead, take notes on common student mistakes and review them as a class at the end of the activity. Encourage students to say as much as they can and to extend the suggested tasks as much as possible.

Other exercises: Completing the other *Review* exercises allows students to check their own ability to understand and use new language. The exercises review the essential content of the unit and include listening, speaking, reading, and writing tasks. Optional activities in the interleaved *Teachers' Notes* can be used to provide further practice as needed. Some general suggestions for presenting the *Review* exercises follow:

➤ Students work individually to complete the review exercises.

➤ Circulate to offer help as needed.

➤ Have students check answers with a partner. Review answers as a class.

➤ Identify any areas of difficulty that may require additional instruction and practice.

Composition: The last activity in each unit asks students to turn back to the full-page illustration at the beginning of the *Review* section. On a separate sheet of paper, students write about the picture. In their workplaces, students may need to write descriptions, short narratives, reports, and / or letters. This activity provides them with practice writing in a safe environment. Ideas specific to each picture and unit are included in the *Teacher's Notes* pages. Some general suggestions follow:

➤ Provide students with concrete approaches to writing about the picture. You may wish to use one of the options included in the *Teacher's Notes*, give students a choice of options, or assign options based on students' levels of proficiency. Model what is expected of students for each option.

➤ Advise students to look back through the unit for help and ideas as they write.

➤ Circulate to offer help as needed.

➤ You may want to keep student compositions that demonstrate effective writing or contain common errors to use as examples for future classes.

➤ If you ordinarily use process-writing techniques in your class, the *Composition* activity is an opportunity to practice peer correction. Students can then revise their drafts to incorporate classmates' suggestions.

Now I can: In the *Now I can* box at the very end of the unit, the objectives from the *Preview* page reappear in the form of a checklist. Having students check off what they are able to do after completing each unit helps them to take responsibility for their own learning and instills confidence and a sense of progress or achievement. General suggestions for using the *Now I can* box follow:

➤ Read the first item in the box out loud. Elicit from the class an example demonstrating that students can do what is described.

➤ In pairs, have students take turns reading each item in the box and giving an example of what they have learned. When students can provide an example, they should check that objective. For the items students weren't able to check, they should look back through the unit for ideas.

➤ When students are finished reviewing with their partners, read each item out loud and elicit an example from the class.

➤ Oral test: You may want to use the *Now I can* box as an informal evaluation. While students are working on the *Composition* activity, you can call them up individually and check their ability with two or three objectives.

➤ Other unit features

Yellow notes: These "notes" are used throughout *Ready to Go* as needed to provide students with additional vocabulary, variations of the vocabulary, or additional information. To help promote correct pronunciation, this element has been recorded on the audiocassette.

➤ To introduce the material, read the words on the yellow language note or play the cassette. Have students listen and repeat with books open.

➤ Note that the material has been recorded twice on the cassette. After each utterance, there is space for student repetition, followed by the recorded word again to confirm and reinforce pronunciation. Students listen to each utterance, repeat the words, and listen for confirmation.

Do it yourself!: Appearing at the end of each two-page spread and applying the language of that spread, *Do it yourself!* is designed to meet the needs of both single-level and multilevel classes. In these communicative and purposeful activities, students use the new vocabulary, social language, and grammar in a variety of creative or personalized ways. *Do it yourself!* helps students bridge the gap between the controlled practice of the textbook page and the natural use of language that will be necessary in the world outside of class.

Some examples of *Do it yourself!* activities are role-plays, discussions, personalized information charts, collaborative activities, and plan-ahead projects, all incorporating language students have just learned. Great care has been taken to ensure that students can perform the tasks successfully with the bare minimum of language presented for active use.

However, students who have richer resources, experience, and ability will also be challenged by the open-ended nature of the tasks.

The interleaved *Teacher's Notes* pages of this Teacher's Edition contain numerous concrete suggestions for presenting the *Do it yourself!* activities. Some general suggestions follow:

➤ Spend as much time as necessary demonstrating the activity for your particular group of students. Keep in mind that the *Do it yourself!* activities are not intended to be a test and that the more support students receive, the more successful they will be in completing the task.

➤ Note that in many *Do it yourself!* activities an example has been provided on the Student's Book page that can be used to demonstrate the activity to the class. The *Teacher's Notes* for each *Do it yourself!* activity offer specific suggestions on how to effectively model each task.

➤ To encourage risk taking and experimentation, avoid correcting students until the end of the activity and praise them for creativity and expressiveness. Encourage students to take the activity in other directions and to extend the suggested tasks as much as possible. Have students say as much as they can.

Interleaved *Teacher's Notes* Pages

This Teacher's Edition contains page-by-page teaching suggestions specific to each new activity interleaved with the corresponding full-color Student's Book pages. The *Teacher's Notes* pages also contain boxed tapescripts of all material recorded on the audiocassettes, suggestions for optional expansion, and listings of potential student output. In addition to the teaching suggestions, answers to the exercises are printed in color directly on the facing Student's Book pages for easy reference.

All teaching suggestions on the interleaved pages should be considered optional. Teachers are encouraged to use the techniques that have been successful for them in the past and to view the teaching suggestions on these pages as a practical menu of additional possibilities.

The interleaved *Teacher's Notes* pages include the following features:

Content: Serving as an at-a-glance summary of the exercise, this feature identifies all the teaching points presented in the exercise and any corresponding yellow language notes, including skills (e.g.,

starting a conversation), the type of new vocabulary presented (e.g. *occupations*), and grammar (e.g., *the present perfect continuous with "for" and "since"*). Note that for lesson planning and compliance with curriculum guidelines, the *Scope and Sequence* chart on pages iv to vii in the Student's Book clearly spells out the following elements for each unit: Lifeskills, Grammar, Social Language, Vocabulary, Civics/Culture Concepts, Math Concepts and Practical Math Skills, Critical Thinking Skills, SCANS Competencies, CASAS Life Skill Competencies, and EFF Content Standards.

Procedure: The *Teacher's Notes* pages offer specific, concrete suggestions for presenting each exercise in the unit. Teachers are encouraged to experiment with their procedure to discover the techniques that work best for their classes.

Options: This element offers teachers many concrete ideas for supplemental activities, adding variety and fun to the lesson while allowing students more time to explore the teaching point. Note that some optional activities may not be appropriate for all settings or all classes. Teachers should use their judgment in selecting material that best meets the needs of their particular group. Optional material suggested in the *Teacher's Notes* includes the following:

➤ Realia: Props, pictures, and real information such as the student's name or job title are important aids in connecting the lesson to the student's real life outside the classroom.

➤ Games: Games in which students must utilize the teaching point in order to play help motivate students by making learning fun. Additionally, variations could also be offered that transform a textbook exercise into a game.

➤ Role-play: Acting out scenarios or conversations offers students the opportunity to rehearse using language in a natural context.

➤ Alternate presentations: Textbook material can often be presented and used in different ways to meet the specific needs of each class. Illustrations are particularly adaptable for different uses.

➤ Collaborative activities: Projects that students can complete together as a class or in groups, such as completing a chart on the board or brainstorming a list of information, encourage students to work together to solve problems and to take more responsibility for their learning.

➤ Graphic organizers: Having students organize content in a chart, diagram, or mind map helps them make sense of new information and makes difficult concepts more accessible. Graphic organizers can also promote interaction and help students efficiently gather and record information or ideas from their classmates. Presenting essential information clearly is a skill that may be helpful to your students in their workplaces.

Challenges: Intended to enrich the learning experience of more advanced groups or students, these optional ideas for supplemental activities increase the level of difficulty by introducing additional vocabulary or alternate methods of expression. As with *Options*, teachers should use their judgment in selecting material that best meets the needs of their particular group.

Field projects: These ideas for field trips and out-of-class assignments connect classroom instruction to the world outside. Each activity requires students to venture into the neighborhood or community to accomplish a specific task. *Field projects* create opportunities for students to use the language they are learning in authentic contexts, interact with native speakers, observe and apply cultural and civic concepts, and become more familiar with community resources. Again, teachers should use their judgment in deciding which of these activities is appropriate for their students and in their community.

Tapescript: A boxed tapescript for each listening comprehension activity is included on the corresponding *Teacher's Notes* page for easy reference. Note that exercises marked with a 🎧 in the Student's Book include a listening component that has been recorded on the audiocassette.

If your students are ready . . . : Specifically targeted to the highly diverse and heterogeneous adult immigrant ESL classroom, these optional notes on language, culture, and civic expectations enrich the language experience of more advanced or academic students in multilevel groups. *Language notes* contain additional information on grammar and American language usage relevant to the lesson. In addition, because information about social customs may be as important as language for immigrant learners, *Culture / Civics notes* offer relevant background information on laws, customs, and traditions in North America. As always, use discretion in choosing which notes to include as some material might be above the level of your group.

READY TO GO ³

Language • Lifeskills • Civics

Joan Saslow

Edwina Hoffman
Series Advisor

Longman

Contents

Scope and sequence

Unit	Lifeskills	Grammar	Social Language	Vocabulary	Civics/Culture Concepts
1 **Your life** page 1	• Engage in small talk • Ask someone to be a reference • Prepare for a job interview • Complete a job application	• The present perfect continuous • Gerunds for describing likes, dislikes, and skills	How to • initiate conversations • give and accept compliments • get to know someone	• Good and bad weather adjectives • Expressions of surprise • Occupations and allied skills	• Appropriate job interview dress and demeanor
2 **The community** page 15	• Request and give directions • Use building diagrams and directories • Use public transportation maps • Demonstrate elevator etiquette	• Imperatives for directions, warnings, requests, and suggestions • Indirect commands	How to • extend and accept invitations • ask for directions • tell and ask others for directions • make plans to meet	• Directions in building interiors • Responses to social invitations	• Appropriate punctuality for social invitations
3 **Technology** page 29	• Discuss a product warranty • Troubleshoot a problem • Use telephone product service lines • Complete a proof-of-purchase card	• The passive voice • Review: Irregular past participles	How to • admit a possible error • reassure a worried person • empathize • express worry about consequences	• Equipment, machines, and appliances • Machine maintenance • Mechanical problems • Computer malfunctions	• Rights afforded by product warranties • Employer expectations that workers report equipment breakdowns
4 **The consumer world** page 43	• Request a brand • Discuss a defective, discontinued, or recalled product and seek resolution • Ask for service in a gas station • Write consumer complaint letters	• Used to • Comparisons with as and not as • Review: Comparative forms	How to • confirm another's opinion • express disappointment • express regret • offer an alternative	• Phrases to describe good and bad quality • Locations in a store • Ways to make good on a complaint • Products for babies and children	• Consumer Product Safety Commission and product safety recalls • Civic responsibility for the environment • EPA rules
5 **Time** page 57	• Discuss payment • Compute pay • Reschedule events • Clarify job expectations • Understand the importance of punctuality	• Verbs followed by infinitives • Verbs followed by objects and infinitives	How to • reschedule events • provide reasons • interrupt politely • ask for repetition • ask for permission • clarify expectations	• Payment options • Wages and hours • Time expressions	• Fair Labor Standards Act: minimum wage and entitlement to overtime pay • Company time vs. personal time

Math Concepts and Practical Math Skills	Critical Thinking Skills	Correlations to National Standards		
		SCANS Competencies	CASAS Life Skill Competencies[1]	EFF Content Standards[2]
• Understand gradations along a continuum • Distinguish between a period of time and a point in time	• Classifies behavior as appropriate and inappropriate	• Interpersonal: Interprets and communicates • Information: Organizes data	0.1.1, 0.1.4, 0.1.5, 0.2.1, 0.2.2, 2.3.3, 2.5.8, 2.7.2, 2.7.3, 3.2.1, 3.5.5, 4.1.1, 4.1.2, 4.1.5, 4.1.6, 4.1.7, 4.1.8, 4.4.1, 4.4.4, 4.8.7, 5.1.2, 5.1.6, 7.1.3, 7.2.1, 7.2.6, 7.4.7, 7.5.1, 7.5.2, 7.5.6, 8.1.1, 8.1.2, 8.3.1, 8.3.2	A full range of EFF Content Standards is included in this unit. The following are emphasized: • Speak So Others Can Understand 1–4 • Plan 1, 2, 4, 5 • Cooperate with Others 1–4 • Take Responsibility for Learning 1, 3, 4, 6
• Understand spatial relationships • Use ordinal numbers • Give and follow sequential directions	• Interprets maps • Analyzes problems depicted in picture • Compares and contrasts map resources	• Information: Acquires and evaluates data related to locations • Interpersonal: Negotiates and plans with culturally diverse companions	0.1.2, 0.1.5, 0.2.3, 0.2.4, 1.1.3, 1.9.4, 2.1.2, 2.1.7, 2.2.1, 2.2.5, 2.6.1, 2.6.3, 2.7.2, 2.7.3, 2.7.4, 2.7.6, 3.5.8, 3.5.9, 4.1.7, 4.4.3, 4.6.2, 4.8.7, 5.1.6, 6.6.5, 6.6.8, 7.1.3, 7.2.1, 7.2.6, 7.4.7, 7.4.8, 7.5.6, 8.3.1, 8.3.2	A full range of EFF Content Standards is included in this unit. The following are emphasized: • Read with Understanding 2–5 • Observe Critically 1–5 • Plan 1–5 • Cooperate with Others 1–4 • Take Responsibility for Learning 1–5
• Understand and apply time limitations and other numerical terms of warranties (miles) • Understand time sensitivity of proof-of-purchase cards	• Interprets a product warranty • Compares and contrasts service receipts	• Information: Acquires and evaluates data • Technology: Maintains equipment and troubleshoots problems	0.1.3, 1.6.4, 1.7.3, 1.7.4, 1.7.5, 1.9.5, 1.9.6, 1.9.7, 2.7.2, 2.7.3, 4.1.7, 4.4.3, 4.5.1, 4.5.4, 4.5.6, 4.5.7, 4.6.4, 4.6.5, 4.8.7, 4.9.4, 5.1.6, 7.1.3, 7.2.1, 7.2.6, 7.3.1, 7.3.2, 7.3.3, 7.3.4, 7.4.7, 7.5.3, 7.5.6, 8.3.1, 8.3.2	A full range of EFF Content Standards is included in this unit. The following are emphasized: • Read with Understanding 1–5 • Solve Problems and Make Decisions 1, 2, 4–6 • Plan 1–5 • Resolve Conflict and Negotiate 1–5 • Take Responsibility for Learning 1–6
• Understand spatial relationships • Understand concept of equivalence of value • Understand U.S. units of measurement (quarts) • Understand motor oil viscosity	• Compares and contrasts consumer behavior in a native country with the U.S.A. • Compares and contrasts present and past life	• Interpersonal: Serves customers • Information: Acquires and evaluates data	0.1.4, 0.1.5, 1.3.1, 1.3.3, 1.3.4, 1.3.7, 1.4.1, 1.6.3, 1.7.1, 1.7.4, 1.9.5, 1.9.6, 1.9.7, 2.7.2, 2.7.3, 4.1.7, 4.6.2, 4.6.4, 4.8.7, 5.1.6, 5.6.2, 5.7.1, 7.1.3, 7.2.1, 7.2.6, 7.3.1, 7.3.2, 7.3.3, 7.3.4, 7.4.7, 7.5.6, 8.2.6, 8.3.1, 8.3.2	A full range of EFF Content Standards is included in this unit. The following are emphasized: • Read with Understanding 1–5 • Solve Problems and Make Decisions 1–6 • Plan 1–5 • Resolve Conflict and Negotiate 1–5 • Take Responsibility for Learning 1–6
• Use addition and subtraction to calculate wage requirements for tipped employees • Calculate time and a half and double time based on hourly rate • Calculate weekly earnings based on hourly wage	• Compares and contrasts payment options • Understands consequences	• Resources: Knows how to allocate time • Information: Interprets and communicates information • Systems: Understands organizational systems	0.1.5, 0.1.6, 1.4.2, 1.4.7, 2.1.3, 2.1.8, 2.2.4, 2.3.1, 2.3.2, 2.5.8, 2.7.2, 2.7.3, 3.1.2, 4.1.3, 4.1.7, 4.2.1, 4.2.2, 4.2.3, 4.2.4, 4.6.3, 4.8.7, 5.1.6, 6.6.6, 7.1.3, 7.2.1, 7.2.3, 7.2.6, 7.4.7, 7.5.6, 8.2.3, 8.2.5, 8.2.6, 8.3.1, 8.3.2	A full range of EFF Content Standards is included in this unit. The following are emphasized: • Read with Understanding 1–5 • Use Math to Solve Problems and Communicate 1–5 • Plan 1–5 • Take Responsibility for Learning 1–6

[1] The corresponding CASAS Life Skill Competency List is available at **www.longman.com/readytogo**.
[2] A more extensive correlation to EFF Content Standards is available at **www.longman.com/readytogo**.

Unit	Lifeskills	Grammar	Social Language	Vocabulary	Civics/Culture Concepts
6 **Supplies and services** page 71	• Use food coupons • Order supplies by phone or online • Use unit pricing • Comparison shop • Determine the "best buy"	• Conclusions with *must* • Exclamations with *What*	How to • agree emphatically • offer suggestions	• Containers • Units of measure • Abbreviations of quantity	• The entitlement of consumers to unit pricing so they can determine the "best buy"
7 **Relation-ships** page 85	• Ask about and understand rules and laws • Offer congratulations or sympathy • Understand a summons for violation of a rule	• Impersonal *it* (with adjectives and infinitives)	How to • express uncertainty • ask someone to be more considerate • apologize • ask a stranger about a rule or law • offer sympathy and express appreciation	• Expressions of uncertainty • Conversation starters • Adjectives of emotion	• Ignorance of the law is no excuse. • The importance of neighborhood etiquette
8 **Health and safety** page 99	• Return an item to the supermarket • Send food back in a restaurant • Fill a prescription • Read directions and warnings • Use over-the-counter medications appropriately	• Review: Possessive adjectives • Review: Possessive nouns • Possessive pronouns	How to • show concern • state one's purpose • confirm information • complain about purchased food	• Complaints about food purchased • Medicine label terms	• The right to return food sold after its sell-by date • The responsibility to use safe food-handling practices at home and on the job
9 **Money** page 113	• Avoid consequences of personal debt • Evaluate bank services • Understand credit and debit cards • Read the fine print • Interpret credit card statements	• Conditional sentences • *Keep* + gerund	How to • offer good and bad financial news • discuss problems with debt • offer advice	• Bank services and accounts • Good and bad financial news • Expressions of satisfaction and dissatisfaction • Complaints about bank services	• Consumer rights to fair credit practices are protected by the Federal Trade Commission.
10 **Your career** page 127	• Phone for an interview • Offer job history and references • Accept positive feedback • Discuss career goals • Praise others	• Review: The simple present tense and the present continuous • Review: The present perfect and the present perfect continuous	How to • move to a first-name basis • accept compliments • explain reasons for actions	• Responses to compliments • On-the-job educational opportunities	• The nature of employee-boss relationships

Math Concepts and Practical Math Skills	Critical Thinking Skills	Correlations to National Standards		
		SCANS Competencies	CASAS Life Skill Competencies[1]	EFF Content Standards[2]
• Convert between unit price and total price • Compare regular prices with specials to determine savings • Appreciate and calculate savings based on buying larger quantity • Understand U.S. units of measurement	• Compares and contrasts values • Draws conclusions • Classifies products by unit of measure	• Interpersonal: Teaches others; Teams with partner • Information: Acquires and evaluates data; Uses computer to process information	0.1.1, 1.1.1, 1.1.4, 1.1.5, 1.1.6, 1.1.7, 1.1.8, 1.1.9, 1.2.1, 1.2.2, 1.2.3, 1.2.4, 1.2.5, 1.3.1, 1.3.3, 1.3.4, 1.3.8, 1.3.9, 1.6.1, 1.7.2, 1.8.5, 1.9.5, 1.9.6, 1.9.7, 2.4.3, 2.4.6, 2.6.4, 2.7.2, 2.7.3, 3.2.1, 3.5.1, 4.1.1, 4.4.3, 4.6.3, 4.7.2, 4.8.7, 4.9.3, 5.1.2, 5.1.6, 6.0.1, 6.0.2	A full range of EFF Content Standards is included in this unit. The following are emphasized: • Observe Critically 1–5 • Use Math to Solve Problems and Communicate 1–6 • Plan 1–5 • Take Responsibility for Learning 1–6
• Interpret signs that stipulate time periods when parking is illegal • Consider relationship between fines and gravity of infractions • Calculate penalties on unpaid fines	• Compares and contrasts customs and laws in a native country and U.S.A.	• Interpersonal: Works on teams and teaches others • Information: Interprets and communicates information	0.1.4, 1.9.1, 1.9.2, 2.2.2, 2.2.3, 2.5.7, 2.7.2, 2.7.3, 4.1.7, 4.6.1, 4.8.7, 5.1.6, 5.3.1, 5.3.2, 5.3.5, 5.3.7, 5.6.1, 7.1.3, 7.2.1, 7.2.6, 7.3.1, 7.3.2, 7.3.3, 7.3.4, 7.4.7, 7.5.3, 7.5.6, 8.1.3, 8.3.1, 8.3.2	A full range of EFF Content Standards is included in this unit. The following are emphasized: • Listen Actively 1–4 • Solve Problems and Make Decisions 1–6 • Plan 1–5 • Guide Others 1–4 • Take Responsibility for Learning 1–6
• Compare package label and calendar date to determine freshness of a food item • Understand medicine dosage, frequency of administration, and maximum daily dosage based on age of patient	• Analyzes medications • Compares food-handling customs • Applies warnings on medications	• Interpersonal: Negotiates and works in teams • Systems: Monitors and corrects performance • Information: Acquires and evaluates data	1.6.3, 1.6.4, 2.6.1, 2.6.3, 2.6.4, 2.7.2, 2.7.3, 3.1.1, 3.1.2, 3.1.3, 3.2.3, 3.3.1, 3.3.2, 3.3.3, 3.4.1, 3.4.2, 3.5.3, 3.5.5, 4.4.6, 4.6.1, 4.8.7, 5.1.6, 6.2.4, 6.2.5, 7.1.3, 7.2.1, 7.2.6, 7.3.1, 7.3.2, 7.3.3, 7.3.4, 7.4.7, 7.5.3, 7.5.6, 8.1.3, 8.2.1, 8.2.2, 8.3.1, 8.3.2	A full range of EFF Content Standards is included in this unit. The following are emphasized: • Speak So Others Can Understand 1–4 • Solve Problems and Make Decisions 1, 3–6 • Plan 1–5 • Guide Others 1–4 • Take Responsibility for Learning 1–6
• Understand concept of a mortgage • Understand concepts of interest and interest rate and how they apply to different bank services and accounts • Decide how much to pay on a monthly credit card bill	• Compares bank services • Solves debt-related problems • Decides how much to pay on a credit card bill	• Interpersonal: Works in teams • Information: Acquires and evaluates data • Systems: Understands organizational systems	1.1.5, 1.1.6, 1.2.1, 1.2.5, 1.3.1, 1.3.2, 1.3.3, 1.3.4, 1.3.6, 1.4.3, 1.4.6, 1.5.1, 1.5.2, 1.5.3, 1.6.2, 1.8.1, 1.8.2, 1.8.3, 1.8.4, 1.8.5, 1.9.5, 1.9.8, 2.1.1, 2.1.4, 2.1.5, 2.2.4, 2.7.2, 2.7.3, 3.2.3, 3.2.4, 4.7.1, 4.8.7, 5.1.6, 6.0.1, 6.0.2, 6.0.3, 6.0.4, 6.2.1, 6.2.2, 6.2.5, 6.3.1, 6.3.2, 6.4.1, 6.4.3	A full range of EFF Content Standards is included in this unit. The following are emphasized: • Read with Understanding 1–5 • Use Math to Solve Problems and Communicate 1–6 • Solve Problems and Make Decisions 1–6 • Plan 1–5 • Take Responsibility for Learning 1–6
• Understand performance review periods (quarterly, yearly)	• Identifies reasons to change jobs	• Information: Interprets and communicates information • Systems: Monitors and corrects performance	1.4.1, 1.4.2, 2.4.1, 2.4.2, 2.7.2, 2.7.3, 4.1.2, 4.1.4, 4.1.5, 4.1.6, 4.1.7, 4.1.8, 4.1.9, 4.4.1, 4.4.2, 4.4.4, 4.6.1, 4.6.2, 4.7.3, 4.8.7, 4.9.1, 5.1.6, 7.1.1, 7.1.2, 7.1.3, 7.2.1, 7.2.6, 7.4.7, 7.5.1, 7.5.2, 7.5.3, 7.5.6, 8.1.1, 8.1.2, 8.3.1, 8.3.2	A full range of EFF Content Standards is included in this unit. The following are emphasized: • Read with Understanding 2–5 • Speak So Others Can Understand 1–4 • Listen Actively 1–4 • Plan 1–5 • Guide Others 1–4 • Take Responsibility for Learning 1–6

[1] The corresponding CASAS Life Skill Competency List is available at **www.longman.com/readytogo**.
[2] A more extensive correlation to EFF Content Standards is available at **www.longman.com/readytogo**.

Acknowledgments

The author wishes to acknowledge with gratitude the following consultants and reviewers—our partners in the development of *Ready to Go*.

Regional Consultant Board

The following people have participated on an ongoing basis in shaping the content and approach of *Ready to Go*:

Ann Belletire, Northern Illinois University–Business and Industry Services, Oak Brook, Illinois • **Sandra Bergman**, Instructional Facilitator, Alternative, Adult, and Continuing Education Program, New York City Board of Education • **Sherie Burnette**, Assistant Dean, Workforce Education, Brookhaven College of the Dallas County Community College District, Farmers Branch, Texas • **Michael Feher**, Boston Chinatown Neighborhood Center, Boston, Massachusetts • **Susan B. Kanter**, Instructional Supervisor, Continuing Education and Contract Training, Houston Community College-Southwest, Houston, Texas • **Brigitte Marshall**, Consultant, Albany, California • **Monica Oliva**, Educational Specialist, Miami-Dade County Public Schools, Miami, Florida • **Mary E. O'Neill**, Coordinator of Community Education, ESL, Northern Virginia Community College—Annandale Campus, Annandale, Virginia • **Grace Tanaka**, Professor of ESL, Santa Ana College School of Continuing Education; ESL Facilitator, Centennial Education Center, Santa Ana, California • **Marcia L. Taylor**, Workplace Instructor, Joblink, Ispat-Inland Inc., East Chicago, Indiana

Reviewers

The following people shared their perspectives and made suggestions either by reviewing manuscript or participating in editorial conferences with the author and editors:

Leslie Jo Adams, Santa Ana College–Centennial Education Center, Santa Ana, California • **Sandra Anderson**, El Monte-Rosemead Adult School, El Monte, California • **Marcy Berquist**, San Diego Community College District, San Diego, California • **Robert Breitbard**, District School Board of Collier County, Naples, Florida • **Ruth Brigham**, A.C.C.E.S.S., Boston, Massachusetts • **Donna Burns**, Mt. San Antonio College, Walnut, California • **Eric Burton**, Downington Area School District, Downington, Pennsylvania • **Michael James Climo**, West Los Angeles College, Culver City, California • **Teresa Costa**, The English Center, Miami, Florida • **Robert Cote**, Miami-Dade County Public Schools, Miami, Florida • **Georgette Davis**, North Orange County Community College District, Orange County, California • **Janet Ennis**, Santa Ana College–Centennial Education Center, Santa Ana, California • **Peggy Fergus**, Northern Illinois University–Business and Industry Services, Oak Brook, Illinois • **Oliva Fernandez**, Hillsborough County Public Schools–Adult & Community Education, Tampa, Florida • **Elizabeth Fitzgerald**, Hialeah Adult & Community Center, Hialeah, Florida • **Marty Furch**, Palomar College, San Diego, California • **Eric Glicker**, North Orange County Community College District, Orange County, California • **Steve Gwynne**, San Diego Community College District, San Diego, California • **Victoria Hathaway**, DePaul University, Chicago, Illinois • **Jeffrey L. Janulis**, Richard J. Daley College, City Colleges of Chicago, Chicago, Illinois • **Mary Karamourtopoulos**, Northern Essex Community College, Haverhill, Massachusetts • **Shirley Kelly**, Brookhaven College of the Dallas County Community College District, Farmers Branch, Texas • **Marilou Kessler**, Jewish Vocational Service–Vocational English Program, Chicago, Illinois • **Henry Kim**, North Orange County Community College District, Orange County, California • **Dr. Maria H. Koonce**, Broward County Public Schools, Ft. Lauderdale, Florida • **John Kostovich**, South Texas Community College–Intensive English Program, McAllen, Texas • **Jacques LaCour**, Mt. Diablo Adult Education, Concord, California • **Beatrice Liebman**, Miami Sunset Adult Center, Miami, Florida • **Doris Lorden**, Wright College–Workforce Training Center, Chicago, Illinois • **Mike Lowman**, Coral Gables Adult Education Center, Coral Gables, Florida • **Lois Maharg**, Delaware Technical and Community College • **Vicki Moore**, El Monte-Rosemead Adult School, El Monte, California • **Deborah Nash**, School Board of Palm Beach County Schools, West Palm Beach, Florida • **Cindy Neubrech**, Mt. San Antonio College, Walnut, California • **Patricia Peabody**, Broward County Public Schools, Ft. Lauderdale, Florida • **Joe A. Perez**, Hillsborough County Public Schools, Tampa, Florida • **Diane Pinkley**, Teacher's College, Columbia University, New York, New York • **Kay Powell**, Santa Ana College–Centennial Education Center, Santa Ana, California • **Wendy Rader**, San Diego Community College District, San Diego, California • **Don Robison**, Jewish Vocational Service–Workplace Literacy, Chicago, Illinois • **Richard Sasso**, Triton College, River Grove, Illinois • **Mary Segovia**, El Monte-Rosemead Adult School, El Monte, California • **Laurie Shapero**, Miami-Dade Community College, Miami, Florida • **Sara Shapiro**, El Monte-Rosemead Adult School, El Monte, California • **Samanthia Spence**, Richland College, Dallas, Texas • **JoAnn Stehy**, North Orange County Community College District, Orange County, California • **Margaret Teske**, Mt. San Antonio College, Walnut, California • **Dung Tran**, North Orange County Community College District, Orange County, California • **Claire Valier**, School District of Palm Beach County, West Palm Beach, Florida • **Catherine M. Waterman**, Rancho Santiago Community College, Santa Ana, California • **James Wilson**, Mt. San Antonio College, Walnut, California

To the teacher

Ready to Go: Language, Lifeskills, Civics is a four-level, standards-based course in English as a second language. *Ready to Go* prepares adults for self-sufficiency in the three principal areas of their lives: the community, the home, and the workplace.

Communicative competence in English is of critical importance in achieving self-sufficiency. *Ready to Go* applies the best of current second language acquisition research to ensure immediate success, rapidly enabling learners to

- understand the spoken and written language of daily life.
- communicate orally and in writing.
- understand the culture and civic expectations of their new environment.
- master lifeskills necessary to survive and thrive in the American community and workplace.

To achieve these goals with efficiency and speed, *Ready to Go* weaves together three integrated strands: language, lifeskills, and civics*, tightly correlating the major state and federal standards with a complete language syllabus and relevant social language.

Course length

Ready to Go is designed to be used in a period of 60 to 90 classroom hours. This period can be shortened or lengthened, based on the needs of the group or the program. The Teacher's Edition gives detailed instructions for tailoring *Ready to Go* to specific settings, circumstances, and student groups.

Components

Student's Book

The *Ready to Go* Student's Book is a complete four-skills text, integrating listening, speaking, reading, and writing, with lifeskills, math skills, civics concepts, and authentic practice understanding native speech and real-life documents. The book contains 10 units, each one followed by a concise review section. For lesson planning and compliance with curriculum guidelines, the Scope and Sequence chart (on pages iv-vii) clearly spells out the following elements for each unit:

- lifeskills
- grammar
- social language
- vocabulary
- civics/culture concepts
- math concepts and practical math skills
- critical thinking skills
- SCANS Competencies
- CASAS Life Skill Competencies
- EFF Content Standards

Further correlations of state and local standards to the *Ready to Go* course can be downloaded at no cost from the *Ready to Go* companion website at www.longman.com/readytogo.

In order to facilitate student-centered instruction, *Ready to Go* uses a variety of grouping strategies: pairs, groups, and whole class. In numerous activities, learners work with others to create a joint product. Those activities are labeled collaborative activities.

*In *Ready to Go*, the term "civics" refers to concepts that introduce learners to expected social behavior in this culture, an understanding of which is essential *before* students can participate fully or truly understand their rights and responsibilities as citizens. The term does not refer to citizenship education.

Two special features of the *Ready to Go* Student's Book are <u>Do it yourself!</u> and <u>Authentic practice</u>.

Because learners have an immediate need to use their new language outside the class, <u>Do it yourself!</u> provides a daily opportunity for students of diverse abilities to put new language into their own words. This affords them a chance to "try their wings" in the safe and supportive environment of the classroom.

<u>Authentic practice</u> activities create a "living language laboratory" within the classroom. Learners practice responding to authentic models of spoken and written English with the limited language they know. In this way, students build their confidence and skill in coping with the language of the real world.

Audiocassettes

Because listening comprehension is a fundamental survival and success skill for new speakers of English, *Ready to Go* includes a comprehensive listening strand in each unit of the Student's Book. In addition to listening comprehension activities, there are numerous other opportunities for learners to practice their listening skills. All exercises that appear on audiocassette are marked with a 🎧 symbol. A transcript of each listening comprehension activity is located on its corresponding Teacher's Edition page, for easy reference.

Teacher's Edition

An interleaved Teacher's Edition provides page-by-page teaching suggestions that add value to the Student's Book. In addition to general and day-by-day teaching suggestions, each teacher's page includes optional activities, challenge activities, and language and culture / civics notes that will help teachers demystify and explain new language and culture concepts to students. Answers to all exercises and the tapescript of each listening comprehension activity are also readily found on all pages.

Workbook

In addition to the ample opportunities for reading and writing practice contained in the Student's Book, the *Ready to Go* Workbook contains further reading and writing exercises. The Workbook is valuable for homework or for in-class activities. An added feature is a test preparation activity for each unit, with CASAS-like and BEST Test-like items which ensure that learners can "bubble in" and cope with the formats of standardized language tests.

Teacher's Resource Binder

A three ring binder contains a wealth of valuable items to enable busy teachers to customize their instruction and make the preparation of supplementary teaching aids unnecessary. The Classroom Booster Pack provided with the Binder features pair-work cards, vocabulary flash cards, grammar self-checks, photo chat cards, and extension activities for daily use. Also included in the Binder are the following additional teacher support materials: Correlations of *Ready to Go* with state and federal standards, Student Progress Checklists, Pre- and Post-Tests and Achievement Tests, and Skills for Test Taking.

Placement Test
A simple-to-administer test places students accurately within the *Ready to Go* series.

Ready to Go Companion Website
The *Ready to Go* companion website (www.longman.com/readytogo) provides numerous additional resources for students and teachers. This no-cost, high-benefit feature includes opportunities for further practice of language and content from the *Ready to Go* Student's Book. For the teacher, there are optional strategies and materials that amplify the *Ready to Go* Teacher's Edition.

Student's Book unit contents
Each unit in the *Ready to Go* Student's Book uses an integrated three-step approach.

1. Practical conversations with integrated vocabulary

   Simple, memorable model conversations that are transferable to learners' own lives permit intensive practice of new vocabulary and key social language. These are followed by lively pair-work activities.

2. Practical grammar

   Essential grammatical structure practice enables learners to manipulate the vocabulary and practical conversations to express ideas of their own.

3. Authentic practice

   An entertaining picture story illustrates the authentic use of spoken target language and leads to a series of interactive comprehension tasks that help students cope with spoken language in the world outside the classroom.

A unique real-world reading enables students to understand culture and civics concepts of their new community and workplace. Then a series of authentic documents provides preparation for coping with the real documents students will encounter in the world outside the classroom.

Review
Following each unit is a three-page, four-skill review for learners to check their progress.

Author

Joan Saslow

Joan Saslow has taught English as a second language and English as a foreign language to adults and young adults in the United States and Chile. She taught workplace English at the General Motors auto assembly plant in Tarrytown, NY; and Adult ESL at Westchester Community College and at Marymount College in New York. In addition, Ms. Saslow taught English and French at the Binational Centers of Valparaíso and Viña del Mar, Chile, and the Catholic University of Valparaíso.

Ms. Saslow is the series director of Longman's popular five-level adult series *True Colors, an EFL Course for Real Communication* and of *True Voices*, a five-level video course. She is the author of *Literacy Plus*, a two-level series that teaches beginning literacy, survival English, and essential civics concepts to adult pre-literate immigrants. She is also author of *English in Context: Reading Comprehension for Science and Technology*, a three-level series for English for special purposes. In addition, Ms. Saslow has been an editor of language teaching materials, a teacher trainer, and a frequent speaker at gatherings of ESL and EFL teachers for over thirty years.

Series advisor

Edwina Hoffman

Edwina Hoffman has taught English for speakers of other languages in South Florida and at the Miccosukee Tribe of Indians, and English as a foreign language in Venezuela. She provided teacher training in a seven-state area for federally funded multi-functional resource centers serving the southeastern part of the United States. Dr. Hoffman taught English composition at Florida International University and graduate ESOL methods at the University of Miami.

Dr. Hoffman is an instructional supervisor with the adult and vocational programs of Miami-Dade County Public Schools in Miami, Florida. She has acted as a consultant, reviewer, and author of adult ESOL materials for over twenty years. A graduate of Middlebury College, Dr. Hoffman's doctoral degree is from Florida International University.

Your life

Note: For the plan-ahead project on page 11, students should bring job applications from their places of employment to class. If possible, you should also bring in several job applications.

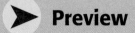 **Preview**

(For general suggestions, see *Introduction*, page Tviii.)

Warm up. How do you start a conversation with someone you don't know?

Procedure:

➤ Before you open the book, provide students with an opportunity to get to know you and each other. As a class, brainstorm and write on the board questions people ask when they meet someone new, such as *What's your name? Where are you from? What do you do?* Have students ask you the questions. Answer each question, modeling for students and telling them something about yourself at the same time. Ask for a volunteer to introduce you to the class. In pairs, have students ask each other the questions on the board and then introduce their partners to the class. Advise students to choose two or three things about their partner to tell the class.

➤ Have students open their books and look at the picture. Ask questions about the picture, such as *Who's in the picture?* (employees) *Where are they?* (at a party) *How can you tell?* (They are eating, drinking, talking, laughing.) *Why are they together?* (They're new.) *What time is it?* (4:15) *What's it like outside?* (It's raining.) If students have difficulty answering these questions, prompt them by asking *What does the sign / banner say in the top left-hand corner?* (*Welcome*, New Employees!) *How are the people dressed?* (in office clothes) *What's on the table?* (food and drinks)

➤ Read the *Warm up* question. Have students look at the picture and imagine what the people are saying. Elicit a variety of ideas from the class, such as *Hello, Nice to meet you, Terrible weather today, Where are you from?*

Option: Have students create a short conversation for one pair or group of people in the picture. Students can add speech balloons to the picture or label the people *A* and *B* or *A, B,* and *C* and write the conversation on a separate piece of paper. You

might wish to make an overhead of the picture and model the activity.

Option: In small groups, have students make a list of things people talk about at parties, such as *the food, the weather, family, work.* Then draw a two-column chart on the board with the headings *With someone you know* and *With someone you don't know.* Have the groups copy the chart and decide where to place each of their topics. For example, students may put *the weather* under *With someone you don't know* and *family* under *With someone you know.*

Option: Ask small groups to discuss whether anything is done to welcome new employees in their native countries. Have each group share with the class. Write any customs on the board. Students can also talk about their workplaces here.

If your students are ready . . .

Culture / Civics note: In North America, it is acceptable to introduce yourself to someone you don't know, regardless of that person's age, position, or gender. It is generally not necessary to wait until you are formally introduced. Introductions typically begin with an exchange of names and a handshake. In other cultures, people might kiss on one or both cheeks, nod, or bow.

When starting a conversation with a stranger, it is common to begin by "breaking the ice" with a neutral topic before talking about more personal information. For example, two people at a party who are meeting for the first time might express their opinions about the music, the food, or the weather before sharing information about their families, jobs, or interests.

Unit 1 objectives

Procedure:

➤ Write *Do you know how to . . . ?* on the board. Ask *Do you know how to . . . ?* with each objective. When students respond positively, elicit examples. Use simple definitions or pictures to convey the meaning of any unknown words. For example, explain that *skills* are things that you can do well, or to convey the meaning of *letter of recommendation,* refer students to the letter on page 4.

➤ Have students check those objectives they already feel comfortable with and circle those they want to work on most.

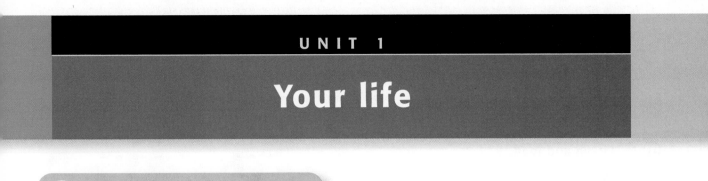

Your life

> **Preview**

Warm up. How do you start a conversation with someone you don't know?

Unit 1 objectives

- Start a conversation with someone you don't know.
- Get to know someone.
- Ask someone for a letter of recommendation.
- Talk about your skills, likes, and dislikes.
- Practice a job interview.
- Fill out an employment application.

Practical conversations

Model 1   Start a conversation with someone you don't know. Make small talk.

A. Listen and read.

A: Nice weather today.

B: Yes, it is. Beautiful.

A: You know, I don't think we've met. I'm Melanie Soto. I work on the third floor.

B: Nice to meet you, Melanie. I'm Luis Cruz.

A: Nice to meet you too. By the way, I like your tie.

B: You do? Thanks!

B. Listen again and repeat.

Vocabulary

Good weather adjectives	Bad weather adjectives

nice	awful
beautiful	terrible
gorgeous	horrible
Add your <u>own</u>: _____	Add your <u>own</u>: _____

C. Pair work. **Meet someone new. Make small talk. Use your <u>own</u> words.**

A: _____ weather today.

B: Yes, it is. _____.

A: You know, I don't think we've met. I'm _____.

B: Nice to meet you, _____. I'm _____.

A: _____. By the way, I like your _____.

B: You do? Thanks.

➤ Practical conversations

(For general suggestions, see *Introduction*, page Tviii.)

Model 1

Content: starting a conversation; making small talk; commenting on the weather; giving a compliment; accepting a compliment

Procedure:

🎧 A. Listen and read.

➤ Read the bar for *Model 1*. Ask students what *small talk* is. If necessary, explain that it is informal conversation that is not usually about important issues, and that we use small talk to get to know people and to be polite.

➤ To set the scene for the conversation, ask questions about the people in the photo, such as *Where are they?* (in a cafeteria) *What are they wearing?* (office clothes) *What are they doing?* (shaking hands) *Do you think they've met before?* (No, because they're shaking hands.)

➤ Play the cassette or read the conversation. After students listen and read, ask comprehension questions such as *What do they talk about first?* (the weather) *Who tells his or her name first?* (the woman, Melanie) *What does Melanie like?* (his tie)

🎧 B. Listen again and repeat.

➤ Play the cassette or read the conversation again. Encourage students to imitate the rhythm, stress, and intonation of the conversation as closely as possible. Correct where necessary, helping students to pronounce the language clearly.

Option: Brainstorm compliments and write them on the board. Have students stand up and walk around the room. Signal to students to stop and pair up with someone nearby. Students introduce themselves and then offer each other a compliment. Allow students about 30 seconds to interact and then signal students to walk around again. Repeat several times, with students interacting with someone different each time.

🎧 Vocabulary

➤ Point to the picture on the left and ask questions, such as *Where is this?* (the beach) *How does the man feel?* (relaxed, happy) *What is the weather like?* (It's sunny.) Point to the picture on the right and ask *How is the weather in this picture?* (It's raining.) *How does the man feel?* (wet, unhappy)

➤ Play the cassette or read the words and have students repeat.

Option: Brainstorm other weather adjectives and write them on the board, such as *sunny, dry, great, rainy, humid, bad.* Have students use the words on the board to create pairs of opposites.

Option: Photocopy the weather forecast for the week from the local newspaper. Have students come up with a comment on the weather for each day of the week.

C. Pair work . . .

➤ Model the conversation with a more advanced student. Play the role of Student B. Demonstrate that, in the second line of the conversation, Student B responds with a weather adjective that is similar in meaning to Student A's adjective. Point out to Student A that any of the vocabulary words can be used in place of *nice* in the first line.

➤ Students practice the conversation with a partner, taking turns playing the roles of Student A and Student B. Circulate and offer help as needed.

Option: Write *classmates, co-workers, neighbors* on the board. Have students practice the conversation playing the three different roles. Point out that Student A can give compliments specific to the situation, such as *I like your office* with a co-worker or *I like your yard* with a neighbor.

Challenge: Have students role-play the conversation in different settings, such as at a party, in the school bookstore, or in the laundry room of an apartment building. Point out that in addition to tailoring the compliment to the situation, Student A can also add explanatory information similar to *I work on the third floor.* For example, at a party Student A could say *I'm a friend of Melanie's,* or in the laundry room *I live in apartment 3B.*

If your students are ready . . .

Culture / Civics note: In North America, compliments are often used to show friendliness or politeness or to make conversation. For example, when meeting someone for the first time, it would be appropriate to compliment the person on an interesting piece of jewelry or clothing, the furnishings of the home, or food served. However, we would not usually compliment a person we have just met on a physical feature, such as eyes, slimness, or attractiveness.

Model 2

Content: getting to know someone; asking questions with *How long...?* and the present perfect continuous; expressing surprise

Procedure:

⌒ A. Listen and read.

➤ Ask questions about the photo, such as *Who's in the picture? Do you remember their names?* (Melanie, Luis) *What are they doing?* (talking and eating)

➤ After students listen to the conversation, check comprehension by asking *How long has the man been working here?* (about a month) *Where did they both work before?* (at Flushing Plumbing Supply) *How do they feel?* (surprised)

➤ Write on the board *It's a small world!* Ask *Have you ever met someone new and then found out that the person knows someone you know? Have you ever met someone new who lived or worked in the same place you did?* Talk about your own experience meeting someone new who had an unexpected connection with you. In groups, have students talk about experiences they've had.

⌒ B. Listen again and repeat.

Option: Divide the class in half. Play the cassette or read the conversation and have half the class repeat Student A's lines and the other half repeat Student B's lines.

⌒ Vocabulary

➤ Have students look at the picture in the *Vocabulary* box. Ask them to describe the man's expression or to speculate about what he just saw or heard.

➤ Play the cassette or read the expressions. Encourage students to repeat using authentic intonation.

➤ Brainstorm other expressions of surprise and write them on the board, such as *No way, I can't believe it, Get out of here, That's impossible.*

C. Pair work...

➤ Model the activity with a more advanced student. Play the role of Student A to demonstrate using words from the box and a way of expressing surprise that are different from those used in the model conversation.

➤ Point out that the verb used in the present perfect continuous in the first line (*How long have you been working here?*) is used in the simple past in the third line (*Where did you work before that?*).

If your students are ready . . .

Culture / Civics note: Although in some countries it is customary to sit down and share a table with someone you don't know, here people are more comfortable if you ask permission first. In a company cafeteria or at a social gathering at work, you can say *May I join you?* In a self-service restaurant, it is appropriate to ask to share a table with someone you don't know only if there are no empty tables. You can say *Do you mind if I sit here?* or *Is this seat taken?* It is not common to ask to join someone you don't know at a table in a restaurant where there are servers.

➤ Do it yourself!

(For general suggestions, see *Introduction*, page Txiii.)

Procedure:

➤ Review the ways of making small talk that students have practiced, such as commenting on the weather, giving compliments, and asking questions with *How long . . . ?* and the present perfect continuous.

➤ Read each speech balloon and ask for volunteers to respond. Eliciting an appropriate response provides students with a context for understanding each phrase. Point out that *Long time, no see!* is informal, or used with friends, and that *I don't think we've met* is used with someone you don't know.

Option: Have students imagine that they are at a welcoming party like the one on page 1. Divide the class in half. One half forms a circle facing outward. The other half forms a circle outside the first circle, facing inward. Each student faces another student. Students facing each other make small talk. After one minute, have the outer circle move counterclockwise one position and the inner circle move clockwise one position. Students then practice beginning a conversation with their new partners. Repeat several times.

A. Listen and read.

A: How long have you been working here?
B: Not long. About a month.
A: Where did you work before that?
B: At Flushing Plumbing Supply.
A: That's incredible! So did I.
B: Wow. It's a small world!

B. Listen again and repeat.

Vocabulary

Ways to express surprise
That's incredible!
That's amazing!
You're kidding!
Add your <u>own</u>: _____

C. Pair work. Get to know a classmate. Use ideas from the box or your <u>own</u> idea.

working here	living in the U.S.	studying English

A: How long have you been _____?
B: _____.
A: Where did you _____ before that?
B: _____.
A: _____.

▶ Do it yourself!

Pair work. Begin a conversation. Make small talk. Use your <u>own</u> words and ideas.

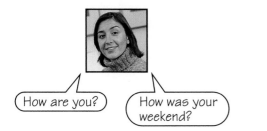

How are you?

How was your weekend?

Long time, no see!

I don't think we've met.

Model 3   Ask someone for a reference.

🎧 **A. Listen and read.**

A: Could you do me a favor?

B: Of course. What is it?

A: Well, I'm applying for a job as a baby-sitter, and I need a reference. Would you mind writing me a letter of recommendation?

B: Not at all. I'd be glad to.

A: Thanks so much. I appreciate it.

🎧 **B. Listen again and repeat.**

To whom it may concern:

Fran Lin has been my student for two years. She is a good worker and is always on time. I can recommend Ms. Lin

🎧 **Vocabulary**

Occupations

a mechanic   an engineer   a plumber   an office manager   a bank teller

Add your <u>own</u>: _____

C. Pair work. Ask for a reference. Use one of the occupations from the vocabulary or use your <u>own</u> occupation.

A: Could you do me a favor?

B: _____. What is it?

A: Well, I'm applying for a job as _____, and I need a reference. Would you mind writing me a letter of recommendation?

B: Not at all. I'd be glad to.

A: ___1___.

---

[1]Thanks

➤ Practical conversations

(For general suggestions, see *Introduction*, page Tviii.)

Model 3

Content: asking for a reference; making polite requests with *Could you . . . ?* and *Would you mind . . . ?*; agreeing to polite requests; occupations

Procedure:

🎧 A–B.

➤ To set the scene for the conversation, ask questions about the photo, such as *Where are the two women?* (in a classroom, in an office) *What do you think their relationship is?* (student and teacher)

➤ Ask questions about the letter, such as *What is this?* (a letter, a letter of recommendation) *What is the student's name?* (Fran Lin) *What are two qualities she has?* (good worker, on time) *Who is writing the letter?* (her teacher) *How do you know?* (Fran Lin has been my student . . .) *Who is the letter to?* Point out that the teacher does not know the name of the person who will read the letter, and that *To whom it may concern* is a standard greeting when the recipient is unknown.

➤ Read the bar for *Model 3.* Ask students what a *reference* is. If necessary, explain that a *reference* is a letter from someone who knows you well and can speak about your skills or ability to do a job.

➤ To draw on students' experiences, ask *Do students in your country ask teachers for letters of recommendation? Have you ever asked a teacher for a recommendation? What other people could you ask for a reference? What are two good qualities that you have? If someone was writing a letter of recommendation for you, what would you want the person to say?*

➤ After playing the cassette or reading the conversation, ask comprehension questions such as *What job is she applying for?* (baby-sitter) *Is her teacher going to write the letter for her?* (yes)

➤ Ask the class what words the student uses to make her request politely. Elicit the responses *Could you . . . ? Would you . . . ? Would you mind . . . ?* Point out that *Thanks so much* and *I appreciate it* are also polite. Ask the class what words the teacher uses to agree politely. Elicit *Of course, Not at all, I'd be glad to.*

Challenge: Copy the letter onto the board. Ask for student input on how to set it up as a business letter. Model standard business-letter format. Use your school's or program's address for the return address and a local business or made-up address for the recipient. Have students finish the letter, adding two more sentences about Fran Lin's qualifications and a name and signature.

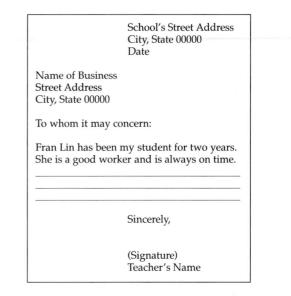

```
                              School's Street Address
                              City, State 00000
                              Date

Name of Business
Street Address
City, State 00000

To whom it may concern:

Fran Lin has been my student for two years.
She is a good worker and is always on time.
_____
_____
_____

                    Sincerely,


                    (Signature)
                    Teacher's Name
```

🎧 Vocabulary

➤ After students listen to and repeat the vocabulary, brainstorm other occupations and write them on the board. Ask about students' occupations in their home countries, their current occupations, and occupations they would like to have. Write *a* or *an* before each occupation, reminding students that *an* is used before singular words that begin with a vowel sound.

➤ Read the occupations on the board and have students repeat after you.

Option: Model for students how to make a four-column chart. Hold up a sheet of paper horizontally. Fold the paper in half twice to create four vertical columns. Have students copy the headings *Name, What did you do in your country?, What do you do now?, What would you like to do?* onto their charts. Students then circulate and ask at least five classmates these questions, filling in their charts with names and occupations.

C. Pair work . . .

➤ Ask students to use their own occupations or occupations they would like to have when they practice the conversation with a partner. Demonstrate by modeling the activity with a more advanced student and playing the role of Student A.

➤ Circulate while students are practicing, providing help with pronunciation as needed.

Model 4

Content: asking for information about someone; using gerunds to talk about skills, likes, and dislikes

Procedure:

🎧 A–B.

➤ With books closed, ask students to think of three or four things they like to do or are good at. On a piece of paper, have students use words, symbols, or pictures to represent these things. Have students share one of these ideas with a partner.

➤ Have students open their books and look at the photo. Ask questions such as *Where are these two people?* (in an office) *How are they dressed?* (in office clothes) *What is the man doing?* (taking notes)

➤ After students listen to the conversation, ask questions such as *Why do you think the woman is here?* (for a job interview) *What is the woman good at?* (working with her hands) *What does she like doing?* (cooking) If students don't use the gerund (*-ing*) form when they respond, say *Yes, you're right* and repeat the answer using the gerund.

➤ Ask *What do you enjoy doing? What are you good at? Is there anything you like doing that you're not good at?*

🎧 Vocabulary

➤ After students listen to and repeat the vocabulary, ask what the words have in common. Elicit the response that in each the first word (or verb) ends in *-ing* and that they are all things people do.

➤ Brainstorm other activities and write them on the board. Write the verbs in the *-ing* form. Then write on the board and have students copy: *I'm good at . . . , I'm not good at. . . , I like . . . , I don't like . . .* Students complete the sentences with the activities in the *Vocabulary* box or on the board. Ask for volunteers to read their sentences to the class.

C. Pair work . . .

➤ Review the meanings of the words in the box. Explain that the words on the left are very positive and that the words on the right are very negative. To convey that the feelings expressed fall along a continuum from very positive to very negative, write the words on the board and draw a face over each, varying the degree of the smile or frown.

➤ Have the students look at the conversation. Ask where in the conversation they will use one of the words from the box. Clarify that the words from the box will be used in Student B's last line.

➤ Have students practice the conversation in pairs.

Option: Write *first day of class, job interview, party* on the board and have students practice the conversation as if they were in these different settings. Point out that in a job interview or other formal situation, it would probably not be appropriate for students to say that they hated or couldn't stand something.

Option: Have students write a sentence about themselves with each word in the box, for example, *I love studying English!* Point out that an exclamation point can be used with *love* and *can't stand* to convey strong emotion.

➤ Do it yourself!

(For general suggestions, see *Introduction*, page Txiii.)

Procedure:

➤ Prepare students by asking questions such as *Who's in the picture?* (John Lee and a woman) *What are they wearing?* (office clothes) *Where are they?* (in a cubicle) *What time is it?* (9:15) *Why is she here?* (for a job interview) *Why do you think so?* (He works in Human Resources.)

➤ Ask for volunteers to present their conversations to the class.

Challenge: Have students create a conversation that is inappropriate in some way. An inappropriate conversation might include a compliment that is too personal, an introduction without a handshake, a request to join someone at a table in a full-service restaurant, or a demand (rather than a polite request) for a reference. As students present their conversations, the class should try to identify the problem.

A. Listen and read.

A: So tell me something about yourself.

B: Well, I really enjoy working with my hands. I'm pretty good at that.

A: What about cooking?

B: Actually, I like cooking, but I'm not very good at it.

B. Listen again and repeat.

Vocabulary

Skills

| driving | fixing cars | working with children | working with people | using a computer |

Add your <u>own</u>: _____

C. Pair work. Discuss your likes and dislikes. Use the vocabulary and the words in the box.

| love | like | enjoy | don't mind | dislike | hate | can't stand |
| **+** | | | | | | **–** |

A: So tell me something about yourself.

B: Well, I really enjoy _____. I'm pretty good at that.

A: What about _____?

B: Actually, I _____.

➤ Do it yourself!

Pair work. **Create a conversation for the people in the picture. Say as much as you can.**

JOHN LEE
Human Resources

REFERENCES

The present perfect continuous

Use the present perfect continuous with <u>for</u> or <u>since</u> to describe activities that began in the past and continue in the present.

I've been working here **for** two months.

Form the present perfect continuous with <u>have been</u> or <u>has been</u> and the continuous (-ing) form of the verb.

She**'s been talking** on the phone **since** 10:00.

Has Martin **been living** here long? Yes, he has. Since 1999.

Where **has** he **been working**? At Micro-tech.

Use **for** with amounts of time: for six years.

Use **since** with specific times and dates: since we met, since May.

A. **Complete the sentences. Fill in the ovals.**

1. How long ____ that telephone call?
   - ⓐ have you been waiting for
   - ⓑ you are waiting for
   - ⓒ you waited for

2. We ____ three hours.
   - ⓐ waited since
   - ⓑ have been waiting for
   - ⓒ waiting for

3. How long ____?
   - ⓐ it has been raining
   - ⓑ has it been raining
   - ⓒ it's raining

4. It ____ Tuesday.
   - ⓐ has been raining for
   - ⓑ been raining since
   - ⓒ has been raining since

B. **Write questions with the words. Use the present perfect continuous.**

1. How long / you / live / in this city?

   How long have you been living in this city?

2. Ellen / work here / longer than Terry?

   Has Ellen been working here longer than Terry?

3. you / take care of children / a long time?

   Have you been taking care of children for a long time?

4. What / you / do / I saw you?

   What have you been doing since I saw you?

➤ Practical grammar

(For general suggestions, see *Introduction*, page Tix.)

The present perfect continuous

Content: the present perfect continuous with *for* and *since*

Procedure:

➤ On the board write *How long have you been living in the United States? How long have you been studying English? How long have you been working at your job?* Have a few students respond. Record two short answers for each question. Include *for* or *since* in the written responses even if the students did not provide them. For example, if a student's response was *two years*, say *You have been living in the United States for two years?* to clarify and then write *for two years.* Point out that living, studying, and working are all activities that students started doing in the past and still do today. Underline *have been living, have been studying,* and *have been working* in the questions and explain that the present perfect continuous is formed with *has / have been* + the *-ing* form of the verb.

➤ Refer to the short answers with *for* and *since* on the board. Explain that *for* is used with an amount or quantity of time (e.g., two years, fifteen minutes), and *since* is used with a specific date or time (e.g., 2001, 9:00). Elicit students' help in converting each *for* answer into a *since* answer and vice versa. Call out several periods of time with *for* and have students use *since* to tell how long; for example, call out *for two years* and elicit *since 2001.* Then do the reverse.

➤ To reinforce use of the present perfect continuous, use activities going on in your classroom as examples. Say *I am teaching right now. I started teaching at (time). I have been teaching for / since ....* Use what individual students are doing as examples to focus on the use of *has* with *he* or *she,* for example, *Radwa has been listening for five minutes.* Write some of these present perfect continuous statements on the board and make them into questions. For example, write *I have been teaching for / since ...* and then *How long have I been teaching?* Draw students' attention to the reversal of the subject and the verb. Have students answer the questions for more practice.

➤ To make sure students know how to answer *yes / no* questions in the present perfect continuous, write on the board the second example from the grammar box, *Has Martin ...* Underline *Yes, he has* in the example. Then change *1999* to a more recent date and elicit a negative response. Next, ask students *Have you been living here long?* Elicit *Yes, I have* and *No, I haven't.*

Option: Write the heading *Present perfect continuous* on the board. Then write the subheadings *Form* and *When used.* Have students read the explanations and examples in the grammar box. Ask how the present perfect continuous is formed. Write *person / people + has / have + been + _____ing* under *Form.* Ask students how a question is formed. Write *(Question word) + has / have + person / people + been + _____ing?* under *Form.* Have students read the sentence at the top of the grammar box. Ask when the present perfect continuous is used. Write *with activities that began in the past and continue in the present* and *with for and since* under *When used.*

A. Complete the sentences ...

➤ To model item 1, write out the question with each possible answer inserted. Have students choose the correct sentence.

➤ Model how to select an answer by filling in the circle with the correct letter.

➤ Advise students that they are looking for an answer that is in the present perfect continuous.

➤ Have students check answers with a partner. Then review as a class.

B. Write questions with ...

➤ Write item 1 on the board and model how to make a question from the words. For example, ask *Do we use have or has with you? Do we say you have or have you?* Review the difference between *yes / no* questions and questions beginning with a question word.

Option: After students complete Exercise B, have them write answers to questions 1, 3, and 4 and then practice asking and answering these questions with a partner.

T6

C. Learn about your classmates' . . .

➤ Students write *yes / no* questions or questions with a question word using the present perfect continuous.

➤ Circulate, making sure questions are correctly formed, have a question mark, and are appropriate.

➤ Have students walk around the classroom and ask at least three other students their questions.

Gerunds for describing likes, dislikes and skills

Procedure:

➤ Tell students that they are going to be using *-ing* words again but in a different way. Have them copy the information you are going to put on the board. Brainstorm verbs in the *-ing* form and write them on the board. At the top of the list, write *Gerunds*. If helpful, explain that a *gerund* is an *-ing* word that is used as a noun.

➤ Have students turn back to page 5. To the left of the gerunds list make a list of ways students can talk about their skills, likes, and dislikes, for example, *I enjoy, I'm good at, I love.* Have students draw lines to connect the words in each list to make true sentences about themselves.

D. Complete each sentence . . .

➤ After students complete the exercise independently, ask for volunteers to read each item to the class. Write the gerunds on the board and advise students to check their spelling.

Note: For a review of how to spell gerunds, refer students to page 150.

➤ Do it yourself!

(For general suggestions, see *Introduction*, page Txiii.)

Procedure:

A–B.

➤ Using gerunds, tell students one thing that you are good at, not good at, like, and don't like to model how they will be filling in their charts. For example, say *I'm good at teaching English, I'm not good at cooking, I like . . . , I don't like . . .* Use true information about yourself, which is more interesting for students and builds rapport.

➤ After students complete their charts, have them sort their answers into gerunds that apply to work situations and those that apply to home or personal life. This will help students prepare for job interviews. In a job interview for a receptionist, for example, it might be interesting to know that a candidate enjoys bicycling, but it is more important to know that he or she enjoys working with people. Have students compare their answers.

Option: Draw a Venn diagram (two overlapping circles) on the board. To demonstrate how the diagram is used, have two volunteers come to the front of the class. Ask the class to tell you how the two students are the same, for example, *brown hair, learning English, in this class.* Write those characteristics in the area where the circles overlap. Then ask how the two students are different, for example, *man / woman, speaks Spanish / speaks Vietnamese, wearing pants / wearing a skirt.* Write these differences in the non-overlapping areas of the circle.

Student A   Student B

In pairs, have students compare and contrast their skills, likes, and dislikes by creating Venn diagrams from their charts.

C. Learn about your classmates' lives and work. Write two questions to ask a classmate. Use the present perfect continuous. Use a question mark (?).

1. _____

2. _____

Gerunds for describing likes, dislikes, and skills

Describe your likes and dislikes with gerunds.	Describe your skills with gerunds.

I like **working** with people.

That's great. We have a good job at the Holiday Hotel.

Tell me something about your skills.

Well, I'm great at **fixing** old cars.

D. Complete each sentence with a gerund.

1. I'm good at ___*organizing*___ . I enjoy ____being____ an administrative assistant.
   organize   be

2. I don't mind ____repairing____ the coffee maker, and you won't have to pay me!
   repair

3. I'm looking for a job as a receptionist. I'm good at ____working____ with people.
   work

4. I really dislike ____getting____ dirty. I'd rather not work in a garage.
   get

See page 150 for spelling rules for the gerund.

► Do it yourself!

A. Personalization. Use gerunds to describe your strengths and weaknesses and your likes and dislikes.

Strengths: *I'm good at*	Weaknesses: *I'm not good at*	Likes: *I like*	Dislikes: *I don't like*

B. Discussion. Talk about your chart with a group.

Authentic practice

A. Read and listen again. Then check True, False, or Maybe.

	True	False	Maybe
1. Mr. Han and Ms. Ramos have been working together for three years.	☐	☑	☐
2. Ms. Ramos's first name is Diana.	☑	☐	☐
3. Ms. Ramos speaks English at A-Mart.	☐	☐	☑
4. Ms. Ramos doesn't want to fill out a questionnaire.	☐	☑	☐

B. Listen. Underline your response.

1. **YOU** <u>Not at all.</u>   **YOU** Not long.

2. **YOU** <u>My supervisor told me about it.</u>   **YOU** It's a small world.

3. **YOU** <u>Of course.</u>   **YOU** I appreciate it.

C. Listen again. Read your response out loud.

➤ Authentic practice

(For general suggestions, see *Introduction,* page Tx.)

Procedure:

🎧

➤ Ask questions about the pictures, such as *Who's in the pictures?* (a man and a woman) *What do they do first?* (shake hands) *Where are they?* (at the Atlas Shoe Company) *What do you think they are talking about?* (a job)

➤ Play the cassette or read the picture story. With books open, students listen and read.

➤ Have students close their books. Ask *yes / no* questions about the conversation, such as *Is the conversation about a salesperson position?* (no, a receptionist position) *Did Ms. Ramos see the ad for the job in a newspaper?* (yes) *Does Ms. Ramos like working with people?* (yes) *Did Ms. Ramos work in a hospital?* (no, in the mail room at A-Mart)

➤ With books open, ask the class to summarize Ms. Ramos's qualifications for the job. Elicit *She has been working in the mail room at A-Mart for three years, She's not bad at organizing and paperwork, Her English has been getting better, She really likes working with people.*

Challenge: Have students imagine what questions might be on the questionnaire that Ms. Ramos is going to fill out. Students can refer to pages 5 and 7 for ideas. First create a couple of questions as a class, such as *Do you enjoy working with people? Are you good at using a computer?* Have students work in pairs to create a questionnaire with at least five questions. Each pair of students can then join another pair and ask the questions on their questionnaire.

🎧 A. Read and listen again . . .

➤ To model the activity, make some of the *yes / no* questions you asked into statements and write them on the board, for example, *This conversation is about a salesperson position.* Ask students which statements are correct, or true, and write *True* next to them. Ask students which statements are wrong, or false, and write *False* next to them. Then write a statement on the board about something that can't be determined from the conversation, such as *Ms. Ramos is from Mexico.* Write *Maybe* next to this statement.

➤ After students listen to the picture story again and complete the exercise, review the answers as a class. Have students change the false statements to make them true.

🎧 B–C.

➤ Read each item in the tapescript out loud or play the cassette. Allow students to listen as many times as necessary to complete the exercise.

➤ Have students check their answers to Exercise B with a partner before they read their responses out loud in Exercise C.

Challenge: Use the prompts for Exercises B and C as a dictation. Have students listen to the tape and write what they hear. Allow students to listen as many times as necessary. Ask volunteers to write the sentences on the board. Make corrections as a class. Students can then practice the prompts and responses with a partner.

Tapescript

1. Would you mind my calling you Diana?

2. How did you hear about this position?

3. Please fill out this questionnaire.

If your students are ready . . .

Culture / Civics note: In formal situations, respect and courtesy are demonstrated by using a person's last name preceded by a title. For example, in the *Authentic practice* conversation on page 8, the interviewer greets Diana Ramos as *Ms. Ramos. Ms.* has become increasingly popular as a general title for any woman, whether married or unmarried. *Miss* is used for an unmarried woman. *Mrs.* is used for a married woman. *Mr.* is used for a man, whether married or unmarried.

Notice that the interviewer asks *By the way, is it OK if I call you Diana?* In the North American workplace, there is a strong belief in equality among co-workers. Co-workers usually call each other by their first names. Formal titles and last names are not generally used, even between the boss and employees. However, when in doubt about how to address someone, it is best to use the formal name and wait for the person to suggest that you use the first name.

An informal job interview

Procedure:

🎧 A–B.

➤ Tell students that they're going to listen to a job interview with a bus driver. Read the selection on the tapescript out loud or play the cassette while students listen with books closed.

➤ Have students open their books. Read the instructions out loud. Refer students to the words for expressing likes and dislikes on page 5. Have students circle the four words in the box on page 5 that are similar to the headings here: *like, don't mind, dislike,* and *hate.* Write these four words on the board with the corresponding headings from Exercise A underneath. Have a volunteer tell something about himself or herself using one of the words from the top line and a gerund, for example, *I like using a computer.* Then have another student use words from the bottom line to tell what the first student likes, doesn't mind, doesn't like, or hates, for example, *She likes using a computer.* Repeat several times to prepare students for the activity and emphasize the difference between talking about likes and dislikes in the first and third person.

➤ Allow students to listen to the conversation as many times as necessary to complete Exercises A and B.

➤ Review the answers as a class and elicit students' help in changing the false answers in Exercise B to make them true.

C. True story...

➤ Model this activity for your students by telling a true story about a job interview that you had. Ask students to put a check mark next to each word in the box that they hear you say. This will help them to notice how and when the words are used.

Challenge: To help students set goals, have students describe their plans for getting a new job in the future, using the words in the box and either *will* or *going to.*

➤ Do it yourself!

(For general suggestions, see *Introduction,* page Txiii.)

Procedure:

A. Write your <u>own</u> response...

➤ Tell students to imagine that Sara Molina is interviewing them for a job. Have students write their responses.

➤ Before students practice with a partner, have a volunteer play the part of Sara Molina and read each speech balloon aloud. Answer each question for yourself, giving students an opportunity to check the appropriateness of their own responses.

B. Culture talk...

➤ To prepare students to discuss, have them make a list of people they call by their first names in their country and a list of people with whom they use a family name and / or title.

➤ Have students share their customs about using first names in small, diverse groups.

Tapescript

[door opens and shuts]

Receptionist: Oh, hello! You surprised me. Have you been waiting long?

Mr. Witherspoon: No, not really. Just since about ten after nine. I have a nine-thirty appointment with Arlene Lopez, and I hate being late.

Receptionist: Well, Arlene's not here yet.

Mr. Witherspoon: That's OK. I don't mind waiting.

Receptionist: That's great. Personally, I can't stand waiting . . . Would you like a cup of coffee while you wait?

Mr. Witherspoon: No, thanks. I'm OK.

[door opens and shuts]

Ms. Lopez: Hi. I got here sooner than I thought.

Receptionist: Arlene, this is . . . I'm sorry. I didn't get your name.

Mr. Witherspoon: Carnell Witherspoon.

Ms. Lopez: Oh, yes. Mr. Witherspoon.

[pause] [door opens, paper shuffles]

Ms. Lopez: Carnell Witherspoon. Do you mind if I call you Carnell? You can call me Arlene. I don't like being too formal.

Mr. Witherspoon: That's fine. Neither do I.

Ms. Lopez: It says here you work for Greenmont Bus. Have you been working there long?

Mr. Witherspoon: Since February.

Ms. Lopez: So how come you're looking for a new job? Don't you like working at Greenmont?

Mr. Witherspoon: Actually, I do. I just need to make some more money, and Greenmont doesn't have anything full-time . . . My wife and I are expecting a baby in December.

Ms. Lopez: What are your hours at Greenmont? This job's real early.

Mr. Witherspoon: How early is that?

Ms. Lopez: Well, the first pickup is at 6:45. You'd have to be here by 6:00 to make it on time.

Mr. Witherspoon: No problem. I like getting up early, and my Greenmont shift doesn't start till 2:00. What time would I get off here?

(Tapescript is continued on page T10.)

A. Listening comprehension. Listen to the job interview with a bus driver. Then listen again and check the things Mr. Witherspoon likes, doesn't mind, doesn't like, or hates.

	Likes	Doesn't mind	Doesn't like	Hates
1. being late	☐	☐	☐	☑
2. waiting	☐	☑	☐	☐
3. being formal	☐	☐	☑	☐
4. working at Greenmont Bus Company	☑	☐	☐	☐
5. getting up early	☑	☐	☐	☐

B. Listen again and write <u>True</u> or <u>False</u>.

1. _____False_____ Mr. Witherspoon has been waiting for a long time.

2. _____False_____ The receptionist was there when Mr. Witherspoon entered.

3. _____True_____ Mr. Witherspoon has been working at Greenmont Bus since February.

4. _____False_____ The Witherspoons had a baby in December.

C. True story. Tell your partner about a job interview you or a friend had. Use words from the box or your <u>own</u> ideas.

a job application   a job   references   a letter of recommendation   an ad

➤ Do it yourself!

A. Write your <u>own</u> response. Then read your interview out loud with a partner.

Hi. I'm Sara Molina. Please call me Sara. What would you like me to call you?

YOU _____

Please tell me a little bit about yourself.

YOU _____

Well, we have several openings right now. When can you give me a list of references?

YOU _____

B. Culture talk. In the country you come from, what are the customs about using first names? Compare cultures with your classmates.

Do's and don'ts for job interviews

🎧 **A.** Read and listen to the letters.

Ask Joan
Culture tips for newcomers

Dear Joan:
I've been living in this country for two years, and I've been taking care of children in my home since I got here. I love working with children, and I'd like to have a full-time job outside the home in a day-care center. I'm writing because I have an interview next week at an employment agency. Joan, this is my first job interview! Any tips for me?

Irene from Moline

Dear Irene:
It sounds like you have great experience for that day-care position. I have only a couple of suggestions. Wear simple, neat clothes. Don't wear a lot of makeup or strong perfume—lots of people don't like that. Bring your references with you. Oh, and just be yourself. I'm sure you'll get the job. Best of luck!

Joan

Dear Joan:
I was an accountant in my country, but I've been driving a taxi since I got here last year. I've also been studying English, and I think I'm ready to start looking for office work while I study for my accountant's license. Do you have any advice for me?

Arturo the accountant

Dear Arturo:
You've learned enough English in one year to restart your career. That's pretty amazing! Congratulations! Be sure to dress neatly and conservatively. Tell the interviewer about your skills and experience. Avoid doing things that might annoy people, like arriving late or chewing gum.

Joan

B. Check <u>Irene</u> or <u>Arturo</u>.

	Irene	Arturo
1. has been driving a taxi	☐	☑
2. has been studying English	☐	☑
3. has been living here for two years	☑	☐
4. has been taking care of children	☑	☐

Ms. Lopez: Let me check . . . It looks like you'd finish here by about 10:00, 10:30 the latest. How's that?

Mr. Witherspoon: Perfect . . . I like having a little break for lunch. By the way, I have references. Would you like to see them?

Ms. Lopez: Yes, thanks.

➤ Authentic practice

(For general suggestions, see *Introduction,* page Tx.)

Do's and don'ts for job interviews

Procedure:

🎧 A. Read and listen to the letters.

➤ Ask students if they have seen advice columns before. If possible, bring in advice columns from a local newspaper. Explain that people write when they have a problem and ask for advice or an opinion about what they should do. The columnist writes back, and the letters are published in the newspaper. Ask students if the newspapers in their countries have advice columns.

➤ Explain that *Ask Joan* is an advice column for people who are new to this country and have questions about cultural expectations.

➤ Play the cassette or read the letters. Students listen and read silently. Pause after the first letter and ask *What is the problem? What will Joan's advice be?* Encourage students to make predictions and then have them listen to the response. Ask *What was Joan's advice?* Repeat for the second letter and response.

➤ Have students close their books and list the *do's* and *don'ts* they can remember from Joan's letters.

Option: To show this unit's grammar in context, have students underline all the examples of the present perfect continuous in the letters and responses, for example, *I've been living.* Then have students circle the gerunds, for example, *working with children.* Note that the letters contain examples of *-ing* words that are neither present perfect continuous nor gerunds. *I'm writing* is present continuous. *That's pretty amazing* is a variation of the phrase *That's amazing* learned on page 3; *amazing* is used as an adjective here, not as a verb or a gerund.

B. Check <u>Irene</u> or <u>Arturo.</u>

➤ Allow students to listen to the letters again, if helpful, and have them complete the exercise.

➤ After students check answers with a partner, have them tell or write two things they have been doing since they came to this country.

If your students are ready . . .

Culture / Civics note: Personal appearance and personal hygiene are important in making a good impression during a job interview. Applicants are expected to dress neatly in clothing appropriate for the job. Clothing should be clean and ironed. Loud colors or revealing clothing should be avoided. Jewelry, cologne, and perfume should be minimal. Before the interview, applicants should be sure to shower or bathe, brush their teeth, shave or neatly trim their beard, and comb or style their hair.

T10

C. What does Joan suggest ...

➤ Have students read the phrases out loud. Reinforce correct pronunciation of the words ending in -ing.

➤ Ask students what kinds of phrases are in the box. Elicit that the phrases are things you should or shouldn't do in an interview and that the first word in each ends in -ing and is a gerund.

➤ Have students write each phrase in the correct column. Review the answers as a class. Discuss why chewing gum, wearing a lot of makeup, and wearing strong perfume are not good ideas.

Option: Students imagine that they have a job interview next week. Have them plan what they will wear and what they will bring.

A pre-employment application

Procedure:

➤ Review the items on the application. If helpful, point out or elicit that the present perfect continuous is used in the question *How long have you been working for this employer?* and that gerunds will be used in filling out the last item on the questionnaire.

➤ Ask students to talk with a partner about their skills and what job they would like to have. Ask for a couple of volunteers to share. Write their desired job and skills on the board. Point out that students should list skills that match the position they are seeking and that they should list their skills using the -ing or gerund form.

➤ Have students complete the form.

➤ Do it yourself!

(For general suggestions, see *Introduction*, page Txiii.)

Procedure:

A. Bring in job applications ...

➤ Collect the applications you asked students to bring in, and add those that you brought.

➤ Have students work in groups of four. Give each group two applications to compare. Ask questions such as *Which is the most difficult to complete? Which asks for the most information? Which asks for skills?*

➤ If there are enough applications, have each student fill one out. If there aren't, have students work in pairs to fill out an application for one of them.

Option: To familiarize students with language used to elicit information on employment applications, have the class generate a list of ten items commonly found on job applications, such as *name, address, date*. On the board, draw a chart like the one below and have students copy it. Have students check off the information that each of their group's two applications contain. Then have students exchange applications with other groups and check off the items that those applications contain.

Field project: Have students create and practice a conversation in which they request a job application. If appropriate, send students in pairs to different neighborhood businesses to ask for applications, or have them to go to a business or company that they do not work for and get an application as an out-of-class assignment.

B. Pair work ...

➤ Ask the groups to brainstorm at least ten interview questions based on the applications. Have all students write the questions.

➤ Divide the number of students present by two. Have students count off from one to this number, starting at one again when the number is reached. Students then pair up with the person who has the same number (and is from a different group) and ask each other their interview questions.

Information	Application 1	Application 2	Application 3	Application 4	Application 5
Name					
Address					
Date					
Current employer					
Current position					
Position desired					
Skills					

C. **What does Joan suggest for job interviews? Write each phrase in the correct column.**

chewing gum	wearing strong perfume
bringing your references	being yourself
being neat	wearing simple, neat clothes
wearing a lot of makeup	being on time

Joan suggests	**Joan advises against**
bringing your references;	chewing gum;
being neat; being yourself;	wearing a lot of makeup;
wearing simple, neat clothes;	wearing strong perfume
being on time	

A pre-employment application

Read the pre-employment application and fill it out for yourself.

Town of Buenavista, Oklahoma
2600 North Main
Buenavista, OK 73129

PRE-EMPLOYMENT APPLICATION

Date of application: _____

_____
Applicant's name
_____
Current mailing address

Are you currently employed? [circle one] **Y / N**   If yes, position: _____

Employer and address: _____

How long have you been working for this employer? _____

If not currently employed, last position held: _____

Dates: from _____ to _____

Describe the type of position you are seeking: _____
_____

Please list your skills (Examples: **driving, repairing equipment, speaking another language, etc.**).
_____

➤ Do it yourself!   A plan-ahead project

A. **Bring in job applications from places such as a supermarket, bank, discount store, or convenience store, or use the one on pages 151 and 152. Fill out an application.**

B. **Pair work. Practice a job interview with a classmate. Use the applications.**

> **Review**

A. Pair work or group work.

- Where are the people?
- What do they want?

Ask and answer questions.
Create conversations.
Tell a story.
Say as much as you can.

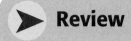 **Review**

(For general suggestions, see *Introduction*, page Txii.)

Procedure:

A. Pair work or group work.

Ask and answer questions.

➤ Ask the class *Where are the people?* (outside the Human Resources cubicle, waiting to talk to someone in Human Resources) *What do they want?* (They want to interview for a job.)

➤ Point to one person in the picture and ask questions such as *What is this person doing? What is this person wearing? How does this person feel? Why do you think so?* Then have students point to different people in the picture and ask each other questions.

Option: As a class, brainstorm and write on the board questions that John Lee might ask the job applicants when he interviews them. Then ask students to choose one applicant in the picture to play the role of. In pairs, students take turns asking each other the interview questions on the board and answering as if they were the character they chose from the picture.

Create conversations.

➤ Ask the class to choose one of the four pairs of people with speech balloons in the picture. Have students label the person on the left *A* and the person on the right *B*. Write *A:* on the board and elicit the class's help in creating the first line of a conversation between the two people. Then write *B:* and elicit a response. Continue adding lines to the conversation as a class, encouraging students to say as much as they can.

➤ With a partner, have students role-play the parts of the other three pairs in the picture. Circulate and listen to the conversations. Use prompts if necessary to help students extend the conversation, such as *What small talk can this person make? What job do you think he or she is applying for? What is he or she good at?* To encourage students to talk more, you may want to have them spend one minute on each of the three pairs; signal when students should move on to the next pair.

Option: When students have finished, write the headings *Small talk, Gerunds, Present perfect continuous* on the board. Ask *Who used small talk? What did you say? Who used gerunds in their conversation? Which ones did you use? Who used the present perfect continuous? Can you give an example?* Write students' examples on the board under the appropriate headings.

Tell a story.

Option: Skills, likes, and dislikes. Have students point to different people in the picture and make up skills, likes, and dislikes for them. Model the activity by pointing to the man on the far left side of the picture and saying *He's good at fixing cars. He likes driving. He doesn't like using a computer.*

Option: How long ...? Have students point to different people in the picture and talk about how long they have been doing different things. Model the activity by pointing to the man with his arms crossed at the bottom of the picture and saying *He has been waiting for two hours. He has been living in the United States for six months. He has also been looking for a job for six months. He has been studying English since he was fifteen.*

Option: Do's and don'ts. Have students point out the do's and don'ts for job interviews that are illustrated in the picture, for example, *Do bring your references, Don't wear a lot of makeup.* Refer students to pages 10 and 11 for ideas.

🎧 B. Listen to the conversation ...

➤ To set the scene, tell students they will hear a conversation between two friends who meet while looking for new jobs.

➤ Read the selection on the tapescript out loud or play the cassette while students listen with books closed.

➤ Have students open their books. Read the instructions out loud. Emphasize that students should listen for what the woman likes and doesn't like.

➤ Read the conversation or play the cassette as many times as necessary for students to complete the exercise.

➤ Ask *What other two things does Cheryl like doing?* (working alone, organizing things)

Option: Have students add two more columns of check boxes with the headings *I like* and *I don't like*. For each item, have students check their own preferences.

C–E.

➤ Students work individually to complete the review exercises.

➤ Circulate to offer help as needed.

➤ Have students check answers with a partner. Review answers as a class.

➤ Identify any areas of difficulty that may require additional practice.

Option: Have students practice Exercises C and D in pairs. One person reads the statement or question and the other reads the response.

Tapescript

Man: Cheryl! I can't believe my eyes!

Woman: Jack? Is that you? What are you doing here?

Man: Looking for a job, just like you, I guess.

Woman: That's right. I really need to change jobs. I've been driving a van for Gold Medal Bread too long. It's time for me to do something else. I like driving and working alone, but I hate getting up in the middle of the night.

Man: Me too. How long have you been working at Gold Medal?

Woman: For two years now. It's time for a change.

Man: What kind of job are you looking for?

Woman: I'm not sure. But I like doing paperwork and I enjoy organizing things and I don't much like working with a lot of people. So I think I'm going to ask for an office job.

B. Listen to the conversation. Then listen again and check the things the woman likes and doesn't like.

	Likes	Doesn't like
1. driving	☑	☐
2. getting up in the middle of the night	☐	☑
3. doing paperwork	☑	☐
4. working with a lot of people	☐	☑

C. Choose <u>your</u> response. Fill in the ovals.

1. "I like that jacket."

   ⓐ It's a small world. ●ⓑ Thanks.

2. "Would you mind driving my daughter to school?"

   ●ⓐ Not at all. ⓑ Do you like driving?

3. "Tell me something about yourself. What do you enjoy doing?"

   ⓐ I haven't been doing that for long. ●ⓑ Cooking.

D. Write responses to the interviewer.

1. **Interviewer:** I'm Eduardo Trent. Do you mind if I call you by your first name?

   YOU _____

2. **Interviewer:** Please tell me something about yourself.

   YOU _____

3. **Interviewer:** Could I see your references?

   YOU _____

E. Write questions with the words. Use the present perfect continuous.

1. How long / you / study English?

   How long have you been studying English?

2. What / he / do / 1999?

   What has he been doing since 1999?

3. Who / work here / the longest?

   Who has been working here the longest?

4. you / wait / long?

   Have you been waiting long?

F. Complete the paragraph with gerunds.

Juan Sepulveda was a pharmacist in his country. Right now he's looking for a part-time job so he can study English and get ready for his licensing exam. He likes _____cooking_____ and _____cleaning_____, and he likes _____working_____ at night
       1. cook   2. clean   3. work

because his English classes are in the afternoon. He doesn't enjoy _____driving_____
                                                        4. drive

and he's not too good at _____fixing_____ office machines, but he doesn't mind
                                 5. fix

_____doing_____ other kinds of office work. Two things he hates _____doing_____
   6. do   7. do

are handling cash and _____taking care of_____ children.
                            8. take care of

G. Fill out the job application for yourself.

Stilton Hotel Corporation
2201 Broadway
Cabo Maria, FL 32862

APPLICATION FOR EMPLOYMENT

_____
Name and current mailing address

_____
Current employer and address

If not currently employed, last employment: _____
                                                     Employer

_____
      Address   Dates (from – to)

Skills: _____

H. Composition. On a separate sheet of paper, write about the picture on page 12. Say as much as you can.

> **Now I can**
> ❑ start a conversation with someone I don't know.
> ❑ get to know someone.
> ❑ ask someone for a letter of recommendation.
> ❑ talk about my skills, likes, and dislikes.
> ❑ have a job interview.
> ❑ fill out an employment application.
> ❑ _____.

F. Complete the paragraph . . .

➤ Students fill in the blanks in the paragraph with the gerund form of the verbs. Check that students drop the *-e* in *driving* and *taking*.

➤ After students complete the exercise, ask *What are Juan's skills? What are his likes? What are his dislikes?*

Option: Have students write a similar paragraph about themselves. Remind them to change the verbs so that they agree with *I* rather than *he*. Collect the paragraphs and read them out loud. Have the class guess who wrote each paragraph.

G. Fill out the job application . . .

Option: After students fill out the application, they can ask a partner interview questions based on the application, for example, *Where do you work now? What was your last job? What are your skills?*

H. Composition . . .

➤ Provide students with concrete approaches to writing about the picture on page 12. Use one of the following options, give students a choice of options, or assign options based on students' levels of proficiency. Model what is expected of students for each option.

➤ Advise students to look back through the unit for help and ideas as they write.

➤ Circulate to offer help as needed.

Option: Have students choose one of the pairs of people in the picture who are talking to each other, label them *A* and *B*, and write an extended conversation for them. Have students use the same format as the model conversations on pages 2 through 5. Students can later role-play their conversations for the class.

Option: Have students number the people in the picture and then, on a separate sheet of paper, write two sentences about each one. To reinforce the grammar points in the unit, one sentence can be about how long the person has been doing something and the other can describe the person's likes, dislikes, or skills using a gerund.

Option: Have students choose one person in the picture on page 12 and tell his or her story in a paragraph similar to Exercise F on page 14. Use a group activity to prepare students for this option. Each group of four will need one sheet of paper and one pen or pencil. Have each group choose one person in the picture whose story they will tell. Explain that they will make up the information they provide. Ask a series of questions for group members to answer about their person, such as *What is this person's name? What was this person's job in his or her country? What is this person doing here? What does this person like? What does this person dislike? What are this person's skills? How long has this person been looking for a job?* The group discusses their answer to each question, but after each question the paper and pen are passed to the right so that a different person is writing each time.

Now I can

➤ Read the first item in the box out loud, *Now I can start a conversation with someone I don't know.* Elicit from the class an example of how to start a conversation with someone you don't know, such as *Terrible weather today.*

➤ In pairs, have students take turns reading each item in the box and giving an example of what they have learned. When students can provide an example, they should check that box. For the items students weren't able to check, they should look back through the unit for ideas.

➤ When students are finished reviewing with their partners, read each item out loud and elicit an example from the class.

Oral test (optional)

You may want to use the *Now I can* box as an informal evaluation. While students are working on the *Composition* activity, you can call them up individually and check their ability with two or three objectives.

The community

Note: For the plan-ahead project on page 25, students should bring a public transportation map, town or city map, or mall or building diagram to class. Encourage students to bring in local maps and diagrams, which may also be used on pages 17 through 19.

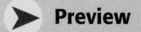 **Preview**

(For general suggestions, see *Introduction,* page Tviii.)

Warm up. What time should the guests arrive?

Procedure:

➤ To activate students' prior knowledge, ask questions such as *How do we invite people to special events?* (in person, by phone, in writing) *What events are written invitations used for?* (weddings, wedding and baby showers, children's birthday parties, surprise parties, company parties) *What information is usually included on a written invitation?* (time, date, place, telephone number, directions / map, occasion, what to bring)

➤ Have students read the invitation. Ask questions such as *What is this?* (an invitation) *What is it for?* (a dinner party) *What time is the party?* (6:30) Elicit or explain that *RSVP* means that you should tell the person who invited you whether you can attend the party or not.

➤ Say *The dinner party is at 6:30. What time should the guests arrive?* Write on the board *6:15, 6:30, 6:45,* and *7:00 or later.* Have students raise their hands for the time they would arrive at the party. Keep a tally on the board. Discuss the results. Explain that in the United States, arriving late, especially for a dinner party, may be considered impolite.

Option: In groups, have students write their own invitations for a party, using the invitation on page 15 as an example. Have a volunteer from each group read the invitation to the class.

If your students are ready . . .

Culture / Civics notes: Written invitations are common for formal events such as birthday parties, weddings, and graduation ceremonies. Invitations generally include a description of the event followed by its date, time, and location. Invitations are usually intended only for those to whom they are addressed. Bringing additional guests of your own without asking the host for permission is impolite. Invitations should be answered promptly, especially if they contain the acronym RSVP (*Répondez s'il vous plaît,* French for *Please reply*). Never accept an invitation unless you really plan to attend. If you are unable to attend, a common reply is *Thank you for the invitation, but I am unable to attend.* Guests are expected to arrive at or close to the scheduled time. Arriving more than 15 or 30 minutes late to a social event is considered impolite.

Although table settings vary depending on the formality of the occasion and the food served, the following basic rules commonly apply. The fork goes on the left side of the plate. The knife goes on the right side of the plate, with the cutting edge toward the plate. The spoon is placed to the right of the knife. The napkin is placed to the left of or under the fork, and the drinking glass goes above the knife.

Unit 2 objectives

Procedure:

➤ After students read the objectives, brainstorm words used to give directions, places in buildings, and forms of public transportation that students already know. Write these words on the board or on a sheet of chart paper and save them for use on pages 16 and 18.

The community

> ## Preview

Warm up. What time should the guests arrive?

A dinner party!
Time: 6:30
Date: May 11
Place: 35 Grove Street
RSVP: 929-3430

Hope you can come!
Marian

Unit 2 objectives

- Extend and accept an invitation and make plans to meet.
- Ask for and give directions within a building.
- Ask for and give assistance on an elevator.
- Use maps, plans, and building directories.
- Ask for and give directions for public transportation.

Practical conversations

Model 1 Ask for and give directions within a building.

A. Listen and read.

A: Excuse me. Can you tell me how to get to the parking garage?

B: Sure. It's on the third floor. Take either the elevator or the escalator to the second floor. Walk to the end of the hall and then go up the stairs.

A: Thanks.

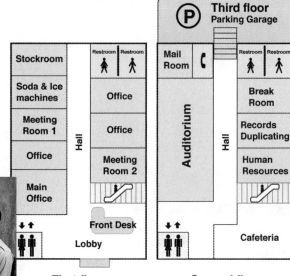

B. Listen again and repeat.

Vocabulary

Directions

Go straight.

Turn right *or* Make a right.

Make your second left.

Go down the hall.

Go to the end of the hall.

Walk down the stairs.

Take the escalator.

Take the elevator.

C. Pair work. Ask for and give directions to places on the building diagram above. Use the vocabulary and your _own_ choices.

A: _____. Can you tell me how to get to _____?

B: ___1___. It's on the _____ floor. _____.

A: Thanks.

[1]Of course, I'd be glad to

16   Unit 2

➤ Practical conversations

(For general suggestions, see *Introduction*, page Tviii.)

Model 1

Content: beginning a conversation; asking for and giving directions within a building

Procedure:

🎧 A–B.

➤ To set the scene for the conversation, ask questions about the photo, such as *Who's in the photo?* (a woman and a building receptionist or security guard) *What is the receptionist doing?* (He's pointing.) *What do you think they are talking about?* (directions, where something is)

➤ Have students compare the places on the diagram with the places in buildings they brainstormed on page 15. Ask *What places on the diagram are also on our list? What are some places on the diagram that are not on our list?* Ask if there are any words on the diagram that are new to students. Provide simple definitions; for example, *Human Resources* is the department in a company that deals with employing, training, and helping people.

➤ After students listen to the conversation, ask comprehension questions such as *Where does the woman want to go?* (to the parking garage) *What floor is it on?* (the third floor) *What should the woman do first?* (Take either the elevator or the escalator to the second floor.)

➤ Have students label the elevator, escalator, and stairs in the diagram.

Challenge: In small groups, ask students to think about what people can do in each place on the diagram. Have students write at least one verb or verb phrase for each place. Elicit examples such as *Soda & Ice Machines—drink, buy; Office—call, write, talk, use the computer.* Focusing on verbs in base form will help students get ready for the *Practical grammar* section of this unit.

🎧 Vocabulary

➤ Compare the vocabulary words to the words used to give directions that students brainstormed on page 15.

➤ As a class, come up with a simple hand gesture for each vocabulary item, such as pointing straight in front of oneself for *Go straight.* Use the steps that follow to help students internalize the vocabulary. Repeat each step several times, moving on to the

next when most of the class seems ready. First, have students use the gestures as they repeat the words. Then have them repeat and use the gestures with books closed. Next, give the directions in a different order and have students respond with the appropriate gesture. Finally, use each gesture and have the class call out the directions.

➤ Review ordinal numbers so that students will be able to give directions in a multi-floor building. Write several numbers on the board and elicit the corresponding ordinal number, for example, 4—*fourth*, 12—*twelfth*, 21—*twenty-first*. Then have students count off from their seats using ordinal numbers.

Note: In addition to *Turn left* and *Make a left*, students may hear *Take a left* when asking for directions outside of class.

Option: Make clear walkways between the rows of desks. Call these *halls.* Have a volunteer start at the front of the class. Point to a walkway and say *Go down the hall. Go to the end of the hall. Turn right. Go straight. Make your second right. Go down the hall.* Repeat with several volunteers. Also, students can give directions for you or each other to follow.

Challenge: Make cards with directions to places in your building. Use only the directions from the *Vocabulary* box, substituting *left* for *right* or using a different ordinal number (e.g., *Make your fourth right.*) as necessary. In pairs, have students follow the directions on their cards to find out which room you have sent them to. Set a five-minute time limit. Ask students where they went when they return. Students can exchange cards and repeat the activity.

C. Pair work ...

➤ Have students look at the diagram in Exercise A and find the front desk on the first floor. Give directions from the front desk to several different places in the building and have the class identify where you sent them.

➤ Model the activity with a more advanced student. Play the role of Student B. Demonstrate giving detailed directions to the place Student A asks about.

Challenge: Give pairs of students a large sheet of paper. Have them draw and label a diagram of the building in which your class is located. If appropriate, allow students to leave class to get a better idea of where places are. When they finish, have students practice the conversation again, this time asking for and giving directions to places in your building.

Model 2

Content: making a polite request; asking for and giving directions in an elevator; talking about locations in a building; complying with a request

Procedure:

🎧 A–B.

➤ Ask questions about the people in the photo, such as *Where are they?* (in an elevator) *What is the woman on the right doing?* (holding the elevator door open for the other woman)

➤ After students listen to the conversation, ask comprehension questions such as *What is the woman on the left doing?* (getting into the elevator) *What question does she ask?* (Going up?) *What question does the woman in the elevator ask?* (Where are you going?) *What floor is the woman on the left going to?* (two, the second floor)

Note: *Going up?* is a reduction. The complete question is *Are you going up?* Students can also use the reduction *Going down?* Also, *What floor?* is another way of asking *Where are you going?* in an elevator.

🎧 Vocabulary

➤ After students repeat the phrases, review the use of *on* and *in* to describe location in buildings. *On* is used to tell which floor. *In* is used to talk about which room or place in the building.

➤ Use the building directory in Exercise C to practice the vocabulary. If necessary, explain that rooms in the 100s are on the first floor, 200s on the second floor, and so on. Ask questions such as *Where are the Executive Offices?* (on the ground floor) *Where is the Human Resources Office?* (in 211) *What floor is it on?* (on the second floor) If students don't use the preposition or use it incorrectly, cue them by responding with a puzzled expression and asking *Where?* When the student self-corrects and says the preposition correctly, repeat the answer, emphasizing the preposition.

C. Pair work . . .

➤ Ask students if any words on the building directory are new to them. Provide simple definitions for any unknown words; for example, *benefits* refers to such things as medical insurance, dental insurance, or a retirement plan that employees receive as a part of their job.

➤ Draw a simple four-story building on the board. Label the basement and first / ground floor through third / top floors. Draw a stick figure to

indicate what floor of the Brimstone Building you're on and a star to indicate where you want to go. Then play the role of Student A and model the conversation with a student.

➤ Have students practice the conversation in pairs. Point out that students don't need to use the prepositions *on* and *in* in the *Pair work* conversation.

If your students are ready . . .

Language note: When talking about destination rather than location, the preposition *to*, rather than *on* or *in*, is used. For example, the response to the question *Where are you going?* is [*I'm going*] *to the basement*, not [*I'm going*] *in the basement*. Often the preposition is dropped in the response: *Where are you going? The basement.*

➤ Do it yourself!

(For general suggestions, see *Introduction*, page Txiii.)

Procedure:

A–B.

➤ If there isn't enough space on the board for all groups to make a building directory or diagram, hand out sheets of chart paper or transparencies and overhead pens.

➤ Refer students to the example of a building diagram on page 16 and the example of a building directory on page 17. In groups, have students create their own building directories or diagrams and then take turns giving directions to places on them, or use one or both of the options that follow.

Option: Bring in enough mall and building diagrams for each group to have one. Have students collaborate to make a building directory based on their diagram. Then have students use the diagram and their directory to practice giving directions within a building and in an elevator.

Option: Have students make a diagram or directory for the building where they work or live or a building they are very familiar with. Display the diagrams and directories on the classroom walls. Have students move around the room asking for and giving directions based on the diagram or directory they are looking at. You may want to have an inside and an outside circle of students rotating in different directions so that students practice with a different partner each time.

A. Listen and read.

A: Hold the elevator, please! Going up?

B: Yes. Where are you going?

A: Two, please.

B: There you go.

A: Thanks.

B. Listen again and repeat.

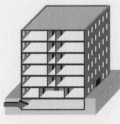

Vocabulary

Building interiors

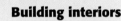

On the top floor.

On the first
(*or* ground) floor.

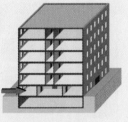

In the basement.

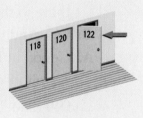

In Room 122.

C. Pair work. Choose a place in the Brimstone Building. Share an elevator ride up or down. Use the vocabulary and the building directory.

A: Hold the elevator, please! Going _____?

B: Yes. Where are you going?

A: _____, please.

B: There you go.

A: ___1___.

¹Thanks so much, I appreciate it

THE BRIMSTONE BUILDING

Executive Offices	Ground floor
Benefits Department	110
Human Resources Office	211
General Manager's Office	212
Medical Services	313
Records Department	Basement

▶ Do it yourself!

A. Collaborative activity. Make a diagram or a building directory on the chalkboard.

B. Discussion. Take turns giving directions to places on the diagram or the directory.

Practical conversations

Model 3   Ask for and give directions for public transportation.

A. **Listen and read.**

A: Hello. Ben's Warehouse.

B: Hello. Could you please tell me how to get there? I'm taking the bus.

A: Where are you now?

B: At the corner of Fulton and Redwood.

A: Well, take the number 6 to Hunter Street and transfer there to the 1.

B: OK. And where do I get off?

A: Get off at Elm. The warehouse is right on the corner. You can't miss it.

B. **Listen again and repeat.**

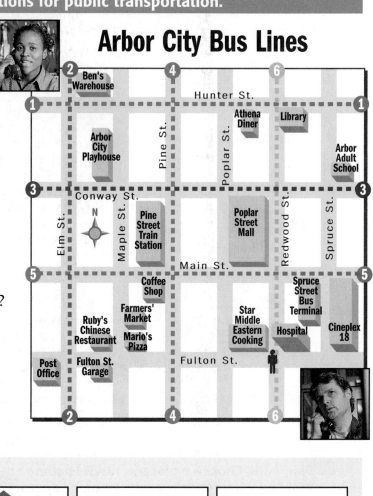

Arbor City Bus Lines

Vocabulary

Directions

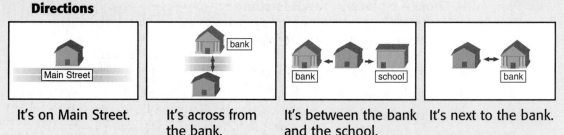

It's on Main Street.   It's across from the bank.   It's between the bank and the school.   It's next to the bank.

C. Pair work. **Get directions from Arbor Adult School to the post office and the hospital.**

A: _____.

B: _____. Could you please tell me how to get there? I'm taking the bus.

A: Where are you now?

B: At _____.

A: Well, take the number _____ to _____ and transfer there to the _____.

B: OK. And where do I get off?

A: Get off at _____. The _____ is _____. You can't miss it.

18   Unit 2

➤ Practical conversations

(For general suggestions, see *Introduction*, page Tviii.)

Model 3

Content: asking for and giving directions for public transportation; describing locations

Procedure:

🎧 A. Listen and read.

➤ Ask students for examples of public transportation (or refer to the list brainstormed on page 15). Elicit responses such as *bus*, *train*, *subway* or *metro*, *trolley*, *streetcar*. Ask what kinds of public transportation your community has. Take an informal poll. Have students who use the bus raise their hand, students who use the train, and so on.

➤ Ask students which types of local transportation post maps for users. Ask where the maps are posted.

➤ Have students look at the map in Exercise A. Ask questions such as *What does the map show?* (bus lines in Arbor City) *How many bus lines are shown?* (six) *What are the bus line numbers?* (1 through 6) Have students point to different streets and places on the map; for example, say *Point to Main Street, Point to Arbor Adult School.*

➤ After students listen to the conversation the first time, have them find on the map the places mentioned in the conversation. Have them point to the corner of Fulton and Redwood, the number 6 bus line, Hunter Street, the number 1 bus line, the corner of Hunter and Elm, and Ben's Warehouse.

➤ Have students place a finger on the corner of Fulton and Redwood. Read the directions slowly and have students follow along on the map.

🎧 B. Listen again and repeat.

➤ When students listen to the conversation the second time, have them trace the directions on the map as they repeat.

➤ Have students close their books. Ask questions such as *Where does the man want to go?* (to Ben's Warehouse) *How is he going to get there?* (by bus) *How many buses does the man have to take?* (two) *Where is Ben's Warehouse?* (at the corner of Hunter and Elm)

🎧 Vocabulary

➤ After students repeat the phrases in the *Vocabulary* box, ask them to describe your school's or program's location using the same directions. Write on the board *The school's on _____, It's across from _____, It's between _____ and _____, It's next to _____.* Elicit students' help in filling in the blanks.

C. Pair work . . .

➤ Have students find and circle on the map the school, the post office, and the hospital.

➤ Practice the directions from the school to the post office as a class. Elicit *Take the number 3 to Elm St and transfer there to the 2. Get off at Fulton.* Then model the conversation with a more advanced student. Play the role of Student A and demonstrate answering the phone as if you work at the post office.

➤ Students practice the conversation with their partners. For further practice, have students call for and give directions from the school to other places on the map.

Option: Give students a starting point and directions to a place on the map. Students follow the directions and then tell you where they ended up. For example, say *You are at the corner of Fulton and Elm. Take the number 2 to Main Street and transfer there to the 5. Get off at Pine. Where are you?* (the coffee shop or train station) Then have students do the same thing with a partner.

Option: Bring in maps for the different forms of public transportation in your community. Have students use them to practice asking for and giving directions.

Field project: If appropriate, have students use the local public transportation maps to plan a short trip. Have groups of students take the trip they have planned outside of class. Even though they have planned the route, have them ask a couple of people for directions along the way. As a class, brainstorm questions students can ask, such as *Can you tell me how to get to . . . ? Where do I get off for . . . ?*

Model 4

Content: extending and accepting an invitation for a social activity; making plans to meet

Procedure:

🎧 A–B.

➤ Ask questions about the photo, such as *Who's talking?* (two couples) *What do you see in the room?* (a child at a desk) *Where do you think they are?* (in a classroom) *Why do you think they're in a classroom?* (Maybe they're at a meeting for parents.)

➤ After students listen to the conversation, ask comprehension questions such as *What does the woman on the left invite the other couple to do?* (have coffee) *When are they going to have coffee?* (Saturday afternoon, around 2:00) *Where are they going to meet?* (at the coffee shop on Main)

➤ Ask the class *How does the woman on the left suggest a time and place to meet?* Have students find and underline in the conversation *How about . . . ?* and *Why don't we . . . ?* If necessary, explain that *around* is a way to give an approximate time.

🎧 Ways to accept an invitation

➤ Have students find *We'd love to*, in blue, in the third line of the conversation. Then have them look at the yellow language note. Explain that these are alternate responses students can use to accept an invitation.

➤ Have volunteers read Student A's first line to you. Respond with a different expression from the box each time. Then have students listen to and repeat the expressions.

🎧 Vocabulary

➤ After students repeat the phrases, brainstorm and write on the board other social activities, such as *go to a game, go to a party, go dancing, go to a museum.*

C. Pair work . . .

➤ Write *I was wondering. Would you like to . . . ?* on the board. Have a volunteer finish the sentence with one of the phrases from the *Vocabulary* box or board, posing the question to another student in the class. That student answers with one of the expressions from the yellow language note and then extends an invitation to a different student. Continue the chain until the new vocabulary has been practiced. Point out that students can say *I'd* (instead of *We'd*) *love to.*

➤ Model the conversation with a more advanced student. Play the role of Student A to demonstrate using *me* instead of *us* in the first line. With the class, look at the map on page 18 for the name of a place and its location.

Option: Make copies of the movie listings from the local newspaper. Have students create a conversation in which they make plans to meet and go to a movie. For further practice, the conversation can also include directions to the movie theater.

Challenge: Use the social activities in the *Vocabulary* box and on the board. In groups, have students talk about who they would and would not invite to do each activity and why. Then lead a class discussion about the appropriateness of inviting different people to various social activities. You may point out, for example, that it would probably not be appropriate to invite your boss or your teacher to go dancing.

If your students are ready . . .

Culture / Civics note: In North America, it is common for social events to include both men and women. In some cultures, social activity is segregated by gender. For example, some cultures prohibit unmarried females from socializing with males who are not related to them or require unmarried females to be accompanied by a family chaperon.

➤ Do it yourself!

(For general suggestions, see *Introduction*, page Txiii.)

Procedure:

A. Personalization . . .

➤ Point out that students can use words from the *Vocabulary* box on page 18 to describe the locations of places they include in their charts.

B. Pair work . . .

➤ If possible, bring in maps of your community and local bus maps for students to refer to in giving directions. Have students give their partner directions to at least two of the places on their chart. Have students give directions from your school or from some other place that they agree on.

Challenge: On the board, write the names and telephone numbers of several local places, such as movie theaters or department stores, that have a recorded message that includes directions. For homework, have students call two of the places on the list and listen to the recorded directions. They should write down the directions and check their accuracy by comparing directions with other students during the following class.

⌒ **A.** **Listen and read.**

> **A:** I was wondering. Would you like to have coffee with us sometime?
>
> **B:** We'd love to. When would be good?
>
> **A:** How about Saturday afternoon? . . . Around 2:00?
>
> **B:** That's fine. Where should we meet?
>
> **A:** Why don't we meet at the coffee shop on Main? It's right across the street from the train station.

⌒ **B.** **Listen again and repeat.**

⌒ **Ways to accept an invitation**

We'd love to.	Sounds great.
That would be nice.	Yes. Let's do that!

⌒ **Vocabulary**

Social activities

go to the movies	go out to eat	go for a walk	go shopping

C. Pair work. **Make plans to meet in Arbor City. Use the map on page 18.**

> **A:** I was wondering. Would you like to _____ with _____ sometime?
>
> **B:** _____. When would be good?
>
> **A:** How about _____? . . . Around _____?
>
> **B:** ___1___. Where should we meet?
>
> **A:** Why don't we meet at _____? It's ___2___.

¹Sure, OK
²on (Main) Street, between, next to

➤ Do it yourself!

A. Personalization. **Complete the chart with activities and places in your town.**

Activity	Place	Location
go to the movies	Metroplex	at the corner of State and First

B. Pair work. **Give your partner directions. You can walk, drive, or take the bus.**

Practical grammar

Directions, warnings, requests, and suggestions

Use imperatives to give instructions or directions.

    Take the number 7 bus to Elm Street.

Use imperatives to give warnings.

    The fire alarm rang. **Don't take** the elevator.

Use imperatives with <u>please</u> for polite requests and written invitations.

    Please bring me the map. (*or* **Bring** me the map, **please**.)

    Please join us for dinner at the Athena Diner for Martha's birthday.

Make suggestions and express invitations with <u>Let's</u>, <u>Let's</u> <u>not</u>, and <u>Why</u> <u>don't</u> . . . ?

    Let's take the bus. **Let's not drive**.

    Why don't we **meet** at 2:00 in the break room?

A. **Read what each person says. Then respond with a direction or a warning, or make a suggestion.**

1. "I don't like my new job."

    YOU _____

2. "Where should we have the meeting?"

    YOU _____

3. "I'd like to see that new movie at the Metroplex."

    YOU _____

4. "I'm hungry."

    YOU _____

Indirect commands

Use <u>ask</u> or <u>tell</u> plus an infinitive to give directions to other people. An infinitive is <u>to</u> plus a verb.

    infinitive

Janet: Laura, please **ask Pete to call** me later.

Laura: OK . . . . Pete, please call Janet later.

➤ Practical grammar

(For general suggestions, see *Introduction*, page Tix.)

Directions, warnings, requests, and suggestions

Content: imperatives; *Let's*, *Let's not*, and *Why don't . . .?*

Procedure:

➤ Have a volunteer stand up. Use imperatives to give the student directions, such as *Go straight, Turn right, Walk to the board*. Then read and discuss the first rule and example in the grammar box. Explain that an imperative is a verb that is used to tell someone to do something. The imperative is the same as the base form of the verb.

➤ Have a different volunteer stand up. Use an imperative to give this student a warning, for example, *Don't open the windows. The heater / air conditioner is on.* Read and discuss the second rule and example in the box.

➤ Have a third volunteer stand up. Use imperatives to make polite requests for this student to comply with, such as *Please come to the front of the class, Please write your name on the board, Please sit down.* Read and discuss the third rule (imperatives with <u>please</u>) and the two examples.

➤ Read the last rule and its examples in the grammar box. Elicit other examples of suggestions with *Let's*, *Let's not*, and *Why don't . . . ?*

A. Read what each person says . . .

➤ Elicit from the class an appropriate response to item 1. Have students complete the rest of the exercise independently.

Option: On the board or on a transparency, draw a large chart like the one that follows. When students have completed Exercise A, ask for several responses to item 1. Write the responses in the appropriate places in the first row of the chart. Elicit students' help in filling in any gaps in this row. Possible answers include *Quit, Don't quit yet, Let's look in the newspaper for a new one, Why don't you talk to your supervisor?* Continue in the same manner with items 2 through 4, or have students work in small groups to fill in the chart.

Situation	Imperative	Don't	Let's Let's not	Why don't . . .?
"I don't like my new job."				
"Where should we have the meeting?"				
"I'd like to see that new movie at the Metroplex."				
"I'm hungry."				

If your students are ready . . .

Language note: Although no subject is written in imperatives, the subject *you* is implied. Writing out *Let us*, the uncontracted form of *Let's*, provides a clue to the subject *we*. The subject of the suggestions beginning with *Why don't* is determined by the pronoun that follows *don't*.

Indirect commands

Content: using *ask* or *tell* to give indirect commands

Procedure:

➤ Write *Indirect commands* on the board. Explain that an indirect command is a way to give directions to someone without speaking to him or her directly. It is a command given through another person; one person tells another person to tell another person to do something. Draw three stick figures on the board and label them *A*, *B*, and *C*. Draw arrows from one to the other as you say *A tells B to tell C to do something.*

➤ Have students look at the pictures. Have three volunteers read the speech balloons. Then read and discuss the explanation below the pictures.

➤ Act out the conversation among Janet, Laura, and Pete with more advanced students. Play the role of Laura. When you read Laura's line, move away from Janet and speak directly to Pete to reinforce that you are relaying Janet's command.

➤ Brainstorm and write on the board several classroom commands such as *Stand up, Walk to the window, Write your name on the board.* Have Student 1 use one of these commands to give directions for Student 2 to relay, for example, Student 1: *Gina, tell Edgar to stand up.* Student 2 (Gina): *Edgar, please stand up.* Edgar then stands up and continues the chain by giving an indirect command to another student.

B. Continue each person's speech . . .

➤ Review the example. Point out that students will begin their sentences with *Please ask* or *Please tell* followed by the person or people indicated below the line. Remind students to add *to* to the verb to make an infinitive.

➤ After students complete items 2 through 5 independently, have students check answers with a partner and then review as a class.

Option: Have students form groups of three. Assign each group one item from Exercise B. Groups practice and then role-play for the class giving, relaying, and complying with the indirect command. For example, Student 1 reads item 2. Student 2 role-plays making a phone call and says *Bill? Walk to the corner of Grand and Third and turn left.* Then Student 3 (Bill) says *Grand and Third . . . turn left. OK. Thanks.*

Challenge: In pairs, have students create three to five situations similar to those given in the speech balloons. Encourage students to think of situations they might encounter at work. Have students write indirect commands for their own situations, or have them exchange commands with another pair.

➤ Do it yourself!

(For general suggestions, see *Introduction*, page Txiii.)

Procedure:

➤ Have volunteers role-play the three people in the pictures and read the speech balloons. Have students label the three people in the pictures *A, B,* and *C.* (The woman is *B,* and students will need to label her twice.) Point out that Person A tells Person B to tell Person C (Mark) how to get to his house.

➤ In groups of three, students practice using indirect commands to give directions from the school to their own houses. Have students rotate so that each person in the group has an opportunity to play the part of Partner A, B, and C.

Option: Have groups write directions from the school to a place in your community. Each person in the group should write down the directions. Then have students form new groups of three. Each person in the new group takes a turn playing the role of Partner A and using an indirect command to relay the directions written by his or her previous group. The student playing the part of Partner C tries to determine where the directions are leading.

B. Continue each person's speech with an indirect command. Use <u>ask</u> or <u>tell</u> and an infinitive.

1. I need some clean mops. _Please ask Mariana to get me some mops from the supply room._

   Mariana / get me some mops / from the supply room

2. Bill needs directions to the office from the warehouse. Please tell him to walk to the corner of Grand and Third and turn left.

   him / walk to the corner of Grand and Third and turn left

3. There's a big spill in the work area. Please ask / tell the maintenance staff to clean it up fast.

   the maintenance staff / clean it up fast

4. The Costas want to have dinner with us at the new Brazilian restaurant. Please ask / tell them to meet us there at 7:30.

   them / meet us there at 7:30

5. John has to pick up the car at 5:00. Please ask / tell him not to forget.

   him / not / forget

➤ Do it yourself!

Form groups of three students. Partner A: Tell Partner B to tell Partner C how to get to your house or to another place in your town.

Take the number 6 bus to Central Avenue. Get off and turn right on Central. Walk two blocks. I'm at 63 Central Avenue. See you and Mark later, OK?

OK!

LATER

Hey, Mark, take the number 6 to Central Avenue. Turn right on Central and go to number 63. It's two blocks.

OK. Great.

Authentic practice

🎧 **A. Read and listen again. Then choose an answer to each question. Fill in the ovals.**

1. Who needs directions?

   ⓐ Pete. ⓑ Ms. Benson.

2. Where's Ms. Benson's house?

   ⓐ In Arbor City. **ⓑ** On Maple Street.

3. What is the house near?

   ⓐ The school. ⓑ Make your second left.

🎧 **B. Listen. Underline your response.**

1. **YOU** <u>The corner of Fulton and Elm.</u> **YOU** I'm taking the bus.

2. **YOU** You can't miss it. **YOU** <u>OK.</u>

3. **YOU** <u>At the Smith Street stop.</u> **YOU** We'd love to.

🎧 **C. Listen again. Read your response out loud.**

➤ Authentic practice

(For general suggestions, see *Introduction*, page Tx.)

Procedure:

🎧

➤ To set the scene for the picture story, ask questions about the pictures, such as *Who's in the pictures?* (a man and a woman) *What are they doing?* (talking on the telephone) *What is the man also doing?* (writing) *What do you think they are talking about?* (directions)

➤ After students listen and read, have them read the speech balloons again and give you directions to Ms. Benson's house from Arbor City. On the board, model writing down directions in shortened form, for example, *Interstate west, Green St. exit.* Then elicit students' help in using the directions to draw a simple map on the board.

➤ Have a volunteer read the directions Ms. Benson gives in the second, third, and fourth boxes. As the student reads the directions, trace the path that Pete will take on your map and add any details not included previously, such as the *North State* and *dead end* signs or the school. Use the map you have drawn to illustrate the meaning of any unknown words. For example, draw Maple Street as a cul-de-sac to illustrate *dead end*. Draw houses on Maple Street and use an arrow to indicate the *next-to-last* house.

🎧 A. Read and listen again ...

➤ After students listen again and complete the exercise, review the answer as a class. Once each correct answer has been identified, talk about why the other answer is incorrect, for example, in item 2, *Ms. Benson's house isn't in Arbor City. It's on Maple Street. Who's in Arbor City?* (Pete)

Option: Have students create additional comprehension questions based on the conversation. Give students an index card and have them write their own comprehension question with two possible answers, for example, *Where does Pete work? (a) At Perillo Plumbing / (b) On Green Street.* Circulate through the room, helping students to formulate their questions correctly. Students take their cards and walk around the room. They find a partner, ask each other their questions, and then exchange cards and find a different partner. Continue until students have had an opportunity to ask and answer several questions.

🎧 B–C.

➤ Have students check answers to Exercise B with a partner before reading their responses out loud in Exercise C.

Option: Once the correct answers have been identified, work as a class to create questions or statements that would require the other response. Write them on the board. Then write the items from the tapescript on the board. Have students practice both sets of questions and responses with a partner.

Challenge: In pairs, have students choose one question or statement and response and add to it to create an extended conversation. Have students write one comprehension question, similar to those in Exercise A, about their conversation. Have volunteers present their conversations to the class and ask their comprehension question.

Tapescript

1. Where are you calling from?

2. You get on the Interstate.

3. And where do I get off?

If your students are ready ...

Culture / Civics note: In many countries, knowing the street address of a place you are looking for is of little help due to a lack of road signs and the haphazard numbering of buildings. However, knowing the street address of a place you are looking for is very helpful in North America. Each building on a street is assigned a number, which is usually posted prominently near the entrance. Numbers are sequential, with odd numbers on one side of the street and even numbers on the other. Nearly all roads are named, with signs posted at intersections identifying each street.

T22

Directions on the elevator

Procedure:

🎧 A. Listening comprehension ...

➤ After students listen to the conversation the first time, ask comprehension questions such as *Where are these people?* (on an elevator) *Where does the first man want to go?* (to the fourth floor) If students have trouble answering the questions, play the cassette or read the tapescript again, pausing periodically to ask questions, for example, *What direction is the elevator going now, up or down?*

➤ After students complete the exercise, review the answers as a class. Discuss the *False* and *Maybe* answers, for example, *The fourth floor is not the top floor. How do you know this?* (because the second man is going to the tenth floor)

🎧 B. Listen again ...

➤ Read the first event, *The man gets on the elevator.* Ask students what happens next. Elicit *The elevator goes down* and have students put a 2 next to this sentence. Have students complete the exercise independently.

➤ When students have finished, ask *What happens first? What happens second?* and so on, and have different students read the sentences in order.

➤ Review the conversation. For example, say *The man is in a hurry. He is looking for the karate school. He has a difficult time finding it.* Then ask *What are the two problems he has?* (He wants to go up to the fourth floor, but the elevator's going down. / The karate school isn't on the fourth floor; it has moved to the basement.)

C. True story ...

➤ Write on the board *Did you ever have a difficult time finding a place?* Answer the question yourself, for example, *Yes, I had a difficult time finding this school the first time I came here.* Have students write in the margin of their books a place they had a difficult time finding.

➤ Write *What happened?* on the board. Point out the problems that might make it difficult to find a place: *reading a map, understanding directions,* and *losing directions.* Brainstorm and write on the board other problems that can make it difficult to find a place, such as *not seeing a sign, not wanting to ask for directions in English, getting off at the wrong bus or subway stop.*

➤ Circle the problem that made it difficult for you to find the place you mentioned, for example, *understanding directions.* Have students circle the problem that made it difficult for them to find

the place they wrote down. (If it is one of the problems on the board, have them write it in their book.)

➤ Tell the class your story, providing details, for example, *The director told me to turn right on First Street, but I thought he said to make the first right.* Ask questions about your story to check comprehension. Encourage students to tell their stories with details.

➤ Do it yourself!

(For general suggestions, see *Introduction*, page Txiii.)

Procedure:

A. Write your own response ...

➤ Explain to students that they should respond to the man in the photo with directions to their house.

➤ Have students read the speech balloons and write their responses.

➤ Before students practice with a partner, have a volunteer interview you. Respond, giving students an opportunity to check the appropriateness of their own responses.

➤ Have students interview each other in pairs to check their responses.

B. Culture talk ...

➤ Elicit or explain that *etiquette* is polite behavior, or how people are expected to act.

➤ Model the activity for students by talking about elevator etiquette in North America. Explain, for example, that people normally face front and don't talk to each other.

➤ Have students discuss elevator etiquette in their countries in small, diverse groups. Circulate and prompt discussion, if necessary, by asking questions such as *Who moves first, the person getting on or the person getting off the elevator? Who pushes the buttons? When do people hold the door for other passengers? Where do people look? Do they talk to each other? What do they talk about?*

➤ Have a spokesperson from each group tell the class how, or if, elevator etiquette differs in the group's cultures.

Tapescript

Man 1: Hold it, please!

Woman 1: Sure.

[elevator doors start to close, are stopped]

(Tapescript is continued on page T24.)

🎧 **A. Listening comprehension. Listen to the conversation. Then listen again and check True, False, or Maybe.**

	True	False	Maybe
1. The man wanted to go to the fourth floor.	☑	☐	☐
2. The fourth floor is the top floor.	☐	☑	☐
3. The woman in the elevator was going to the fourth floor.	☐	☑	☐
4. The man is a karate teacher.	☐	☐	☑

🎧 **B. Listen again and put the events in order.**

1. _4_ He goes to the fourth floor.
2. _3_ The elevator goes up.
3. _1_ The man gets on the elevator.
4. _2_ The elevator goes down.
5. _5_ He gets off the elevator.

C. True story. Did you ever have a difficult time finding a place? What happened? Use the ideas in the box or your own idea. Tell the story to your partner.

reading a map   understanding directions   losing directions

➤ Do it yourself!

A. Write your own response. Then read your conversation out loud with a partner.

I just realized I have no idea how to get to your place. Can you give me directions?

YOU _____

Please give me directions from the school.

YOU _____

Great. Thanks. Would you mind giving me the number of your house again?

YOU _____

B. Culture talk. In the country you come from, what is elevator etiquette? Compare cultures with your classmates.

Elevator etiquette and social etiquette

A. Read and listen to the letters.

Ask Joan
Culture tips for newcomers

Dear Joan:
I don't understand something that happened to me today. In the elevator at work this morning, the other people in the elevator looked at me and then moved away from me. I get the feeling I did something wrong, but I don't know what it was.

Otis Schindler

Dear Otis:
You don't give me much information, so let me tell you some of the "unwritten rules" of elevator etiquette. First of all, face front. Second, if there are only a few people in the elevator, don't stand too near any of the other passengers. It makes people very uncomfortable. And if the floor buttons are only on one side of the car and you're standing in front of

them, offer to press buttons for passengers on the other side of the car. The simplest way to do this is to say, "What floor?" or "Where are you going?" If someone asks *you* that question, answer with a floor number, not the name of the place you are going to.

That should do it!

Joan

Dear Joan:
Last week a co-worker invited me to a party at her house. I'm very nervous about the party. First of all, in my religion we don't drink alcoholic beverages, and I think many people drink alcohol here. Is it rude or unfriendly to ask for a nonalcoholic drink? Also, the invitation is for 6 o'clock. In my country, we never get to a

party at the exact time of the invitation — we get there later. Please tell me what to do. Hurry, Joan. The party is this Sunday!

Nervous Nadia

Dear Nadia:
You can stop worrying. Your co-worker will offer a variety of beverages. Many people in this country don't drink alcoholic beverages either, so when your host offers a drink, just ask for fruit juice or soda. No one will think that's unusual. You didn't say if the party was a dinner party. If the party is a sit-down dinner, and the invitation is for 6:00, it's impolite to arrive after about 6:15. Enjoy yourself, make new friends, and have fun!

Joan

B. Read Joan's advice again. Read the statements and check <u>True</u> or <u>False</u>.

		True	False
1.	Don't stand very near people in an elevator.	☑	☐
2.	Stand with your back to the door.	☐	☑
3.	It's OK to ask for juice when some people are drinking alcohol.	☑	☐
4.	It doesn't matter what time you arrive at a dinner party.	☐	☑

Tapescript (*continued from page T23*)

Man 1: Wow! Thanks. I'm in a real hurry.

Woman 1: No problem. What floor?

Man 1: Four, please.

Woman 1: Uh-oh. This elevator's going down.

Man 1: You're kidding! Oh, well . . .

[elevator stops]

Woman 1: Well, this is my floor. Have a nice day.

Man 1: You too.

[elevator doors open and close] [pause] [doors open]

Man 2: Going up?

Man 1: Yup.

Man 2: Great. Could you hit 10, please?

Man 1: Sure. No problem.

[elevator doors close, elevator goes up]
[doors open, footsteps as man walks up and down hallway looking for the karate school]

Man 1: [to woman in hallway] Excuse me. I'm looking for the karate school.

Woman 2: The karate school? They moved to the basement. Just get back on the elevator and hit B. That'll take you right there.

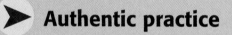

➤ Authentic practice

(For general suggestions, see *Introduction*, page Tx.)

Elevator etiquette and social etiquette

Procedure:

🎧 A. Read and listen to the letters.

➤ Tell students that the two *Ask Joan* letters will ask for advice on how to act in an elevator and at a party.

➤ As students read and listen to the letters, pause after each letter and ask the class to identify the writer's problem(s) or Joan's advice.

➤ With books closed, have students listen to the letters again.

➤ Draw on the board two t-charts with the headings *Do's* and *Don'ts*. Label one *In an elevator* and the other *At a party*. Fill in the charts with the advice students can recall from Joan's letters, for example, *In an elevator: Do face front, Don't stand too near any of the other passengers.*

Option: Explain that pausing in the right places when they read out loud will make students easier to understand. Have students make slash (/) marks over the commas, periods, and question marks in Joan's letter to Otis. Play the cassette or read the letter and have students observe the pauses after punctuation. Then have students read the letter to a partner and practice pausing in the appropriate places.

Challenge: Have students circle the imperatives in the letters. Make a list on the board. Imperatives include *let me tell you, face front, don't stand too near, offer to press buttons.*

B. Read Joan's advice again . . .

➤ Working individually, students mark each item *True* or *False*. Have students check answers with a partner and then review as a class.

➤ For each of the two false answers (items 2 and 4), have students find and underline the sentence in Joan's letters that shows that the item is false: *First of all, face front* and *If the party is a sit-down dinner . . . 6:30.*

Note: *It doesn't matter* in item 4 may be unfamiliar to students. If students don't understand, rephrase it as *It's not important.*

If your students are ready . . .

Culture / Civics note: In North America, respecting the personal space of others is highly important. When North Americans are talking to or standing next to each other, they unconsciously tend to keep a specific distance apart. The space required varies according to the relationship of the people involved and the situation. For example, when talking to friends, the average person maintains a distance of about one arm's length. If this space is violated, most people feel very uncomfortable and back away to re-establish a more comfortable distance.

Written directions to a place

Procedure:

➤ Read the description of the situation in bold out loud.

➤ Have students look at the map and locate Paul's house, Nadia's house, and the Luna Italian Restaurant. Have students locate bus lines 1, 2, and 3.

➤ To make sure students understand the task, ask questions such as *Where are Tran and Nadia going?* (to Paul's house) *Where is Nadia going from?* (her house) *Where is Tran going from?* (the Luna Italian Restaurant) *How can they get there?* (walk, drive, or take a bus)

➤ Explain that students should complete the letter to the right of the map, writing either to Tran or to Nadia and providing directions, a date, and a time. For help with giving directions, refer students to page 18. Review the *Writing tip.* Then circulate through the room as students work individually, checking their use of capital letters and periods.

➤ Have students check answers with a partner who chose the same co-worker.

➤ Have students read their directions to a partner who chose the other co-worker. The partner traces the directions on the map as they are read.

Option: On a sheet of paper, have students write a letter with directions for the co-worker they didn't choose.

Option: Students imagine that they are Nadia and invite Paul to dinner. On a sheet of paper, students write a letter to Paul from Nadia with directions from the restaurant to her house.

➤ Do it yourself!

(For general suggestions, see *Introduction*, page Txiii.)

Procedure:

A–B.

➤ Have students take out the maps and diagrams they brought in, or have them turn to page 153. If possible, bring in maps or print them from the Internet.

➤ Have students work with a partner who has a different map or diagram. Students compare maps. To prompt discussion, give students specific suggestions about what to look for, such as what the map shows, symbols, use of color, orientation (north, south, east, west).

➤ Have students circle a starting point and a destination on their maps. Students give directions to their partners. After both partners have given directions, they exchange maps and find a new partner. Students use the starting point and destination on the map to give directions to a new partner. Repeat until students have had an opportunity to use several maps.

Field project: If appropriate, plan a field trip to a mall. Give each pair of students a blank index card. Have students use the mall directory and diagram to write directions on their card to one shop or place in the mall. They should write the name of the shop or place on the back of the card. Have each pair walk to the place they chose to check the accuracy of their directions. Set an appropriate time limit. When students return, have pairs exchange cards and follow the directions on the card they receive. When they arrive at their destination, they should look at the back of the card to see if they followed the directions correctly. The pair then returns to the directory and exchanges cards with another pair of students. Send students out several times with different cards. Later, have students ask salespeople or security guards for directions to different places in the mall. They can also use the elevator and ask other passengers *Going up? Going down? Where are you going? What floor?*

Written directions to a place

Paul wants to invite two co-workers, Tran and Nadia, to dinner at his house. Write directions for one of Paul's co-workers. Nadia is going to Paul's from home. Tran is going directly from the Luna Italian Restaurant. They can walk, drive, or take a bus.

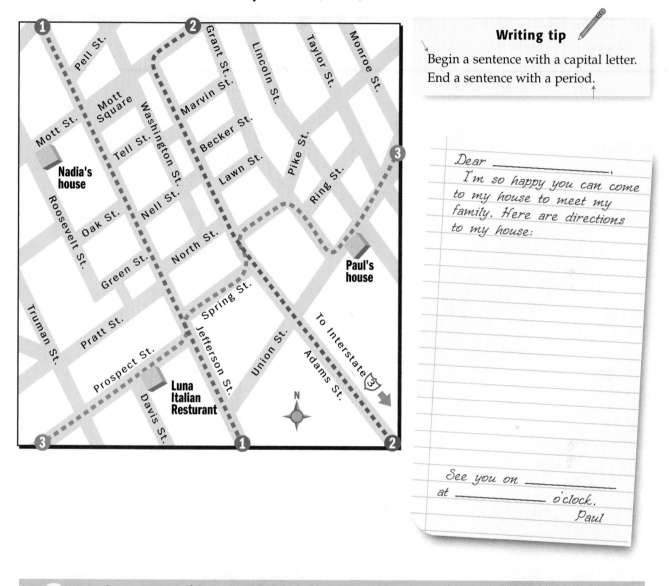

Writing tip

Begin a sentence with a capital letter. End a sentence with a period.

> *Dear* _____,
> *I'm so happy you can come to my house to meet my family. Here are directions to my house:*
>
> *See you on* _____ *at* _____ *o'clock.*
> *Paul*

► Do it yourself! A plan-ahead project

A. Bring in public transportation maps, town or city maps, or mall or building diagrams. Or use the one on page 153.

B. Discussion. Compare maps. Give directions to your classmates to places on the map.

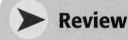 Review

(For general suggestions, see *Introduction*, page Txii.)

Procedure:

A. Pair work or group work.

➤ Have students take turns pointing to and naming as many things as they can in the picture.

Ask and answer questions.

➤ Point out the two questions asked in the directions. Ask *Where are the people?* Elicit the response *at a mall.* Hold up the textbook, point to the man in the upper right corner of the picture, and ask *Where is this person?* Elicit an appropriate response, such as *on the second floor.* Point to the same man and ask *What is he doing?* Elicit the response *talking on the telephone.* Then have students take turns pointing to different people in the picture and asking their partners *Where is this person? What is he or she doing?*

Option: Give students one minute to study the picture and remember all they can about it. Then have students close their books and form small groups. Ask questions about the picture and keep a record of the correct answers. After each question, allow the groups time to discuss and record the group's answer on a sheet of paper. Possible questions include *How many people are cleaning the floor?* (two) *Is the person on the escalator a man or a woman?* (a woman) *Is she going up or down?* (up) *What street is the mall on?* (Union Street) When you have finished asking questions, have students open their books. Review the answers as a class, and have each group add up the number of correct responses it has.

Create conversations.

➤ Hold up the textbook and point to the two women cleaning the floor. Play the role of the woman on the left and ask *I was wondering. Would you like to go to the movies with me later?* Elicit from the class an appropriate response for the woman on the right, such as *I'd love to. What time?* Respond, and then elicit from the class an appropriate next line for the woman on the right.

➤ In pairs, have students choose two people in the picture and create a conversation for them. Ask for volunteers to role-play their conversations for the class.

Option: Have pairs write one line of conversation for each person in the picture. Students can add speech balloons for the people who don't already have them and draw thought balloons for the people who aren't interacting with someone else. Then each pair of students joins another pair. Pairs take turns reading their lines and guessing who in the picture is speaking.

Option: Have students locate the different pairs of people talking to each other in the picture. Working with a partner, students create the first line of a conversation for five different pairs in the picture, for example, for the woman at the information booth, *Excuse me. Can you tell me where Dinah's is?* Then, each pair of students joins another pair. They take turns pointing to a person in the picture and saying the line they've prepared. The other pair of students gives a response, such as *No problem. It's down the hall, on the right.*

Tell a story.

Option: Describe the mall. Have students describe the mall. Review vocabulary words they can use, such as *the escalator, the elevator, the end of the hall, on the first* (or *ground*) *floor, across from, between, next to.*

Option: Create a character. Point to one person in the picture and relate the details of his or her life. For example, for the woman who is cleaning the floor and asking her co-worker to the movies, say *Her name is Elizabeth. She's from Mexico. She has been working at the mall for six months. She doesn't mind cleaning, but she loves working with children . . .* Then have students tell the story of at least one person in the picture to a partner. Explain that they will need to make up the information they relate.

Option: Tell shoppers' plans. Point to one shopper in the picture and explain what he or she is doing at the mall. For example, for the woman on the escalator, say *She's going to the department store on the second floor. She's going to a party on Saturday, and she's looking for a new dress.* Then, in pairs, students take turns telling what different shoppers in the picture are doing at the mall. Circulate through the room, encouraging students to make up as much as possible about each person's situation.

⌕ B. Listen to the conversation...

➤ Tell students they are going to listen first to a boss giving his assistant instructions for the next day, and then to the assistant announcing the instructions to the workers.

➤ Read the selection on the tapescript out loud or play the cassette while students listen with books closed.

➤ After students listen to the conversation the first time, ask who is giving indirect commands (Ben).

➤ Have students open their books. Read the instructions out loud. Have volunteers read items 1 through 7 out loud so that students know what to listen for.

➤ Read the tapescript or play the cassette again. Students check the boxes next to the imperatives that they hear.

C–E.

➤ Students work individually to complete the review exercises.

➤ Circulate to offer help as needed.

➤ Have students check answers with a partner. Review answers as a class.

➤ Identify any areas of difficulty that may require additional instruction and practice.

Option: For Exercise D, have students write directions from their houses or apartments to other familiar places in your community.

Tapescript

Ben: [on interoffice phone] Mary? Ben. Have you got a minute? I need to give you some instructions for tomorrow, and I don't have much time.

Mary: Sure, Ben. Would you mind if I got a pencil and paper? I don't want to miss anything this time. I'll be right back.

Ben: OK. [pause] [phone is put down, man whistles as he waits]

Mary: OK. I'm back. Shoot.

Ben: Get Ron to open up a little early tomorrow. The truck's coming in around seven, and I want to be open when it gets there. Ask Phil to leave the keys on my desk. I'll need them later. And be sure that Nan checks the cartons when they come off the truck. And when the cartons are unloaded, tell Ivan to put two cartons of the new laundry detergent in my office. Oh, and please ask Tim not to put cheese on my sandwich. I really hate that cheese he bought. Have you got all that?

Mary: Sure thing. Bye, Ben.

Ben: See you later.

Mary: [over a public address system] Attention, everyone. I've got tomorrow's orders. Listen carefully. Any questions, give me a call at 322. OK, Ron, please open up a little early tomorrow. The truck'll be here around seven. Phil, after Ron opens up, get the keys from him and leave them on Ben's desk. Nan, be sure to check the cartons while they're offloading the truck. Let's see. Oh, yes, Ivan—please put two cartons of the new detergent in Ben's office. He wants to check that the labels are better this time. And Tim, Ben says he hates the new cheese and not to put any on his sandwich. OK, guys. That's about it. Over and out.

B. Listen to the conversation about instructions for the next day. Read the statements and listen again. Check the directions, warnings, and requests you hear.

1. ☑ Open the building early.
2. ☐ Close the building late.
3. ☑ Leave the keys on Ben's desk.
4. ☑ Check the cartons.

5. ☑ Put two cartons of detergent in Ben's office.
6. ☐ Check the labels on the detergent.
7. ☑ Don't put cheese on the sandwich.

C. Choose your response. Fill in the ovals.

1. "I was wondering, would you like to have coffee after work?"
   - ⓐ Sure. When would be good?
   - ⓑ Sure. I don't know how to get there.

2. "Excuse me. Can you tell me how to get to the warehouse?"
   - ⓐ Where are you now?
   - ⓑ Tell him to take the bus.

3. "You can't miss it."
   - ⓐ Where are you going?
   - ⓑ Thanks. See you then.

4. "Why don't we meet in the break room?"
   - ⓐ I don't know.
   - ⓑ That's fine.

D. Write directions from your house or apartment to your supermarket. Begin each new sentence with a capital letter. End each sentence with a period.

_____

_____

_____

E. Write a response to each statement or question. Use your own words.

1. "I was wondering. Where would you like to have the meeting?"

   (YOU) _____

2. "Hold the elevator, please!"

   (YOU) _____

3. "Why don't we meet at the Farmers' Market on Maple Street?"

   (YOU) _____

F. Look at the building plan. Read the statements and check <u>True</u> or <u>False</u>.

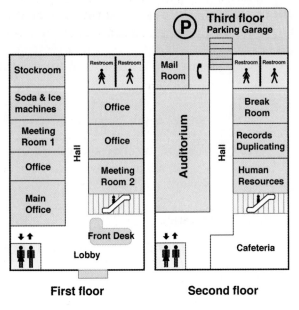

First floor   Second floor

		True	False
1.	The main office is on the first floor.	☑	☐
2.	The cafeteria is next to the parking garage.	☐	☑
3.	The break room is down the hall from the stockroom.	☐	☑
4.	Access to the parking garage is at the end of the first floor hall.	☐	☑
5.	To get to the Human Resources department from the first floor, take the elevator or the escalator.	☑	☐

G. Composition. **On a separate sheet of paper, write about the picture on page 26. Say as much as you can.**

> **Now I can**
> ☐ extend and accept an invitation and make plans to meet.
> ☐ ask for and give directions within a building.
> ☐ ask for and give assistance on an elevator.
> ☐ use maps, plans, and building directories.
> ☐ ask for and give directions for public transportation.
> ☐ _____ .

F. Look at the building plan . . .

Option: Have students change the false sentences to make them true. Then have students write two additional true statements based on the building plan.

Option: Have students create a building directory based on the map.

G. Composition . . .

➤ Provide students with concrete approaches to writing about the picture on page 26. Use one of the following options, give students a choice of options, or assign options based on students' levels of proficiency. Model what is expected of students for each option.

➤ Advise students to look back through the unit for help and ideas as they write.

➤ Circulate to offer help as needed.

Option: Review *there is / are.* Have students write sentences about the picture using *there is / are*, for example, *There is an elevator across from the information booth, There is a telephone on the second floor.*

Option: Have students create a building plan for the first floor of the mall.

Option: Have students choose one of the pairs of people who are talking to each other in the picture on page 26, label them *A* and *B*, and write an extended conversation for them.

Option: Have students imagine that they are one of the people in the picture and describe themselves in a paragraph, for example, *I have worked at the mall for a year. I really enjoy working with people, so my job is perfect for me. I answer people's questions and give directions . . .* Collect the paragraphs and read each one aloud. Students try to determine which person in the picture is speaking.

Now I can

➤ Read the first item in the box out loud, *Now I can extend and accept an invitation and make plans to meet.* Elicit from the class an example of how to extend an invitation, accept an invitation, or make plans to meet, such as *Would you like to go out to eat with me sometime?*

➤ In pairs, have students take turns reading each item in the box and giving an example of what they have learned. When students can provide an example, they should check that box. For the items students weren't able to check, they should look back through the unit for ideas.

➤ When students are finished reviewing with their partners, read each item out loud and elicit an example from the class.

Oral test (optional)

You may want to use the *Now I can* box as an informal evaluation. While students are working on the *Composition* activity, you can call them up individually and check their ability with two or three objectives.

Technology

Note: For the plan-ahead project on page 39, students should bring to class a warranty from a product they have purchased. These warranties can also be used on page 31.

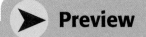 **Preview**

(For general suggestions, see *Introduction*, page Tviii.)

Warm up. What's a warranty?

Procedure:

➤ Have students read the warranty. Ask questions such as *What is the name of the company?* (MicroTastic) *What product is the warranty for?* (a microwave oven) *What number do you call for service?* (1-800-MTASTIC) *For how long does the warranty cover all defective parts?* (one year) *Is there any charge for parts or labor during this time?* (no) *For how long does the warranty cover the magnetron tube?* (three additional years) *Is there any charge for replacing the magnetron tube?* (Yes. You have to pay the labor costs, but there is no charge for the part.)

➤ Ask *What's a warranty?* Elicit or explain that it is a written promise that a company will fix or replace something if it breaks after you have bought it.

➤ Ask students if any of them have recently purchased a product that came with a warranty. Brainstorm and write on the board a list of products that typically have warranties—such as *computers, refrigerators, tools*—and a list of products that don't normally come with warranties—such as *clothes, food, shampoo*.

➤ In small groups, have students make a list of what kind of information is usually given in a warranty, such as *the name of the company, the name of the product, a telephone number, the length of the warranty,* and *what the company will replace or repair.*

If your students are ready . . .

Culture / Civics note: Most major purchases, such as cars, appliances, and electronic items, come with a *warranty*. This is a written promise that the seller or manufacturer will repair or replace the product if it breaks or does not work correctly. There is no additional charge for a warranty; it is included in the price of the product.

Sellers are required by law to provide a copy of the warranty for you to read before you buy. As the amount of coverage that a warranty provides varies greatly, it is important to read the warranty carefully. Warranties specify conditions under which the company will repair the product, replace it, or refund your money. Most warranties are valid for only a fixed period of time, such as one year, beginning from the date of purchase.

Unit 3 objectives

Procedure:

➤ Choose one difficult word from each objective and write a simple definition on the board. For example, for *troubleshoot,* write *try to solve a difficult problem.* Write only the definitions, not the words, and don't write them in order. Label the definitions *a* through *e.*

➤ Say the five words you've chosen and have students underline them in their books. Students read the objectives and use context clues to try to match the words with the definitions. Students write the letter of the definition next to the objective that contains the matching word.

➤ Discuss the meanings of the words and of each objective.

➤ Ask *Which objectives are related to feelings?* Elicit *admitting an error, reassuring someone,* and *expressing frustration.* Ask students which situation is most difficult for them.

Technology

> **Preview**

Warm up. What's a warranty?

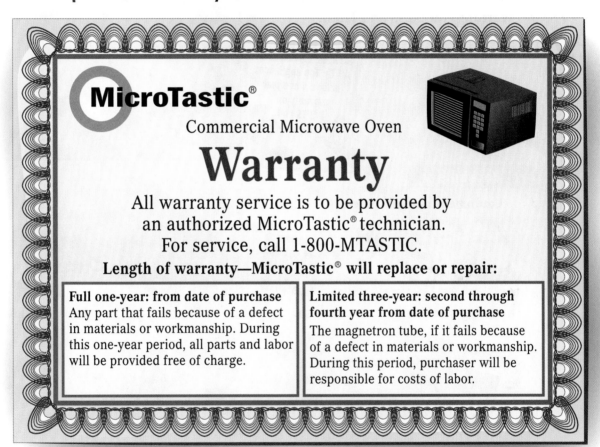

MicroTastic®

Commercial Microwave Oven

Warranty

All warranty service is to be provided by
an authorized MicroTastic® technician.
For service, call 1-800-MTASTIC.

Length of warranty—MicroTastic® will replace or repair:

Full one-year: from date of purchase Any part that fails because of a defect in materials or workmanship. During this one-year period, all parts and labor will be provided free of charge.	**Limited three-year: second through fourth year from date of purchase** The magnetron tube, if it fails because of a defect in materials or workmanship. During this period, purchaser will be responsible for costs of labor.

Unit 3 objectives

- Read and understand a product warranty.
- Admit a possible error.
- Reassure someone.
- Express frustration with equipment malfunctions.
- Troubleshoot a problem.

Model 1   Discuss a warranty.

A. Listen and read.

> **A:** I wonder if this freezer is still under warranty.
> **B:** When was it purchased?
> **A:** About six months ago.
> **B:** No problem. It has a one-year warranty on parts and labor.

B. Listen again and repeat.

All Tip Top appliances include a one-year warranty on PARTS and LABOR.

Vocabulary

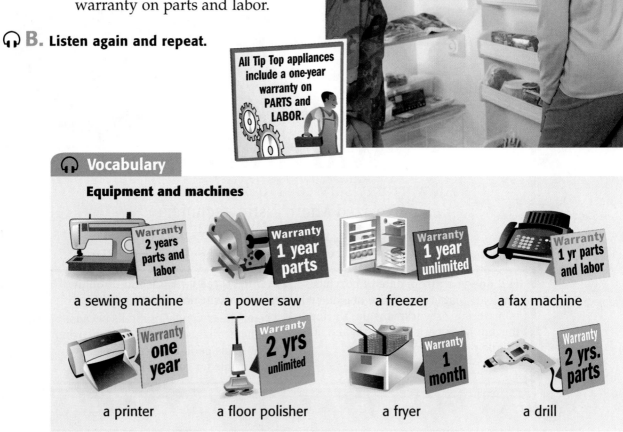

Equipment and machines

Warranty 2 years parts and labor — a sewing machine

Warranty 1 year parts — a power saw

Warranty 1 year unlimited — a freezer

Warranty 1 yr parts and labor — a fax machine

Warranty one year — a printer

Warranty 2 yrs unlimited — a floor polisher

Warranty 1 month — a fryer

Warranty 2 yrs. parts — a drill

C. Pair work. Discuss a warranty. Use the vocabulary or your _own_ machines and warranties.

> **A:** I wonder if this _____ is still under warranty.
> **B:** When was it purchased?
> **A:** _____.
> **B:** _____. It has _____ warranty.

➤ Practical conversations

(For general suggestions, see *Introduction*, page Tviii.)

Model 1

Content: making an inquiry with *I wonder*; using *ago* to tell how far back in the past something happened; discussing warranties on equipment and machines; the passive voice

Procedure:

🎧 A–B.

➤ To set the scene for the conversation, ask questions about the photo and freezer label, such as *What are the women doing?* (looking inside the freezer) *What brand is the freezer?* (Tip Top) *Does the freezer have a warranty?* (yes)

➤ After students listen to the conversation, check comprehension by asking questions such as *When was the freezer purchased?* (about six months ago) *What is the length of the warranty?* (one year) *What does the warranty cover?* (parts and labor)

➤ Explain the difference between *parts* and *labor*. *Parts* are the separate pieces that a machine or piece of equipment is made of. *Labor* is the work that a repairperson does to fix a machine or piece of equipment.

➤ Have students explain in their own words what the warranty means, for example, *The company promises to fix the freezer if it breaks during the first year. There will be no charge for new parts or for the work.*

➤ To make sure students understand *I wonder*, brainstorm several inquiries with *I wonder*, for example, *I wonder if the weather will be nice tomorrow, I wonder if (a student's name) likes studying English.*

➤ To make sure students understand the use of *ago*, ask what the date was six months ago. Model the use of *ago* by making statements about yourself, such as *I moved to this city three years ago, I started teaching English nine years ago.* Have students use *ago* to answer questions such as *When did you move to this country? When did you start learning English? When did you learn to drive?*

🎧 Vocabulary

➤ After students listen to and repeat the vocabulary, ask questions about the pictures in the box, such as *How long is the warranty on the sewing*

machine? (two years) *What does the warranty on the power saw cover?* (parts)

➤ Explain that *unlimited* is another way to state that a warranty includes parts and labor for a given period of time. With a partner, have students take turns reading out loud the terms of the warranties for the equipment and machines. Point out that the terms of warranties, as well as the wording, can vary greatly.

➤ Have students discuss with a partner which machines they have used or purchased. Write the machines on the board. Take a poll of how many students have used each machine.

Option: As a class, show the results of the poll on a bar chart like the one that follows. Elicit students' help in drawing the bar for *sewing machine*. Ask *What do the numbers on the left represent?* (the number of students) *How many students have used a sewing machine before?* Begin drawing a line up from sewing machine, asking the class to tell you when to stop. When the appropriate height is reached, make a bar from the line. Have volunteers come up to the board to draw the bars for the other equipment and machines. When the bar chart is finished, erase any other poll results that are on the board. Then call on students to interpret the chart; for example, ask *How many students have used a fryer before?*

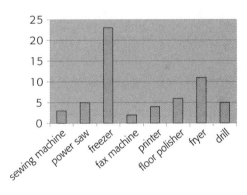

C. Pair work ...

➤ Model the activity with a more advanced student. Play the role of Student A to demonstrate substituting a product from the *Vocabulary* box for *freezer*. Prompt Student B to find the product in the box and give the accurate length of the warranty.

Note: If Student A responds with a period of time that is longer than the terms of the warranty, Student B will not be able to use a response such as *No problem.* You may wish to brainstorm responses Student B can use if the machine was purchased too long ago and the warranty is not valid or good anymore, for example, *Too bad* or *Oh, no. It has a one-year warranty.*

Model 2

Content: admitting a possible error; asking for clarification; giving advice about what to do when something is broken; reassuring someone

Procedure:

🎧 A–B.

➤ To activate prior knowledge, ask students to share with a partner an experience when they broke something. To prompt discussion, ask questions such as *What did you break? Whose was it? How did you feel? What did you do?*

➤ Ask questions about the photo, such as *What is the man on the left holding?* (a machine) Have students look at his expression and speculate about how he feels and what problem he has.

➤ After students listen to the conversation, ask comprehension questions such as *What did the man on the left break?* (the sander) Elicit or explain that a *sander* is an electric tool used for making surfaces smooth. Then ask *How does he feel about breaking the sander?* (worried, scared) *Why is he worried?* (He doesn't want to get in trouble.) *What advice does his co-worker give?* (to tell someone)

➤ Point to the man on the left and say *He is worried that he will get into trouble for breaking the sander. What could happen to him?* Elicit responses such as *He could lose his job* or *He could have to pay for the sander.*

➤ Have students practice using *you'd better* to strongly suggest that someone do something. Brainstorm sentences with *you'd better* that parents might say to their children, such as *You'd better do your homework, You'd better wash the dishes.* Explain that *Maybe you'd better* is a less forceful way of offering advice.

➤ Make sure students understand that *fault* refers to responsibility for something bad that has happened.

➤ Ask students the meaning of *speak up.* Elicit responses such as *talk about it, tell someone, say something.* Discuss other situations when it's good to speak up.

🎧 Vocabulary

➤ Have students close their books. Ask *What can you do when something at work is broken?* Brainstorm ideas and write them on the board.

➤ Have students open their books and listen to and repeat the vocabulary. Compare the solutions in the *Vocabulary* box to the ones on the board.

C. Pair work . . .

➤ Have students practice the conversation with a partner. Point out that Student A will use *the* with one of the machines pictured or one of the machines on page 30 and that Student B will give advice using one of the phrases from the *Vocabulary* box.

➤ Have students practice again, this time using machines they have at work.

If your students are ready . . .

Culture / Civics note: In the North American workplace, employees are expected to speak up when they note equipment problems on the job, even if they contributed to the breakdown. Admitting mistakes is considered a positive trait. For unintentional mistakes, the emphasis is usually on fixing the problem and restoring productivity rather than assigning blame or punishment. Concealing or ignoring problems, especially those that hurt productivity, is considered a much greater offense than making the original mistake.

➤ Do it yourself!

(For general suggestions, see *Introduction*, page Txiii.)

Procedure:

A–B.

➤ If you or the students have brought in warranties, have students use them to fill in their charts. If students do not know the terms of warranties for machines they have, they can ask about machines classmates have. If students have warranties at home, they can complete their charts outside of class.

➤ Have students compare their charts and identify the machines with the best warranties.

If your students are ready . . .

Culture / Civics note: The ability to use money carefully and wisely is highly valued in North America. Buying used goods is one popular method of saving money here, and there is no shame attached to this practice. In particular, automobiles are often bought used, as buying a one- or two-year-old car can be significantly less expensive than buying a new car. One drawback to purchasing used goods is that they may not be covered by a warranty. Thrift stores, resale shops, consignment stores, online auctions, flea markets, and yard sales are good sources of used products.

A. Listen and read.

> **A:** Uh-oh. I'm going to get in trouble.
> **B:** What do you mean?
> **A:** Well, I think I broke this sander.
> **B:** Maybe you'd better tell someone.
> **A:** I don't know. They'll think it's my fault.
> **B:** Don't worry. It's always good to speak up.

B. Listen again and repeat.

Vocabulary

What to do when something is broken

| call the manager | call the help line | call maintenance | ask someone for help |

C. **Pair work. Express concern about breaking something. Talk about what to do. Use these machines or the ones on page 30. Or use your _own_ machines.**

> **A:** Uh-oh. I'm going to get in trouble.
> **B:** What do you mean?
> **A:** Well, I think I broke _____.
> **B:** Maybe you'd better _____.
> **A:** I don't know. They'll think it's my fault.
> **B:** Don't worry. It's always good to speak up.

➤ Do it yourself!

A. **Personalization. Complete the chart with machines or equipment you have, or a friend has.**

Machine	New / Used	Warranty?	Terms
my car	☐ ☑	☑	6 months or 3000 miles
1.	☐ ☐	☐	
2.	☐ ☐	☐	

B. **Discussion. Talk about the information on your chart.**

Model 3   Express frustration with an equipment malfunction. Empathize.

A. Listen and read.

A: Can you believe it? This hose is clogged again.

B: You're kidding. When was it serviced?

A: Just last week.

B: That's ridiculous. What a waste of time!

A: You can say that again! Let's write up a repair or replace order.

B. Listen again and repeat.

Machine maintenance

serviced
cleaned
fixed

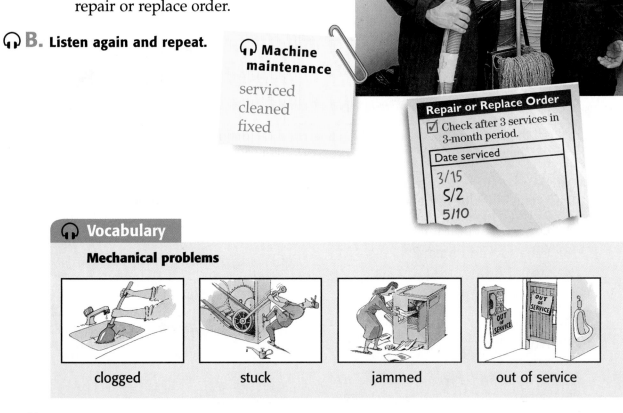

Repair or Replace Order

☑ Check after 3 services in 3-month period.

Date serviced
3/15
5/2
5/10

Vocabulary

Mechanical problems

clogged	stuck	jammed	out of service

C. Pair work. Decide to write up a repair or replace order. Use these machines and equipment or your <u>own</u> machines and equipment.

copier	sink	sewing machine	toilet	vacuum cleaner

A: Can you believe it? The _____ is _____ again.

B: You're kidding. When was it _____?

A: ____1____.

B: That's ridiculous. What a waste of time!

A: _____. Let's write up a repair or replace order.

[1]About (two) days / weeks ago

➤ Practical conversations

(For general suggestions, see *Introduction*, page Tviii.)

Model 3

Content: expressing frustration with an equipment malfunction; describing a mechanical problem; talking about machine maintenance; empathizing; the passive voice

Procedure:

🎧 A–B.

➤ With books closed, explain that *frustration* is the feeling of being upset or angry because you can't control or change a situation. Ask students what causes them to feel frustrated. Ask students what they do when they are frustrated.

➤ Read the bar for *Model 3* aloud. Make sure students understand that a *malfunction* is a problem in the way a machine works and that *empathize* is to understand someone else's feelings and problems.

➤ Ask questions about the photo, such as *What are the maintenance workers looking at?* (a hose, a commercial vacuum cleaner) *What's on the wall behind them?* (repair or replace order forms)

➤ Have students look at the repair or replace order below the photo. Ask *How many times has the vacuum cleaner been serviced?* (three times) *On what dates was it serviced?* (3/15, 5/2, and 5/10)

➤ After students listen to the conversation, ask comprehension questions such as *What is the problem?* (The hose is clogged.) *Have there been problems with this vacuum cleaner before?* (yes) *When was the last problem?* (last week)

➤ Have students underline the word *frustration* in the *Model 3* bar and then underline in the conversation the different ways frustration is expressed: *Can you believe it?*, *You're kidding*, *That's ridiculous*, *What a waste of time!* Have students circle the word *Empathize* in the *Model 3* bar and then circle *You can say that again!* in the conversation.

🎧 Machine maintenance

➤ After students repeat the words, point out that *cleaned* or *fixed* can be substituted for *serviced* in the conversation. Explain that to keep machines working well, they must be cleaned and serviced regularly and that, when broken, they need to be fixed. Elicit or explain the meaning of *serviced* as looked at or examined and fixed if necessary. Ask students for another word for *fixed*. Elicit *repaired*.

➤ Point out that all three words end in *-ed*. Have students underline *-ed* in each word, in anticipation of learning the passive voice later in the unit.

🎧 Vocabulary

➤ After students listen to and repeat the vocabulary, brainstorm and write on the board at least two machines or pieces of equipment that can have each problem, for example, *clogged: toilets, sinks, bathtubs, hoses.*

Option: Throw a light ball or beanbag to a student and call out a kind of machine, such as *a copier.* The student responds with a mechanical problem that a copier could have, such as *It's jammed,* and tosses the ball back. Throw the ball to another student and call out a different machine. Repeat several times.

C. Pair work . . .

➤ Model the activity with a more advanced student. Play the role of Student A to demonstrate using a machine from the box or board and the new vocabulary. Point out that Student B can insert *serviced, cleaned,* or *fixed* in the blank.

Challenge: Have partners practice a version of the conversation until they have memorized it. Have volunteers present their conversations to the class. Encourage students to be dramatic, exaggerating their frustration. Have students use props if available.

Model 4

Content: inquiring about a problem; talking about computer activities and malfunctions; troubleshooting a problem

Procedure:

🎧 A–B.

➤ To activate students' prior knowledge and to learn about students' experience with computers, take a poll. Say *If you have used a computer, raise your hand.* Write on the board *used a computer* and the number of positive responses. Continue, asking students to raise their hands if they have *sent e-mail messages, used the Internet, typed a document on the computer, printed a document.* Tally the responses. Discuss the results.

➤ Ask questions about the photo, such as *Where are the women?* (in an office or computer lab) *How does the woman on the right look?* (frustrated) *What do you think they are talking about?* (a computer problem)

➤ After students listen to the conversation, ask questions such as *What's the problem with the computer?* (It crashed.) *What does the woman on the right need to do?* (order supplies) *What suggestion does the woman on the left make?* (to try restarting the computer)

🎧 Computer malfunctions

➤ After students repeat the words, ask what the words mean. If necessary, explain that *frozen* means that nothing on the screen will move or respond to clicking or typing. The rest of the words refer to general computer malfunctions and mean that the computer isn't working. Ask the class *Have you ever experienced a computer malfunction? What did you do? Then what happened?*

🎧 Vocabulary

➤ After students listen to and repeat the vocabulary, ask questions about each activity, for example, *In what business do you order supplies? What do you order?*

➤ Brainstorm and write on the board other activities computers are used for, such as *buy something online, check / send e-mail, balance bank accounts, check the weather, print labels.* Ask students what they use computers for at work and at home.

Option: If appropriate based on your poll, have students use a Venn diagram to compare their computer use at work and at home. (Refer to page T7 for an example of a Venn diagram.) On the board, draw two overlapping circles and label the first one *At work* and the second *At home*. Model the activity by listing in the appropriate places on the Venn diagram computer activities you do at work, at home,

and in both places. For example, write *order supplies* on the left side of the diagram and *balance my checking account* on the right side. In the area where the circles overlap, write *send e-mail*.

C. Pair work . . .

➤ Model the activity with a more advanced student. Play the role of Student B to demonstrate using a computer malfunction from the yellow language note in the first blank and a computer activity from the *Vocabulary* box or board in the second blank. Refer Student A to the *Vocabulary* box on page 31 for different ways of giving advice on what to do.

Field project: If students have limited experience with computers, take them to the school's computer lab or to a public library. Familiarize them with the basics of using a computer, including how to turn the computer on and off, how to use the mouse, how to open and close programs, and so on. Then guide the class through a specific task, such as doing the tutorial for a software application, setting up a free e-mail account, using a search engine to find news on their countries, checking the weather, or using a Web site that has games or activities for ESL students.

➤ Do it yourself!

(For general suggestions, see *Introduction*, page Txiii.)

Procedure:

A. Pair work . . .

Note: The mechanical problems are listed in the simple present here. On page 32, the past participles were given.

➤ Ask *Do you have any problems with machines at work or at home? What is the problem?* Talk about the meaning of the example, *My camera jams.*

➤ Have students complete the chart. Refer them to the illustrations of equipment and machines on pages 30 and 31 and of mechanical problems on page 32.

B. Discussion . . .

➤ Model the activity by talking about your own experience with a machine malfunctioning.

➤ Ask questions to prompt discussion, such as *What machine did you have a problem with? What was the problem? What did you do? Was the problem fixed? Were you frustrated? Did anyone empathize with you?*

➤ Refer students to the *Vocabulary* box on page 31 for help in discussing how they solved the problem.

A. Listen and read.

> **A:** What's the matter?
> **B:** My computer crashed. And I need to order supplies.
> **A:** Did you try restarting it?
> **B:** Yes, I did. But that didn't help.
> **A:** Maybe you'd better tell someone.

B. Listen again and repeat.

Computer malfunctions

crashed	is broken
is down	is frozen
isn't working	

Vocabulary

Computer activities

File Folders
Price: $13.99 **ORDER**
Unit: 100/box

detergent ..... 3 cartons
paper towels .... 15 rolls
cleanser .... 2 boxes

Aircraft	T- 343
Dep. Time	06:45pm
Arr. Time	08:17pm
Total Stops	None
Aircraft	MP267
Dep. Time	07:00am
Arr. Time	09:37am
Total Stops	None

Starflight Diner
Hamburger plate 4.95
Salad 2.95
Coffee .80
  .61
Tax $9.31
Total
Thank you!

Ace Electr
Memo
To: Edward Stone
From: Miriam Yu
CC: Anita Cordova
Date: 5/11/03
Re: New stock ro

order supplies   check stock   make reservations   print receipts   write memos

C. Pair work. Discuss a computer problem. Use activities from the vocabulary or your own computer activities.

> **A:** What's the matter?
> **B:** My computer _____. And I need to _____.
> **A:** Did you try restarting it?
> **B:** Yes, I did. But that didn't help.
> **A:** Well, maybe you'd better ____1____.

[1]call the help line, ask someone for help

➤ Do it yourself!

A. Pair work. Complete the chart about problems with two of your machines.

B. Discussion. Talk about what you did when a machine malfunctioned.

Machine	sticks	clogs	jams	crashes
my camera	☐	☐	☑	☐
1.	☐	☐	☐	☐
2.	☐	☐	☐	☐

Practical grammar

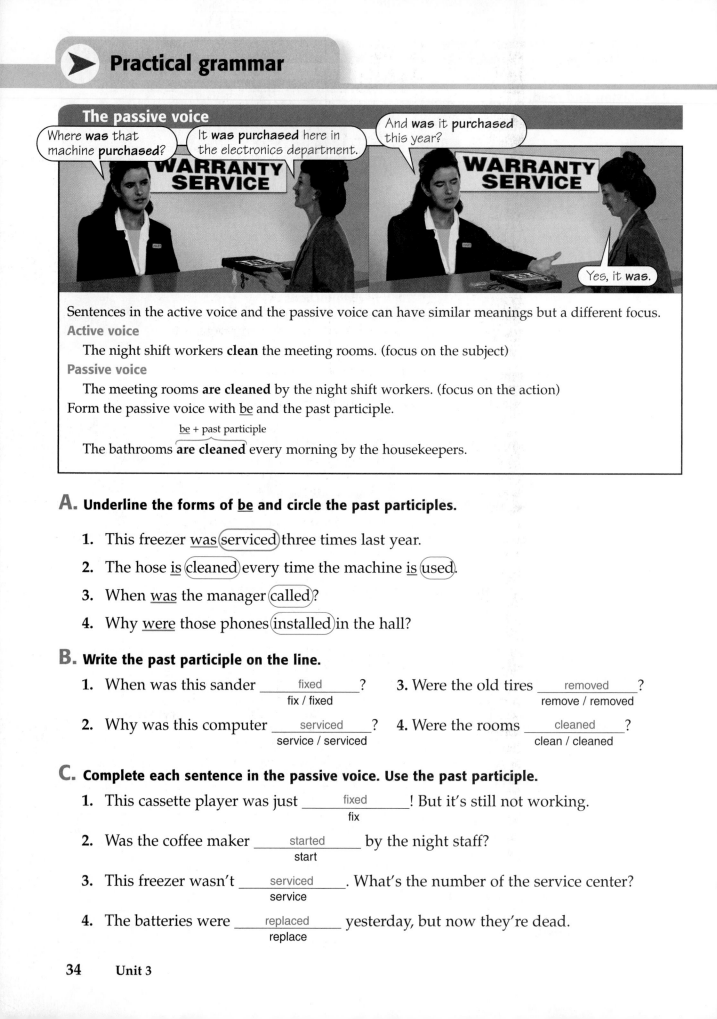

Where **was** that machine **purchased**?

It **was purchased** here in the electronics department.

And **was** it **purchased** this year?

Yes, it **was**.

Sentences in the active voice and the passive voice can have similar meanings but a different focus.

Active voice

   The night shift workers **clean** the meeting rooms. (focus on the subject)

Passive voice

   The meeting rooms **are cleaned** by the night shift workers. (focus on the action)

Form the passive voice with **be** and the past participle.

        be + past participle

   The bathrooms **are cleaned** every morning by the housekeepers.

A. Underline the forms of be and circle the past participles.

1. This freezer <u>was</u> serviced three times last year.

2. The hose <u>is</u> cleaned every time the machine <u>is</u> used.

3. When <u>was</u> the manager called?

4. Why <u>were</u> those phones installed in the hall?

B. Write the past participle on the line.

1. When was this sander ____fixed____ ?
   fix / fixed

2. Why was this computer ____serviced____ ?
   service / serviced

3. Were the old tires ____removed____ ?
   remove / removed

4. Were the rooms ____cleaned____ ?
   clean / cleaned

C. Complete each sentence in the passive voice. Use the past participle.

1. This cassette player was just ____fixed____ ! But it's still not working.
   fix

2. Was the coffee maker ____started____ by the night staff?
   start

3. This freezer wasn't ____serviced____ . What's the number of the service center?
   service

4. The batteries were ____replaced____ yesterday, but now they're dead.
   replace

➤ Practical grammar

(For general suggestions, see *Introduction*, page Tix.)

The passive voice

Procedure:

➤ Write on the board (*Your school's or program's name*) *offers this class*. Draw a box around *this class* and then an arrow to the beginning of a new sentence. Write *This class is offered by (your school's or program's name)*. Write *Active voice* above the first example and *Passive voice* above the second. Explain that in the first sentence the focus is on the school or program and that in the second sentence the focus is on *offered*, or the action. Underline *offers* in the first sentence and *is offered* in the second.

➤ Read and discuss the examples in the box. Make sure students understand that the passive is formed with the verb *be* + the past participle. Elicit the present and past forms of the verb *be* from students. Point out that past participles for regular verbs end in *-ed*. Brainstorm a few examples on the board.

➤ Give a student a command that involves acting on an object; for example, say *Maria, turn off the lights*. Then ask *What happened to the lights?* Write on the board *The lights* and elicit the class's help in finishing the sentence with the passive voice. Write *were turned off by Maria* on the board. Give similar commands to several different students, asking what happened to the object after each, and practice forming the passive voice as a class.

A. Underline the forms of <u>be</u> ...

➤ Use the passive voice examples on the board to model the activity. For example, in *This class is offered by (your school's or program's name)*, underline *is* and circle *offered*. In *The lights were turned off by Maria*, underline *were* and circle *turned off*. Then write the sentence from item 1 on the board. Ask *What is the form of <u>be</u>?* Elicit and underline *was* in the sentence. Ask *What is the past participle?* Elicit and circle *serviced* in the sentence.

➤ After students complete the exercise individually, review the answers as a class. Then read item 1 again and ask *Who serviced the freezer three times last year?* Elicit the response that we do not know who serviced the freezer. Read item 2 and ask *Who cleans the hose? Who uses the machine?* Point out that the passive voice is most often used when it is not known or not important to know who performs an action.

Option: Point out the examples of the passive voice in the model conversations on pages 30 and 32, such as *When was it purchased?* Have students underline the forms of *be* and circle the past participles.

B–C.

➤ Students complete the exercises individually. Have students check answers with a partner, or review as a class.

Note: In Exercise C, students may be unfamiliar with the use of *dead* to mean not working in item 4.

Option: For Exercise B, have students create answers to the questions and then ask and answer the questions with a partner.

If your students are ready ...

Language note: The passive voice can be formed only from a sentence in the active voice that contains an object of the verb. The object is moved into the subject position to form the passive.

The passive can be used to avoid saying who did something. For example, if my co-worker puts too much paper in the printer and jams it, I can report the problem to my supervisor by saying *The copier is jammed because too much paper was added.* In this way, someone can speak up about a problem without assigning blame or feeling uncomfortable about telling on someone else.

D. Complete each sentence...

➤ Point out that the questions are in the passive voice and that the answers should be also. Have students underline the forms of *be* and circle the participles in the questions.

➤ Do item 1 as a class. Students complete items 2 through 4 individually and then check their work by reading the questions and answers with a partner.

Irregular past participles: Review

Procedure:

🎧

➤ Have students listen to and then repeat the three forms of each verb. Ask which verbs have the same form for the simple past and the past participle. Elicit *bring, buy, make, sell, send.*

➤ Point to the date or some other information you have already written on the board. Say *I wrote the date at the beginning of class.* Then say *The date was written at the beginning of class.* Using verbs from the grammar box, write a couple of sentences in the simple past on the board and as a class change them to the passive voice, for example, *She bought the computer last week.* ➝ *The computer was bought last week.*

E. Complete each sentence...

➤ Write item 1 (without the answer) on the board. Have students find the verb *write* in the box. Ask *What is the past participle of <u>write</u>?* (written) Redirect students' attention to the board and elicit the correct form of *be* for item 1. Write the answer on the line.

➤ Students complete items 2 through 4 individually. Review as a class, making sure students have used a form of *be* in the past. If necessary, point out the phrases, such as *a week ago* and *last time,* that indicate past tense.

Option: Using the irregular verbs from the box and the equipment and machines vocabulary on page 30, have students write one positive statement, one negative statement, and one question in the passive voice, for example, *The drill was bought six months ago, The sewing machine wasn't made in the United States, When was the printer given to you?*

➤ Do it yourself!

(For general suggestions, see *Introduction,* page Txiii.)

Procedure:

➤ Have students look at the service receipts. Ask for the names of the two auto repair shops. Have students find *Services(s) performed* on both receipts. Have volunteers read the services performed at each shop.

➤ Write on the board *What work was done at Vinny's?* and *What work was done at Maisie's?* Read the first question and ask a volunteer to respond by reading the first speech balloon. Read the second question and ask another volunteer to respond by reading the second speech balloon.

➤ With a partner, students continue comparing the other services performed at the two auto repair shops. Point out that the verbs used are all regular, so the past participles will end in *-ed.*

➤ When students are finished, ask *What was done at both Vinny's and Maisie's?* Elicit *A state inspection was performed.*

Option: Have students bring in service receipts from their workplaces or from places in your community such as repair shops, dry cleaners, medical or dental offices, and customer service counters. In small groups, have students share their receipts and talk about the services that were performed.

D. Complete each sentence in the passive voice.

1. **A:** When was the filter changed?

   B: It ___was changed___ last week.

2. **A:** Where was the truck purchased?

   B: It ___was purchased___ at Trucks, Inc.

3. **A:** Was the thermostat adjusted?

   B: Yes, it ___was adjusted___ this morning.

4. **A:** Were the phones moved?

   B: Yes, they ___were moved___ by Ann.

Irregular past participles: Review

The following verbs have irregular past participles.

🎧 Verb	Simple past	Past participle	🎧 Verb	Simple past	Past participle
begin	began	**begun**	give	gave	**given**
break	broke	**broken**	make	made	**made**
bring	brought	**brought**	sell	sold	**sold**
buy	bought	**bought**	send	sent	**sent**
choose	chose	**chosen**	take	took	**taken**
drive	drove	**driven**	write	wrote	**written**

A more complete list of irregular past participles can be found on page 148.

E. Complete each sentence in the passive voice.

1. The repair or replace order _was written_ a week ago.

write

2. Where ___was___ the car ___brought___ for repairs last time?

bring

3. When ___was___ this washing machine ___bought___?

buy

4. That floor polisher ___was___ not ___broken___ the day before yesterday.

break

➤ Do it yourself!

Pair work. Look at the service receipts for two cars. Compare what was done by Vinny's Car Repair and Maisie's Garage.

VINNY'S *Car Repair*

024986

Date: March 5, 2003

Model: Monsoon van, model year 1999

Services performed	
☐ replace wipers	
☑ change oil	☑ perform State Inspection
☑ clean air filter	
☑ replace fan belt	

Maisie's Garage

030355

DATE March 5, 2003

SERVICE RECORD Skyview sedan   MODEL YEAR 2000

SERVICE PERFORMED
☑ rotate tires   ☑ perform State Inspection
☑ replace left tail light bulb   ☑ recharge freon (air conditioner)

DROP-OFF   PICK-UP   CUSTOMER PHONE NUMBER

At Vinny's, the air filter was cleaned.

At Maisie's, the tires were rotated.

Authentic practice

🎧 **A. Read and listen again. Then check <u>True</u>, <u>False</u>, or <u>Maybe</u>.**

	True	False	Maybe
1. The wires were broken before.	☑	☐	☐
2. The cooks will reconnect the wires.	☐	☑	☐
3. The worker who broke the wires will speak up.	☐	☐	☑

🎧 **B. Listen. Underline <u>your</u> response.**

1. **YOU** Is it clogged?   **YOU** <u>What do you mean?</u>

2. **YOU** <u>That's ridiculous.</u>   **YOU** Now it won't work at all.

3. **YOU** What a waste of time.   **YOU** <u>Great. Let's start now.</u>

🎧 **C. Listen again. Read <u>your</u> response out loud.**

➤ Authentic practice

(For general suggestions, see *Introduction,* page Tx.)

Procedure:

🎧
➤ Have students look at the burner with wires coming out of it in the first picture. Ask what other appliances and machines have wires, such as *stereos, light fixtures, car engines.*

➤ After students read and listen, check comprehension by asking questions such as *Where are the women?* (at work in a restaurant or cafeteria) *What is broken?* (the wires to the burner) *Who broke the wires?* (the woman on the left, Laura) *What does the woman on the right first suggest?* (trying to reconnect the wires)

➤ Have students circle *in hot water* in picture 1 and *a big deal* and *in a jiffy* in picture 2. Have a volunteer read each speech balloon that contains one of these expressions. Encourage students to speculate about what the expressions mean based on the context. As a class, come up with simple definitions for each expression, for example, *in trouble, serious, very quickly.*

➤ Draw a chart on the board like this one.

Action	+	−
Trying to reconnect the wires		
Not doing anything		
Speaking up		

➤ Elicit and list on the chart the three actions that are suggested in the picture story—*trying to reconnect the wires, not doing anything / cooking with the other three burners,* and *speaking up.* Ask students to think of a positive and a negative result for each action. For example, for *trying to reconnect the wires,* the positive result could be *The problem is fixed,* and the negative result could be *They get in trouble.*

➤ When the chart is complete, ask students which solution they think is best. Ask *What would you do if you were in this situation?* Ask students to predict what Laura, the woman in the picture story, will do.

➤ Have students close their books and retell the story in their own words to a partner.

Challenge: In pairs, have students role-play a conversation in which the cook reports the problem to her supervisor. Have volunteers present their conversations to the class.

🎧 A. Read and listen again . . .

➤ Have students read and listen again and answer the items. Then have them find and underline in the picture story a sentence that supports each answer. To demonstrate, have a volunteer read and answer item 1. When the student says that the item is true, ask *How do we know?* The class finds and underlines *This is the third time I've done that.* Have students work with a partner to find sentences to support items 2 and 3, and then review as a class.

🎧 B–C.

➤ Read each item in the tapescript out loud or play the cassette as many times as necessary for students to complete the exercise.

➤ Review the answers before having students read their responses out loud.

➤ Read each item from the tapescript again, and ask the class to restate it in their own words; for example, for *I'm really in hot water now,* students might say *I'm really in trouble now.*

Tapescript

1. I'm really in hot water now.
2. It's really a big deal. It'll take two hours to fix.
3. No problem. We can do it in a jiffy.

Technical assistance on the telephone

Procedure:

🎧 **A.** Listening comprehension...

➤ If necessary, familiarize students with computer terminology before they listen to the conversation. Use a computer in your classroom or a picture of a computer to point out the *screen*, *mouse*, *keyboard*, and *control* and *escape keys*.

➤ Tell students that they are going to listen to a man call a help line about a computer problem. With books closed, students listen to the conversation.

➤ Have volunteers read the items out loud before students listen to the conversation again and check the boxes.

➤ After reviewing the answers, have students change item 3 to make it true.

B. True story...

➤ Tell your own story about having a machine or piece of equipment serviced or repaired. Then ask *What did I have repaired? Did I send it to a service center, take it to a repair shop, or fix it myself?*

➤ Ask *What have you had serviced or repaired?* Have students write the name of a machine or piece of equipment in the margin. Ask *Did you send it to a service center, take it to a repair shop, or fix it yourself?* Have students circle the caption that tells what they did. If necessary, brainstorm other possibilities. Then students tell their stories to a partner.

Option: With books closed, brainstorm a list of machines and write it on the board. Bring in telephone books, or ask students to bring telephone books in. Have students search for repair shops or service centers that fix each type of machine. Have students write down each shop's name and telephone number. Point out that service may be abbreviated as *svc*. Discuss other abbreviations that students find. If appropriate, have students call one of the shops and ask for directions.

Challenge: Have students retell their partners' stories, using the passive voice. For example, if one student told the story *I broke my stereo last month. I took it to a repair shop...*, his or her partner would say *The stereo was broken last month. It was taken to a repair shop...*

➤ Do it yourself!

(For general suggestions, see *Introduction*, page Txiii.)

Procedure:

A. Write your own response...

➤ Say *The man in the photo is your co-worker. He admits to you an error he has made. Find out what happened. Empathize with him. Then give him advice.*

➤ Have students read the speech balloons and write their responses.

➤ Have a volunteer read any one of the three responses. Ask the class which speech balloon the response goes with. Then have students take turns reading their responses out of order to a partner and having their partners match each response with the appropriate speech balloon.

➤ Have students take turns practicing their conversations with a partner.

B. Culture talk...

➤ Write on the board *1. Do people tell a supervisor when they make a mistake? 2. Do people tell a supervisor about their co-workers' mistakes?* Ask students to think about their workplaces in their home countries. Give each student a slip of paper. Have them write *Yes* or *No* to each question. Have volunteers collect the slips of paper and tally the responses on the board. Discuss the results as a class.

➤ Read the directions out loud. Ask students to imagine that the mistake described in Exercise A was made by a worker in their home country. In small, diverse groups, have students discuss what the worker would probably do.

Option: Have students imagine themselves in the situations described in the model conversation on page 31 and in the picture story on page 36. Have students discuss with their groups what they would have done in their home countries.

Tapescript

Man: Oh, no! It crashed again. Judy, where's that number for the computer service center? Oh, thanks. 1-800-555-3333.

[man dials as he says each number]

(Tapescript is continued on page T38.)

A. **Listening comprehension. Listen to the conversation about a computer problem. Then listen again and check <u>True</u>, <u>False</u>, or <u>Maybe</u>.**

	True	False	Maybe
1. The computer crashed.	☑	☐	☐
2. The computer was purchased at Electronics World.	☐	☐	☑
3. Holding down the control key helps for a while.	☐	☑	☐
4. The computer needs more memory.	☐	☐	☑

B. **True story. Tell your partner about a machine or piece of equipment that was serviced or repaired.**

I sent it to a service center.

I took it to a repair shop.

I fixed it myself.

➤ Do it yourself!

A. **Write your <u>own</u> response. Then read your conversation out loud with a partner.**

I'm definitely in big trouble now.

YOU _____

The hose was clogged. I disconnected it, but I forgot to turn off the machine. Now there's dirt all over the floor.

YOU _____

Maybe I should just say I found it like this when I got here. Then no one will know who made the mess.

YOU _____

B. **Culture talk. In the country you come from, how do you tell a supervisor that you made a mistake? Compare cultures with your classmates.**

Speak up about equipment breakdowns.

🎧 **A.** Read and listen to the letters.

Ask Joan
Culture tips for newcomers

Dear Joan:

I'm a cafeteria worker in a manufacturing plant. I like my job. I was hired only six months ago, and last week I was promoted! I have a problem, though, and I hope you can help me with it.

I am responsible for purchasing all supplies and preparing breakfast for the first shift. I come in early, and there's not much time to clean up and get ready. Sometimes I work too fast. When I try to clean under the burners, I sometimes disconnect the wires by mistake. This has already happened three times, and I'm afraid to tell the manager that I did it again today. She might think I'm not careful with the equipment.

I can't fix the wires myself, and I can't do all the cooking if I don't have all the burners working. What should I do? I don't want to get in trouble or lose my job.

I really need advice.

Laura

Dear Laura:

You have no idea how many letters like yours I receive! Many workers are afraid to tell their managers when something breaks. So instead of reporting a problem, workers often avoid working with the machine, probably hoping that someone else will solve the problem for them.

Remember: Managers want the work to get done. If you are having a problem with equipment, just speak up. Your manager will help you. She can probably show you how to clean under the burner without breaking the electrical connection. Don't worry. Your concern about the equipment will be rewarded, not blamed!

Joan

B. **Choose an answer to each question. Fill in the ovals.**

1. What's the problem?

    ⓐ A worker is afraid to speak up about a problem.   ⓑ The stove is dirty.

2. How often has this problem occurred?

    ⓐ Once.   ⓑ Several times.

3. What advice does Joan give?

    ⓐ Blame the manager.   ⓑ Tell the manager.

Tapescript *(continued from page T37)*

Recorded message: Welcome to the Electronics World Service Center, the largest computer service center in the state. If you have a touchtone phone, please touch 1 now. If you have a rotary phone, please stay on the line. A technician will be with you shortly to walk you through our telephone service. [beep]

Recorded message: To speed our response, please enter your 15-digit model number at the sound of the tone. [beep]

[eight telephone tones]

Man: Oops. [beep]

Recorded message: That is not a valid model number. Please try again.

[fifteen telephone tones]

Recorded message: Thank you. To speak to a technician, touch zero now. [beep] [music]

Trish: This is Trish. How can I help you?

Man: I have a problem with my laptop. When I use the mouse, the computer crashes.

Trish: Let me ask you a few questions. When was your computer purchased?

Man: About six months ago. It's still under warranty.

Trish: Thank you. That's good. Now, first of all: Are you sure that the mouse and the keyboard are connected?

Man: Let me check. . . . Yes, they are.

Trish: And have you tried holding down the control and escape keys?

Man: Yes. But that doesn't help at all.

Trish: And have you tried shutting down and restarting the computer?

Man: Yes. And that works. But sooner or later, if I use the mouse, the computer crashes again.

Trish: It sounds like the computer needs to be serviced. Are you in Maplewood?

Man: Yes, I am. Not far from the service center.

Trish: Can you bring the computer in to the center tomorrow? We can have a look at it. I'm not sure what the problem is. It might need more memory.

Man: Thanks. I'll bring it in tomorrow.

Authentic practice

(For general suggestions, see *Introduction*, page Tx.)

Speak up about equipment breakdowns.

Procedure:

A. Read and listen to the letters.

➤ Have students look back at the picture story on page 36. Ask students to recall what the problem was. Explain that the *Ask Joan* letter is from Laura, the woman who broke the burner wires in the picture story.

➤ After students read and listen to the letters, check comprehension by asking questions such as *What do some workers do instead of reporting a problem?* (avoid working with the machine) *What do managers want?* (for the work to get done) *What is Joan's advice?* (to speak up)

➤ Discuss how Laura can tell her manager about the problem with the burners. As a class, draft what she should say on the board.

B. Choose an answer . . .

➤ After students complete the exercise individually, have them check answers with a partner.

Challenge: In groups, have students write a letter to Joan from the man who broke the sander in the model conversation on page 31. Write on the board *Worker's name? Job? Length of time employed? Responsibilities? Error?* Have volunteers read the model conversation on page 31 out loud. As a class, note on the board the information provided in the conversation. Each group then makes up the information not provided. Using this information and the letter from Laura as a model, groups write letters to Joan.

C. What's your advice . . .

➤ Ask questions about the picture, such as *Where does the man on the right work?* (at Bright Laundry Service) *What mistake did he make?* (He put too much soap in the washing machine.) *What should he do?* Brainstorm and write on the board a list of possible solutions to the problem, such as *Turn off the machine* or *Ask someone for help.*

➤ Practice making suggestions to the worker as a class. Have volunteers use the ideas on the board with the prompts in the speech balloons. Point out that the *-ing* form of the verb must be used with *Try* _____. Then, have partners practice giving and responding to advice.

Option: In small groups, have students think of another situation in which a person makes a mistake at work and causes a problem, for example, *In the break room, someone puts a metal spoon in the microwave. Sparks and then smoke come out of the microwave.* Have each group write or draw its situation on the board. When all groups' situations are on the board, have a volunteer from each group read or describe its situation. If necessary, ask the group questions to clarify the situation. Then have each group choose one of the situations, not their own, and brainstorm suggestions they could make to the person. Have groups use the situation they have chosen and their list of suggestions to create a conversation. Have groups present a role-play of the situation to the class. During the presentations, have the other students write down one suggestion they hear in each conversation.

Product warranties and proof-of-purchase cards

Procedure:

➤ Have students look at the form on the right. Have a volunteer read the directions in parentheses under *Proof of purchase.* Ask what a proof of purchase is for and what you do with it. Explain that this form is sometimes called a *product registration card.*

➤ After students read the documents and answer the questions, have them check answers with a partner and / or review as a class. Then ask additional questions about the documents, such as *What does the warranty cover in the first year?* (parts and labor) *When was the microwave oven purchased?* (January 1, 2002) *Who purchased the microwave oven?* (Tina Park) *Where can she find a list of customer service centers?* (on the back of the card)

Challenge: Have students imagine that Tina Park has a problem with her microwave oven. In pairs, students create a telephone conversation between Tina Park and a customer service representative. Brainstorm and write on the board what information the customer service representative should ask for, such as *model number, when purchased, where purchased, whether or not she sent in the proof-of-purchase card, what the problem is, if it has been serviced before.* Have volunteers role-play their conversations for the class.

➤ Do it yourself!

(For general suggestions, see *Introduction,* page Txiii.)

Procedure:

➤ Have students look at the warranties they brought to class or at a warranty on page 154 and ask *What's the warranty for? How long is it good for? Is there a customer service number? What is it? Are parts covered? Is labor covered? Is there a proof-of-purchase or product registration card?* Pause between each question and allow students time to locate the information on their warranty and tell their partners the answer.

➤ Draw a chart on the board like the one here and have each pair of students copy it, or provide handouts. Have students fill in the information for their own and their partners' warranties, then have pairs exchange warranties. Continue until pairs have filled in their charts. Circulate, providing help as necessary.

Name of product	Length of warranty	Customer service number	Parts covered?	Labor covered?	Conditions

➤ Have students use their charts to compare warranties. To prompt discussion, ask questions such as *Which warranties are better? Why? Which warranty would you not like to have? Why not? Do any of the warranties have proof-of-purchase cards to fill out?*

C. What's your advice? Look at the picture. Tell the worker what to do.

Why don't you _____?

Try _____.

Don't be afraid to _____.

Product warranties and proof-of-purchase cards

Read the warranty and proof-of-purchase card. Answer the questions.

MicroTastic®
Commercial Microwave Oven

Warranty

All warranty service is to be provided by
an authorized MicroTastic® technician.
For service, call 1-800-MTASTIC.

Length of warranty—MicroTastic® will replace or repair:

Full one-year: from date of purchase Any part that fails because of a defect in materials or workmanship. During this one-year period, all parts and labor will be provided free of charge.	**Limited three-year: second through fourth year from date of purchase** The magnetron tube, if it fails because of a defect in materials or workmanship. During this period, purchaser will be responsible for costs of labor.

MicroTastic®

Microwave Oven Models MTMO 3400 and 3405

PROOF OF PURCHASE
(MUST BE SENT IN WITHIN ONE MONTH OF PURCHASE
TO ACTIVATE WARRANTY)

Your name _Tina Park_

Your address _131 Stanley Street, Pine Plains, New Jersey 07077_

Where was your MicroTastic® microwave oven purchased?
City Wide Electronics, 2 Central Ave., North Orange, NJ 07079

When was it purchased? _January 1, 2002_

If your MicroTastic® microwave oven needs to be serviced,
call the authorized Customer Service Center nearest you.
A complete list can be found on the back of this card.

1. Under the terms of the warranty, who has to provide service for the microwave?

_____

2. What does the purchaser have to do to activate the warranty? _____

_____

3. Who will pay for the cost of labor if the magnetron tube is replaced in 2003?

_____

➤ Do it yourself! A plan-ahead project

What's the warranty for?

How long is it good for?

**Pair work. Bring in a product warranty from a product
you purchased. If you don't have a warranty, use one on
page 154. Compare warranties with a classmate.**

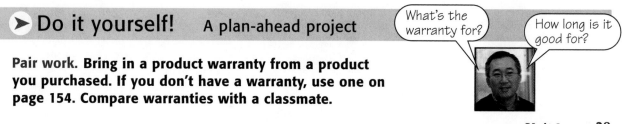

 **Review**

(For general suggestions, see *Introduction*, page Txii.)

Procedure:

A. Pair work or group work.

Ask and answer questions.

➤ Ask general questions about the picture, such as *What is the name of this store?* (Bestway) *What is sold at Bestway?* (appliances) *What is at the back of the store?* (a service center) *How many employees are in the picture?* (four)

➤ Have students take turns pointing to and naming the different machines in the picture. Then have the pairs label in their books all the machines they know. Review as a class. Write the machines on the board and have students check their spelling.

➤ Ask *Which two machines in the picture have problems?* (the coffee maker, the cash register) In pairs, have students describe the problem with each machine. Review as a class.

Create conversations.

➤ Have students look at the two people at the top of the page. Play the role of the customer with the coffee maker, and have a more advanced student come to the front of the room and play the role of the employee behind the counter. Initiate a conversation; for example, say *Excuse me. This coffee maker is broken.* If necessary, the class can help the student playing the role of the employee to respond. Continue the conversation for as long as possible, with each of you making a tally mark on the board every time you speak. When finished, count the marks.

➤ In pairs, have students create conversations for the other two scenes—in the vacuum cleaner department and at the cash register—and keep track of how many times they speak. Explain that the goal is to say as much as you can. Have pairs count their tally marks and report how many times they spoke.

Option: Have pairs create a third conversation, either between the female employee at the cash register and the male employee pointing toward the manager's office or between a customer on the telephone and a store employee.

Tell a story.

➤ Have a student time you while you talk about the picture for one minute. Then, in pairs or small groups, each student talks about the picture for one minute. Encourage students to describe each of the three scenes in the picture and to say as much as they can. Tell students to continue talking until you say *Stop*, indicating that the minute is up.

Option: Bingo game. Have students make a Bingo board with sixteen squares, four across and four down, or provide handouts. Write the following list of words on the board: *cash register, returned, warranties, coffee maker, headache, manager, activated, service counter, clogged, buttons, serviced, charge, suggested, stuck, jammed, bought, problem, try, vacuum cleaner, trouble.* Have students choose sixteen of these words / phrases, and write them one to a box, in any order. Once students have filled in their boards, read the story that follows. Students mark off their boxes as they hear the words in the story. When a student marks off four words across, down, or vertically, he or she calls out *Bingo*, interrupting the story. Have the student read his or her words. Check them, and then continue reading until another student calls *Bingo*.

> *What a day! Everything went wrong at once. First I jammed the cash register by pushing two buttons at once. Marvin came over and told me to try turning the key, so I did, but the machine was still stuck. Then Carlo suggested we tell the manager, but I was afraid I'd get into trouble. I've broken the register before. While we tried to fix the problem, one of the customers clogged a vacuum cleaner by sucking up the packing foam that came in the box. Well, the vacuums have warranties, but the customer hadn't bought it yet, so we didn't know if we should charge him to have it serviced. Meanwhile, Tim was at the service counter where a coffee maker was returned because it was broken. But the woman had never activated the warranty. So she started yelling at Tim, and I got a headache.*

🎧 B. Listen to the conversation . . .

➤ Tell students that they're going to listen to a conversation between an employee and a customer at an electronics repair shop.

➤ After students listen to the conversation the first time, ask *What machine does the customer have a problem with?* (a fax machine) Then review the meanings of *crashes, clogs, sticks,* and *jams.* Have a volunteer read the four items whose malfunctions students will listen for.

Option: Discuss feelings related to problems with machines and equipment. Ask *How do you feel when a machine or piece of equipment doesn't work? How do you feel when something you just bought doesn't work? What do you do? How do you feel when you have to explain the problem to someone at the store? To someone on the phone?*

C–E.

➤ Students work individually to complete the review exercises.

➤ Circulate to offer help as needed.

➤ Have students check answers with a partner. Review answers as a class.

➤ Identify any areas of difficulty that may require additional instruction and practice.

Tapescript

Woman: Can I help you?

Man: Yes, thanks. I bought this fax machine here and I have a problem with it. Actually, I have several problems.

Woman: What's the matter?

Man: Well, first, the paper jams.

Woman: [writes] paper . . . jams. Yes, and what else?

Man: Well, second, the button sticks.

Woman: What do you mean?

Man: I have to press the fax button at least four times to get the machine to send a fax. And the toner is a problem too. The hose that the toner goes through gets clogged up, and the warning light goes on.

Woman: Is the fax machine connected to a computer?

Man: Yes, it is.

Woman: Can you send a fax through the computer?

Man: Yes, I can. But then the computer crashes.

Woman: I'm so sorry. It sounds like you have a lot of problems!

Man: You can say *that* again.

	crashes	clogs	sticks	jams
1. the paper	☐	☐	☐	☑
2. the fax button	☐	☐	☑	☐
3. the toner hose	☐	☑	☐	☐
4. the computer	☑	☐	☐	☐

C. **Choose your response. Fill in the ovals.**

1. "Can you believe it? This drill is still under warranty."

   ⓐ That's too bad.   ⬤ⓑ That's great.

2. "I'm afraid I'm going to get in trouble."

   ⓐ What a waste of time.   ⬤ⓑ Don't worry. It's always good to speak up.

3. "Now it won't work at all."

   ⬤ⓐ That's ridiculous.   ⓑ About six months ago.

4. "Uh-oh."

   ⓐ You're kidding.   ⬤ⓑ What's the matter?

D. **Write the past participle on the line.**

1. The fryer was _____made_____ in Taiwan.
   make / made

2. This car was _____given_____ to me by my husband.
   gave / given

3. The best printers are _____sold_____ at Martin Electronics.
   sell / sold

4. Was the repair or replace order _____written_____ by the night shift?
   wrote / written

E. **Complete each sentence in the passive voice.**

1. The fax machines _____were brought_____ to the shop on May 1.
   bring

2. The sander _____was broken_____ by the painters last week.
   break

3. The proof of purchase _____was sent_____ to the company yesterday.
   send

4. The coffee maker _____was repaired_____ by the cafeteria manager.
   repair

F. Write a response to each statement. Use your **own** words.

1. "I'm really in hot water now!"

   _____

2. "Maybe I should just try to do the work by hand. I don't want anyone to know that I broke the sewing machine."

   _____

3. "I think you should speak up. You won't be blamed."

   _____

G. Read the warranty. If you buy a Spiffy Floor Polisher today, what repairs will the company make under the warranty five years from today? Check the repairs.

Spiffy Floor Polisher PRODUCT WARRANTY

Full one-year
from date of purchase: Any part that fails because of a defect in materials or workmanship.

Lifetime
from date of purchase: The engine, if it fails because of a defect in materials or workmanship. Spiffy will be responsible for all costs.

1. ☐ the handle   2. ☐ the belts   3. ☑ the engine

H. Composition. On a separate sheet of paper, write about the picture on page 40. Say as much as you can.

> **Now I can**
> ☐ read and understand a product warranty.
> ☐ admit a possible error.
> ☐ reassure someone.
> ☐ express frustration with equipment malfunctions.
> ☐ troubleshoot a problem.
> ☐ _____ .

F–G.

➤ Students work individually to complete the review exercises.

➤ Circulate to offer help as needed.

➤ Have students check answers with a partner. Review answers as a class.

➤ Identify any areas of difficulty that may require additional instruction and practice.

H. Composition...

➤ Provide students with concrete approaches to writing about the picture on page 40. Use one of the options that follow, give students a choice of options, or assign options based on students' levels of proficiency. Model what is expected of students for each option.

➤ Advise students to look back through the unit for help and ideas as they write.

➤ Circulate to offer help as needed.

Option: Have students create a simple warranty and proof-of-purchase card for the lawn mower.

Option: Have students imagine that they are Bestway customers and have purchased something that isn't working. The employee at the service center doesn't know whether the product should be repaired or replaced. He asks them to write down their name, phone number, and the details of their purchase—what was bought, when it was bought, what the problem is, if the machine has been serviced before, what the length and terms of the warranty are, and whether they activated the warranty—so that the manager can call them later.

Challenge: Have students write an *Ask Joan* letter from the female employee at the cash register. Advise students to include the employee's name, position, how long she has worked at Bestway, her responsibilities, and the mistake she made. Have students use the letter from Laura on page 38 as a model.

Now I can

➤ Read the first item in the box out loud, *Now I can read and understand a product warranty.* Elicit from the class an example of how to read and understand a product warranty; for example, a student could point to the warranty on page 29 and say *The microwave has a one-year warranty on parts and labor.*

➤ In pairs, have students take turns reading each item in the box and giving an example of what they have learned. When students can provide an example, they should check that box. For the items students weren't able to check, they should look back through the unit for ideas.

➤ When students are finished reviewing with their partners, read each item out loud and elicit an example from the class.

Oral test (optional)

You may want to use the *Now I can* box as an informal evaluation. While students are working on the *Composition* activity, you can call them up individually and check their ability with two or three objectives.

The consumer world

➤ Preview

(For general suggestions, see *Introduction*, page Tviii.)

Warm up. What's the problem?

Procedure:

➤ Ask questions about the photos, such as *Who's talking?* (a man and a woman) *What do you think they're talking about?* (the notice, the Infant World high chair)

➤ Have students look at the notice from the Consumer Product Safety Commission. Have a volunteer read the notice. Ask questions such as *What product is pictured?* (a high chair) *What company makes the high chair?* (Infant World Inc.) *What's wrong with the high chair?* (It's defective.)

➤ Elicit or explain the meaning of *defective* as not made correctly or not working correctly. Then have students find and circle the words *recalled* and *recall* in the notice. Ask *What's a "recall"?* Have students try to determine the meaning of *recall* from the context. If necessary, explain that a *recall* occurs when a company asks people to return a product they bought because there is a problem with it.

➤ To activate students' prior knowledge, ask *Where can you hear about product recalls? Have you ever purchased something that was recalled? What was it? Was the product repaired or replaced, or did you get a refund? Why is it especially important to know about recalls of products for babies? Are products recalled in your country?*

➤ Brainstorm and write on the board a list of types of products that are often recalled. As a class, think of specific problems for a couple of the products, for example, for a car, *the brake pedal sticks*. Review the vocabulary *clogs, crashes, freezes, jams,* and *sticks* from pages 32 and 33.

➤ Summarize and check comprehension by reading the *Warm up* question and having students give an answer to a partner. Circulate and listen to students' answers.

If your students are ready . . .

Culture / Civics note: The United States Consumer Product Safety Commission and the Product Safety Bureau of Health Canada are government agencies that protect consumers from dangerous products. These agencies work with industry to develop product safety standards, collect information about unsafe products, and announce product recalls.

A product *recall* is a request by a manufacturer for consumers and sellers to return defective or unsafe products so that the manufacturer can fix the problem, replace the product, or offer a refund. Recall announcements are posted in stores that originally sold the product and are reported in newspapers, in popular magazines, on news programs, and on the Internet.

Unit 4 objectives

Procedure:

➤ Read the objectives. Discuss any unfamiliar vocabulary; for example, *discontinued* means not made or produced anymore.

➤ Explain that a *consumer* is someone who buys and uses products and services. Have students underline in the objectives the skills that will give them more protection as a consumer. Students should underline *Discuss a defective, discontinued, or recalled product; Understand and act on a product safety recall; Write a consumer complaint letter.*

The consumer world

Preview

Warm up. What's the problem?

Consumer Product Safety Commission

Defective high chair recalled. CPSC and Infant World Inc. announce recall of high chair.

Infant World high chair

Unit 4 objectives

- Discuss a defective, discontinued, or recalled product.
- Ask for and provide service at a gas station.
- Understand and act on a product safety recall.
- Write and respond to a consumer complaint letter.

Model 1 Discuss a defective item.

A. Listen and read.

A: Hi, Ed. Could you have a look at these faucets?

B: Sure. No problem.

A: The salespeople have been complaining about them.

B: Well, no wonder. They're not up to code.

B. Listen again and repeat.

Poor quality

not up to code
defective
not too good
below standard
no good

Vocabulary

Buyers and sellers

a customer   a dealer   a salesperson

C. Pair work. Ask your partner to check the quality of these products or the quality of products you make on your job.

cookies   shower heads   shoes   zippers

A: Hi, _____. Could you have a look at these _____?

B: Sure. No problem.

A: _____ have been complaining about them.

B: Well, no wonder. They're _____.

➤ Practical conversations

(For general suggestions, see *Introduction*, page Tviii.)

Model 1

Content: asking someone to check the quality of a product; reporting complaints from buyers and sellers; discussing a defective item

Procedure:

🎧 A–B.

➤ To set the scene for the conversation, ask questions about the photo, such as *What does the sign on the wall say?* (Quality Control) *What are the men looking at?* (faucets)

➤ After students listen to the conversation, check comprehension by asking questions such as *Who works in the quality-control department?* (Ed, the man on the right) *Who has been complaining about the faucets?* (the salespeople) *What is the problem with the faucets?* (They're not up to code.)

🎧 Poor quality

➤ Review other ways to describe poor quality that can be substituted for *not up to code* in the conversation. Point out that *not up to code* and *below standard* refer to rules or laws not being followed in making something. Remind students that *defective* means not made correctly or not working correctly.

➤ To activate students' prior knowledge, ask *In your jobs, are there codes, standards, or guidelines that have to be followed?* Ask *Why do we have codes and standards?* (for safety, to protect consumers)

🎧 Vocabulary

➤ After students listen to and repeat the vocabulary words, write the headings *Buyers* and *Sellers* on the board. Ask *Is a customer a buyer or a seller?* Write *a customer* under *Buyers*. Then ask *Is a salesperson a buyer or a seller?* Write *a salesperson* under *Sellers*. Explain that a dealer buys and sells a particular product. Write *a dealer* under both *Buyers* and *Sellers*. Brainstorm other words for buyers and sellers and add them to the lists, for example, *a consumer, a client, a cashier, a sales representative / rep.*

C. Pair work ...

➤ Have students look at the products in the pictures. As a class, match an expression of poor quality with each product. Point out, for example, that *defective* is appropriate only with the manufactured products, not with *cookies*.

➤ Ask *What products do you make, package, or sell at work?* Brainstorm additional products and write them on the board in plural form.

➤ Write *a customer—customers* on the board. Have students tell you the plural forms of the other words for buyers and sellers, the ones in the *Vocabulary* box and on the board.

➤ Model the activity with a more advanced student. Play the role of Student A. Demonstrate using one of the products pictured in Student A's first line and the plural of a buyer or seller in Student A's second line. If necessary, prompt Student B to choose a phrase from the yellow language note.

If your students are ready ...

Culture / Civics note: A building code is a set of rules for builders that are designed to protect the health, safety, and general welfare of the public. For example, building codes require that construction materials such as faucets, pipes, and concrete meet specified standards of quality and performance. To ensure the safety and durability of a structure, building codes also specify the manner in which materials must be assembled. In addition, codes require fire safety systems such as sprinklers, fire alarms, and fire escapes. Generally, each local area has its own building code, which is adopted, modified, and enforced by local government.

Model 2

Content: requesting a brand; offering an alternative; describing locations in a store; *used to*; comparisons with *as* and *not as*

Procedure:

⌒ A–B.

➤ Ask questions about the photo, such as *Where are these two people?* (in a hardware store) *Who is the customer?* (the woman) *Who is the salesperson?* (the man) *What are they looking at?* (saws)

➤ After students listen to the conversation, ask questions such as *What brand of tools is the woman looking for?* (Atlas) *Does the store have them?* (no) *Did the store have them before?* (yes) *What brand does the store have now?* (Hercules)

⌒ Locations in a store

➤ Use your classroom to demonstrate the locations. Count off the aisles between the desks and have them represent aisles in a store. Point down for *downstairs* and up for *upstairs*.

➤ After students listen and repeat, read each phrase again and have the class point to locations in the classroom to convey *over here / there, in aisle 2, downstairs, upstairs, in the back / front.* Repeat several times, changing the order in which you read the locations.

➤ Ask where different objects in your classroom are, eliciting the locations taught here.

Option: On the board, draw a diagram of the aisles in a hardware store. Write the products found in each aisle on the diagram; for example,

BACK OF STORE

drills	power drills	faucets	vacuum cleaners	ant traps
saws		shower heads	mops	locks
hammers	power saws			paint
1	2	3	4	5

FRONT OF STORE

Ask where different items are located. For example, ask *Where are the power drills?* and elicit *They're in the back, in aisle 2.* To practice *over here / there,* draw a stick figure on the diagram, ask where an item is located, and elicit *over here* or *over there.* Erase the stick figure, draw a new one in a different location, and repeat.

C. Pair work …

➤ Ask students how *No-Mor* is normally spelled. Point out that companies sometimes use different spellings of ordinary words as product names, perhaps to get customers' attention.

➤ Model the activity. Play the role of Student B to demonstrate offering the alternative brand of the product Student A asks for and choosing a location from the yellow language note.

➤ Do it yourself!

(For general suggestions, see *Introduction*, page Txiii.)

Procedure:

A–B.

➤ Describe your own experience buying a poor-quality or defective product. Then ask *What product did I buy? What was the problem with it? Where did I buy it? / What was the dealer's name? What did I do?*

➤ Have students complete the first line of the chart about a product they bought. Then have them describe their experience to a partner. As they listen to their partners' experiences, have students fill in the second line of their chart.

➤ Ask *What did you do about the defective product?* Have students discuss with their partners.

Option: Have students make a chart for conducting a poll or survey, or provide handouts. Have students draw eight columns and ten rows and write one of the following eight responses to *What did you do about the defective product?* at the top of each row: *exchanged it, took it to a repair shop, sent it to a service center, fixed it myself, called the dealer, wrote a letter of complaint, did nothing, threw it away.* Students then walk around the room and ask ten different students *What did you do about the defective product you bought?* They write each student's name to the left of a row and check the box for the response he or she gives. When they are finished, students tally the results and determine the most common response.

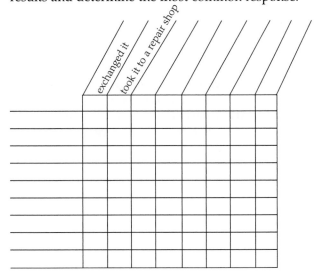

🎧 **A.** **Listen and read.**

A: Do you carry Atlas tools?

B: No. We used to carry them, but we don't anymore.

A: Oh, that's a shame. What brand *do* you carry?

B: Hercules. They're just as good and not as expensive.

A: Really?

B: Yes. They're over here. Would you like to have a look?

🎧 **B.** **Listen again and repeat.**

C. Pair work. **Discuss brands that the store carries. Use these products or your <u>own</u> ideas.**

A: Do you carry _____?

B: No. We used to carry them, but we don't anymore.

A: _____. What brand *do* you carry?

B: _____. They're just as good and not as expensive.

A: _____?

B: ___¹___. They're _____. Would you like to have a look?

¹Sure

🎧 **Locations in a store**

over here / over there
in aisle 2
downstairs / upstairs
in the back / in the front

➤ **Do it yourself!**

I called the dealer and complained.

I exchanged it for something else.

A. Collaborative activity. **Complete the chart about defective products you bought.**

I took it back to the dealer.

Product	Problem	Dealer's name
Primary Paint	*wrong color on label*	*Hardware Mart*
1.		
2.		

B. Discussion. **What did you do about the defective product?**

Practical conversations

Model 3 Explain about a discontinued product.

A. Listen and read.

A: Excuse me. I'm looking for the Speedy shower heads.

B: I'm sorry. Those were discontinued. They didn't meet EPA rules.

A: That's too bad. They were really great.

B: That's what everyone said. But I can show you something else.

B. Listen again and repeat.

Good quality
great
fantastic
effective
convenient

Vocabulary

Products that have to meet EPA rules and other environmental standards

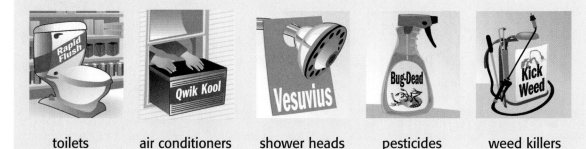

toilets   air conditioners   shower heads   pesticides   weed killers

C. Pair work. Tell a customer about a discontinued product. Use the vocabulary or other brands and products you know.

A: Excuse me. I'm looking for the _____.

B: I'm sorry. Those were discontinued. They didn't meet EPA rules.

A: ____1____. They were _____.

B: ____2____.

[1] You're kidding; Oh, that's a shame
[2] You can say that again; Don't worry. I can show you something else

➤ Practical conversations

(For general suggestions, see *Introduction*, page Tviii.)

Model 3

Content: explaining about a discontinued product; expressing disappointment; describing good quality; offering an alternative

Procedure:

⌖ A-B.

➤ Ask questions about the photo, such as *Where are the people?* (in a hardware store) *What are they looking at?* (shower heads)

➤ Ask what *EPA* stands for. If necessary, explain that it stands for Environmental Protection Agency and that this is the department of the U.S. government that is responsible for protecting the air, water, and land.

➤ After students listen to the conversation, ask comprehension questions such as *What is the customer looking for?* (Speedy shower heads) *What happened to the Speedy brand?* (It was discontinued.) *Why?* (Their shower heads didn't meet EPA rules.)

➤ Ask *Why does the EPA have rules about shower heads?* (because this agency is responsible for protecting the water supply; to keep people from using too much water) *Why didn't the Speedy shower heads meet EPA rules?* (probably because they used too much water)

⌖ Good quality

➤ Review other ways to describe good quality that can be substituted for *great* in the conversation. Point out that *great* and *fantastic* are very positive. Explain that a product is *effective* if it does what it is supposed to do and that a product is *convenient* if it makes something easier or saves you time. Ask students to name products they use that are effective. Ask students to think of a machine or product they use daily that makes their lives easier or is convenient.

➤ Brainstorm and write on the board other words to describe good quality, such as *excellent*, *reliable*, and *dependable*.

⌖ Vocabulary

➤ Have students repeat the vocabulary words and the brand names. Ask how *Qwik Kool* is normally spelled.

➤ Brainstorm and write on the board other products that have to meet environmental standards, such as *faucets, motor oil, batteries.* Say *Think of products that could use too much water or that could contaminate, or have a bad effect on, the air, water, or land.*

C. Pair work . . .

➤ As a class, brainstorm alternative responses for the first blank in Student A's last line and for Student B's last line. Then have students practice the conversation.

Field project: If appropriate, have students go to a store that sells hardware and / or small appliances and look for the types of products from the *Vocabulary* box and board. Have students check the labels to see if any note EPA rules or environmental standards. For any labels that do, have students write down the type of product and brand name. For additional practice, have students ask for the location of two different products, and ask a salesperson the difference between two different brands of the same product. Students should practice asking questions before they take the trip and report their findings when they return.

If your students are ready . . .

Culture / Civics note: The United States Environmental Protection Agency, or EPA, is a government agency responsible for protecting and improving the quality of the natural environment. The EPA develops and enforces national pollution-control regulations and works with industries to promote pollution prevention programs and the conservation of renewable resources. Environment Canada is the Canadian equivalent of this agency.

T46

Model 4

Content: discussing a product safety recall; offering to make good; requesting a different resolution; agreeing; using *so long as* to state a condition; products for babies and children

Procedure:

🎧 A–B.

➤ Have students look at the photos and the notice. Ask *Have you seen this before?* (yes) *Where?* (on page 43) *What can you remember from our discussion? What is a "recall"?* (when a company asks people to return a product they bought because there is a problem with it)

➤ After students listen to the conversation, check comprehension by asking questions such as *What type of product was recalled?* (a high chair) *What does the salesperson offer?* (a replacement) *What does the woman ask for instead?* (a credit)

➤ Ask *What does the woman need to get a credit?* (her receipt) *Can she get a credit if she doesn't have her receipt?* (no) Explain that she can get a credit only if, or *so long as*, she has her receipt.

🎧 Ways to make good

➤ Write *a replacement, a credit, a refund* on the board. Ask *If the woman in the conversation accepted a replacement, what would she get?* Write *a new high chair* next to *a replacement*. Say *The woman in the conversation wants a credit. What will she get?* Write *a slip of paper for the amount of money she spent* next to *a credit*. Explain that she can use it to buy something else at the store. Ask *If the woman in the conversation got a refund, what would she get?* Write *her money back* next to *a refund*.

🎧 Vocabulary

➤ After students repeat the vocabulary words, brainstorm and write on the board other products for babies or children that students know, such as *a changing table, a baby monitor, a swing*.

C. Pair work ...

➤ Read the conversation out loud, pausing at each blank substitution line and eliciting an appropriate word or phrase from the class. If necessary, prompt students to choose a product from the *Vocabulary* box in the second line of the conversation and two different ways to make good from the yellow language note in the third and fourth lines of the conversation. When you get to the last line, elicit a variety of possible responses from the class.

Option: If possible, have students look at the U.S. Consumer Product Safety Commission Web site at www.cpsc.gov. Have students look at actual recalls of products for babies and children. Have them choose one recall and find as much as they can of the following information: the type of product, the brand name, the model number, the problem with the product, when the product was sold, how much it cost, who to contact, and what to do about the recall.

If your students are ready ...

Culture / Civics note: In the United States and Canada, children riding in automobiles are required by law to use passenger restraint systems such as car seats, booster seats, and seat belts. The type of safety restraint required depends on the child's age and size. Laws governing child passenger safety vary by state or province.

➤ Do it yourself!

(For general suggestions, see *Introduction*, page Txiii.)

Procedure:

➤ Have students look at the photos and read the man's speech balloon. Ask *Who is the man?* (a salesperson) *Who is the woman?* (a customer)

➤ In pairs, have students read the four model conversations from this unit again. Before they begin, have them decide who will read Student A's lines and who will read Student B's lines. Also, have students review the yellow language notes on pages 44 through 47.

➤ Have students choose a product and create a phone conversation between the two people pictured. Suggest that students talk about a defective product, a brand the store doesn't carry anymore, a discontinued product, or a product recall. Have volunteers present their conversations to the class.

A. Listen and read.

A: Customer Service. How can I help you?

B: I bought a high chair from you, and I heard there's been a recall.

A: Yes, that's true. Please bring it in and we'll give you a replacement.

B: Can I get a credit instead?

A: Absolutely. So long as you have your receipt.

B. Listen again and repeat.

Consumer Product Safety Commission

Defective high chair recalled. CPSC and Infant World Inc. announce recall of high chair.

Infant World high chair

Ways to make good

a replacement
a credit
a refund

Vocabulary

Products for babies and children

a stroller   a crib   a car seat   a high chair

C. Pair work. Discuss a product safety recall. Offer to make good. Use the vocabulary or your **own** ideas.

A: Customer Service. _____?

B: I bought a _____ from you, and I heard there's been a recall.

A: Yes, that's true. Please bring it in and we'll give you a _____.

B: Can I get a _____ instead?

A: ____1____.   [1]Of course, Sure, That's fine, No problem

➤ Do it yourself!

How can I help you?

Pair work. Create a phone conversation about one of the products. Use your <u>own</u> ideas. Say as much as you can.

Used to

Do you still carry the Infant World stroller?

*No. We **used to carry** it, but it was recalled.*

Use <u>used to</u> and a verb to talk about something that happened in the past but no longer happens.

Dora Mee **used to live** in China. Now she lives in the United States.

I
You
He, She
We } **used to shop** at Infant World.
You
They
Pedro and Pilar

Questions

Did you **use to** live in Peru?	Yes, I did.
Where did Dora Mee **use to** live?	In China.
Do you carry Atlas tools?	No, but we **used to**.

A. **Read and write about Dora Mee's life in China and the United States.**

in China	in the United States
1. lived in a small town	lives in a large city
2. worked in a hospital	works in a factory
3. ordered supplies	checks quality
4. took a bus to work	drives to work

1. *She used to live in a small town. Now she lives in a large city.*

2. She used to work in a hospital. Now she works in a factory.

3. She used to order supplies. Now she checks quality.

4. She used to take a bus to work. Now she drives to work.

B. **Look at Dora's chart for ideas. Then complete the chart about yourself.**

in my home country	in the United States
1. /	/
2. /	/

C. **Pair work. Ask your partner what he or she used to do and what he or she does now. Then tell the class about your partner.**

➤ Practical grammar

(For general suggestions, see *Introduction*, page Tix.)

Used to

Content: statements and questions with *used to*

Procedure:

➤ Use *used to* to talk about your own life. Provide several examples. For example, say *I used to live in California. Now I live in New York. I used to work in an office. Now I teach.*

➤ Ask questions about the examples you gave: *Did I use to live in California? Do I live in California now? Where did I use to work? Do I work in an office now?*

➤ Have students look at the picture and read the speech balloons. Explain that *We used to carry it* means that we carried it before, but we don't carry it now / anymore. As a class, read and discuss the information in the box. Point out that there is no *d* on *use* in the questions because *did* tells us that the question is in the past. Write on the board *Dora Mee didn't use to live in the United States.* Point out that there is no *d* on *use* in a negative sentence either.

➤ Write *I used to + verb* on the board. Have students think of something that they did in the past but that they no longer do, for example, *I used to live in El Salvador.* Note several responses and use them to ask questions, for example, *Did Gabriel use to live in El Salvador? Where did Myung use to work?* Use the same notes to ask questions with *Do you . . . ?* For example, *Gabriel, do you live in El Salvador now?* Point out the last example under *Questions* in the box and elicit the student's answer *No, but I used to.*

A. Read and write about . . .

➤ Have students circle *lived* in item 1 on the chart. Then have them circle *used to live* in the example and point out that we don't put *live* in the past because *used* already tells us that the sentence is in the past.

➤ After students complete the exercise, have them exchange books and check a partner's work. Instruct students to make sure that the first sentence in each item has *used to* + the verb in the base form, not in the past tense. As a class, review the base forms of the verbs in the exercise before partners check each other's work.

B–C.

➤ After students complete the chart about themselves, they ask each other *What did you use to do?* and *What do you do now?* You may wish to have students think of more specific questions to ask, such as *Where did you use to shop? Where do you shop now? Did you use to walk to work?*

➤ After students practice asking and answering the questions with a partner, have them share with the class something their partners used to do and something their partners do now.

Option: Say *I used to buy Brand X. Now I buy Brand Y because . . .* Then have students discuss brands they used to buy and brands they buy now. Give examples of types of products to talk about, such as cookies, shampoos, detergents. Have students tell why they changed brands. Circulate as students discuss, listening to make sure students use correct verb forms.

Challenge: Have students think about a job they used to have. Have them write sentences with *used to* about their duties and responsibilities at that job, for example, *I used to order supplies, I used to fix office machines.* Point out that they might need to write sentences like these on a job application or use them in an interview. Encourage students to be specific.

Comparisons with as and not as

Procedure:

➤ Have two students who are tall and roughly the same height and one student who is shorter come to the front of the room. Say *(Student 1) is as tall as (Student 2). (Student 3) is not as tall as (Student 2). (Student 3) isn't as tall as (Student 1).* Use other students or objects in the classroom to give more examples of comparisons with *as* and *not as*.

➤ Have volunteers read the examples in the box. Ask *Which tools are better, Safe-Tee tools or Topnotch tools?* (They're the same quality.) *Which spray is more effective, Kick Weed or Bug-Dead?* (Bug-Dead) *Were these tools stronger before or are they stronger now?* (before) Then ask *How many times is as used in each sentence?* (twice)

➤ In groups, have students use *as* and *not as* to make comparisons among themselves or using objects in the classroom. Before students begin, elicit a couple of comparisons to write on the board and serve as a model. Circulate, listening to make sure students are forming their comparisons correctly and providing help as needed.

D. Write comparisons...

➤ Have students look at the example and circle *as* both times it occurs in the sentence. Point out that to make sentences from the words, students will need to add *is* or *are* and *as* twice.

If your students are ready...

Language note: All the sentences in the grammar box and in Exercise D use the verb *be* and an adjective. With other verbs, the pattern is the same, but an adverb is used to make the comparison instead of an adjective (e.g., *Maria doesn't weigh as much as Dmitri*).

Comparative forms: Review

Procedure:

➤ Remind students that they can also make comparisons using comparative forms with *than*. Point out that comparative forms end in *-er* or have *more* or *less* in front of them and that there are some irregular comparatives, such as *better* and *worse*.

E. Write comparisons...

➤ Ask students if they prefer old cars or new cars. Have students look at the words in the box and then ask why. Read the example. If students can form other comparisons about old and new cars, they should write their own sentences to the right of the example. Have students read their sentences.

If your students are ready...

Language note: Following are rules for forming the comparative of adjectives.

• For one-syllable adjectives and two-syllable adjectives ending in *-y*, use adjective + *-er*. The spelling rules for adding *-er* are as follows.

  1. Add *-er* to one-syllable adjectives.
     cheap   cheaper

  2. If the adjective ends in *-e*, add *-r*.
     late   later

  3. If a two-syllable adjective ends in a consonant and *-y*, change *y* to *i* before adding *-er*.
     spicy   spicier

  4. If the adjective ends in a consonant-vowel-consonant (CVC), double the final consonant before adding *-er*.
     big   bigger
     Exception: Don't double the consonant in words ending in *-w* or *-y*.
     slow   slower

• For most other adjectives of two or more syllables, use *more* + adjective and *less* + adjective.

➤ Do it yourself!

(For general suggestions, see *Introduction*, page Txiii.)

Procedure:

A–B.

➤ Write the headings *Food, Public transportation,* and *Weather* on the board. Brainstorm adjectives to describe each, for example, for *Public transportation: fast, slow, clean, dirty, convenient, dependable.*

➤ Have students use the adjectives to describe the food, public transportation, and weather where they used to live, filling in the first column of empty boxes.

➤ Then have students use *as, not as,* or the comparative forms of the adjectives to compare this country's food, public transportation, and weather to that where they used to live.

Challenge: Have students use the information on their chart and their own ideas to write sentences comparing where they used to live with this country. For example, *The weather in this country is not as cold as the weather in Russia, Russia is bigger than the United States.* Remind students to use a capital letter at the beginning and a period at the end of each sentence.

Comparisons with <u>as</u> and <u>not as</u>

Safe-Tee tools are **as good as** Topnotch tools. | These tools are **not as strong as** they used to be.
Kick Weed is**n't as effective as** Bug-Dead.

D. Write comparisons with <u>as</u> and <u>not as</u>.

1. Lifeline strollers / not safe / Krafty strollers.
   Lifeline strollers are not as safe as Krafty strollers.

2. The hand drill / not fast / the power drill.
   The hand drill is not as fast as the power drill.

3. Small neighborhood stores / not convenient / chain stores.
   Small neighborhood stores are not as convenient as chain stores.

4. Pesticides / dangerous / weed killers.
   Pesticides are as dangerous as weed killers.

Comparative forms: Review

| cheaper | more convenient / less convenient | better |

E. Write comparisons using comparative forms. Use your <u>own</u> opinions.

1. old cars / new cars
   Old cars are cheaper than new cars.

2. television / radio

3. power tools / hand tools

See page 149 for a list of irregular comparative and superlative forms of adjectives.

➤ Do it yourself!

The weather in this country is not as hot as the weather in Ecuador.

A. Personalization. Compare the country where you used to live with this country.

	Where I used to live	This country	
food	spicy	not as spicy	
food			
public transportation			
weather			

B. Discussion. Talk to your classmates about your life in the past and your life now.

Authentic practice

A. Read and listen again. Then complete each sentence.

1. The kind of gas the customer asked for was _____ regular _____.

2. The attendant told him he also needed _____ oil _____.

3. The brand of oil the service station used to carry is _____ Auto-Lube _____.

4. The attendant suggested that the customer check his _____ tires _____.

B. Listen. Underline _your_ response.

1. **YOU** Absolutely.   **YOU** <u>Do you carry Auto-Lube?</u>

2. **YOU** So long as you have the receipt.   **YOU** <u>Yes, please.</u>

3. **YOU** <u>Really?</u>   **YOU** OK, please check the oil.

C. Listen again. Read _your_ response out loud.

➤ Authentic practice

(For general suggestions, see *Introduction*, page Tx.)

Procedure:

🎧

➤ To activate students' prior knowledge, ask questions about service stations, such as *What can you do at a service station?* (get gas, get your oil checked, get oil, clean your windshields / windows, get air in your tires, use the restroom, buy drinks or snacks) *What is "self-service"?* (You pump the gas yourself.) *What is "full-service"?* (An attendant pumps the gas.) *How many grades of gas can you choose from?* (usually three) *What are the names of some of the gas stations in our area? Is gas more or less expensive here than it is in your country?*

➤ After students have read and listened to the story, ask *What are the three things that the customer gets done at the service station?* (gets gas, gets the oil checked / gets oil, gets air in his tires) *Which oil is better, Auto-Lube or Regal?* (Regal, *or* They're the same quality.)

➤ Ask the class *What is "a quart of 15 w 40"?* If necessary, explain that the customer is asking for a type of motor oil. Point out that a quart is a unit of liquid measurement and that the metric system is not used in the United States.

➤ Have students close their books. Read the following lines and ask who says each one, an attendant at a service station or a customer: *Fill it up, Pull up to the pump, You're down a quart, Give me a quart of 15 w 40, Check the oil?* Make sure to read *Check the oil?* with question intonation.

Option: In groups, have students discuss the differences between gas stations here and those in their native countries. To prompt discussion, ask questions such as *Did you use to have a car in your country? Where did you use to buy gas? Are gas stations in your country self-service or full-service? Is gas cheaper or more expensive in your country? Are service stations here more or less convenient than in your country? Why?*

Field project: Have students who drive pay attention to the following information the next time they are at a service station and then report to the class: *Does the station have self-service, full-service, or both? What is the difference in price? How many grades of gas are offered? What are the names? What are the prices?* If there are mechanics or service station attendants in the class, have them talk about routine car maintenance, such as how often to have your oil changed,

what kind of oil to use, how often to have your tires rotated, and so on.

🎧 A. Read and listen again . . .

Note: For item 4, students may also answer *tire pressure* or *air pressure in tires*.

Option: In pairs, have students create their own item 5, for example, *The brand of oil the service station now carries is _____ .* Have students close their books. Ask for volunteers to read their items. Elicit the correct answers from the class.

🎧 B–C.

➤ Review the answers before having students read responses out loud. Ask *When you read your responses, are you an attendant or a customer?* (a customer)

Tapescript

1. Yes, sir?

2. Check the oil?

3. You're down a quart.

If your students are ready . . .

Culture / Civics note: Canada uses the metric system of measurement; the United States does not. In the United States, motor oil is usually sold in quart containers. For an approximate conversion of quarts to liters, multiply the amount in quarts by 0.95. Gasoline is measured in U.S. gallons (which are smaller than UK imperial gallons). To convert gallons to liters, multiply the amount in gallons by 3.8.

In North America, motor oil is classified according to its viscosity, or thickness. Containers of motor oil are labeled with numbers; the lower the number, the thinner the oil. The type of oil required depends on the type of vehicle you are driving, how you use your vehicle, and the outdoor temperature that you're driving in. For example, thinner oil is required for lower temperatures while thicker oil is better for higher temperatures.

In the *Authentic practice* conversation on page 50, the customer asks for *15 w 40* motor oil, a commonly used, mid-range oil. The *15 w* indicates the viscosity of the oil at cold temperatures. (Five grades are available: 5 w, 10 w, 15 w, 20 w, and 25 w.) The *40* refers to the viscosity of the oil at engine operating temperatures. (The five grades are: 20, 30, 40, 50, and 60.)

Product safety recalls

Procedure:

🎧 A. Listening comprehension . . .

➤ Tell students that they will hear two announcements about product recalls. To review, ask *What is a "recall"?* (when a company asks people to return a product they bought because there is a problem with it)

➤ Have students read the items before listening to the announcements again.

➤ Pause between the announcements and allow students to complete the items. Read each item in the tapescript out loud or play the cassette as many times as necessary for students to complete the exercise.

B. True story . . .

➤ To model the activity, talk about a product safety recall that you have heard or read about.

➤ Have students discuss in groups. If students have trouble thinking of product recalls, use the Consumer Product Safety commission Web site, www.cpsc.gov, as a resource.

➤ Each group tells the class about one recall, describing the problem with the product, what the company is offering / offered, and what purchasers should do / had to do.

➤ Do it yourself!

(For general suggestions, see *Introduction*, page Txiii.)

Procedure:

A. Write your <u>own</u> response . . .

➤ *Say Imagine that you are a salesperson. The man in the picture is a customer. He is calling you about a recalled product.* Point out that students should use the information from Announcement 2, in the *Listening comprehension* activity, in writing their responses.

➤ Have volunteers read the speech balloons. Read the second speech balloon again. Then point to the first response line and ask *What do you have to do here?* (ask for the model number, say that the company is offering a repair kit)

➤ Working individually, students write their own responses to complete the conversation. To check answers, have students read their conversations out loud with a partner. Have volunteers role-play their conversations for the class.

B. Culture talk . . .

➤ Write all the countries (or regions) represented in class in different areas on the board. Have students form groups next to their countries. If there are many students from the same country, write that country's name more than once.

➤ Ask *In the country you come from, how do customers deal with defective products?* Remind students of the vocabulary: *replacement, credit, refund, service center, repair shop, fix it yourself.* Have students discuss and write their ideas on the board. To prompt discussion, ask questions such as *Does your country have a government agency similar to the Consumer Product Safety Commission? Did you hear or read about product safety recalls in your country? Is it easier or more difficult to return or exchange products in your country?*

➤ Have students return to their seats. A representative from each group reads the group's response. Encourage the class to ask questions.

Tapescript

Announcement 1

The U.S. Environmental Protection Agency, the EPA, is announcing a consumer product recall for two widely used home pesticide products because of container problems. The spray container that the Smith Company uses for its Bug-Dead insect spray and its Kick Weed weed killer can malfunction and expose the user to pesticides.

The Smith Company has voluntarily stopped shipment and use of the Atomic Spray and is asking that all Bug-Dead and Kick Weed in this container be returned to the place of purchase for a full refund.

The products affected by this recall are only those sold in the Atomic Spray container. Other packages are not affected by this recall.

Announcement 2

The Jones Company announced today a four-state recall of its new infant carrier. The model affected is the Gran Turismo that bears the following model number: 1311-X. The company says that the handle is defective, and when a baby is in the carrier, the handle can rotate suddenly, causing the baby to fall out to the ground, suffering serious injury.

Jones is offering a free repair kit to address the problem. Jones Chairman Ann Stern says, "It's an easy repair to make, and it is designed to protect your baby from very serious injury." To arrange for the repair kit, call Jones's toll-free recall line: 1-877-555-4500. Once again, that's 1-877-555-4500.

A. Listening comprehension. Listen to the announcements. Then listen again and complete each sentence. Fill in the ovals.

Announcement 1

1. The problem is ____.

ⓐ a pesticide   ⓑ a container

2. The company is offering ____.

ⓐ a recall   ⓑ a refund

3. Purchasers should ____.

ⓐ return the product   ⓑ expose the user to pesticides

Announcement 2

1. The problem is ____.

ⓐ a four-state recall   ⓑ an infant carrier

2. The company is offering ____.

ⓐ a refund   ⓑ a repair kit

3. Purchasers should ____.

ⓐ call a toll-free number   ⓑ return the product

B. True story. In a group, discuss product safety recalls that you have heard or read about.

➤ Do it yourself!

A. Write your own response. Then read your conversation out loud with a partner.

Hello, I'm calling about the Jones Gran Turismo infant carrier that was recalled.

YOU _____

It's model 1311-X. What do I have to do to get the repair kit?

YOU _____

What a shame that infant carrier was recalled! It was so convenient.

YOU _____

B. Culture talk. In the country you come from, how do customers deal with defective products? Compare cultures with your classmates.

Environmental protection laws

 A. Read and listen to the letters.

Ask Joan
Culture tips for newcomers

Dear Joan:
I work in a parking garage with some people from the country where I used to live. Sometimes we earn a little extra money running errands and doing favors for our customers, and the boss says that's OK. Well, last week one of my co-workers changed the oil in a customer's car, and he threw the container with the used oil right in the garbage so that it wouldn't make a mess. He closed the container very tight to keep the garage clean.

When the owner of the garage saw the container with the old oil in the garbage, he was very angry. He said he was going to fire my friend! Joan, I don't understand what the big deal is. It was just one container of oil, and he threw it in the garbage, not on the street. The garage owner said it was against the law to throw motor oil in the garbage, that you have to recycle it.

I don't understand. What could one little container of oil do?

Confused in Kentucky

Dear Confused:
In this country we have strict rules about what things you can throw into the garbage and what things you cannot. The U.S. Environmental Protection Agency, the EPA, sets standards, and these rules help us protect the environment. People who violate the rules have to pay large fines. No wonder your boss was so angry!

Used motor oil can get into our water supply and seriously damage it. Some other things that can hurt the environment are batteries, pesticides, weed killers, and other chemicals. Batteries and used motor oil have to be recycled. Your boss can tell you where to find recycling bins. Pesticides, weed killers, and other chemicals have to be disposed of properly. Be sure to read the directions on the containers.

One little container of oil is a small thing, but if everyone threw one container of used oil into the garbage, the problem would be very serious.

Joan

B. Choose an answer to each question. Fill in the ovals.

1. What's the problem?
   - ⓐ The oil wasn't disposed of properly.
   - ⓑ The boss had to pay a fine.

2. What can used motor oil do?
   - ⓐ Make a mess in the garbage.
   - ⓑ Damage the water we drink.

3. What is a <u>fine</u>?
   - ⓐ Money you have to pay when you break a rule.
   - ⓑ The environment.

➤ Authentic practice

(For general suggestions, see *Introduction*, page Tx.)

Environmental protection laws

Procedure:

🎧 A. Read and listen to the letters.

➤ Pause after the first letter. Check comprehension by asking questions such as *Where does Confused in Kentucky work?* (in a parking garage) *How do the parking attendants make extra money?* (running errands and doing favors for customers) *How did the co-worker get in trouble?* (He threw used oil from a customer's car in the garbage.) *How did the owner of the garage react?* (He was very angry.)

➤ After students read and listen to Joan's response, ask *Who makes rules about what you can and cannot throw into the garbage?* (the EPA) *What happens if you don't follow the rules?* (You have to pay large fines.) *What can used motor oil damage?* (the water supply) *What other things can hurt the environment?* (batteries, pesticides, weed killers, and other chemicals)

Option: There are several synonyms in the letters. With a partner, have students find in the letters the following words or phrases: *threw in the garbage, serious problem, rules, damage.* Then have them find and circle words or phrases that have the same meaning. As a class, review the answers: *disposed of, big deal, standards* or *laws, hurt.*

B. Choose an answer . . .

➤ After students complete the exercise individually, have them check answers with a partner.

Field project: If appropriate, have students go to an auto parts store or gardening center and look for disposal directions on containers of oil, pesticides, or weed killers. Students take notes and then, in groups, make a sign to post in an auto repair shop or in the office of a landscape / gardening business. On their signs, students use words and pictures to show how to dispose of the product properly.

If your students are ready . . .

Language note: Conjunctions are used to combine two sentences. The most common conjunctions are *and* and *but*. In the *Ask Joan* letters, *and* is used to combine sentences four times, and *but* is used as a conjunction once. Examples: *Sometimes we earn a little extra money running errands and doing favors for our customers, <u>and</u> the boss says that's OK; One little container of oil is a small thing, <u>but</u> if everyone threw one container of used oil into the garbage . . .* When using conjunctions to combine sentences, a comma is placed at the end of the first sentence, before the conjunction.

C. What's your advice . . .

➤ Have students look at the pictures. Ask *What is the man throwing in the garbage?* (a car battery) *What is the woman throwing in the garbage?* (weed killer and pesticide) Review ways to give advice, such as *Maybe you'd better . . .* and *Why don't you . . . ?*

➤ Have students look back at Joan's letter on page 52. Have students read the second-to-last paragraph and underline two ways to find out how to properly dispose of products that can hurt the environment. Review, making sure students found *Your boss can tell you where to find recycling bins* and *Be sure to read the directions on the container.*

➤ Students complete the items individually and then read their advice to a partner.

Option: Ask students if they have to dispose of any harmful or dangerous materials at work or at home. As a class, make a chart like this one.

Item	Proper disposal
Used medical supplies	Medical waste container
Transmission fluid	Recycling container

Consumer complaint letters and responses

Procedure:

A. Read the consumer complaint letter . . .

➤ Ask *What is a complaint?* Elicit the response that it is a statement in which you say that you are unhappy or not satisfied with something.

➤ Have students read the complaint letter individually. Then check comprehension by asking questions such as *What product is Peter Plummer unhappy with?* (the Enviro-Flush toilet) *What toilet did Plumb Good use to carry?* (the Vesuvius toilet) *Why was the Vesuvius toilet discontinued?* (It didn't meet EPA guidelines for water conservation.) *What is the problem with the Enviro-Flush toilet?* (It has to be flushed four times.)

➤ Explain that *P.S.* is an abbreviation that stands for *post script*, a Latin phrase meaning to write after. It is used to add a note after the end of a letter.

➤ Have students read the dealer's response individually. Then check comprehension by asking questions such as *Why can't the dealer give a refund?* (because the toilet is used) *What does the company offer?* (a discount on Mr. Plummer's next purchase)

B. On a separate sheet of paper . . .

➤ Have students think of something they bought that they were dissatisfied with. Using Peter Plummer's letter as a model, students write their own complaint letters. Have students begin their letters in the same way, *I'm writing to complain about . . . ,* and include the sentence *I am very dissatisfied with . . . because . . .* Brainstorm and write on the board other information students can include in their letters, such as *what was purchased, when it was purchased, what the problem is, how you would like the company to make good.* Have students copy this list and make notes regarding their own purchase before they begin writing their letters.

Option: Have students write their letters using standard business-letter format. Refer to page T4. Have students include the date, their return address, and the recipient's address. If possible, have students use telephone books or the Internet to find the store's or dealer's address.

➤ Do it yourself!

(For general suggestions, see *Introduction*, page Txiii.)

Procedure:

⌖ Ways to make good on a complaint

➤ After students listen to and repeat the phrases, have them explain each way to make good by referring to the situation with Peter Plummer and the Enviro-Flush toilet; for example, if Plumb Good offered a refund, he would get his money back.

➤ Have students look at the letter from Plumb Good again. Ask *What is another way to make good on a complaint?* Elicit the response *offer a discount on the customer's next purchase.*

➤ Have students exchange complaint letters written in Exercise B with a partner.

➤ Students read their partners' letters and write a response, using the letter from Plumb Good Plumbing Supply as a model. Have students begin their letters in the same way: *I am sorry that you are dissatisfied with the . . . you purchased from us,* and include an explanation and an offer to make good.

Option: If appropriate, have students send complaint letters they wrote for recent purchases. Have students bring to class any responses they receive. Read the letters to the class and ask how the company offered to make good on the complaint.

What's your advice? Tell each person what to do.

1. YOU _____

2. YOU _____

Consumer complaint letters and responses

A. Read the customer complaint letter and the dealer's answer.

Sir or Madam:

I'm writing to complain about the Enviro-Flush toilet I recently purchased at Plumb Good. You used to carry the Vesuvius toilet and it was a very good toilet. It's a shame you don't carry that brand anymore. Your sales staff said that Vesuvius didn't meet EPA guidelines for water conservation and that Enviro-Flush was just as good.

I am <u>very</u> dissatisfied with the Enviro-Flush toilet because I have to flush it four times instead of only once. Please tell me, how is this saving water?

Sincerely,
Peter Plummer

P.S. I have three children. This toilet is <u>not</u> convenient for us.

PLUMB GOOD PLUMBING SUPPLY

1600 South Freemont
Flushing, MI 48433

Dear Mr. Plummer:

I am sorry that you are dissatisfied with the toilet you purchased from us. I'm sure you understand, however, that Plumb Good Plumbing Supply must comply with all EPA standards. Although we cannot, of course, give a refund on a used toilet, we'd be happy to offer you a discount on the next purchase you make at our store.

Sincerely,

Manny Diamante

Manny Diamante

For extra practice, go to page 155.

B. On a separate sheet of paper, write a complaint letter about something you bought.

➤ Do it yourself!

Collaborative activity. Read your partner's letter of complaint. On a separate sheet of paper, write a response letter to your partner. Offer to make good.

🎧 **Ways to make good on a complaint**

offer a refund
offer an exchange
offer store credit
offer a repair

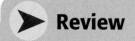

Review

(For general suggestions, see *Introduction*, page Txii.)

Procedure:

A. Pair work or group work.

Note: The *Refunds & Exchanges* sign contains an ampersand. If necessary, point out that this symbol means *and*.

➤ Students take turns pointing to things in the picture and naming them, for example, *a high chair, shower heads, toilets, strollers, cribs, a car seat, tools.*

➤ Have students list everything they can name in the picture.

➤ Help students with any vocabulary they don't know, for example, *bunk beds, wrench, urinal.*

Option: Alphabet game. One group begins by saying a word or phrase from their list that begins with an *A*, such as *Atlas brand tools*. The next group says an item from the picture that begins with a *B*, such as *baby.* Continue through the end of the alphabet, with groups taking turns naming something in the picture that begins with the next letter. Groups earn a point each time they give an appropriate word or phrase.

Ask and answer questions.

➤ Ask *Who are the employees?* Have students identify the three employees in the picture. Ask *How many customers are there?* (seven, including the baby)

➤ Point to the customer at the bottom of the page and ask *What does she want?* Elicit an appropriate response, such as *She bought Be Gone Paint Remover, and there's been a recall. She wants a refund.* Students point to the other customers in the picture and discuss with their partners what the people want.

Create conversations.

➤ Have pairs number the speech balloons and, on a separate sheet of paper, write one line of conversation for each person in the picure.

➤ Then have pairs choose one of the four scenes in the picture and create an extended conversation. Remind students to refer to the four model conversations on pages 44 through 47 for help and ideas.

➤ Have volunteers role-play their conversations for the class.

Tell a story.

Option: Describe locations. Have students play the role of the salesperson near the products for babies and children or of the male employee behind the counter. Students describe the locations of products in the store, using vocabulary such as *over here, over there, in the back, in the front, across from, between, next to.*

Option: Create a character. Have students choose a person in the picture and talk about his or her life now and in the past. Remind students to use *used to* and tell them that they will need to make up the information about the person's life.

Option: Announce a recall. Have students create a recall announcement for Be Gone Paint Remover. Have students include the problem with the paint remover, what the company is offering, and what purchasers should do.

🎧 B. Listen to the conversation...

➤ Tell students that they are going to listen to a conversation between a wife and a husband about a product recall.

➤ After students listen to the conversation the first time, have students read items 1 through 4, so that they will know what to listen for. Allow students to listen to the conversation as many additional times as necessary to complete the exercise.

➤ Have students check answers with a partner. Then have pairs change the false statements to make them true.

➤ Ask additional comprehension questions such as *What product was recalled?* (tomato soup) *What's the problem with it?* (bacteria) *What should purchasers do?* (take the soup back to the place of purchase for a refund)

Challenge: Write the sentence *Food isn't as safe as it used to be* on the board. Ask students if they think this is true. In groups, have students think of other things that were better in the past and write one or two similar sentences, for example, *Salespeople aren't as helpful as they used to be.* Then have students think of things that are better now than they were in the past. Provide an example, such as *Computers are cheaper than they used to be,* and have students write one or two similar sentences. Have groups write one of each type of sentence on the board. Read and discuss the sentences as a class.

C–D.

➤ Students work individually to complete the review exercises.

➤ Circulate to offer help as needed.

➤ Have students check answers with a partner. Review answers as a class.

➤ Identify any areas of difficulty that may require additional instruction and practice.

Challenge: For Exercise D, have students use the information in the chart to write a short letter of recommendation for Ines Ramirez, for example, *I have known Ines Ramirez for 10 years. She used to live in Mexico. She used to teach mathematics in a primary school. Now she lives in Denver, Colorado. She teaches Spanish in a high school. She really enjoys working with children . . .* Encourage students to add information not included in the chart.

Tapescript

Wife: Listen to this, honey.

Husband: What is it?

Wife: You know that tomato soup we bought yesterday at Foods of the World?

Husband: Mm-hmm.

Wife: Well, it's been recalled.

Husband: How do you know?

Wife: I just saw it on the news. Not five minutes ago. There's a nationwide recall. Every can of soup. Can you believe it?

Husband: What's wrong with it?

Wife: Something about bacteria. They said it's really dangerous.

Husband: You didn't eat any of it, did you?

Wife: No, thank goodness. They said to bring the soup back to the place of purchase for a refund.

Husband: It's really a shame, isn't it? Food isn't as safe as it used to be.

Listen to the conversation between a wife and a husband about a product recall. Read the statements and listen again. Check True or False.

	True	False
1. The product is something to eat.	☑	☐
2. They bought it five minutes ago.	☐	☑
3. They got a recall notice in the mail.	☐	☑
4. The dealer will give them a refund.	☑	☐

C. **Choose your response. Fill in the ovals.**

1. "People are complaining about these zippers."

   ⓐ It's no wonder. They're defective.　　ⓑ What brand do you carry?

2. "The Rapid-Flush toilets were discontinued."

   ⓐ Absolutely.　　　　　　　　　　ⓑ That's a shame.

3. "Can I get a credit?"

   ⓐ Sure. No problem.　　　　　　　ⓑ We don't anymore.

D. **Read about Ines Ramirez. Then write about what she used to do and what she does now.**

in the past	now
1. lived in Mexico	lives in Denver, Colorado
2. worked in a primary school	works in a high school
3. taught mathematics	teaches Spanish
4. lived in a house	lives in an apartment

1. *She used to live in Mexico. Now she lives in Denver, Colorado.*

2. She used to work in a primary school. Now she works in a high school.

3. She used to teach mathematics. Now she teaches Spanish.

4. She used to live in a house. Now she lives in an apartment.

E. **Write comparisons with <u>as</u> and <u>not as</u>. Use your <u>own</u> opinion.**

1. Chinese food / spicy / Mexican food.

   _____

2. weather in the fall / warm / weather in the spring.

   _____

3. Buses / convenient / trains.

   _____

F. **Write a response to each statement or question. Use your <u>own</u> words.**

1. "You used to carry Best Loaf bread. Why don't you carry it anymore?"

   _____

2. "My tires are a little low. Do you have an air pump?"

   _____

3. "I'm down a quart of oil."

   _____

G. **Composition. On a separate sheet of paper, write about the picture on page 54. Say as much as you can.**

Now I can
❏ discuss a defective, discontinued, or recalled product.
❏ ask for and provide service at a gas station.
❏ understand and act on a product safety recall.
❏ write and respond to a consumer complaint letter.
❏ _____.

E–F.

➤ Students work individually to complete the review exercises.

➤ Circulate to offer help as needed.

➤ Have students check answers with a partner. Review answers as a class.

➤ Identify any areas of difficulty that may require additional instruction and practice.

Option: For Exercise E, give students a list of topics to use in creating additional comparisons with *as* and *not as*. Possible topics include *countries, movies, sports*. Provide an example such as *Soccer is not as dangerous as hockey*. Have volunteers write sentences on the board. Read each comparison and have students raise their hands if they agree with the statement. Then have students who disagree raise their hands. Keep a tally on the board of the responses to each comparison. Discuss the results as a class.

Challenge: Have students create a bar graph or a pie chart showing the class's responses to one of the comparisons. For example,

Soccer is not as dangerous as hockey.

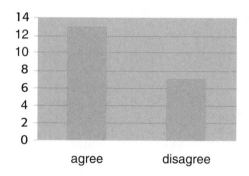

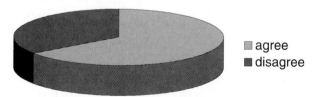

G. Composition ...

➤ Provide students with concrete approaches to writing about the picture on page 54. Use one of the following options, give students a choice of options, or assign options based on students' levels of proficiency. Model what is expected of students for each option.

➤ Advise students to look back through the unit for help and ideas as they write.

➤ Circulate to offer help as needed.

Option: Have students write sentences comparing products in the picture. Have students use the brand names in the picture and add their own brand names. For example, *The Sleepy Time crib is safer than the Infant World crib*.

Option: Have students write an extended conversation for one group of people in the picture. Have students refer to the model conversations on pages 44 through 47 for an example of the form to use.

Option: Have students write a complaint letter about one of the products in the picture on page 54. Before they write, have students decide on a product, a purchase date, a problem with the product, and how they would like the dealer to make good. Students may also include the length and terms of the warranty and whether the product has been serviced before.

Now I can

➤ Read the first item in the box out loud, *Now I can discuss a defective, discontinued, or recalled product*. Elicit from the class an example of how to discuss a defective, discontinued, or recalled product, such as *The shower heads are not up to code*.

➤ In pairs, have students take turns reading each item in the box and giving an example of what they have learned. When students can provide an example, they should check that box. For the items students weren't able to check, they should look back through the unit for ideas.

➤ When students are finished reviewing with their partners, read each item out loud and elicit an example from the class.

Oral test (optional)

You may want to use the *Now I can* box as an informal evaluation. While students are working on the *Composition* activity, you can call them up individually and check their ability with two or three objectives.

Time

Note: For the plan-ahead project on page 67, students should bring want ads from the local newspaper to class. These ads can also be used on page 59.

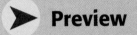 **Preview**

(For general suggestions, see *Introduction*, page Tviii.)

Warm up. What's "minimum wage"?

Procedure:

➤ Ask *What is this? Where is this information from?* If necessary, explain that it is a drawing of a window on a computer screen and that the information is from a Web site, or place on the Internet where you can find information about a variety of subjects.

➤ Ask *What does this Web site give information about?* (the Fair Labor Standards Act) Ask *What does "fair" mean?* (acceptable, right, equal) *What is "labor"?* (work) *What are "standards"?* (rules) Then elicit or explain that an *act* is a law. Encourage students to put this information together and speculate about what the Fair Labor Standards Act is (a law that regulates work practices).

➤ Have students look at the text on the computer screen. Explain that pay is one work practice that the government wants to make sure is fair. Direct students' attention to the title of the text. Ask *What is "minimum wage"? What is the minimum wage now?* If necessary, explain that a minimum wage is the lowest amount of money that a worker can earn per hour in many jobs. The current minimum wage is $5.15 per hour.

➤ Have students read the information about minimum wage. Then check comprehension by asking questions such as *Who doesn't get minimum wage or overtime?* (executives, administrative and professional employees, teachers, and so on) *How much do employers have to pay employees who receive tips?* (at least $2.13 per hour) *What if $2.13 per hour plus tips does not add up to $5.15 per hour?* (The employer has to pay the difference.) *If an employee works more than 40 hours in a week, how much does the employer have to pay for the extra hours?* (1½ times the employee's regular hourly pay)

➤ Brainstorm occupations that receive tips, such as *restaurant workers, taxi drivers, hotel employees, delivery people.*

Option: Introduce or review computer-related vocabulary, such as *screen, window, icon, scroll bar, cursor.*

Option: Have the class choose five new words from the text on the computer screen. Have students underline these words in their books. Have volunteers read the sentences that contain the new words. Encourage students to use context to determine the meaning of each word. As a class, create simple definitions for the words, for example, *overtime: more than 40 hours worked in a week.* Have students copy the definitions from the board.

Challenge: Have students calculate how much an employee has to make in tips each hour so that the employer doesn't have to pay more than $2.13 ($3.02). Have students calculate how much an employee has to make in tips during an eight-hour day so that the employer doesn't have to pay more than $2.13 per hour ($24.16). Ask *How much is overtime pay for a worker who earns minimum wage?* ($7.73 per hour)

Unit 5 objectives

Procedure:

➤ Read the objectives. Define any words that are unfamiliar to students; for example, *punctual* means on time.

➤ As a class, choose one of the objectives. Find out what related information students already know. For example, for *Talk about your own time and company time,* ask *What is "your own time"?* (the time you spend outside of work) *What is "company time"?* (the time you spend at work) *What do you do on your own time? What do you do on company time?* Then find out what questions students have related to the objective, for example, *Is it OK to make personal phone calls on company time? Is it OK to read a magazine at work if you are not busy?* Write the questions on a large sheet of paper and keep them for students to answer at the end of the unit.

Time

> **Preview**

Warm up. What's "minimum wage"?

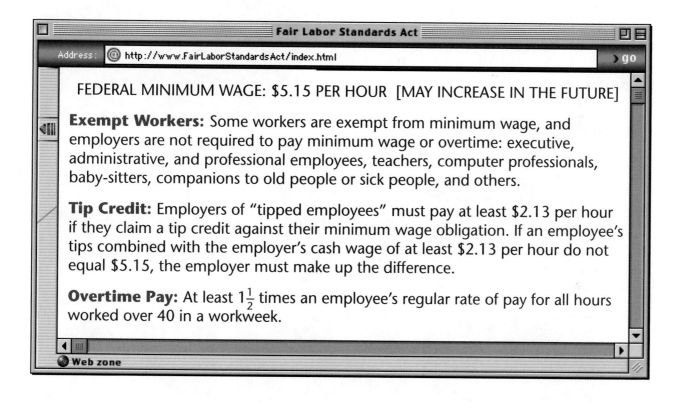

Fair Labor Standards Act

Address: @ http://www.FairLaborStandardsAct/index.html › go

FEDERAL MINIMUM WAGE: $5.15 PER HOUR [MAY INCREASE IN THE FUTURE]

Exempt Workers: Some workers are exempt from minimum wage, and employers are not required to pay minimum wage or overtime: executive, administrative, and professional employees, teachers, computer professionals, baby-sitters, companions to old people or sick people, and others.

Tip Credit: Employers of "tipped employees" must pay at least $2.13 per hour if they claim a tip credit against their minimum wage obligation. If an employee's tips combined with the employer's cash wage of at least $2.13 per hour do not equal $5.15, the employer must make up the difference.

Overtime Pay: At least $1\frac{1}{2}$ times an employee's regular rate of pay for all hours worked over 40 in a workweek.

Web zone

Unit 5 objectives

- Discuss payment, hours, and overtime pay.
- Reschedule an event.
- Talk about your own time and company time.
- Understand your employer's expectations.
- Understand why it's important to be punctual on the job.

Model 1   Discuss payment options.

🎧 **A.** **Listen and read.**

A: I really need to find a job. Tell me, what are you doing these days, Nicole?

B: I'm working as a baby-sitter.

A: A baby-sitter? That's great! Full-time or part-time?

B: Full-time, live-in.

A: How are you paid?

B: By the hour, plus room and board.

🎧 **B.** **Listen again and repeat.**

🎧 **Vocabulary**

Occupations and payment options

a gardener:
paid by the hour

a messenger:
paid by the job

a companion:
paid by the week

a waiter / waitress:
paid by the hour, plus tips

a mover:
paid by the hour, plus tips

a taxi driver:
paid by the trip, plus tips

C. **Pair work.** **Discuss jobs and payment options. Use the vocabulary or your <u>own</u> jobs.**

A: I really need to find a job. Tell me, what are you doing these days, _____?

B: I'm working as _____.

A: ____1____. Full-time or part-time?

B: _____.

A: How are you paid?

B: By the _____.

[1] Really?; Wow!; You're kidding; Sounds great; That's fantastic!

➤ Practical conversations

(For general suggestions, see *Introduction*, page Tviii.)

Model 1

Content: asking about someone else's job; talking about current employment; expressing enthusiasm; discussing work hours and payment options; *need* followed by an infinitive

Procedure:

🎧 A–B.

➤ To set the scene for the conversation, ask questions about the people in the photo, such as *Where are they?* (at a restaurant) *Do you think they're friends or an employer and an employee?* (friends) *Why do you think so?* (They're eating together. They're wearing casual clothes.)

➤ After students listen to the conversation, check comprehension by asking questions such as *Who needs a job?* (the woman on the left) *What is Nicole's job?* (baby-sitter) *Does she work full-time or part-time?* (full-time, live-in) *How is she paid?* (by the hour, plus room and board)

➤ Elicit from the class the meanings of words and phrases that may be unfamiliar, such as *full-time, part-time, live-in, room and board.* If necessary, provide simple definitions; for example, *room and board* is a room to sleep in and food.

➤ Point out that the statement *I really need to find a job* suggests that the following question *Tell me, what are you doing these days, Nicole?* is asked not only out of curiosity or to make conversation, but also as a way to find out about employment possibilities or opportunities.

🎧 Vocabulary

➤ After students listen to and repeat the vocabulary, ask them to describe what a person in each occupation does, for example, *A waiter or waitress takes orders and serves food.*

➤ Discuss the different payment options. Elicit explanations from students. If necessary, explain that *by the hour* means that you get paid a certain amount of money for each hour of work you do, *by the job* means that you get paid a certain amount of money for each job you complete, and so on.

➤ Point out that a waiter / waitress is also called *a server.*

C. Pair work ...

➤ Talk about you current employment situation. For example, say *I'm working as an ESL teacher. I'm working part-time. I'm paid by the course.* Then ask several students the following questions: *What are you doing these days? Are you working full-time or part-time? How are you paid?* For the first question, if students don't answer with *I'm working as a / an . . . ,* restate their answer, as if to verify that you heard correctly. Say *You're working as a / an . . . ?*

➤ Model the conversation with a volunteer. Play the role of Student A. For Student A's second line, say *Really?* or *You're kidding* and *That's fantastic!* to demonstrate that students can use their own words.

Option: Provide students with an opportunity to explore employment possibilities. Have students walk around the room and practice the conversation with three different partners. Students take turns reading the roles of Students A and B with each partner.

If your students are ready ...

Culture / Civics note: In North America, it is customary to give a small amount of money, called a *tip,* for certain services. Some service workers earn a very low hourly wage and make most of their income from tips. The amount of the tip depends on the quality of the service performed. For example, wait staff at a full-service restaurant generally receive 15 percent of the amount of the check if the service is satisfactory. A larger tip may be given if the service is above average and less (or none at all) if service is poor. Some other tipped employees include hotel / airport porters ($1.00–$2.00 per bag), hairdressers (15 to 20 percent of the bill), and taxi drivers (15 percent of the fare). Tips should *never* be offered to police officers, customs officials, postal workers, driver's test examiners, or anyone else working in a government or public service job. Offering a tip will be viewed as attempting a bribe, which is illegal.

Model 2

Content: talking about work hours and overtime pay; making polite requests

Procedure:

🎧 A–B.

➤ Have students cover up the conversation and look only at the photo. In pairs, students describe what is happening, for example, *Two people are sitting at a table in a restaurant. The man is reading from a sheet of paper. The woman is writing in a notebook.* Elicit descriptions from volunteers until it becomes clear that this is probably an interview. Then ask *What do you think they are talking about?* Elicit responses, and then have students read the bar for *Model 2*.

➤ After students listen to the conversation, ask questions such as *What are the hours?* (eight to five, with an hour for lunch) *What is the regular pay?* (minimum wage) *What is the overtime pay?* (time and a half) *What is the pay for Sundays and holidays?* (double time) *If the woman gets the job, how will she be paid?* (by the hour)

➤ Point out that *Could you please . . . ?* and *I'd like to . . .* are polite ways to make a request and are appropriate to use in an interview.

🎧 Vocabulary

➤ After students listen and repeat, demonstrate how time and a half and double time are calculated. Explain that *time* refers to the hourly wage, so *time and a half* is the hourly wage + half the hourly wage, in this case $5.15 + $2.58 = $7.73. *Double* means twice, or two times, so double time is $5.15 + $5.15 = $10.30.

Option: Have students calculate time and a half and double time for a job that pays $6.50 per hour ($9.75, $13.00). Then have students calculate time and a half and double time for their own hourly wages.

C. Pair work . . .

➤ Have students read the two want ads. Have students find and circle the abbreviations */hr.* and *pt.-time.* Ask what the abbreviations stand for (per hour, part-time).

➤ Have students look at the two ads. For each ad, ask *What are the hours?* (for the parking attendant, 7 a.m. to 3 p.m. or 3 p.m. to 11 p.m. with a one-hour break) *What is the pay?* (for the parking attendant, minimum wage, or $5.15, plus tips and time and a half for overtime)

➤ Have pairs practice the conversation.

Option: Use the want ads brought in by students or ads that you've brought in. Have students look for more abbreviations and write them on the board. Elicit or explain the meaning of each abbreviation.

Option: Have students look for the word *shifts* in the ad for a parking attendant. Ask *What are the two shifts?* (first: 7 a.m. to 3 p.m., second: 3 p.m. to 11 p.m.) Elicit or explain that a *shift* is one of three eight-hour periods when a particular group of employees is at work. Mention that factory workers and hospital workers often work in shifts rather than from 9:00 to 5:00, which are usual office hours. Ask what shifts students in the class work. Brainstorm other words used to describe shifts, such as *day, evening, night, first, second, third, early, late.* Ask students what shift they prefer to work and why.

➤ Do it yourself!

(For general suggestions, see *Introduction,* page Txiii.)

Procedure:

➤ On the board, make a chart like the one on page 59 but with several more rows. Ask one student *What are you doing these days?* Fill in the first box under *Occupations* with the response. Then ask the same student *How are you paid?* Fill in the first box under *How paid?* with the response. Next, have the student come up to the board to ask a second student the same questions and fill in the second row of the chart. If a student gives an occupation and payment option already included in the chart, a check mark is made to the right of that row. The chain continues until all the occupations and payment options in the class are represented on the chart. If you have students who are regularly paid a fixed amount, introduce the word *salaried.*

➤ Encourage students to make generalizations based on the information in the chart, for example, *People who work in restaurants and hotels are paid by the hour and also get tips.*

Option: Have students make their own charts like the one in the book but with five to ten rows. Students walk around and ask about classmates' occupations and how they are paid.

Option: Have students add to their charts columns for *Full-time or part-time?* and *What shift?*

A. Listen and read.

A: What are the hours?

B: Eight to five and an hour for lunch.

A: And could you please tell me what the pay is?

B: We pay minimum wage, time and a half for overtime, and double time on Sundays and holidays.

A: Could you repeat that, please? I'd like to make a note of it.

B. Listen again and repeat.

Vocabulary

Wages and hours

minimum wage: $5.15 per hour   time and a half: $7.73   double time: $10.30

C. Pair work. Talk about hours and overtime pay. Use the ads or your own hours and pay.

A: What are the hours?

B: _____.

A: And could you please tell me what the pay is?

B: We pay _____ and _____.

A: _____?

PARKING ATTENDANT

Minimum wage $5.15/hr. + tips
Overtime pay: time and a half
Shifts: first: 7am to 3pm with
 one-hour break for lunch.
second: 3pm to 11pm with
 one-hour break for dinner.

• BEAUTICIAN'S ASSISTANT •

Pt.-time Immediate
Responsibilities: wash clients'
hair. Salary: $4.80/hr.
plus tips. Hours: Tuesdays
& Wednesdays 11:00 a.m. to
4:00 p.m. Experienced only.

➤ Do it yourself!

Collaborative activity. Make a list of the occupations of the students in the class. Write the list on the chalkboard.

Occupations	How paid?
live-in home health aide	by the month + room and board

Model 3   Reschedule an event with a co-worker or a friend. Explain the reason.

🎧 **A.** Listen and read.

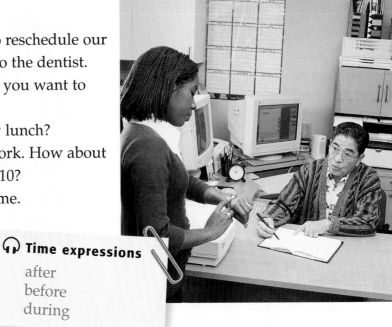

> **A:** I'm sorry, but I have to reschedule our meeting. I have to go to the dentist.
> **B:** No problem. When do you want to reschedule?
> **A:** How's tomorrow, after lunch?
> **B:** Actually, that won't work. How about tomorrow morning at 10?
> **A:** Yeah. That's good for me.

🎧 **B.** Listen again and repeat.

🎧 **Time expressions**

after
before
during

🎧 **Vocabulary**

Reasons to reschedule events

I have a problem at home.

I have a family problem.

I'm not feeling well.

I have to run an errand.

C. Pair work. **Reschedule an event from the box. Give your <u>own</u> reason.**

lunch	appointment	meeting	dinner

> **A:** I'm sorry, but I have to reschedule our _____. I _____.
> **B:** ____1____. When do you want to reschedule?
> **A:** How's _____?
> **B:** Actually, that won't work. How about _____?
> **A:** ____2____.

¹Sure, OK, That's fine
²Sure, That's fine, Sounds great

➤ Practical conversations

(For general suggestions, see *Introduction*, page Tviii.)

Model 3

Content: rescheduling an event with a co-worker or a friend; explaining the reason; proposing a time to meet; *want* followed by an infinitive

Procedure:

🎧 A–B.

➤ Ask questions about the people in the photo, such as *Where are they?* (in an office) *What is the woman doing?* (looking at her watch) *What does the man have in front of him?* (a planner, or date book)

➤ After students listen to the conversation, ask questions such as *Who needs to reschedule the meeting?* (the woman) *Why?* (She has to go to the dentist.) *When does the woman suggest they meet?* (tomorrow after lunch) *When does the man suggest they meet?* (tomorrow morning at 10)

➤ Point out that the woman apologizes before she asks to change the day and time of the meeting, as rescheduling an event may not be convenient for the other people involved. Also, *How's . . . ?* and *How about . . . ?* are two ways to suggest a time and / or place for an event.

🎧 Time expressions

➤ After students repeat the words, tell them what you did before class, what you are doing now during class, and what you are going to do after class. Emphasize the words *before, during,* and *after* and give times to reinforce the meanings of the words. For example, *Before class, at 3:00, I picked up my kids from school.* Then have students relate their own activities before, during, and after class to a partner.

🎧 Vocabulary

➤ After students repeat the vocabulary, make sure that they understand what *an errand* is by asking for examples, such as *go to the cleaners, the bank, the post office.*

➤ Brainstorm and write on the board other reasons to reschedule events. Have students think about situations in their own lives that might cause them to have to reschedule, for example, *I have to work overtime, I have a doctor's appointment, My baby-sitter isn't feeling well.*

C. Pair work . . .

➤ Copy the conversation on the board. Point to each blank substitution line and elicit a variety of appropriate words or phrases from the class. For example, point to the first blank and elicit *lunch, appointment, meeting, dinner.*

➤ Point out that *I have to run an errand* is an appropriate reason for rescheduling a social event but not a business meeting.

➤ Students then practice the conversation in pairs.

Model 4

Content: asking for permission; clarifying expectations; giving a condition with *unless*; discussing personal activities and personal time; *need* followed by an infinitive; *expect* followed by an object and an infinitive

Procedure:

🎧 A–B.

➤ Have students listen to the conversation with their books closed.

➤ Check comprehension by asking questions such as *Who's speaking?* (two men, an employee and a supervisor or boss) *Where are they?* (at work) *What does the first speaker ask for permission to do?* (speak to his friend) *What is the second speaker's answer?* (Do that on your own time.)

➤ Have students look at the photo. Ask *Which man is the supervisor?* (the man on the right) *Who is the man in the doorway?* (the employee's friend)

➤ To make the meaning of *unless* clear, read the last line in the conversation *Well, unless it's an emergency, we expect* . . . Then read it again, substituting *if it's not* for *unless it's.*

Option: Have students practice *unless* by thinking about conditions parents might give their children. Write on the board *Unless you get good grades in school, you can't watch TV.* Read this example and then rephrase it, saying *If you don't get good grades in school, you* . . . Elicit similar sentences from the class.

🎧 Personal time . . .

➤ Have students listen to and repeat the phrases.

🎧 Vocabulary

➤ After students repeat the vocabulary, brainstorm and write on the board other personal activities, such as *get a soda, check my e-mail, have something to eat.*

➤ Elicit or explain that *Human Resources* is the department in a company that deals with employing, training, and helping people. Ask *What do employees speak to Human Resources about?* (training classes, medical insurance, sick days)

C. Pair work . . .

➤ Model the activity with a more advanced student. Play the role of Student A. Demonstrate choosing a personal activity from the *Vocabulary* box or board for the first line and answering negatively in Student A's second line.

➤ Do it yourself!

(For general suggestions, see *Introduction*, page Txiii.)

Procedure:

➤ Write item 1 on the board. Ask *Is it OK to read the newspaper on company time? What's your opinion?* Discuss as a class, eliciting the response that, in most cases, reading the newspaper is something you should do on your own time. Point out that many employers have strict rules that prohibit non-work-related activities during working hours. Next to *read the newspaper*, write *on your own time.*

➤ Working in groups of three, have each student in a group assume the role of either the facilitator (who asks questions and gets everyone in the group to respond), the recorder (who notes the group's opinion on each item), or the reporter (who reports the group's opinions to the class). The groups discuss items 2 through 5 and any others they want to add. Encourage students to discuss each item until they reach an opinion that everyone in the group can agree with or accept.

➤ While the groups are discussing, make a three-column chart on the board with the headings *Activities, On company time, On your own time.* List items 2 through 5 in the first column. When the groups are finished, read item 2 and have the reporter from each group give the group's opinion. To the right of *get a cup of coffee*, make a check mark indicating each group's response, either under *On company time* or *On your own time.* Continue in the same manner with items 3 through 5.

➤ Ask what other activities students discussed. Add these to the chart. Have students change roles within their groups. Then give the groups time to talk about any activities on the chart that they hadn't discussed before. The reporters from each group give the group's opinion in the same manner as before.

➤ As a class, discuss the activities that groups had different opinions about. Ask groups who answered differently to explain their opinions.

Note: Groups' opinions may vary, as different activities may be more or less appropriate depending on the type of workplace. For example, it's probably OK to get a cup of coffee on company time in an office but probably not OK in a factory.

A. Listen and read.

A: I need to speak to my friend. Is that a problem?

B: Is it an emergency?

A: No, not really.

B: Well, unless it's an emergency, we expect you to do that on your own time. Why don't you do that at lunch time?

B. Listen again and repeat.

Personal time

on your own time
at break time
at lunch time
after closing time

Vocabulary

Personal activities

make a phone call

speak to Human Resources

go to the restroom

C. Pair work. Ask for permission. Use the vocabulary or your <u>own</u> activities.

A: I need to _____. Is that a problem?

B: Is it an emergency?

A: _____.

B: Well, unless it's an emergency, we expect you to do that on your own time. Why don't you do that _____?

➤ Do it yourself!

What's your opinion? What's OK to do on company time? What should you do on your own time? Discuss with a partner or a group.

1. read the newspaper
2. get a cup of coffee
3. go to the restroom
4. go to the dentist
5. use the Internet
6. other: _____

Verbs followed by infinitives

Infinitive

I **need to make** a phone call. Is that a problem?

Well, actually it is. You should
Infinitive
plan to do that on your own time, not on company time.

Use infinitives after the following verbs: <u>be sure</u>, <u>decide</u>, <u>forget</u>, <u>need</u>, <u>plan</u>, <u>remember</u>, <u>want</u>.

Lynn **decided to look for** a new job.

They **forgot to reschedule** the meeting.

Remember to dispose of pesticides properly.

A. Complete the paragraph with verbs and infinitives.

Pennsylvania Pipe Company

Policies and Procedures

Time off with pay

When you _____ decide to take _____ a personal day, _____ be sure to ask _____
       1. decide / take   2. be sure / ask

your manager in advance. Let him or her know that you _____ need to be _____
                                                3. need / be

out of the office. Also, _____ don't forget to tell _____ your manager when you
                      4. not forget / tell

_____ plan to return _____ to work.
      5. plan / return

Pennsylvania Pipe

See page 149 for a list of verbs followed by infinitives.

Verbs followed by objects and infinitives

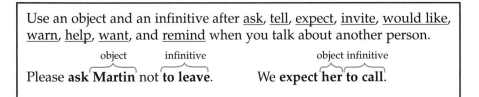

Use an object and an infinitive after <u>ask</u>, <u>tell</u>, <u>expect</u>, <u>invite</u>, <u>would like</u>, <u>warn</u>, <u>help</u>, <u>want</u>, and <u>remind</u> when you talk about another person.

object   infinitive   object infinitive

Please **ask Martin** not **to leave**.   We **expect her to call**.

➤ Practical grammar

(For general suggestions, see *Introduction*, page Tix.)

Verbs followed by infinitives

Procedure:
➤ Explain that an infinitive is the base form of a verb, used with *to*. Write examples of infinitives on the board, such as *to talk, to eat, to drive*. Elicit more examples from students.

➤ Have two students read the speech balloons in the grammar box. Ask *What are the two infinitives?* (to make, to do) *What verb does to make follow?* (need) *What verb does to do follow?* (plan)

➤ Read the explanation and examples in the grammar box. Ask the class questions to prompt use of the new structure, such as *What do you need to do tomorrow? What do you plan to do on the weekend? What do you want to do in the future? What did you forget to do last week?* Have students answer in complete sentences. If necessary, restate responses that lack *to* using question intonation, expressing interest in the answer, for example, *You want to move to Texas? Really? Why is that?* Call on individual students to recall what other students need, plan, want, or forgot to do; for example, ask *What does Ali need to do tomorrow?* (He needs to . . .)

➤ Write the verbs *be sure, decide, forget, need, plan, remember, want* on the board. To make sure students know their meanings, elicit from students original sentences using each verb followed by an infinitive, for example, *Be sure to make phone calls on your own time.*

➤ Write *not need* and *not want* on the board. Elicit a couple of negative sentences, such as *I don't need to speak to Human Resources.*

A. Complete the paragraph . . .
➤ Have students look at item 1. Ask if *decide* is one of the verbs listed in the grammar box. Since it is, ask *What do you need to use with take?* (to) Elicit the correct answer, *decide to take*, from the class and write it on the board. Have students complete items 2 through 5.

Option: Have students imagine that they are employees of Pennsylvania Pipe Company and write a note to their manager requesting a personal day, for example, *I want to take a personal day next Friday. I need to go to the doctor. I plan to return to work on Monday.*

Verbs followed by objects and infinitives

Note: Students practiced *ask* or *tell* followed by an object and an infinitive when they learned indirect commands in Unit 2.

➤ Read only the list of verbs from the box. Review the meanings of any verbs students are unfamiliar with. Provide examples and encourage students to determine the meaning from context; for example, *We expect you to make phone calls on your own time* means *We think that you should make phone calls . . .*

➤ Have students read the explanation and examples in the box. Explain that these verbs are followed by an object and then an infinitive. To give students an idea of what an *object* is, have them look at the list of objects in Exercise B on page 63.

➤ Model the structure by talking about your expectations and hopes for the class, for example, *I expect you to arrive on time to class, I would like you to participate in class and group discussions, I don't want you to miss class.*

Challenge: Write on the board *Please don't ask Martin to leave* and *Please ask Martin not to leave*. Ask the class to speculate about the difference in meaning between the two sentences. Say *If I say to you, "Please don't ask Martin to leave," what do I want you to do?* (not to say anything to Martin about leaving) *If I say to you, "Please ask Martin not to leave," what do I want you to do?* (to talk to Martin and ask him to stay) Then write *I didn't remind him to turn off his computer* and *I reminded him not to turn off his computer*. Have small groups discuss the difference in meaning between the two sentences. Review as a class. Elicit that the first sentence means that I didn't tell him that he should turn off his computer, while the second sentence means that I did tell him that he shouldn't turn off his computer.

If your students are ready . . .

Language note: Some sentences with verbs followed by infinitives and verbs followed by objects and infinitives are made negative in only one way: either by making the main verb negative or by making the infinitive negative. For example, with *invite*, the main verb is made negative: *I didn't invite him to go to the movies with us.* We wouldn't say *I invited him not to go . . .* With *be sure*, the infinitive is made negative: *Be sure not to read the newspaper on company time.* We wouldn't say *Don't be sure . . .*

B. Write your <u>own</u> sentences...

➤ Read the example. Ask what change was made to *ask.* Elicit the response that *-ed* was added or that it was changed to past tense.

➤ Students choose one word or phrase from each list to create their own sentences, making changes to the verbs as necessary.

➤ Students read their sentences to a partner. Then volunteers read their sentences to the class.

Note: You may want to refer students to a more complete list of verbs followed by objects and infinitives on page 150.

Option: In groups of four, have students make round-robin sentences. The first student chooses a subject, the second a verb, the third an object, and the fourth an infinitive phrase. Then the first student repeats the entire sentence, and the second student starts a new sentence. Continue until all four students have started a sentence.

➤ Do it yourself!

(For general suggestions, see *Introduction*, page Txiii.)

A–B.

➤ On a sheet of paper, have students write *at work, at home, at school* and make short lists of who they see and talk to in each place, for example, for *at school, teacher* and *classmates.*

➤ Have students look at the exercise. Give examples of what people expect of you in each place, for example, for *at work, The director expects me to prepare for my classes.*

➤ After students write their own sentences about expectations people have of them, have them compare their sentences with a partner. To encourage more discussion, ask questions such as *Are there any conflicts between the expectations different people have of you?* Give an example: *What if your boss expects you to come to work on time, and your children expect you to help them get ready for school? Are some expectations more important to meet than others?*

Option: Have students prioritize the expectations people have of them. Have students number the sentences they wrote from 1 to 3, with 1 being the most important.

B. Write your <u>own</u> sentences with these subjects, verbs, objects, and infinitive phrases.

Subjects	Verbs	Objects	Infinitive phrases
I	expect	us	to call
You	want	her	to tell me
She	invite	him	to reschedule lunch
He	remind	you	not to park in the small lot
Ivan	warn	us	to pay us by the hour
Ms. Smith	ask	them	to give him a tip
We	tell	Glenda	to get time and a half
They	would like	Alan	to make a note of that

1. *He asked Glenda to reschedule lunch.*

2. _____

3. _____

4. _____

5. _____

6. _____

See page 150 for a list of list of verbs followed by objects and infinitives.

➤ Do it yourself!

A. **Personalization.** What do people expect you to do? Write about expectations people have of you at work, at home, and at school.

at work

My boss expects me to come to work on time.

at work

_____

at home

_____

at school

_____

B. **Discussion.** Compare your answers with a partner or a group.

Authentic practice

① Well, congratulations on your promotion to bell captain, Ramon. That didn't take long . . . only two months, right?

Right. I feel very lucky.

On the contrary. We're lucky to have you.

② Now, bell captains are expected to get in a little early, before the shift starts.

If you know you're going to be late, please call in as early as possible.

③ And if you're planning to ask for time off, we like to have advance warning so we can get a replacement.

I understand.

Sometimes it's not easy to find a backup on short notice.

④ Excuse the interruption, Fran. I have to postpone our lunch meeting again.

Two porters called in sick, and I've got to see who can fill in for them.

A. Read and listen again. Then choose the word or phrase that has the same meaning.

1. Sometimes it's not easy to find a <u>backup</u> on short notice.

   ⓐ a replacement   ⓑ a porter

2. Sometimes it's not easy to find a backup <u>on short notice</u>.

   ⓐ with a lot of time   ⓑ with only a little time

3. I have to <u>postpone</u> our lunch meeting again.

   ⓐ reschedule for an earlier time   ⓑ reschedule for a later time

B. Listen. Underline your response.

1. (YOU) <u>Thanks so much.</u>   (YOU) From porter to bell captain.

2. (YOU) <u>Absolutely.</u>   (YOU) That's very dangerous.

3. (YOU) <u>That's OK. What's up?</u>   (YOU) On the contrary.

C. Listen again. Read your response out loud.

➤ Authentic practice

(For general suggestions, see *Introduction*, page Tx.)

Procedure:

🎧
➤ Have students look at the uniform that the man in the first picture is wearing. Ask *What kind of uniform is he wearing?* (porter / bellhop, doorman, elevator operator) *Where do you think he works?* (at a hotel, in an apartment building)

➤ Read the conversation out loud or play the cassette. With books open, students read and listen. Then have students find and circle the two job titles mentioned in the picture story (bell captain, porters). Ask *What do porters do?* (carry guests' bags to their rooms) *What do bell captains do?* (supervise the porters, or bellhops) *What job is Ramon going to have now?* (bell captain) *What job did he probably have before?* (porter) *What is a "promotion"?* (a move to a more important job in the same workplace)

➤ In pairs, have students talk about Fran's expectations of Ramon. Have them write three sentences beginning with *She expects him to . . .* For example, *She expects him to get in a little early.* Review as a class, and then brainstorm and write on the board other expectations Ramon's supervisor might have of him, for example, *She expects him to make phone calls on his own time, She expects him to help new porters.*

Option: Have students find and underline the infinitive phrases in the picture story: *to have you, to get in a little early, to ask for time off, to have advance warning, to find a backup.*

🎧 A. Read and listen again . . .
➤ After students read and listen again, have them look at the underlined words and phrases in items 1 through 3. Have students find and draw a box around these words and phrases in pictures 3 and 4.

➤ Have students read all the speech balloons in picture 3. Then ask *What does the supervisor expect Ramon to do before taking time off?* (to give advance warning) *What does "give advance warning" mean?* (tell them before) *Why?* (so that they can get a replacement) *What's a "replacement"?* (a backup, another person to do the same job) *Is it easy to get a replacement?* (no) *Is it more difficult with a lot of time or with a little time?* (with a little time) Have students answer items 1 and 2 individually.

➤ Have students read the speech balloons in picture 4. Ask *Can the man in the doorway meet with Fran at lunch today?* (no) *Is he probably going to meet with her some other time?* (yes) *Yesterday or tomorrow?* (tomorrow) Have students answer item 3 individually.

Option: After reviewing the answers, have students use each underlined word or phrase in an original sentence.

🎧 B–C.
➤ Before playing the cassette or reading the tapescript, have students read the response options for each item.

➤ Allow students to listen to the items as many times as necessary to complete the exercise.

➤ Have students check answers with a partner before they read their responses out loud.

Tapescript

1. Congratulations on your promotion.
2. Please give me advance warning if you need to reschedule.
3. Excuse the interruption.

If your students are ready . . .

Culture / Civics note: Company policies regarding time off differ greatly. Some companies offer employees a specified amount of paid time off from work each year for vacations, taking care of personal matters, and recovering from illness. With other companies, time off is unpaid. Most companies require employees to make requests for time off as far in advance as possible. By notifying a manager in advance, the employee allows the employer time to find a substitute worker. For sick days, employees are generally expected to notify a supervisor of the nature of their illness and the number of days they are likely to be absent from work. Employees should also notify their supervisor if they know that they are going to be late to work.

Clarifying employers' instructions

Procedure:

🎧 A. Listening comprehension . . .

➤ Tell students that they are going to listen to a conversation between an employer and a baby-sitter. Before reading the selection on the tape-script out loud or playing the cassette, brainstorm and write on the board expectations employers might have of baby-sitters, such as *to arrive on time, to call if there is a problem.* Include what an employer expects a baby-sitter not to do, such as *not to make personal phone calls, not to invite friends to the house.*

➤ After students listen to the conversation the first time, have volunteers read each item out loud so that students will know what to listen for. Play the cassette or read the conversation and have students check Mr. Gomez's expectations for the baby-sitter.

➤ Ask questions about the conversation, such as *How is Sara paid?* (by the hour) *What is her pay?* ($8 per hour before 11 p.m., $10 per hour after 11 p.m.) *Does she make more or less than minimum wage?* (more) *What does Mr. Gomez expect Lisa to do on school nights?* (to do her homework or read) *When should Sara call Mr. Gomez?* (if Jaime's fever is over 100 or he says he feels sick)

Challenge: In groups, have students compare what is expected of a baby-sitter in their countries with the expectations described in the conversation.

B. True story . . .

➤ Make a list similar to the one in Exercise A of four responsibilities you have at home and four responsibilities you have at work, for example, at home, *to pay the bills.* Begin each item with *to.* Then have students make their own lists.

➤ For each item on your lists, tell the class who expects you to do this, for example, *My family expects me to pay the bills.* Have students talk about the items on their lists in the same way.

➤ Do it yourself!

(For general suggestions, see *Introduction,* page Txiii.)

Procedure:

A. Write your <u>own</u> response . . .

➤ Explain to students that the man in the photo is a supervisor and that they should respond to his offer of part-time work.

➤ Students read the speech balloons and complete the activity individually.

➤ Review as a class. Read each speech balloon and elicit a variety of appropriate responses.

➤ Students read their conversations out loud with a partner and then change roles to practice both parts.

B. Culture talk . . .

➤ Read the question and elicit a response from a volunteer. Ask questions to clarify or find out more about the response.

➤ In groups, students respond to the question. Encourage them to ask for clarification of or more information about each other's responses.

Option: Have students bring in from their places of employment forms used to request time off in advance or forms used to report an absence. If they don't know already, have students find out the procedure for calling in sick at their places of employment. In groups, have students read and discuss the forms and talk about what to do if they're not feeling well and can't go to work.

Challenge: Have students role-play a telephone conversation in which an employee calls in sick to a supervisor. Students prepare their conversations with a partner. They then join another pair and present their role-plays to each other.

Tapescript

Mr. Gomez: Thanks for coming to baby-sit on such short notice, Sara.

Sara: No problem, Mr. Gomez. I've been looking for some part-time work. Feel free to call me anytime.

Mr. Gomez: Great! Now, let's see. I can't remember how much you charge.

Sara: Eight dollars an hour before 11:00 p.m., $10 after.

Mr. Gomez: That's fair. Oh, Lisa asked if she could have a pizza. I'll leave you some money to order one. And I'll leave a couple of extra dollars for the delivery man. Be sure to give him a tip.

Sara: I will. Thanks.

Mr. Gomez: There are just a couple of things you need to know. First, please remind Lisa to do her homework. You don't actually have to do anything, just be sure she sits down to do her work early on. Otherwise she gets too tired.

(Tapescript is continued on page T66.)

A. Listening comprehension. Listen to the conversation between an employer and a baby-sitter. Listen again and check what Mr. Gomez expects the baby-sitter to do.

Mr. Gomez expects the baby-sitter

1. ☑ to order pizza.
2. ☑ to give the delivery man a tip.
3. ☑ to remind Lisa to do her homework.
4. ☐ to help Lisa with her homework.
5. ☐ to watch TV with Lisa.
6. ☐ to remind Jaime to do his homework.
7. ☐ to call him if Jaime has a cold.

B. True story. What are your responsibilities at home or at work? What do other people expect you to do? Tell your partner or your group.

➤ Do it yourself!

A. Write your <u>own</u> response. Then read your conversation out loud with a partner.

> You said you were looking for some part-time work. I have something for you.

YOU _____

> Charlie called in sick. Do you think you could fill in for him? We could pay you overtime ... time and a half.

YOU _____

> Any questions?

YOU _____

B. Culture talk. In the country you come from, do you have to tell an employer in advance that you can't come to work? Compare cultures with your classmates.

Punctuality and consideration of others

 A. Read and listen to the letters.

Ask Joan
Culture tips for newcomers

Dear Joan:
I wrote you a few months ago to ask when to arrive at a dinner party that was scheduled for 6:00, and you told me to arrive by about 6:15. Joan, I trusted your advice, and now I'm in big trouble at work!

I had my performance review yesterday, and my supervisor said I was a great worker, but that I can't get a raise until I am more punctual. I was afraid to ask him to explain, but I don't understand. I always follow your advice, and when my lunch or my break is over, I always go right back to work in fifteen or twenty minutes. Am I doing something wrong?

Nadia, even more nervous

Dear Nadia:
At work it's very important to be punctual. No employer will tolerate lateness because it causes problems for the whole team. If you are not on time at your job, someone else will have to do your work.

Your supervisor expects you to come in on time, return from breaks and lunch on time, and do personal business on your own time, not company time. If for some reason you have an emergency or you can't be on time, be sure to give your boss as much advance warning as possible, so he or she can plan to fill in with someone who can do your job temporarily.

If you follow these rules and keep being a good worker, I'm sure you'll get a raise in no time!

Joan

B. Choose an answer to each question. Fill in the ovals.

1. What's the problem?

  ⓐ Nadia isn't punctual. **ⓑ** Nadia does personal business on company time.

2. Nadia's lunch hour ends at 1:10. When does her boss expect her to be at her desk?

  ⓐ 1:10 **ⓑ** 1:30

3. What should Nadia do if she has an emergency and can't be on time for work?

  ⓐ call her boss first **ⓑ** come in late and then explain the problem

C. What's your advice? Tell each co-worker what to do.

My son has a fever, and the school nurse asked me to come get him. But my shift is just starting. What should I do?

I need to run across the street to pick up a couple of videos. It'll only take 15 minutes. What do you think?

1. **YOU** _____ 2. **YOU** _____

Tapescript *(continued from page T65)*

Sara: OK. Great. What if she asks to watch TV?

Mr. Gomez: Absolutely not. We expect her to do her homework or to read on school nights. TV is for the weekends. No exceptions.

Sara: What about Jaime?

Mr. Gomez: Thanks for asking. He has a bad cold. Could you check his temperature around 8:30 and call me if he has a fever? The thermometer is in the upstairs bathroom.

Sara: Sure. Did you leave the number where you can be reached?

Mr. Gomez: Yes. On the kitchen table. But you don't have to call me unless Jaime's fever is over 100 or he says he feels sick.

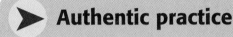

➤ Authentic practice

(For general suggestions, see *Introduction*, page Tx.)

Punctuality and consideration of others

Procedure:

🎧 A. Read and listen to the letters.

➤ Before playing the cassette or reading the letters, ask *What time does your work start? What time do you arrive at work?*

➤ As students listen to and read the letters, pause at the end of each paragraph and ask the class to retell the main information in their own words.

➤ After reading Joan's letter, ask *What four things does Nadia's supervisor expect her to do?* (to come in on time, to return from breaks and lunch on time, to do personal business on her own time, to give advance warning if she can't be on time) Write these four expectations on the board. Ask *How good are you at meeting these expectations at work?* Have students rate their own performance on each expectation as *great, good, not too good,* or *poor*.

Option: Have students underline the infinitives in the letters: *to ask, to arrive, to explain, to be, to come, to give, to fill in.* They should easily identify those that follow the verbs and objects they have worked with in this unit. Review the pronunciation of infinitives. Explain that the *to* is said very quickly and may sound like *t*.

B. Choose an answer...

➤ After students complete the activity individually, review the answers as a class.

➤ Then ask additional comprehension questions such as *When does Nadia go back to work after her lunch or break?* (in fifteen or twenty minutes) *Why?* (because of Joan's advice about when to arrive at a dinner party) *Is Nadia a bad worker?* (No, she's a good worker.) *What does she need to do to get a raise?* (to be more punctual)

C. What's your advice...

➤ Have students look at the drawings and read the speech balloons. Ask *What's the problem?*

➤ Have student take turns reading the speech balloons and giving advice with a partner.

➤ When students are finished, read each speech balloon out loud and elicit a variety of responses from the class.

Option: Have pairs create their own speech balloon describing a similar situation and asking for advice. Volunteers read their speech balloons out loud and elicit advice from the class.

If your students are ready...

Language note: In English, we often drop words that are repeated in parallel structure. In Joan's response, she writes: *Your supervisor expects you to come in on time, return from breaks and lunch on time, and do personal business on your own time, not company time.* This is really a combination of sentences: Your supervisor expects you to come in on time. Your supervisor expects you to return from lunch and to return from breaks on time. Your supervisor expects you to do personal business on your own time, not company time. Native speakers simply delete all the repeated words if they are exactly the same.

Culture / Civics note: Americans and Canadians are very conscious of time and considerable importance is placed on punctuality. In the workplace, being on time is viewed as a demonstration of responsibility, respect, and competence. Employees are expected to begin and end work at the exact time that they are scheduled and to return promptly from break periods. For social engagements, the degree of punctuality depends on the occasion and whether a latecomer would disrupt the event. For example, if friends make plans to meet in front of a movie theater, it is rude to be more than a few minutes late. However, at a gathering with a large number of guests, it is acceptable to arrive up to a half hour after the specified time.

Overtime pay

Procedure:

A. Read about the minimum wage...

➤ Have students read the information. Then ask *Do you remember looking at this information at the beginning of the unit? What do you remember from our discussion?* With their partners, students say as much as they can about the information from the Fair Labor Standards Act. Say *Imagine that you are explaining the information to someone who has never seen it before.*

➤ Ask each pair to say something to the class about the information from the Fair Labor Standards Act, for example, *Standards are rules* or *Employers don't have to pay teachers overtime.* Tell the class that each pair must say something new and not repeat what another pair has already said.

Option: Review the five words the class defined in the optional activity on page 57. Have students use the words in sentences, for example, *I want to work overtime because I would like to send my family in Mexico more money.*

B. Read these want ads.

➤ Have a different volunteer read each ad. If necessary, elicit from the class the meanings of abbreviations as they are encountered.

➤ Ask questions about the ads, such as *Which jobs pay more?* (nurse, sales rep) *Which jobs require training or experience?* (nurse, sales rep, second secretarial position) *How is the waiter / waitress job paid?* (by the hour, plus tips) *What is the pay for the short-order cook job?* (minimum wage, time and a half for overtime, and double time on Sundays and holidays) *Which job are you more qualified for? Which job would you like to have?*

C. Read about the people...

➤ Have a volunteer read item 1. Have students look at the ad for the nurse's job. Ask *What is the pay?* ($24 per hour) Ask *How many hours did Raul work?* (56) Write *$24 per hour* and *56 hours* on the board. Elicit from the class how to figure out how much Raul earned last week. Write on the board *$24 × 56 = $1344.* Ask *Is item 1 true or false?* (false)

➤ Have students complete items 2 and 3 with a partner. For item 2, refer students to the *Vocabulary* box on page 59 for time and a half and double time pay based on minimum wage. If necessary, point out that for item 2 students will have to calculate how much Golda earned from Monday to Friday, how much she earned on Saturday, and how much she earned on Sunday and then add the three amounts together.

➤ Do it yourself!

(For general suggestions, see *Introduction*, page Txiii.)

Procedure:

A. Bring in want ads...

➤ On the board, make a chart like the one below. Use the want ads on page 67 to fill in the chart as a class.

➤ Have students make a chart with the same column headings and at least five rows. Students use the wants ads that they have brought in to fill in information on at least five different jobs.

B. Discussion...

➤ Students compare their charts with a partner. To prompt discussion, write questions on the board such as *Which jobs pay by the hour? Which jobs pay by the week? What other payment options are there? Which jobs require experience?*

➤ From their own or their partner's chart, have students choose a job that they are qualified for or interested in. With their partners, students talk about how their skills, likes, and / or dislikes make this a good job for them, for example, *I am interested in the sales rep job because I like driving and I'm good at working with people.*

Challenge: If appropriate, have students call to inquire about jobs listed in the want ads they brought in. Before students call, have them decide which jobs they are qualified for or interested in. Then have them rehearse questions about pay, hours, requirements, how and where to apply, and so on.

Job	Pay per hour	Pay per week	Other form of payment	OT?	Hours?	Experience required?
Nurse	$24					
Waitress / Waiter	$4.50 + tips				FT / PT / weekends	
Short-order cook	$5.15			Time + 1/2; 2 × on Sun.		
Sales rep	$12.50 to $50				M–F 5–9:30 p.m., Sat. 10–2	yes

A. Read about the minimum wage taken from the Fair Labor Standards Act.

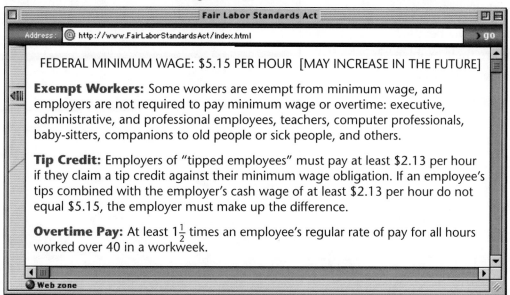

```
┌──────────────────── Fair Labor Standards Act ─────────────────────┐
│ Address: @ http://www.FairLaborStandardsAct/index.html      ⟩ go  │
│                                                                    │
│  FEDERAL MINIMUM WAGE: $5.15 PER HOUR  [MAY INCREASE IN THE FUTURE] │
│                                                                    │
│  Exempt Workers: Some workers are exempt from minimum wage, and    │
│  employers are not required to pay minimum wage or overtime: executive, │
│  administrative, and professional employees, teachers, computer professionals, │
│  baby-sitters, companions to old people or sick people, and others.│
│                                                                    │
│  Tip Credit: Employers of "tipped employees" must pay at least $2.13 per hour │
│  if they claim a tip credit against their minimum wage obligation. If an employee's │
│  tips combined with the employer's cash wage of at least $2.13 per hour do not │
│  equal $5.15, the employer must make up the difference.            │
│                                                                    │
│  Overtime Pay: At least 1½ times an employee's regular rate of pay for all hours │
│  worked over 40 in a workweek.                                     │
│                                                                    │
│ Web zone                                                           │
└────────────────────────────────────────────────────────────────────┘
```

For extra practice, go to page 156.

B. Read these want ads.

Help Wanted	Help Wanted	Help Wanted
NURSE—LPN or RN Medicaid # needed. $24/hr. Private home. 914 555 8700	**WAITRESS/WAITER** PT/FT/WEEKENDS $4.50 / + tips; FT (40 hrs per wk) **SHORT-ORDER COOK** Also wanted Minimum wage. Time + 1/2 for OT, 2x on Sundays and Holidays. Apply in person at Cindy's Diner, 28 Chambers St.	** Sales Reps ** Earn $12.50 to $50 per hour. Must have 3 yrs experience. Evenings: 5–9:30 & Saturdays: 10–2 p.m. Call 201 555 4360
Now Hiring **OFFICE MGMT/SECRETARY** FT position. Casual environment. Will train right person. Must be responsible. 621-9555		**SECRETARY** Full-time; phones, MS Word, Accts Receivable & Payable experience. Please call:

C. Read about the people who got the jobs and how much they earned.
Then check **T** (true), **F** (false), or **?** (not enough information to answer).

	T	F	?
1. Raul Santini got the nurse's job. Last week he worked 56 hours. He earned $1536.	☐	☑	☐
2. Golda Moskowitz got the short-order cook's job. She worked 40 hours from Monday to Friday and 6 hours on Saturday and on Sunday. She earned $314.18.	☑	☐	☐
3. Ken Park got the sales rep's job. He worked 35 hours last week. He earned $1050.	☐	☐	☑

➤ Do it yourself!   A plan-ahead project

A. Bring in want ads from your local newspaper. Find a job that pays by the hour, one that pays by the week, and one other kind.

B. Discussion. Compare ads with your classmates.

Review

A. Pair work or group work.

- Where are the people?
- What are their problems?

Ask and answer questions.

Create conversations.

Tell a story.

Say as much as you can.

Morning Shift:
7am–3pm

Afternoon Shift:
3pm–11pm

EXIT

BACK-UP

HUMAN RESOURCES

Job Opportunities This Week

Non-exempt
Van driver
sal.: $24/hr.

Exempt
Computer technical
support
sal.: $44,500/year

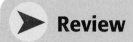
➤ Review

(For general suggestions, see *Introduction,* page Txii.)

Procedure:

A. Pair work or group work.

Option: To encourage students to pay more attention to environmental print they encounter daily and see it as an opportunity to practice reading in English, have students read all the text in the picture, for example, the shift times, the *Exit* and *Human Resources* signs, and the job opportunities. Then have students think about the reading they do at work and make a list. Students' lists might include *signs, notices, schedules, forms.*

Ask and answer questions.

➤ Have students take turns asking each other questions about the picture. Model the activity with a more advanced student. Hold up the textbook and point to the woman at the bottom of the page. Ask *Where is she?* (in the break room) The student answers and then asks you a question, such as *What job is paid by the hour?* (van driver) Model one more question and answer and then have students ask and answer questions with a partner. Point out the two questions asked in the directions and suggest that students ask where different people in the picture are and what problems they have.

Create conversations.

➤ Divide the class into three groups. Provide each group with a space on the board or a piece of chart paper. In each group, one student assumes the role of facilitator and another the role of recorder. Group 1 brainstorms ideas for a telephone conversation between the supervisor and the woman with the alligator in her basement. Group 2 brainstorms ideas for a conversation between the two men in the hall near the Human Resources cubicle, and Group 3 brainstorms ideas for a conversation between the two men in the Human Resources cubicle, the one at the desk and the one at the entrance.

➤ Within each group, students pair up and create a conversation. Suggest that students think of names for the people in their conversations.

➤ When the pairs have created and practiced their conversations, have students form new groups. Each new group consists of a pair from Group 1, a pair from Group 2, and a pair from Group 3. Each pair role-plays its conversation for its new group.

Tell a story.

Option: Create a character. Write on the board *be sure, decide, forget, need, plan, remember, want.* Point to the man at the time clock. Say *He has decided to ask for a shift change. He wants to work the morning shift. He wants to spend more time with his children. He forgot to ask yesterday, but he plans to ask today.* Have students choose a person in the picture and use as many of the verbs followed by infinitives as they can to talk about the person's life.

Option: Discuss expectations. Have students tell what the supervisor (the woman on the phone in the cubicle on the left) expects of her employees. If helpful, write on the board *She expects them to . . .* Alternatively, have students play the role of the Human Resources representative and tell an applicant the expectations for the computer technical support or van driver job; write on the board *We expect you to . . .*

T68

B. Listen to the conversation...

➤ Tell students that they are going to listen to a conversation about wages and hours.

➤ After students listen to the conversation the first time, have them read the questions so that they will know what to listen for. Allow students to listen to the conversation as many times as necessary to complete the exercise.

➤ Have students check answers with a partner. Then have pairs write questions for the incorrect answers; for example, for item 1, they might write *Which job is full-time?*

Challenge: Play the cassette or read the tapescript one more time. Tell students to try to remember what is said, but don't allow them to take any notes. Have students try to re-create the conversation with a partner.

C–E.

➤ Students work individually to complete the review exercises.

➤ Circulate to offer help as needed.

➤ Have students check answers with a partner. Review answers as a class.

➤ Identify any areas of difficulty that may require additional instruction and practice.

Option: For Exercise E, have students practice the questions and their responses with a partner.

Option: For Exercise E, have students choose one question and response and create an extended conversation.

Tapescript

Woman: I'm looking for a job.

Man: Certainly. What kind of position are you looking for, full-time or part-time?

Woman: That depends. What do you have available?

Man: Well, we have a couple of openings right now. Both are managerial positions. One's a mailroom manager, and the other's a cafeteria manager. Are you interested?

Woman: Could you give me some idea of the pay?

Man: The full-time mailroom position pays $600 a week. The part-time cafeteria manager pays $340 for 20 hours a week. But there's unlimited overtime available at $27 an hour, so if you work a full 35-hour week, the cafeteria job is a better deal. Also, if you don't always want to work so many hours, the cafeteria job gives you more flexibility. What do you think?

Woman: Well, right now the money is more important to me than the flexibility.

1. Which job is part-time?

   ⓐ the cafeteria manager   ⓑ the mailroom manager

2. What's the weekly pay for the mailroom manager?

   ⓐ $600.00   ⓑ $340.00

3. Which is more important to the applicant?

   ⓐ flexibility   ⓑ money

C. Complete each sentence. Fill in the ovals.

1. A waiter or a waitress gets a salary plus _____.

   ⓐ tips   ⓑ minimum wage

2. The hours are _____ with a one-hour break for lunch.

   ⓐ 9 to 5   ⓑ $4.80

3. Don't do that on _____.

   ⓐ Human Resources   ⓑ company time

4. I have to run _____.

   ⓐ an errand   ⓑ an emergency

D. Complete each sentence with an object and an infinitive. Use your **own** ideas.

1. She invited *her mother to go shopping.*

2. Peter reminded _____

3. They always ask _____

4. The baby-sitter warned _____

5. We would like _____

6. His children expect _____

E. Read each sentence. Write your **own** response.

1. "How do you get paid on your new job?"

   (YOU) _____

2. "What are you doing these days?"

   (YOU) _____

3. "I'm sorry, but I'm going to have to reschedule."

   (YOU) _____

F. **Write your expectations of your boss, your teacher, and one other person.**
Use your <u>own</u> ideas.

1. my boss *I expect my boss to give me a raise this year.*

2. my boss _____

3. my teacher _____

4. _____

G. Read the ads.

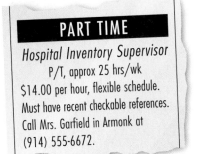

Now read about each person. Choose a job for each one. Fill in the ovals.

1. Lucinda Apu is a night student at a technical college. She needs a part-time job. Which job is better for her?

   (a) hospital inventory supervisor   (b) teacher's aide

2. Luis Leon needs to earn $350 per week. He has a child at home and only has a baby-sitter two days a week. Which job is better for him?

   (a) hospital inventory supervisor   (b) teacher's aide

H. Composition. **On a separate sheet of paper, write about the picture on page 68.**
Say as much as you can.

Now I can
❏ discuss payment, hours, and overtime pay.
❏ reschedule an event.
❏ talk about my own time and company time.
❏ understand my employer's expectations.
❏ understand why it's important to be
   punctual on the job.
❏ _____ .

F. Write your expectations . . .

➤ Preface the activity by saying *On page 63 you wrote and talked about other people's expectations of you. Now you are going to write and talk about your expectations of other people.*

➤ Have students decide who the person in item 4 is, for example, husband or wife, neighbor.

➤ Have students read their answers to items 2 through 4 with a partner. Then have them talk about other expectations they have of these three people.

Option: Write on the board *I expect my teacher . . .* Have students write on the board how they finished this sentence in item 3. Then brainstorm students' responsibilities. As a class, choose the five most important expectations of a good teacher and of good students. Have volunteers make posters with each list. One poster might say *We expect a good teacher to start class on time, to be prepared . . .* The other poster might say *We expect good students to be punctual, to participate in class . . .* Display the posters.

G. Read the ads.

➤ Have students read the ads out loud with a partner, pronouncing the words that are abbreviated.

➤ After students complete the exercise individually, review the answers as a class. For each item, ask why the job is better for the person described.

➤ Have students discuss with their partners which of the two jobs would be better for them and why.

H. Composition . . .

➤ Provide students with concrete approaches to writing about the picture on page 68. Use one of the options that follow, give students a choice of options, or assign options based on students' levels of proficiency. Model what is expected of students for each option.

➤ Advise students to look back through the unit for help and ideas as they write.

➤ Circulate to offer help as needed.

Option: Have students write an extended conversation between the Human Resources representative and the woman he is interviewing. Have students refer to the model conversation on page 59 for ideas.

Option: Students imagine that they are the Human Resources representative and that the company has decided to place ads in the newspaper for the two job openings. Have students choose one of the jobs and fill out the form on page 162. Students make up

additional information about the job in order to fill all 20 boxes.

Challenge: Have students look at the picture on page 68 and imagine that they are the supervisor on duty. Explain that one of the supervisor's responsibilities is to write a *Change of shift report*. In it, the supervisor describes what happened during the shift and reports absences, replacements, and so on. Have students copy the following form from the board, or provide handouts. Students fill out the form for the supervisor at the end of the morning shift.

Change of shift report

Supervisor's name:_____

Date: _____

Shift: _____

Employee absences: Please list employees affected and explain reasons.

Replacements: Please list backups called in.

Requests to leave early: Please give reason.

New employees hired: List name, position, hours, and pay.

New jobs open: List position and pay.

Other issues or concerns:

Now I can

➤ Have students answer the questions the class wrote when the objectives were discussed on page 57.

➤ Read the first item in the box out loud, *Now I can discuss payment, hours, and overtime pay.* Elicit from the class an example of how to discuss payment, hours, or overtime pay, such as *Could you please tell me what the pay is?*

➤ In pairs, have students take turns reading each item in the box and giving an example of what they have learned. When students can provide an example, they should check that box. For the items students weren't able to check, they should look back through the unit for ideas.

➤ When students are finished reviewing with their partners, read each item out loud and elicit an example from the class.

Oral test (optional)

You may want to use the *Now I can* box as an informal evaluation. While students are working on the *Composition* activity, you can call them up individually and check their ability with two or three objectives.

Supplies and services

Note: Have students bring to class coupons and catalogs, for use on pages 72 through 74, and empty food and drink containers, for use on page 80. Students will need to go to a grocery store for the plan-ahead project on page 79.

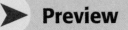 **Preview**

(For general suggestions, see *Introduction*, page Tviii.)

Warm up. Which is the best buy?

Procedure:

➤ Draw on students' prior experience by asking them questions about their own buying habits, such as *Who does the shopping in your household? How do you decide what products to buy? Is price an important consideration? What other things do you consider? How can you tell which product is the cheapest?*

➤ Have students look at the picture. Ask questions such as *What kind of food is this?* (pasta sauce) *Where is it?* (on a shelf in the grocery store) *How can you tell?* (There are prices on the shelf.) *What are the brands?* (Old World, Healthy Acres, Mama's Own)

➤ Write the three brand names as headings on the board. Have students cover up the pricing information and look only at the containers of sauce. As a class, compare the three sauces. Elicit and write on the board information about each brand of sauce. For example, if a student says *Old World and Healthy Acres are tomato sauce. Mama's Own is cheese sauce,* write *tomato* under *Old World* and *Healthy Acres* and *cheese* under *Mama's Own.* Ask students which sauce they would buy based on the information on the board and why.

➤ Have students look at the pricing information. Ask how much each container of sauce costs. Then ask *What are the prices on the right?* (the unit prices) *The unit price is the price per . . . ?* (ounce) Demonstrate how the unit price is calculated. Write *$2.76* on the board. Ask *How many ounces are in the jar of Old World pasta sauce?* (12 ounces) Write *12 ounces* on the board and then *$2.76 ÷ 12 = $.23.*

➤ Ask *Which container of sauce is cheapest?* (Mama's Own) *Which sauce has the lowest unit price?* (Mama's Own) Point out that, in this case, the product with the lowest price also has the lowest unit price. Ask *Why?* If necessary, explain that this is because the containers of sauce are all the same size, 12 ounces. Ask *When is it helpful to compare the unit prices?* (when the products are different sizes)

➤ Ask *Which pasta sauce is the best buy? Why? Which pasta sauce would you buy? Is price the most important consideration? Is price more important than taste? Is price more important than nutrition?*

Option: Have students calculate the unit price for a 12-ounce jar of pasta sauce that costs $3.48 ($.29).

Unit 6 objectives

Procedure:

➤ Have students read the objectives. *Ask What will this unit help you do?* (be a better shopper, find the best prices) *What does a good shopper do?* (compares prices, looks for sales, uses coupons) *What are some ways that you as a shopper can save money? What can you do with the money you save?*

Supplies and services

> Preview

Warm up. Which is the best buy?

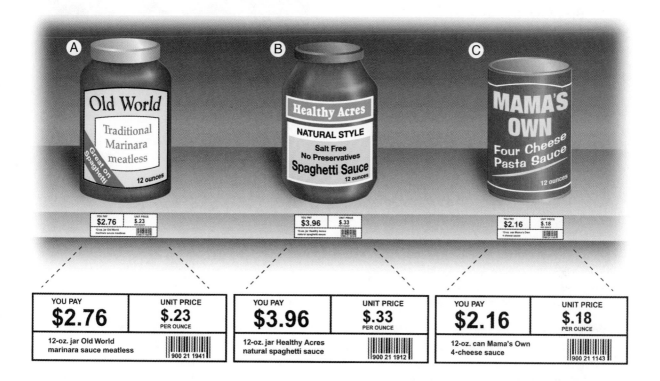

A		B		C	
YOU PAY	**UNIT PRICE**	**YOU PAY**	**UNIT PRICE**	**YOU PAY**	**UNIT PRICE**
$2.76	**$.23** PER OUNCE	**$3.96**	**$.33** PER OUNCE	**$2.16**	**$.18** PER OUNCE
12-oz. jar Old World marinara sauce meatless	900 21 1941	12-oz. jar Healthy Acres natural spaghetti sauce	900 21 1912	12-oz. can Mama's Own 4-cheese sauce	900 21 1143

Unit 6 objectives

- Determine the best buy.
- Talk about bargains.
- Order supplies online and by phone.
- Understand and use unit pricing.

Model 1   Talk about bargains.

A. Listen and read.

A: What a bargain! Three cans of tuna for a dollar!

B: Really? They're usually 89 cents each. That must be a mistake.

A: No. Look at the coupon. It's a seven-ounce can.

B: Wow, that *is* a bargain.

A: You can say *that* again!

B. Listen again and repeat.

Vocabulary

How food is sold

a can   a loaf   a box   a package   a container

C. Pair work. Describe a bargain. Use the coupons or your own ideas.

Bargains: This week only.   All are FOODWAY BRAND.

12-oz. pkg
Cheddar cheese
3 for $1.59
Reg. $.99 ea.

32-oz. bottle
Apple juice
2 for $1.29
Reg. $.89 ea.

1-gal. cont.
Milk
2 for $3.29
Reg. $2.49 ea.

1-pint jar
Tomato sauce
3 for $3.00
Reg. $1.59 ea.

10-lb. bag
Potatoes
2 for $2.99
Reg. $2.99 ea.

A: What a bargain! _____ for _____!

B: Really? _____ usually _____. That must be a mistake.

A: No. Look at the coupon. It's a _____.

B: Wow, that *is* a bargain.

A: You can say *that* again!

Practical conversations

(For general suggestions, see *Introduction*, page Tviii.)

Model 1

Content: talking about bargains; reading coupons; describing quantities and how food is sold; exclamations with *What*; conclusions with *must*

Procedure:

🎧 A–B.

➤ To set the scene for the conversation, ask questions about the photo, such as *Where is this couple?* (at the supermarket or grocery store) *What is the man holding?* (three cans) *What do you think they are looking at?* (a shopping list, an advertising circular, a coupon)

➤ After students listen to the conversation, check comprehension by asking questions such as *How much is the tuna?* (three cans for a dollar) *What size can?* (seven ounces) *Why does the woman think the price is a mistake?* (because it's so low) *What is the regular price?* (89 cents per can) *Where is the cheaper price listed?* (on the coupon)

➤ Have students read the conversation again silently. Then ask *What is a bargain?* (something bought cheaply or for less than its usual price) *What is a coupon?* (a small piece of printed paper that gives you the right to pay less for something) If students have trouble with the meaning of *coupon*, show coupons you or the students have brought in. Ask *Where can you find coupons?* (in the mail, in the newspaper, in advertising circulars at the front of the store) Ask students if they use coupons. Have them save any coupons they find and bring them to class.

Option: Have students calculate how much three cans of tuna would cost at the regular price. ($2.67) Then ask *How much do you save with the coupon?* ($1.67)

🎧 Vocabulary

➤ For each of the vocabulary words, have groups brainstorm food items that are sold this way; for example, for *a can*, students might list *tuna, soup, beans, corn.*

Option: Have groups brainstorm food items that are sold in *a bottle, a jar,* and *a bag.* Use the pictures in Exercise C to illustrate the meanings of these words, if necessary.

C. Pair work . . .

➤ Have a different volunteer read each coupon. If necessary, elicit from the class the meanings of abbreviations as they are encountered.

➤ Copy the conversation on the board. Read the conversation, pausing at each blank substitution line. Using the first coupon, have the class provide the correct word or phrase for each blank. The class should give the answers *Three packages, a dollar fifty-nine, They're, 99 cents each, twelve-ounce package.*

➤ Students then practice the conversation in pairs, using the other coupons or their own ideas. Point out that *Wow, that is a bargain* stresses the word *is*, indicating agreement with the other speaker.

Challenge: With their partners, have students calculate how much two or three of each product would cost at the regular price. Then have them determine how much is saved by using the coupon. For example, three packages of cheese at $.99 would cost $2.97; the savings with the coupon is $1.38. Then have students calculate the total savings if all the coupons are used ($8.32).

If your students are ready . . .

Culture / Civics note: In North America, there are many ways that shoppers can save money at the supermarket. Most supermarkets hold weekly sales with discounted prices on selected items. These sales are advertised in printed circulars found at the entrance to the store and in Sunday newspapers. Stores and manufacturers also offer discounts in the form of *coupons*: pieces of paper that the customer presents to the cashier to pay less money for a specified item. Coupons are often included with Sunday newspapers, in popular magazines, and inside product packaging. Most major supermarkets and drugstore chains also offer a savings club card. Presenting this card to the cashier allows members to take advantage of sales available only to club members.

Model 2

Content: making a suggestion; explaining how to order things by phone or online; acknowledging a good idea

Procedure:

🎧 A–B.

➤ Ask questions about the picture, such as *What is this?* (a computer screen, a window, a Web site) *What is sold on this Web site?* (pencils, fax machines, clipboards, paperclips)

➤ After students listen to the conversation, ask questions such as *What does the woman on the left need to do?* (go shopping for office supplies) *What does the woman on the right suggest?* (ordering supplies by phone or online) *What Web site sells office supplies?* (paperclips.com)

➤ Ask *How much will the phone call to 1-800-NOTEPAD cost?* If necessary, explain that calls to telephone numbers with the area code 800 are toll free.

➤ Elicit or explain the meanings of *online* and *log on. Online* means over the Internet, and to *log on* to a Web site is to go to the site by typing in its address. Brainstorm, write on the board, and discuss the meaning of other terms related to using the Internet, such as *Web browser, Web address, search, click.*

➤ Ask who has ordered something by phone and who has ordered something online. If many students have experience ordering by phone or online, have students discuss in groups what they ordered, how, from what company, and if there were any problems. If few students have ordered by phone or online, ask those students to share their experience with the class.

🎧 Vocabulary

➤ After students listen to and repeat the vocabulary, brainstorm and write on the board other things that students or people they know have ordered by phone or online, such as *books, CDs, furniture.*

C. Pair work . . .

➤ Ask students what they think can be ordered using each phone number or Web address. Point out that companies try to get telephone numbers and Web addresses that are easy to remember and make obvious what they sell. Ask students if the companies they work for have 800 numbers and / or Web sites and what the numbers and addresses are.

➤ Have students match a telephone number and Web site from the box with each vocabulary word. For example, for *clothes,* you can call *1-800-CLOTHES* or log on to *yourclosets.com.*

➤ Read the first line of the conversation four times, inserting each of the vocabulary words. Each time, have the class respond by reading the second line of the conversation chorally. Listen to make sure that the class says *Order them* for *clothes, auto parts,* and *uniforms,* and *Order it* for *safety equipment.*

Option: Use catalogs that you or the students have brought in. Give each pair a catalog and have them find the 800 number and Web address that customers use to place an order. Have students practice the conversation again using this information.

Option: Have students look at their telephones at home and figure out the numbers for the three 800 numbers that are given in letters in Exercise C.

Field project: If possible, have students use computers to learn more about ordering online. Have students choose a product and have the class follow step-by-step instructions to do a search for that product. Demonstrate how to click on the different sites found and how to go back to the page of search results. Then choose an online shopping site and have students select a couple of products. Point out the *Add to shopping cart* icon. Tell students how to add the products they've selected to their carts. Next have them *Proceed to checkout* to see what information they have to provide to place an order online and what the shipping costs are.

If your students are ready . . .

Language note: Most Web addresses for companies end in *.com.* Addresses for public agencies may end in *.org,* those for universities in *.edu.* Most Web addresses begin with *www. Paperclips.com* would actually be *www.paperclips.com.*

➤ Do it yourself!

(For general suggestions, see *Introduction,* page Txiii.)

Procedure:

A–B.

➤ Model the activity for students. Draw the chart on the board. Fill in the first row according to your own buying habits. Talk about why you prefer to buy each item at a store, by telephone, or online, and where you get the best bargains.

A. Listen and read.

A: I need to go shopping for office supplies.

B: Can I make a suggestion? Order them by phone or online.

A: How?

B: Call 1-800-NOTEPAD or log on to paperclips.com.

A: Hey, why didn't *I* think of that?

B. Listen again and repeat.

Vocabulary

Things to order by phone or online

| clothes | auto parts | uniforms | safety equipment |

C. Pair work. Make suggestions. Use the vocabulary and the information in the box.

1-800-CLOTHES	1-800-ANYTHING	your_closets.com
1-800-555-CARPART	auto_parts.com	safety_first.com

A: I need to go shopping for _____.

B: Can I make a suggestion? Order _____ by phone or online.

A: ___1___?

B: Call _____ or log on to _____.

A: Hey, why didn't *I* think of that?　　¹What do you mean

➤ Do it yourself!

A. What do you buy at a store, by phone, or online? Complete the chart.

At a store	By telephone	Online
cleaning supplies		

B. Discussion. Where do you get the best bargains? Compare opinions with your classmates.

➤ Practical grammar

Conclusions with must

A gallon of ice cream for $2.00? That **must be** a mistake. It usually costs five something.

You're right. It **must not be** the gallon container.

Use <u>must</u> and <u>must not</u> to guess a reason for something you are almost sure of.

I see Linda on the bus every day at 7:30. She **must work** the early shift.

A. Match each statement with a conclusion. Write the letter on the line.

1. Arlene bought 24 cans of cleanser. __b__
2. She always buys shoes at Harry's. __c__
3. My boss was going to call, but he didn't. __a__
4. Roger never goes to the store for parts. __e__
5. The waiters only earn $3.50 per hour. __d__

a. He must not have my number.
b. It must be cheaper by the case.
c. They must have great bargains.
d. They must get a lot in tips.
e. He must shop by phone or online.

B. Complete each conclusion. Use <u>must</u> and the verb.

1. What a great price for that soup! It _____must be_____ on sale.
   _be_
2. Pilar always orders online. She _____must have_____ her own computer.
   have
3. Ilhan buys only Golden Fields bread. He _____must like_____ that brand.
   like
4. The nurses always shop there. They _____must offer_____ the largest selection.
   offer
5. That package is cheaper than this one. This _____must not be_____ the best buy.
   not be

Exclamations with What

What beautiful cheese!

And **what** great prices!

What a nice tie!

$6⁹⁹ $5⁹⁹ $4⁹⁹

➤ Practical grammar

(For general suggestions, see *Introduction*, page Tix.)

Conclusions with <u>must</u>

Content: conclusions with *must* and *must not*

Procedure:

➤ Say *(Name of absent student) is not here today. Why do you think he or she's not here?* Elicit from the class several possible reasons and write them on the board. Then point to the reasons and ask *Which one is probably the real reason he or she's not here?* Elicit a response from the class and then ask *Are you almost sure?* If, for example, your class agrees that the absent student is most likely sick, circle this response on the board and then write next to it *She must be sick.*

➤ Make two other observations about your students. Write sentences that students can draw obvious conclusions from, for example, *Esther is yawning, George is looking at Ismael's book.* Ask *Why do you think so?* and elicit conclusions with *must* or *must not*, for example, *She must be tired, George must not have his book.*

➤ Have two students read the speech balloons in the grammar box out loud. As a class, read and discuss the explanation and example on the right.

Option: Have students create additional examples with a partner. Circulate and check students' examples for correctness. Have students add one or two examples to the space in the grammar box.

A. Match each statement ...

➤ Have students cover up the conclusions on the right and look only at the statements. Have a volunteer read item 1. Ask *Why do you think she bought 24 cans of cleanser?* Elicit ideas. If students don't use *must* when they guess a reason, rephrase their response. Say *So you think it must ...* Have students look at the answer choices on the right and identify the correct conclusion. If necessary, explain that a case contains 24 items.

➤ Students complete items 2 through 5 individually and then check answers with a partner.

Note: For item 2, the subject pronoun *They* in answer (c) refers to *the people at Harry's.*

B. Complete each conclusion ...

➤ Read item 1 and elicit the correct answer, *must be*, from the class.

➤ Students complete items 2 through 5 individually and then check answers with a partner.

Challenge: Have students write a sentence about a classmate on a slip of paper, for example, *Lars got a new job* or *Yelena is wearing her coat.* Students take their slips of paper and walk around the room. Students pair up, read their sentences, and use *must* or *must not* to draw conclusions from each other's sentences. For example, if one student reads the sentence *Lars got a new job*, the other could draw the conclusion *He must be happy.* Students then exchange slips of paper, find a new partner, and repeat the activity. Direct students to sit down once they have exchanged sentences with five different partners.

Exclamations with <u>What</u>

Procedure:

➤ Use exclamations with *What* to give compliments to students in your classroom. Say, for example, *What a beautiful sweater! What gorgeous earrings! What a nice shirt!*

➤ Have volunteers read the speech balloons in the grammar box. Encourage students to read with expression.

➤ Point out that *a* or *an* is used when describing a singular count noun, *What <u>a</u> nice tie!* You may wish to explain by writing *tie* on the board and eliciting the plural *ties.* Then write *cheese* on the board and make sure students understand that there is no plural form. Write *a tie*, and then write *a cheese* and cross out the article *a.*

➤ Brainstorm on the board adjectives students can use to describe things they like, such as *gorgeous, great, cool, fantastic.*

➤ Have students walk around the room and use exclamations with *What* and the adjectives on the board to compliment each other, for example, *What cool shoes! What nice handwriting!*

Option: If you or the students have brought in catalogs, have students look through them with a partner and use exclamations with *What* to comment on the products; for example, *What a nice table!* Before students begin, brainstorm and write on the board adjectives students can use to describe products they don't like, such as *awful, terrible, horrible.* Remind students to use *an* with *awful* and singular count nouns.

C. Complete each exclamation ...

Note: Although the examples in the grammar box on page 74 include adjectives before the noun, an adjective is not necessary, for example, *What fun! What a day!*

➤ Have students cover up the speech balloons. For each picture, elicit exclamations with *What* from the class, for example, for item 1, *What a beautiful car!* or for item 2, *What a nice computer!*

➤ Explain that students should complete the exclamations with *What* or with *What* and the adjective below the line. Remind students to use *a* or *an* with singular count nouns such as *car* and *loaf*.

➤ Review by having different students read each speech balloon. Encourage students to read with expression.

Challenge: With a partner, students choose one picture and create an extended conversation based on the speech balloon(s). Encourage students to look at the model conversations in this and previous units for ideas. To model the activity, have students look at item 4. Then read the following conversation with a more advanced student:

Woman: Look, dear. I won two movie tickets. What luck!

Man: Great! We'll go tonight. What fun!

Woman: I wonder if we can get a baby-sitter.

Man: I don't know. It's not easy to find a baby-sitter on short notice.

Woman: You can say *that* again! Maybe we'd better go next week.

Have volunteers role-play their conversations for the class.

➤ Do it yourself!

(For general suggestions, see *Introduction*, page Txiii.)

Procedure:

➤ Ask *How do you feel when you receive a package or box in the mail?* Elicit responses such as *happy, excited, curious.*

➤ Have students look at the photos and read the speech balloons. Then, in pairs, have them say something about each box using an exclamation with *What.* Have them use *must* to make guesses about what's in each box.

➤ Have each pair share with the class something they said about one of the boxes.

Option: Put some items that students will be able to describe in a box. Have a volunteer go to the front of the class, choose an item from the box (without showing it to the class), and describe the item, for example, *It's small. It's a piece of paper. You find it in the newspaper. You use it at the supermarket to get a cheaper price.* Students use *must* to guess what the item is, for example, *It must be a coupon.* The student who guesses correctly goes up to the front of the class and chooses a different item from the box to describe.

C. Complete each exclamation with **What**.

What a great
_____
1. great
car! It must be really expensive.

Look at this screen!
What fabulous
_____
2. fabulous
prices! Let's order from them.

What a gigantic
_____
3. gigantic
loaf of bread! We'll never finish it.

Look, dear. I won two movie tickets. What luck!

Great! We'll go tonight.
What _____ fun!
4.

I can't believe this.
What low
_____
5. low
salaries!

This place is pretty expensive. But
what delicious
_____
6. delicious
food!

➤ Do it yourself!

Say something about each box. Then guess what's in it.

What a big box from Notepad!

NOTEPAD OFFICE SUPPLIES

Hey, it must be the new printer!

Authentic practice

A. Read and listen again. Then check <u>True</u>, <u>False</u>, or <u>Maybe</u>.

	True	False	Maybe
1. The boy wants Star cheese.	☐	☑	☐
2. The clerk understands unit pricing.	☑	☐	☐
3. The father thinks Star cheese tastes better than Wow Cow.	☐	☑	☐
4. The big package of Wow Cow costs less per pound than the small package.	☑	☐	☐

B. Listen. Underline <u>your</u> response.

1. (YOU) <u>Right! What a difference!</u>   (YOU) What's in it?

2. (YOU) I won't buy it.   (YOU) <u>You can say *that* again.</u>

3. (YOU) <u>Not always.</u>   (YOU) That's a shame.

C. Listen again. Read <u>your</u> response out loud.

➤ Authentic practice

(For general suggestions, see *Introduction*, page Tx.)

Procedure:

🎧

Note: The procedure for the picture story is different in this unit to help students develop strategies for improving listening comprehension.

➤ Have students listen with books closed. Then ask questions such as *How many people are speaking?* (three) *Who are they?* (a child, a father, a store clerk) *What does the child want?* (Wow Cow cheese) *Which brand does the father decide to buy?* (Wow Cow) *What size?* (the big package)

➤ Have students look at the picture story. Ask questions about the pictures, such as *Where are the father and son?* (at a supermarket) *How can you tell?* (the food, the display case, the shopping cart) *What is the child doing in the first picture?* (pointing at cheese) *What is the father doing in the second picture?* (comparing two packages of cheese) Point to the clerk and ask *How can you tell that he works at the store?* (He's wearing an apron.) *What is the child doing in the last picture?* (raising his arms / cheering) Ask *Does seeing the pictures help you better understand what happened?*

➤ Have students listen again with books open. Ask *Is it easier to understand when you can read along?* (yes, probably) *Why?* (because you can listen and see the written words) *Why is it a good idea to practice listening and not read along at the same time?* (When you listen to someone talking, there are no written words to look at.) *What words or phrases were difficult to understand when you were only listening?* Have students underline these words and phrases in the picture story. Elicit words and phrases students had trouble with and write them on the board. Try to identify patterns, such as difficulty understanding a particular speaker, with new expressions like *no-brainer,* or understanding numbers.

➤ Write on the board and discuss the following listening comprehension strategies: *using context to guess about meaning, asking for repetition, asking for clarification, taking notes, listening to the news or talk radio for more practice.* Explain *context* as what you see, what you know about a situation, and what is said before and after the word or phrases you don't understand. Brainstorm and write on the board ways to ask for repetition and clarification, such as *Could you repeat that, please? I'd like to make*

a note of it and *What do you mean?* Discuss when taking notes is appropriate, for example, when talking on the phone or during an interview. Ask students to choose one listening strategy to practice before the next class.

➤ Have students look at picture 1. Ask *Why is it difficult to compare the prices of the two brands of cheese?* (because they come in different-sized packages) Have students look at picture 2. Ask *How does looking at the unit price make it easier to compare?* (because it gives the price per pound for both brands) *How much is Wow Cow per pound?* ($6.56) *How much is Star per pound?* ($4.16) *Which brand does the father want to buy?* (Star)

➤ Have students look at picture 4. Ask *How much is Wow Cow per pound if you buy the big package?* ($3.20) Have students calculate how much you save per pound if you buy the big package. ($3.36) As a class, discuss *Why does the big package cost less per pound? Why do you get a discount, or lower price, for buying more? Is it always better to buy the bigger package so that you can get the discount?*

Option: In groups, have students compare food shopping in the United States and in their home countries. Ask *In the country you come from, who usually does the food shopping? Do people shop at supermarkets or in small stores? Do the stores give unit prices? Is there a discount for buying larger quantities?*

🎧 A–C.

➤ Have students check answers with a partner before reading their responses out loud in Exercise C.

Tapescript

1. If you just check the unit price labels, it'll be easier to figure the best buy.
2. What a no-brainer!
3. The bigger the better.

If your students are ready . . .

Culture / Civics note: In North America, buying larger quantities of a product can often result in a lower unit price. For example, in the *Authentic practice* conversation on page 76, the Wow Cow 12-slice package of cheese is priced at $6.56 per pound, but the much larger package is priced at only $3.20 per pound. Some supermarkets have a special aisle with bulk quantities of products for sale at a discounted price, and there are also discount stores that specialize in bulk goods.

Ordering supplies online

Procedure:

🎧 A. Listening comprehension ...

➤ Have students listen to the conversation with books open. Before students listen, have them read the directions. Then ask *What will the conversation be about?* (ordering supplies online) Point to the pictures and ask *What are these?* (computer screens) Explain that one of the speakers in the conversation will move from one screen to the next, in order, by clicking on certain items. Use a mouse, if available, to demonstrate clicking.

➤ Ask *At a workplace, who is usually responsible for ordering supplies?* (a secretary, an office manager, an administrative assistant) Ask if any students are responsible for ordering supplies at their workplaces.

Option: After students listen to the conversation the first time, but before they look at Exercise B, have them listen again and practice taking notes as a listening strategy. Tell students to imagine that they are on the telephone with Maritza, the second speaker, and that she is explaining to them how to order supplies online. They are taking notes so that they'll be able to order when they get off the phone.

🎧 B. Listen again ...

➤ Allow students to listen to the conversation as many times as necessary to complete the exercise. Have students also fill in the company's name and address on the last screen.

➤ After reviewing the answers as a class, have students use the pictures and items they have circled to tell a partner how to order supplies online. Remind students to use *Click on . . .* Have students begin their directions with *Log on to . . .* or *Type in . . .* and a Web address from the book (*paperclips.com, pencilpoint.com*), an actual Web address, or one they make up. Point out that with *Type in . . .* students should include the *www* at the beginning of the address.

C. Answer the questions ...

Option: Have students calculate the per-pencil savings and the total savings when 5000 pencils are purchased ($.07, $350). Read Maritza's line *Well, the more you order, the cheaper they are* and Gloria's response *That's true, but what are we going to do with 5,000 pencils? We don't have room for all those pencils!* Ask students if they would follow Maritza's advice and order more to get the discount, or if they think Gloria is right to order only 500 pencils.

➤ Do it yourself!

(For general suggestions, see *Introduction*, page Txiii.)

Procedure:

A. Write your own response ...

➤ Explain to students that they should give the man in the photo advice about what brand of tuna to buy.

➤ Students read the speech balloons and complete the activity individually. Circulate to offer help as needed.

➤ Students read their conversations out loud with a partner and then change roles to practice both parts.

B. Culture talk ...

➤ Have students look back at the picture story on page 76. Ask *What brand of cheese did the son want?* (Wow Cow) *What brand of cheese did the father buy?* (Wow Cow) *Why did the son want Wow Cow cheese?* (because Big Bunny, a character on TV, eats Wow Cow) Ask the class to speculate about how the child in the picture story would have reacted if the father had decided to buy Star cheese.

➤ Before groups discuss, ask questions to give students ideas about what to say, for example, *In the country you come from, do children go shopping with their parents? Do they ask for certain products? Do parents buy what their children want? How do children react when they don't get what they want?*

Tapescript

Gloria: Maritza, I'm sick and tired of going out every time we need supplies. It's such a waste of time.
Maritza: You can say *that* again. Why don't you just order online?
Gloria: Excuse me?
Maritza: It's the twenty-first century, girl. You've got a computer on your desk. Use it.
Gloria: But I've never ordered online. Can you walk me through it?
Maritza: With pleasure. OK. What do you need to order?
Gloria: I need pencils for the office.
Maritza: Pencils. OK. Type in www.pencilpoint.com. [pause] Now "Go." [pause] Great.
[pause, screen 1]
Gloria: Cool. Look at that.
Maritza: Which kind do you want?
Gloria: Let's see . . . Standard Round is good.

(Tapescript is continued on page T78.)

A. Listening comprehension. Listen to the conversation about ordering supplies online.

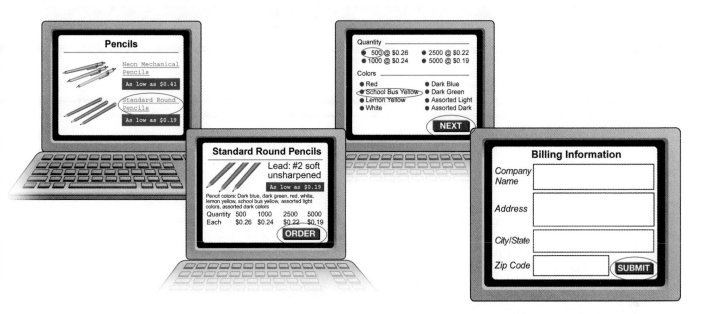

B. Listen again. Circle the item or items on each screen that Gloria clicks on.

C. Answer the questions about Gloria's order.

1. What did she order? _____ Standard Round Pencils _____

2. How many? What color? _____ 500, School Bus Yellow _____

➤ Do it yourself!

A. Write your own response. Then read your conversation out loud with a partner.

Look—Happy Fish tuna costs twice as much as the Deep Blue. But the cans are the same size.

YOU _____

Which one should I buy?

YOU _____

Why?

YOU _____

B. Culture talk. In the country you come from, what is the children's role in choosing foods for the family? Compare cultures with your classmates.

Authentic practice

Unit pricing

A. Read about unit pricing from a consumer information Web site.

Consumer Information

Address: @ http://www.consumerinformation   › go

Using Unit Pricing

Use unit pricing to find the best buys!
It takes some know-how to find the best buys at the supermarket. When shopping for food, you have to consider nutrition, personal tastes, storage space, quality, convenience, and economy. Which product is most economical? Unit pricing helps you compare prices!

What is unit pricing?
Unit pricing is a way to compare prices. The package price tells how much you pay for a food item. The unit price is the price of a "unit" in a package.

A "unit" can be an individual piece, a square foot, an ounce, a pound, or a quart. For example, the unit price shows you the cost of each ounce in a can of tuna. The package price—the price you pay—is the price of the whole can. You can use unit pricing to compare costs of different sizes and brands—without doing arithmetic.

When to use unit pricing
Using unit pricing can help strengthen your food dollar and help you save money. You can use unit pricing to compare costs of any package size or brand of similar items. But remember, unit pricing will not help you compare nutritional value, quality, or convenience, and it can't give you information on family tastes.

Web zone

B. Read the statements about unit pricing. Then check <u>True</u> or <u>False</u>.

		True	False
1.	Unit pricing tells you which product to buy.	☐	☑
2.	Unit pricing can help you compare prices of similar foods in different-size packages.	☑	☐
3.	The unit price is the price of the package.	☐	☑
4.	To get the unit price of a product, you have to do arithmetic.	☐	☑
5.	Unit pricing gives you information about how convenient a product is or whether you will like it.	☐	☑

Tapescript (continued from page T77)

Maritza: Click on that.
[pause, screen 2]
Gloria: Oh, yeah. Those look great. I'll order them.
Maritza: Great. Just click on "Order."
[pause, screen 3]
Gloria: Let's see. How many should I get?
Maritza: Well, the more you order, the cheaper they are.
Gloria: That's true, but what are we going to do with 5000 pencils? We don't have room for all those pencils! Hmmm. . . . there's not that much difference in price between 500 and a thousand. I'll just get 500 this time.
Maritza: OK. Click on "500." . . . Now, color?
Gloria: Oh . . . School Bus Yellow. That sounds cute. I think I'll click on that. Or maybe Assorted Dark would be a better idea. No, on second thought, I'll take all School Bus Yellow.
Maritza: OK. Click on that. Now click "Next."
[pause, screen 4]
Gloria: Just type in the name of the company?
Maritza: Yup.
Gloria: [typing] ABC Oil Company . . . 2200 Main Street . . . Dallas, Texas . . . 75219. That's it?
Maritza: Now click "Submit." Easy as pie.

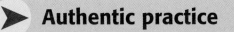

➤ Authentic practice

(For general suggestions, see *Introduction*, page Tx.)

Unit pricing

Procedure:

A. Read about unit pricing . . .

➤ Have students read the first section of text, *Use unit pricing to find the best buys!* Then ask *What are the six things to consider when shopping for food?* (nutrition, personal tastes, storage space, quality, convenience, economy) List these considerations on the board and discuss the meaning of each. Next, on a sheet of paper, have students list these considerations in order of importance to them, the most important one first. Have each student tell which consideration is most important to him or her. Record the results on the board. See which consideration the class identifies as most important.

➤ Have students read the second section of text, *What is unit pricing?* Ask students to explain unit pricing to a partner in their own words.

➤ Have students read the last section of text, *When to use unit pricing.* Then ask the class *What does unit pricing help you do?* (save money, compare costs of any package size or brand of similar items) *What does unit pricing not help you do?* (compare nutritional value, quality, convenience; give you information on family tastes)

Option: Demonstrate the units of measure mentioned in the reading. For example, bring in a square foot of aluminum foil, a pound of flour, and a quart container of milk.

Challenge: Draw a two-column chart on the board with the headings *Noun* and *Adjective*. Under the heading *Noun* write the following words from the reading: *nutrition, taste, space, convenience, economy, information.* In pairs, students fill in the right-hand column of the chart with the adjective forms of each noun: *nutritious / nutritional, tasty, spacious, convenient, economical, informative.* Allow students to use dictionaries, if available, pointing out that they should look for the abbreviation *adj.* After reviewing the adjective forms as a class, have students use each adjective in a comparative sentence, for example, *Apple juice is more nutritious than soda.*

B. Read the statements . . .

➤ After students complete the exercise individually, have them work with a partner to change the false statements to make them true.

C. Discussion ...

➤ Write on the board the six things from the reading on page 78 to consider when shopping for food: *nutrition, personal taste, storage space, quality, convenience, economy.* Have students write the six considerations on a sheet of paper. In groups, students compare the three brands of sauce on each of the considerations and write down the one they would choose based on that consideration alone. For example, for *nutrition*, a student might choose *Healthy Acres* because it doesn't have salt or preservatives.

➤ Have students put stars next to the two considerations that are most important to them. Have them look at their papers and decide which sauce to buy.

➤ Students tell their groups which sauce they chose and why.

➤ Survey the class. For each brand of pasta sauce, have students who chose that brand raise their hand. Tally the results. Have students who chose the most popular brand give reasons why they chose it.

Challenge: In groups, have students create a radio or print advertisement for one of the three brands of pasta sauce. The ads shoud highlight one or more of the six things to consider when shopping for food.

➤ Do it yourself!

(For general suggestions, see *Introduction*, page Txiii.)

Procedure:

A–B.

➤ Preview the activity by asking *Do you buy the products listed? What brand do you usually buy? About how much do you spend? Where do you shop?*

➤ Model the activity by copying the chart headings on the board and listing *pasta sauce* as the first product. Ask the class for the *Brand and package price* of the first jar of sauce in Exercise C (Old World brand $2.76). Then ask for the *Unit price from shelf* for Old World brand sauce ($.23 per ounce).

➤ Ask students to complete the chart on their next trip to the supermarket. Have them find the information for chicken soup, even though it is used as an example.

➤ When students have completed the activity, post four large charts, one for each product, like the one that follows. Ask students to write on the charts the information they found.

Brand of chicken soup	Package price	Unit price from shelf

➤ Divide the class into four groups. Have the groups rotate so that each group has an opportunity to look at and discuss each chart. Groups look at each chart and discuss which brand is the best buy based on the unit price.

Option: To prepare students for the activities on page 80, have them find the unit prices for five additional products of their choice. Then draw on the board a two-column chart with the headings *Product* and *Unit of measure* and have students copy it. Students list the products from their charts in Exercise A and the five additional products they chose. In the right-hand column, students write what units the products were sold in. For example, for *chicken soup*, students write *per fluid ounce*. For *potatoes*, students might write *per pound*.

C. Discussion. Look at the unit price labels for tomato sauce. Compare the products. Then decide which sauce to buy. Explain your answer to a partner or a group.

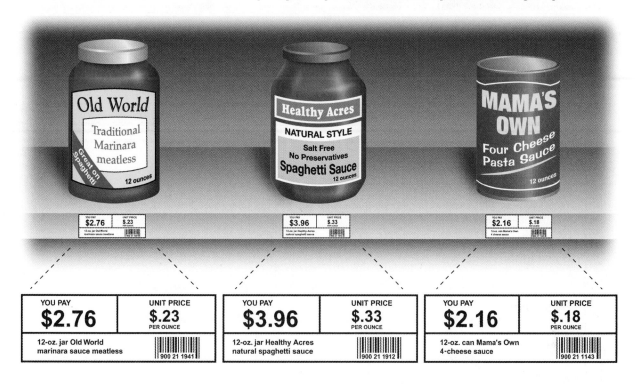

YOU PAY	UNIT PRICE
$2.76	**$.23** PER OUNCE
12-oz. jar Old World marinara sauce meatless	‖‖‖‖‖‖‖‖‖ 900 21 1941

YOU PAY	UNIT PRICE
$3.96	**$.33** PER OUNCE
12-oz. jar Healthy Acres natural spaghetti sauce	‖‖‖‖‖‖‖‖‖ 900 21 1912

YOU PAY	UNIT PRICE
$2.16	**$.18** PER OUNCE
12-oz. can Mama's Own 4-cheese sauce	‖‖‖‖‖‖‖‖‖ 900 21 1143

> ➤ Do it yourself!   A plan-ahead project

A. Go to the store. Choose one example of each product. Look at the package price and the unit price on the shelf. Write them on the chart.

Product	Brand and package price	Unit price from shelf
Chicken soup	*Grandma's brand 89¢*	*$.09 per fluid ounce*
Chicken soup		
Laundry detergent		
Cooking oil		
Rice		

B. Discussion. Compare information with the class.

Authentic practice

Units of measure

A. Read about how to use unit pricing from the Web site.

Consumer Information

Address: @ http://www.consumerinformation

Using Unit Pricing

How do I use unit pricing?
When you compare product prices, compare what you pay per unit instead of what the package price is. You may see different kinds of unit prices.

Unit of measure	Products
By weight	
Ounce, Pound	Solids: canned and packaged goods, frozen foods, produce, meats, poultry
By volume	
Fluid ounce, Pint, Quart, Gallon	Liquids: oils, milk, juices, syrups, soft drinks
Count	
(number of items in the package)	facial tissues, tea bags, trash bags, napkins, soap pads
Square feet	
(area = length x width)	food wrap, paper towels, toilet paper

Where can I find unit pricing?
In the supermarket, look for unit price shelf tags below each product. For example:

YOU PAY	UNIT PRICE
$1.69	**$1.50** PER POUND

18-oz. CRISPY FLAKES
12 0-1098765432 12345678

900 21 1941

Is biggest best?
Not always! In the supermarket, larger sizes are usually more economical than smaller sizes, but not always. You have to consider nutrition, convenience, family tastes, quality, storage space, and economy. So use unit pricing to compare costs. Then choose the size and brand that suit your needs best.

Web zone

B. Collaborative activity. Complete the chart with a group. For each unit of measure, list the products that group members buy. Then compare charts with other groups.

Unit of measure	Products
Ounce	
Pound	
Fluid ounce	
Pint	

Unit of measure	Products
Quart	
Gallon	
Count	
Square feet	

➤ Authentic practice

(For general suggestions, see *Introduction*, page Tx.)

Units of measure

Procedure:

A. Read about how ...

➤ Ask *In the country you come from, how is meat measured? How is juice measured? How is aluminum foil or plastic wrap measured?*

➤ Have students look at the information on the computer screen. Ask *Where are the units of measure listed?* (on the left) *Where are the products listed?* (on the right) Have students scan the reading to find how *meats, juices,* and *food wrap* are measured in the United States (ounces, pounds; fluid ounces, pints, quarts, gallons; square feet)

➤ Demonstrate the meaning of each way of measuring. For *By weight,* hold a heavy object in one hand and a light object in the other. Lower the hand holding the heavy object and ask *Which object weighs more?* For *By volume*, bring in an empty container such as a juice or soft drink bottle. Fill the bottle with water and explain that the volume is the three-dimensional space that the water fills. Read and point out the unit of measure on the label of the bottle, for example, *12 fluid ounces.* For *Count,* bring in an item that is sold by count, such as a box of tea bags. Read and point out on the box the number of tea bags the box contains. Then open the box and take out several tea bags one at a time, counting out loud. For *Square feet,* use a ruler to draw on the board a rectangle that is two feet long and one foot wide. Label the length and the width. Write *2 feet × 1 foot = 2 square feet.* Draw a line down the middle of the rectangle and show how big one square foot is.

➤ Ask about the unit of measure for specific products in the categories listed—such as *apples, vegetable oil*—and for items that are similar to those listed—such as *pork, water, sandwich bags.* You may also want to bring in empty containers to show units of measure on a variety of products.

➤ Ask *Are unit prices usually higher or lower for larger size packages?* (lower) *Is it always a good idea to buy the larger size?* Ask where on the screen students can find information to help them answer this question. (under the heading "Is biggest best?") Have students read this last section independently.

Option: Write on the board a list of several two-dimensional objects that can be found in your classroom; for example, desk tops, the board, the door, the floor, a window. Have students use rulers to practice estimating how many square feet these objects are. When measuring, have students round off to the nearest foot.

B. Collaborative activity ...

➤ This activity will be most successful if students are able to read the units of measure on a variety of product labels. If possible, bring in or have students bring in several empty food and drink containers or supermarket circulars that show units of measure. Before students begin completing their charts, write the units of measure from the chart on the board. Have students look at the containers or circulars and find the abbreviations for each unit of measure. Have volunteers write the abbreviations on the board.

➤ After students have completed their charts, ask *What products are measured in ounces?* Have each group tell one product. Repeat with the other units of measure.

Option: Instead of bringing in empty containers or advertising circulars, take a class trip to the supermarket, or have students complete the chart at home so that they can look at the labels of products in their cupboards to see what units of measure are used.

Option: If it is not convenient or appropriate to bring in containers or circulars or to complete the chart outside of class, students can use the products listed in Exercise A, products from the *Do it yourself!* activity on page 79, and / or products that they and their group members buy that are similar to those in Exercise A or that they know the units of measure for.

If your students are ready ...

Culture / Civics note: The United States remains one of the few countries that has not adopted the metric system as the standard for measurement. Some common traditional-to-metric conversion values include:

1 pound (lb.) = 454 grams (g)
1 ounce (oz.) = 28 g
1 fluid ounce (fl. oz.) = 30 milliliters (ml)
1 pint (pt.) = 473 ml
1 quart (qt.) = 946 ml
1 gallon (gal.) = 3.8 liters (l)
1 square foot (sq. ft.) = 929 square centimeters (sq. cm)

T80

Ordering supplies by mail

Procedure:

A. Look at the order form ...

➤ Ask questions about the order form, such as *What information do you have to provide at the top of the form?* (your name [submitted by], the company's name, the company's address [billing address]) *What can you order using this form?* (binders, clips, pens) If available, show students a binder and some clips. Measure the thickness of the binder and show students what size it is (e.g., one inch, two inches). Point out that the material the binder is made of is vinyl.

➤ Ask questions about the items that can be ordered, such as *How much is a two-inch black vinyl binder?* ($3.39) *How much is a box of mini clips?* ($1.19) *How much are a dozen fine, blue markers?* ($11.99) *What is the item number for the jumbo clips?* (C3401) *What is the item number for the medium, black ballpoint pens?* (P3402)

➤ Have students place a sheet of paper under the row beginning with item *B3401* so that they are looking only at this first row. Ask *What item is this information for?* (a binder) *What is the item number?* (B3401) *What do you think you write under "QTY"?* (how many you want) *How are the binders sold?* (each, individually) *What color is this binder?* (black) *What size is it?* (one inch) *How much does one binder cost?* ($2.39) *If you order two binders, what is the total cost?* ($4.78) If helpful, ask the class similar questions about other rows.

Option: Demonstrate the difference between fine-point and medium-point pens by drawing on the board a thin line and then a thicker line. Show students a ballpoint pen and a marker. Ask students to take out a pen and describe it by color, point size, and type, for example, *I have a blue, medium ballpoint pen.*

B. Discussion ...

➤ Have students find and circle each abbreviation on the form. Have them write the meanings for as many of the abbreviations as they can.

➤ Have students stand up and find a partner to compare answers with. If after comparing with one partner students still don't have all the answers, they find another partner to check answers with.

➤ Review as a class. Then ask *How many items are in a dozen?* (12) *What products are sold by the dozen?* (markers, pens, eggs, doughnuts)

C. Now fill out the order form ...

Challenge: Give groups a budget, such as $350, for ordering supplies. Tell them to order as many supplies as they can without spending more than the specified amount.

➤ Do it yourself!

(For general suggestions, see *Introduction*, page Txiii.)

Procedure:

➤ In groups, students think of one advantage and one disadvantage of each way of buying supplies.

➤ Have students in each group agree on the best way to buy supplies and make an extended list of advantages. Have each group read its list to the class.

Option: As a class, discuss whether the advantages and disadvantages of each way of ordering supplies are different for companies and for individual consumers.

Option: If appropriate, ask the person responsible for ordering supplies for your school or department to visit your class. Have students brainstorm questions to ask before he or she arrives, for example, *How often do you order supplies? What do you order? How are the supplies purchased—at a store, by telephone, by mail, or online? What catalog or Web site do you use? How much can you spend? How much do you pay in shipping costs?*

A. Look at the order form for office supplies.

ℝ Robinson Office Products					Order form

Submitted by _____
ABC Oil Company
Company name

2200 Main Street, Dallas, Texas 75219
Billing address

Item	QTY	UM	Description	Price	Total
BINDERS					
B3401	_	EA	Binder vinyl 1" black	$2.39	_____
B3402	_	EA	Binder vinyl 2" black	$3.39	_____
B3403	_	EA	Binder vinyl 1" white	$2.39	_____
B3404	_	EA	Binder vinyl 2" white	$3.39	_____
CLIPS					
C3401	_	BX	Clips jumbo smooth	$2.29	_____
C3402	_	BX	Clips mini smooth	$1.19	_____
PENS					
P3401	_	DZ	Fine markers blue	$11.99	_____
P3402	_	DZ	Ballpoint medium black	$10.99	_____

B. Discussion. What do the abbreviations mean? Explain to a partner or a group.

1. QTY _____quantity_____
2. UM _____unit of measure_____
3. EA _____each_____
4. BX _____box_____
5. DZ _____dozen_____

C. Now fill out the order form. Order supplies for ABC Oil Company at 2200 Main Street in Dallas, Texas 75219. Choose your supplies and use your <u>own</u> name.

For extra practice, go to page 157.

➤ Do it yourself!

Discussion. How do you buy supplies? First make notes about your ideas on the chart. Then discuss the advantages and disadvantages of each way.

Going to the store	
advantage *You can see the product.*	disadvantage *It takes a lot of time.*
advantage	disadvantage
Ordering by mail from a catalogue	
advantage	disadvantage
Shopping online	
advantage	disadvantage

Review

(For general suggestions, see *Introduction*, page Txii.)

Procedure:

A. Pair work or group work.

Challenge: Have students use the signs on the wall to calculate the unit price for one ounce of Carioca Coffee ($.26), one ounce of Florida's Best Natural Orange Juice (approximately $.04), and one Country Napkins brand napkin (approximately $.01).

Ask and answer questions.

➤ Ask the class general questions about the picture, such as *Where are the people?* (in a grocery store or supermarket) *What employees are in the picture?* (a cashier and a manager) *What are the bargains in this store?* (the five products advertised on the wall and the Nature's Grain bread)

➤ Have students point to people in the picture and ask their partners *What is this person doing?* or *What is he or she buying?* Students can also ask and answer questions about the package prices of different products, for example, *How much is the Cola Cola?* ($3.99 for six cans)

Option: Have students list all the products that they can see in the picture or that are advertised on the wall. Students write the unit of measure next to each product, for example, *Salerno Spaghetti—pound.* For some products, students will need to speculate about the unit of measure based on the information on page 80 or their own experience; for example, *Nature's Grain bread—ounce.* Then have partners compare answers by asking each other *What is the unit of measure for . . . ?*

Create conversations.

➤ In pairs, have students create a conversation for either the manager and woman shaking hands under the *Help Wanted* sign, the two customers looking at the signs on the wall, the cashier and the customer who is paying, or the customer who is paying and her son. Have students label the pair they choose *A* and *B*. Students write their conversations in the same format as the model conversations.

➤ Pairs copy each line of their conversations onto a slip of paper, mix up the order of the slips, and give them to another pair. The other pair must then put the conversation back in the correct order.

➤ Each pair reads the conversation they put in order to the pair who wrote the conversation and guesses who is being portrayed.

Tell a story.

Option: Draw conclusions. Have students look at what the woman who is paying bought and talk about what meal each product *must be* for, for example, *The milk and cereal must be for breakfast.*

Option: Give a tour. Have students imagine that they are the store's manager. Explain that the woman in the red jacket wants to apply for the job as assistant manager. They should take her on a tour of the store, describing what is sold, where things are, and what this week's bargains are. They can also introduce her to the cashier and tell her about pay, hours, expectations, and so on. Encourage students to say as much as they can.

🎧 B. Listen to the conversation . . .

➤ Tell students that they are going to listen to a conversation about ordering supplies.

➤ After students listen to the conversation the first time, have them read the statements so that they will know what to listen for.

➤ Allow students to listen to the conversation as many times as necessary to complete the exercise. Review the answers as a class. Then have students change the false statements to make them true.

Option: Have students imagine that they are the employee who takes orders at 1-800-AUTOFIX. Students listen again and write down the product, the model year, the 15-digit code number from the back of the catalog, the quantity, and the charge for overnight delivery.

C–F.

➤ Students work individually to complete the review exercises.

➤ Circulate to offer help as needed.

➤ Have students check answers with a partner. Review answers as a class.

➤ Identify any areas of difficulty that may require additional instruction and practice.

Tapescript

Man 1: Did you order those hoses? I'm almost out, and next week I've got five Monsoon customers coming in with defective air conditioners. It's the same old story. That Monsoon ventilation system's a lemon.

Man 2: You can say *that* again. Well, I totally forgot. And now there's no way to get an order here in time.

Man 1: Well, I have this catalog from 1-800-AUTOFIX. I think they'll overnight stuff. It costs a little more, but it's worth it.

Man 2: Let's check it out. Hand me that catalog. . . . Let's see. Monsoon, 2000 model, ventilator hose. Great. Here it is. I'll call.

[touchtone sounds]

Lorraine: Hello. 1-800-AUTOFIX, fast service, low prices. This is Lorraine. How can I help you?

Man 2: I need to order Monsoon ventilator hoses, 2000 model year.

Lorraine: OK, sir. Could you please read me the 15-digit code number on the back of the catalog?

Man 2: [turning pages] Sure. 0-6778934-3321-456.

Lorraine: OK. What quantity were you looking for? The more you buy, the cheaper they are.

Man 2: Let's see. I'll take two dozen.

Lorraine: OK. And can we send that by regular mail? That takes approximately ten business days.

Man 2: Actually, no. I need overnight delivery. How much will that cost?

Lorraine: Overnight delivery is $18.99. Do you want us to send it overnight?

Man 2: Yes. I need them right away.

Lorraine: Would you like to order something else? The delivery charge would be the same.

Man 2: No, thanks. That's all I need to order today.

B. Listen to the conversation about ordering supplies. Read the statements and listen again. Check **True** or **False**.

		True	False
1.	The men repair car air conditioners.	☑	☐
2.	They can't fix the problem because they don't have enough parts.	☑	☐
3.	They order hoses online.	☐	☑
4.	The company is going to send the parts by regular mail.	☐	☑
5.	The man orders more parts because delivery is a bargain.	☐	☑

C. Match the abbreviation with the word. Write the letter on the line.

1. __b__ DZ   **a.** quantity

2. __d__ EA   **b.** one dozen (12)

3. __c__ UM   **c.** unit of measure

4. __a__ QTY   **d.** each

D. Write the name of each kind of package.

1. _____a box_____   2. ___a container___   3. _____a can_____   4. ___a package___

E. Write a response to each statement.

1. "I have no time to go to the store."

   _____

2. "What a bargain!"

   _____

F. Write a conclusion with **must**.

1. Jose Antonio always buys milk in two-gallon containers.

   _____

2. Look at this huge box. What's in it?

   _____

3. Claire wants to be a teacher.

   _____

G. Complete each exclamation with <u>What</u>.

1. _____ can of soup! How much does it cost?
   big

2. _____ food. Let's eat here again.
   wonderful

H. Choose the correct answer to each question about unit pricing. Fill in the ovals.

1. What does unit pricing tell you?

   ⓐ Which product to buy.

   ⓑ The cost of each unit of a product.

2. What is the advantage of unit pricing?

   ⓐ It helps you compare prices of products in different-size containers.

   ⓑ It tells you the package price.

3. What CANNOT be learned from a unit price?

   ⓐ The price of a unit of the product.

   ⓑ The best product.

I. Which peaches have the lower unit price? Fill in the oval.

ⓐ Orchard's Pride   ⓑ Tasty Fruit

YOU PAY	UNIT PRICE
$2.49	**$.21** per fluid ounce
12-oz. can Orchard's Pride cling peaches in heavy syrup	900 42 0818

YOU PAY	UNIT PRICE
$2.99	**$.18** per fluid ounce
17-oz. can Tasty Fruit cling peaches in heavy syrup	900 21 1912

J. Composition. On a separate sheet of paper, write about the picture on page 82. Say as much as you can.

> **Now I can**
> ❏ determine the best buy.
> ❏ talk about bargains.
> ❏ order supplies online and by phone.
> ❏ understand and use unit pricing.
> ❏ _____.

G–I.

➤ Students work individually to complete the review exercises.

➤ Circulate to offer help as needed.

➤ Have students check answers with a partner. Review answers as a class.

➤ Identify any areas of difficulty that may require additional instruction and practice.

J. Composition . . .

➤ Provide students with concrete approaches to writing about the picture on page 82. Use one of the following options, give students a choice of options, or assign options based on students' levels of proficiency. Model what is expected of students for each option.

➤ Advise students to look back through the unit for help and ideas as they write.

➤ Circulate to offer help as needed.

Option: Have students write the shopping list of the woman who is paying for her groceries; for example, *spaghetti, bread, cereal.*

Option: Have students write a job announcement for the assistant manager position. Have them include as much information as possible, such as hours, shifts, pay, overtime pay, expectations, skills.

Option: One person in a group begins by writing a sentence about the picture on a sheet of paper. This person then passes the sheet of paper to the person on his or her right, who reads what is written and adds another sentence. If a student can't think of a new sentence, the group can help, but he or she must be the one to write the sentence. Groups continue passing the sheet of paper and adding sentences until they can no longer write anything new.

Now I can

➤ Read the first item in the box out loud, *Now I can determine the best buy.* Elicit from the class an example of how to determine the best buy, such as *It's easy to compare prices and find the best buy if you look at the unit price labels.*

➤ In pairs, have students take turns reading each item in the box and giving an example of what they have learned. When students can provide an example, they should check that objective. For the items students weren't able to check, they should look back through the unit for ideas.

➤ When students are finished reviewing with their partners, read each item out loud and elicit an example from the class.

Oral test (optional)

You may want to use the *Now I can* box as an informal evaluation. While students are working on the *Composition* activity, you can call them up individually and check their ability with two or three objectives.

Relationships

➤ Preview

(For general suggestions, see *Introduction*, page Tviii.)

Warm up. What's the problem?

Procedure:

➤ Ask questions about the picture, such as *What do the signs say?* (No parking between signs, No parking Monday through Friday 6:00 a.m. to 6:00 p.m.) *What's the problem in the picture?* (A car is parked between the "No parking" signs.) *What's the police officer doing?* (writing a ticket)

➤ To access students' prior experience, ask *Have you or has anyone in your family gotten a parking ticket? Why? How much did you have to pay? What are the parking restrictions in your neighborhood? Near your work? Near the school?*

Field project: If appropriate, have students look at parking signs in the neighborhood around your school. Have students note street names and rules. Set a time limit, such as 15 minutes. When students return to class, have them work in groups to write sentences on chart paper explaining the parking rules in the area, for example, *You can't park on New Street between 6:00 a.m. and 8:00 a.m. and between 4:00 p.m. and 6:00 p.m.* Have each group present to the class its rules about parking near the school.

Unit 7 objectives

Procedure:

➤ Read the objectives. For each objective, discuss the meaning of any unfamiliar words and then elicit examples from students. For example, for *Ask about and understand rules and laws,* students might say *Can I park here?* or *You can't park on New Street between 6:00 a.m. and 8:00 a.m. and between 4:00 p.m. and 6:00 p.m.* When the class can't think of an example, provide one; for example, for *Ask someone to be more considerate,* say *Could you please turn down the TV? It's too loud. I can't sleep.*

➤ As a class, identify situations that call for apologizing, making small talk, offering congratulations, and expressing sympathy.

➤ Have students underline the two objectives that are most useful or interesting to them. Have students tell a partner why they chose those two objectives.

Relationships

> **Preview**

Warm up. What's the problem?

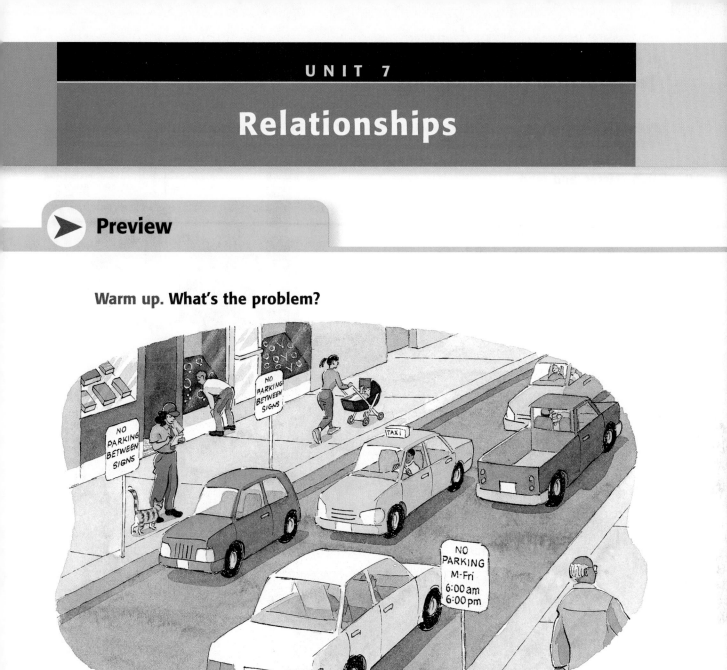

Unit 7 objectives

- Ask about and understand rules and laws.
- Ask someone to be more considerate.
- Apologize for inconsiderate behavior.
- Understand personal responsibility to know and obey rules and laws.
- Make small talk.
- Congratulate someone on good news.
- Express sympathy and offer to help.

| Model 1 | Ask someone to be more considerate. Apologize for your behavior. |

🎧 **A.** **Listen and read.**

> A: Excuse me. Would it be possible for you to turn down the music? It's after 11:00.
> B: Oh, I'm sorry. I didn't realize that.
> A: Thanks. I appreciate it.
> B: You're welcome.

🎧 **B.** **Listen again and repeat.**

🎧 **Vocabulary**

Difficult requests

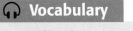

 to turn down the music

 to park somewhere else

 to get off the phone

 to put out the cigarette

 to move the truck

 to close the window

C. **Pair work.** **Ask someone to do something. Use the vocabulary and the reasons in the box. Or use your _own_ reasons.**

I can't get into my driveway.	It's very cold in here.
It's too loud to work.	I'm having trouble sleeping.
That's my parking space.	I'm allergic to smoke.
I'm waiting for an important call.	It's really late.

> A: Excuse me. Would it be possible for you to _____? _____.
> B: Oh, I'm sorry. I didn't realize that.
> A: ____1____.
> B: ____2____.

[1]Thanks so much [2]Not at all, No problem

➤ Practical conversations

(For general suggestions, see *Introduction*, page Tviii.)

Model 1

Content: asking someone to be more considerate; giving a reason for the request; apologizing for inconsiderate behavior

Procedure:

🎧 A–B.

➤ To set the scene for the conversation, ask questions about the photo, such as *Are these men the same age?* (No. The man is on the left is older.) *What is happening in the photo?* (The older man is at the door. The younger man is answering the door.) *What gesture is the older man making with his hand?* (Students should imitate the gesture.) *What does the gesture mean?* (to keep the noise down)

➤ After students listen to the conversation, check comprehension by asking *What time is it?* (after 11:00) *What does the older man ask the younger man to do?* (to turn down the music) *How does the younger man respond?* (He apologizes, or says he's sorry.)

➤ In groups, have students brainstorm problems with neighbors, such as *loud parties, arguments, barking dogs, not taking care of the yard*. Draw on the board a three-column chart with the headings *Inconsiderate behavior, Request,* and *Reason*. Have each group write one of their problems on the board under the heading *Inconsiderate behavior*.

🎧 Vocabulary

➤ After students listen to and repeat the vocabulary, have them look at the chart on the board. For each problem students listed under *Inconsiderate behavior*, brainstorm a request for someone to be more considerate and write it under *Request* in the second column. For example, for *loud parties*, you could ask someone *to turn down the music* or *to keep the noise down*.

➤ Read each request the class generated and have students repeat.

C. Pair work ...

➤ Have volunteers read the reasons in the box out loud. Elicit or explain the meanings of *driveway* and *allergic*. If necessary, draw on the board and explain *driveway* as the place for cars between a house and the street. For *allergic*, point to the cigarette on page 86 and / or the cat on page 85 and pretend to sneeze.

➤ Have students match each request from the *Vocabulary* box with a reason. Point out that there is more than one possible reason for each request. To review, call on students and ask *Why do you want me ... ?* and complete the question with one of the requests from the *Vocabulary* box. Students answer with one of the reasons from the box in Exercise C, for example, *Why do you want me to turn down the music?* (It's too loud to work.)

➤ Have students look at the chart on the board. Brainstorm a reason for each request and write it in the third column under *Reason*. For example, for *to turn down the music*, students might say *I can't sleep* or *I have a job interview tomorrow morning*.

➤ Point out that in the first line of the conversation, Student A should use a request and a reason from page 86 or from the board.

Option: As a class, discuss polite ways to ask someone to be more considerate. Copy on the board the model conversation, in which the man asks his neighbor to be more considerate about noise. Ask students to identify polite language that Speaker A uses to express his complaint. Underline this language and point out that the man begins with a polite apology (*Excuse me*); phrases his complaint as a request, not as a demand (*Would it be possible for you to turn down the music?* instead of *Turn down the music*); offers a reason for his complaint (*It's after 11:00*); and expresses his appreciation when the man agrees to turn down the music (*Thanks. I appreciate it*).

If your students are ready ...

Language note: *Would it be possible for you to ... ?* is a very polite way to make a request. *Would you mind _____ ing ... ?, Could you (please) ... ?,* and *Can you ... ?* can also be used to ask someone to do something. When making a difficult request of someone you don't know very well, *Would it be possible for you to ... ?* is most appropriate.

Culture / Civics note: Americans and Canadians generally expect consideration from others and feel entitled to speak up when a friend, acquaintance, neighbor, or even a stranger is behaving inconsiderately. Because considerable value is placed on preserving harmony in interpersonal relationships, complaints are usually made in a calm, non-confrontational, friendly manner.

T86

Model 2

Content: asking about rules and laws; admitting that you're not sure; making a suggestion to ask someone else; impersonal *it*

Procedure:

🎧 A–B.

➤ Have students cover up the conversation and describe the photos in pairs. One partner says as much as he or she can about the larger, square photo. The other partner says as much as he or she can about the round photo. For example, for the square photo, a student might say *An older woman is driving the car. She is asking a younger woman a question. The younger woman is pointing to a man . . .*

➤ Ask *What do you think the woman in the car is asking? Have you ever asked someone for information while driving? Who did you ask? How did you get the person's attention? What did you want to know?*

➤ After students listen to the conversation, ask questions such as *What does the woman in the car want to know?* (if it's legal to park there) *Does the woman on the right know?* (She's not sure.) *Does the man know?* (He thinks it's OK, but he's not really sure.)

➤ Have students underline *to tell you the truth* and *as far as I know* in the conversation. Explain that *to tell you the truth* is used when admitting something. The woman in the street admits that she doesn't know the answer to the driver's question. Explain that *as far as I know* is used when you think something is true, but you are not sure.

🎧 To say you're not sure

➤ After students listen to and repeat the phrases, write the phrases on the board from left to right in the following order: *I'm not positive, I'm not sure, I don't know, I have no idea.* Point out that *I'm not positive* and *I'm not sure* indicate that you have some knowledge of a situation and can make a guess about the answer to a question, while *I don't know* and *I have no idea* indicate that you know nothing about a situation and can't even make a guess.

🎧 Vocabulary

➤ After students listen to and repeat the vocabulary, discuss whether or not it's legal in your community *to let a dog off the leash* and *to make a right turn on red.* Discuss any special provisions. For example, there may be certain parks where dogs are allowed to run free, or you may be able to make a right turn on red unless it's posted that you can't.

➤ Brainstorm and write on the board other things that might be against the rules or the law in your community, such as *to use a cell phone while driving* or *to ride a bicycle or motorcycle without a helmet.*

C. Group work . . .

➤ Model the conversation with two more advanced students. Play the role of Student A. Demonstrate repeating the same possibly illegal activity in Student A's second line. If necessary, prompt Student B to use a phrase from the yellow language note for the first blank and to use *him, her,* or Student C's name in the second blank. Turn toward Student C when you read Student A's second line.

➤ Have students practice the conversation in groups of three. Have volunteers act out their conversations in front of the class.

➤ Do it yourself!

(For general suggestions, see *Introduction,* page Txiii.)

Procedure:

➤ Write on the board several statements beginning with *It's illegal here,* for example, *It's illegal here to smoke in any public building* or *It's illegal here to ride in a car and not wear a seatbelt.* Write some statements that are true for your community or state and some that are false. In groups, students read and discuss each statement, deciding whether they think it's true or false.

➤ Groups report their answers for each statement. Discuss the correct answers as a class. Then students complete the exercise, listing things they were surprised to learn are illegal here.

Option: Students form groups with other students from the same country. Together they make a list of things that the class might be surprised to learn are illegal in their country. Groups read their lists to the class.

Field project: Brainstorm and write on the board a list of questions about local rules and laws. Have students begin their questions with *Is it legal to . . . ?* They might say, for example, *Is it legal to make a right turn on red? Is it legal to burn trash or leaves? Is it legal to smoke in restaurants?* Depending on the number of questions generated, assign one question per student or one question to every few students. Explain that students should try to find an answer to their question by the next class meeting. Suggest that students ask neighbors, co-workers, community members, or school staff.

A. Listen and read.

A: Excuse me. Is it legal to park here?

B: Well, to tell you the truth, I'm not sure. Why don't you ask him?

A: Excuse me. Is it OK to park here?

C: As far as I know, it is.

B. Listen again and repeat.

To say you're not sure

I'm not sure.
I don't know.
I have no idea.
I'm not positive.

Vocabulary

Things that might be against the rules or the law

to put the trash cans here   to let a dog off the leash   to make a right turn on red

C. Group work. Ask two people about rules or the law. Use the vocabulary or your own question about rules or the law.

A: _____1_____. Is it legal to _____?

B: Well, to tell you the truth, _____. Why don't you ask _____?

A: _____. Is it OK for me to _____?

C: As far as I know, it is.

¹I was wondering

➤ Do it yourself!

Collaborative activity. Make a list of things you were surprised to learn are illegal here. Then discuss your list with other groups.

It's illegal here to let a dog off the leash.

_____

_____

_____

Practical conversations

Model 3   Make small talk. Talk about good news.

A. Listen and read.

A: Hey, Steve. How are things?

B: Pretty good. What about you?

A: Great, actually. I just got engaged.

B: Congratulations. I'm really happy to hear that.

B. Listen again and repeat.

To start a conversation

How are things?	How are you?
How's it going?	What's up?
How're you doing?	What's new?

Vocabulary

Happy occasions

get engaged   get married   have a baby   have a grandchild get a promotion

C. Pair work. Make small talk about a happy event in your life or the life of a relative. Use the vocabulary or your <u>own</u> happy event.

A: Hey, _____. _____?

B: ____1____. What about you?

A: Great, actually. _____.

B: Congratulations. I'm really happy to hear that.

[1]OK, Fantastic

→ Practical conversations

(For general suggestions, see *Introduction*, page Tviii.)

Model 3

Content: starting a conversation; making small talk; talking about good news; using *just* to talk about something that happened very recently

Procedure:

🎧 A–B.

➤ Ask questions about the photo, such as *What are the two men doing?* (talking, smiling) *How do they feel?* (happy)

➤ After students listen to the conversation, ask questions such as *Which man is Steve?* (the man on the right) *What good news does the man on the left have?* (He just got engaged.)

🎧 To start a conversation

➤ After students listen to and repeat the questions, point out that some ways to start a conversation are less formal than others. *How are you?* and *How are you doing?* are more appropriate than *What's up?* or *How's it going?* when you don't know the person you are speaking to very well.

🎧 Vocabulary

➤ After students listen to and repeat the phrases, ask them to circle the occasions they have experienced themselves. Have them put a star next to any occasion that they experienced recently. Then have students note below the photos any family members who have recently experienced these happy events.

➤ Ask students if they or their family members have recently experienced any other happy occasions, for example, *graduate, get a new job, buy a new home*. Write these occasions on the board.

C. Pair work . . .

➤ Elicit the past tense of the happy occasions listed in the book and on the board, for example, *got engaged, had a baby, graduated*.

➤ Model the activity with a more advanced student. Play the role of Student A. Demonstrate using one of the questions from the yellow language note in Student A's first line. For Student A's second line, talk about a happy event in the life of a relative; for example, say *My sister-in-law just had a baby*.

➤ Have students walk around the room and practice the conversation with at least two different partners.

Option: Ask students to bring in photos of happy occasions in their lives, such as weddings, birthdays, and graduations. In groups, students show and talk about their photos, for example, *This is when I got married, This is when my daughter graduated from high school*. Encourage students to say as much as they can about each photo. Model the activity by showing and talking about photos of happy events in your life.

Challenge: In groups, have students compare engagement and marriage customs in their home countries. Then ask students what they know about engagement and marriage customs in North America and discuss as a class.

Field project: If appropriate, have students go to a stationery store or any store with a large selection of greeting cards. Ask students to make a list of happy and unhappy occasions that they find greeting cards for. Have students look for a card for each of the happy occasions in the *Vocabulary* box. Students write down the happy occasion and, next to it, one line from the card that they understand and might use to congratulate someone on good news. When students return to class, have volunteers read the lines they wrote down for each occasion. As a class, discuss the meaning and / or appropriateness of each.

Model 4

Content: asking about how someone feels; talking about bad news; offering sympathy and help

Procedure:

🎧 A–B.

➤ Have students look at the photo and speculate about how the woman on the right feels and why she feels this way.

➤ After students listen to the conversation, point to the woman on the right and ask *What is her bad news?* (Her sister and brother-in-law are getting a divorce.)

➤ In pairs, have students discuss who they feel comfortable talking to when they have bad news.

Option: Under the heading *Language expression*, write the sentences from the conversation on the board separately: *You look upset; Is there anything wrong?; Well, actually, my sister and brother-in-law are getting a divorce; Oh, I'm so sorry to hear that; Is there anything I can do?;* and *Not really. But thanks for offering.* Under the heading *Purpose*, write, in random order, what the different sentences in the conversation accomplish: *Notice someone's feelings, Ask about how someone feels, Tell bad news, Express sympathy, Offer help, Express thanks.* Students match each language expression with its purpose.

🎧 Unhappy feelings

➤ After students listen to and repeat the words, explain that they are all ways that you feel when something bad has happened to you or to someone else.

➤ Ask *When do you feel unhappy?* Elicit a variety of responses from the class.

🎧 Vocabulary

➤ After students listen to and repeat the vocabulary, ask them to think about an unhappy event in their lives or in the life of a family member or friend. Elicit examples from a couple of volunteers.

➤ If students or their family members have recently experienced any other unhappy occasions, such as *break up with a boyfriend or girlfriend, have an illness in the family,* write them on the board.

Note: *Get divorced* has the same meaning as *get a divorce.*

C. Pair work . . .

➤ Elicit the past tense of the unhappy occasions listed in the book and on the board, for example, *had a death in the family, got separated, lost a job.* Point

out that if a separation or divorce is in process, students should say *is / are getting separated* or *getting divorced,* as in the model conversation.

➤ Model the activity with a more advanced student. Play the role of Student B. If necessary, prompt Student A to choose an unhappy feeling from the yellow language note. For Student B's first line, talk about an unhappy event in the life of a friend or family member, for example, *My husband lost his job.* For Student B's second line, point out that *But* in the next sentence indicates that a negative response is needed in the blank.

➤ Do it yourself!

(For general suggestions, see *Introduction*, page Txiii.)

Procedure:

➤ Ask questions about the picture, such as *What is the man thinking about?* (the death of a family member or friend) *How does he probably feel?* (upset, down, sad, depressed) *What can the woman say to express sympathy?* (I'm so sorry to hear that.) *To offer help?* (Is there anything I can do?)

➤ Students create a conversation for the man and the woman. Have volunteers role-play their conversations for the class.

Challenge: In diverse groups, have students compare customs surrounding death in their home countries. Then ask students what they know about how death is dealt with in North America and discuss as a class.

If your students are ready . . .

Culture / Civics note: Funeral rituals and mourning etiquette differ greatly in ethnically diverse North America. Generally speaking, however, expressions of condolence and offers of support are appropriate and appreciated. When learning that someone has suffered a loss, it is common to express sympathy by saying *I'm so sorry.* Sending a short, handwritten letter or a card with a few personal words, giving flowers, or making a charitable donation in the name of the deceased are also common. In addition, offers of help—such as bringing meals, baby-sitting children, or caring for pets—are welcome gestures. The funeral may be for family members only or open to the public. Death announcements are usually printed in the local newspaper. If the hours and location of the funeral are printed, then anyone wishing to pay their respects may attend.

A. **Listen and read.**

A: You look upset. Is there anything wrong?

B: Well, actually, my sister and my brother-in-law are getting a divorce.

A: Oh, I'm so sorry to hear that. Is there anything I can do?

B: Not really. But thanks for offering. I appreciate it.

B. **Listen again and repeat.**

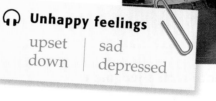

Unhappy feelings

| upset | sad |
| down | depressed |

Vocabulary

Unhappy occasions

have a death in the family

get separated

get a divorce

get laid off *or* lose a job

C. Pair work. **Talk about an unhappy event. Offer sympathy and help.**

A: You look _____. Is there anything wrong?

B: Well, actually, _____.

A: Oh, I'm so sorry to hear that. Is there anything I can do?

B: _____. But thanks for offering. I appreciate it.

➤ Do it yourself!

Pair work. **Create a conversation for the people. Say as much as you can.**

Impersonal it

It's wrong to throw trash on the ground.

Oh, I'm sorry.

Express judgments with <u>It is</u> + an adjective and an infinitive. Here are some adjectives of judgment:

polite	right	inconvenient
impolite	great	possible
rude	hard	impossible
important	easy	good
wrong	convenient	bad

A. **Complete each sentence with a judgment.**

1. ___It's___ bad ____to be____ rude to your neighbors.
    <small>be</small>

2. ___It's___ important ____to learn____ all the rules.
    <small>learn</small>

3. ___It's___ rude ____to play____ music too loud.
    <small>play</small>

4. ___It's___ wrong ____to put____ trash on the street.
    <small>put</small>

5. ___It's___ very convenient ____to park____ in your own driveway.
    <small>park</small>

6. ___It's___ not difficult ____to get____ a promotion here.
    <small>get</small>

B. **Write a question from the cues. Then ask your partner each question. Your partner answers in his or her own words.**

1. legal / park in a bus stop?

    A: _Is it legal to park in a bus stop?_

    B: _____

2. possible / get a divorce in all countries?

    A: Is it possible to get a divorce in all countries?

    B: _____

3. easy / ask your neighbor to move his or her car?

    A: Is it easy to ask your neighbor to move his or her car?

    B: _____

➤ Practical grammar

(For general suggestions, see *Introduction,* page Tix.)

Impersonal *it*

Content: expressing judgments with *It is* + an adjective and an infinitive

Procedure:

➤ Read the adjectives in the grammar box and have students repeat. Review the meanings of any that are unfamiliar. If necessary, provide simple definitions; for example, *polite* is acting or speaking in a way that is appropriate or correct for the social situation you are in.

➤ Draw on the board a two-column chart with the headings *Positive (+) judgments* and *Negative (–) judgments.* In pairs, have students decide which column of the chart each adjective belongs in; for example, *polite* should be written under *Positive (+) judgments* and *impolite* under *Negative (–) judgments.*

➤ Have students look at the picture. Ask two volunteers to read the speech balloons. Write on the board *It's wrong to throw trash on the ground.* Ask *Who says this?* (a mother, or a baby-sitter) *Who does she say it to?* (a child) Have a volunteer read the explanation in the grammar box. Point to the sentence on the board. Underline *It's* and then ask *What's the adjective?* (wrong) *What's the infinitive?* (to throw) Underline and label *wrong* and *to throw.*

➤ Have groups create four original sentences using *It is* + an adjective from the box and an infinitive, for example, *It is important to understand rules and laws.* Remind students that an *infinitive* is *to* + the base form of a verb. Groups choose one of their sentences to read to the class. After each group reads its sentence, have students who agree with the judgment raise their hands, and then have students who disagree raise their hands.

Option: Have students match each adjective with its opposite. Elicit the pairs of opposites from the class and write them on the board: *polite—impolite, rude; right—wrong; easy—hard; convenient—inconvenient; possible—impossible; good—bad.* As a class, come up with opposites for *great* and *important,* such as *terrible* and *unimportant.* Point out that some opposites are formed by adding *im-, in-, un-,* or *il- (illegal)* to the beginning of the original word.

A. Complete each sentence . . .

Option: After students complete the exercise, introduce the terms *strongly agree, agree, disagree,* and *strongly disagree.* Have students read items 1 through 5 again, decide how they feel about each one, and write one of the new terms to the right of each sentence. Then students read each sentence to a partner, checking their answers, and discuss how strongly they agree or disagree with each judgment.

B. Write a question . . .

➤ Have groups change the four original sentences they wrote previously into questions by reversing the order of *it* and *is* and adding question marks, for example, *Is it important to understand rules and laws?* Each group reads one of its questions (not the same one read earlier in statement form) and calls on another group to answer.

➤ For items 1 through 5, students use the cues to write questions.

➤ Before students ask and answer the questions with a partner, review ways students can say that they're not sure by having them look back at the yellow language note on page 87. Point out that students can preface their answers with *To tell you the truth* and can also use *As far as I know, it is.*

Option: For further practice, have students rewrite the statements in Exercise A as questions and then ask and answer the questions with a partner. For example, for item 1, Student A asks *Is it bad to be rude to your neighbors?* Student B might respond *Yes, it's terrible to be rude to your neighbors.*

If your students are ready . . .

Culture / Civics note: Littering—or leaving pieces of paper, garbage, or other waste material in a public place—is not acceptable in the United States and Canada. It is also illegal, and those caught littering can be given large fines. Waste material should be placed in trash receptacles provided in most public parks, city streets, and buildings. In many cities, pet owners must clean up any mess that their pets leave in public areas.

C. Rewrite each sentence ...

➤ If helpful, point out that each sentence begins with a gerund, or -*ing* word. Remind students that they used gerunds to talk about their skills, likes, and dislikes in Unit 1. Write on the board *I'm good at working with people,* and then underline *working with people* and label it *gerund.*

➤ Write item 1 on the board and circle *illegal.* Then have students circle the adjectives in items 2 through 5. Point to the underlined gerund in item 1. Explain that in each item students will change the gerund to an infinitive. Cross out *Parking here* and write *to park here* above it. Write on the board *It's +* (adjective) *+ infinitive.* Elicit from the class the answer to item 1, *It's illegal to park here.*

Option: Have students rewrite the sentences from Exercise A on page 90 so that they begin with a gerund and end with the adjective, for example, *Being rude to your neighbors is bad.*

Challenge: Have students rewrite the questions from Exercise B on pages 90 and 91 using a gerund instead of an infinitive, for example, *Is parking in a bus stop legal?*

➤ Do it yourself!

(For general suggestions, see *Introduction,* page Txiii.)

Procedure:

A–B.

➤ Make sure that students understand the difference between customs and laws. Explain that a *custom* is something that is done in a particular society because it is traditional. A *law* is a rule that people in a particular country, city, or state must obey or follow. Write on the board *not asking a co-worker about salary or religion* and *walking across the street in an area that is not marked for walking.* Have student read the examples. Then ask *Which one is a custom in this country?* (not asking a co-worker about salary or religion) *Which one is against the law?* (jaywalking)

➤ Have students work in groups with classmates from the same or similar backgrounds. Draw on the board two two-column charts, one for *Customs* and one for *Laws.* On each chart, write the headings *My country* and *This country.* Have each group copy the charts. To provide a model, write *OK to ask a co-worker about salary or religion* under *My country* on the *Customs* chart. Write *impolite to ask those questions* under *This country* on the same chart. On the *Laws* chart, write *legal to cross the street wherever you want* under *My country* and *against the law to jaywalk* under *This country.* Groups fill in their charts with differences between their home country and this country in customs and laws.

➤ Students use one idea from each of their group's charts to complete Exercise A.

➤ If possible, have each group join another group of students from a different cultural background. Groups present their charts to each other and discuss.

Option: For extra practice comparing customs and laws, have students look at the recycling poster on page 158 and then compare recycling practices and regulations in their home countries and here.

Challenge: Have students use their group's charts to write one paragraph comparing customs and one paragraph comparing laws in their country and this country.

Field project: Have students pick up a driver's manual from the local department of motor vehicles. Have students scan the booklets for traffic rules that are different from those in their countries. If helpful, divide the pages among groups of students. Have each group post a list of traffic and / or parking laws that newcomers might not know.

4. wrong / let your dog off the leash?

   A: Is it wrong to let your dog off the leash?

   B: _____

5. good / get married when you're very young?

   A: Is it good to get married when you're very young?

   B: _____

C. Rewrite each sentence. Express the ideas in another way.

1. Parking here is illegal. *It's illegal to park here.*

2. Playing music late at night is rude. It's rude to play music late at night.

   _____

3. Getting a divorce is terrible. It's terrible to get a divorce.

   _____

4. Is driving a truck hard? Is it hard to drive a truck?

   _____

5. Was calling my supervisor at home impolite? Was it impolite to call my supervisor

   at home?

➤ Do it yourself!

A. Personalization. Compare customs and laws in your country and in this country.

Custom	*In my country, it's OK to ask a co-worker about salary or religion. In this country, those questions are impolite.*
Law	*In my country, it's legal to cross the street wherever you want. Here, jaywalking is against the law.*
Custom	_____
	_____
Law	_____
	_____
	_____

B. Discussion. Compare customs and laws with your classmates. How are they different?

For extra practice, go to page 158.

Authentic practice

🎧 **A.** **Read and listen again. Choose the word or phrase closer in meaning to the underlined word or phrase. Fill in the ovals.**

1. "Listen to that <u>racket</u>."

   ⓐ work   ● noise

2. "Why don't you just ask them <u>to keep it down</u>?"

   ● to talk less loudly   ⓑ to make noise

3. "I'm sure they don't even realize <u>they're bothering you</u>."

   ⓐ they're helping you   ● they're making it difficult for you

4. "Could I ask you two <u>a big favor</u>?"

   ● to do something for me   ⓑ a question

🎧 **B.** **Listen. Underline your response.**

1. **YOU** I have no idea.   **YOU** <u>Yes. Would it be possible for you to close the door?</u>

2. **YOU** As far as I know it is.   **YOU** <u>Are you sure?</u>

3. **YOU** <u>I'm sorry. I didn't realize that.</u>   **YOU** I'm glad to hear that.

🎧 **C.** **Listen again. Read your response out loud.**

➤ Authentic practice

(For general suggestions, see *Introduction*, page Tx.)

Procedure:

🎧

➤ Ask *Is there anything that your co-workers do that bothers you or makes it difficult for you to get your work done?* Note one or two students' situations on the board, for example, *The person who works the afternoon shift is always late. I can't leave until she arrives, so my kids are home alone after school.*

➤ After students listen to and read the picture story, check comprehension by asking questions such as *Who has a problem?* (the woman wearing a gray sweater) *What's the problem?* (She can't work because there's too much talking.) *What suggestion does her co-worker make?* (asking Jim and Marie to keep it down, asking them to close the door) *How do Jim and Marie react when she asks them to close the door?* (They say they're sorry, say they had no idea they were bothering her, say they're glad she spoke up.)

➤ Ask *Is it rude to speak up at work when something is bothering you?* (no, as long as you are polite about it) Have students find and underline in the picture story the polite language that the woman in the gray sweater uses when she talks to her co-workers about the noise. Students should underline *Could I ask you two a big favor?; Well, I hate to complain, but; do you think it would be possible to.*

➤ Have students look at the situations that are on the board. Using the language students underlined in picture 3, have pairs come up with polite ways their classmates can speak up about problems they have with co-workers, for example, *I hate to complain, but could you please try to get to work on time? I really need to get home by 3:30 to take care of my kids.*

Option: Ask *Where does the woman in the picture story talk to her co-workers about the problem?* (in the break room or kitchen) *Are there any other people in the room?* (no) *Why is this a good place to talk about the problem?* (It's away from work and from supervisors or other co-workers.) *At your work, where is a good place to talk to a co-worker about a problem?* (outside the building, in the cafeteria, in an office) *How can you make someone feel more comfortable when talking about a problem?* (by discussing the problem privately, sitting down, speaking in a friendly voice, using polite language)

🎧 A. Read and listen again...

➤ Before students read and listen again, have them circle in the picture story the phrases that are underlined in items 1 through 4. Explain that as students listen, they should pay particular attention to the circled phrases and what is said right before and after them.

➤ Students read and listen to the picture story again and then complete Exercise A individually.

➤ Review the answers as a class. If students have trouble determining the meaning of the phrases from the context, read the items substituting each answer choice for the underlined phrase. Then ask students which sentence makes more sense, based on their understanding of what happens in the picture story. For example, say *Listen to that work. Listen to that noise. Which sentence makes more sense?*

🎧 B–C.

➤ Before playing the cassette or reading the items from the tapescript, have students find *a big deal* in picture 2. Write on the board the last two sentences from this speech balloon, *Just ask them politely. Don't make it a big deal.* Underline *make it a big deal* in the second sentence. Then elicit alternative endings to this sentence, such as *Don't get upset or angry.*

➤ Allow students to listen as many times as necessary to complete the activity. Have students check their answers to Exercise B with a partner before they read their responses out loud in Exercise C.

Tapescript

1. Are we bothering you?
2. Just ask them. Don't make it a big deal.
3. Your radio is really loud. I'm having trouble working.

If your students are ready...

Language note: When speaking up about a problem, it is customary for native English speakers to avoid confrontation by using polite language. One method is to use language that suggests the speaker's own responsibility for the difficult situation. In the picture story on page 92, the woman making a complaint puts the focus on herself: *Could I ask . . . a big favor? I hate to complain; I have trouble concentrating.* By using *I* instead of *you*, she suggests that maybe she is the one who is making things difficult and helps to avoid bad feelings between herself and her co-workers.

Neighborhood etiquette

Procedure:

🎧 A. Listening comprehension ...

➤ Tell students that they are going to listen to two separate conversations between neighbors.

➤ After students listen the first time, ask *What's the same in both conversations?* (Someone has a problem with a neighbor and makes a polite request.)

🎧 B. Now listen ...

➤ Pause between each conversation to allow students to answer the questions. Play the cassette or read each conversation as many times as necessary for students to complete the exercise.

➤ Have students check answers with a partner. Then review as a class.

Challenge: Play the cassette or read each conversation again and have students write down three examples of polite language used by Mark or Phil to speak up about a problem. Possible answers include *I just wanted to make a request, I hate to complain, Do you think there's some way to . . . ?, I've got to ask you a big favor, It's hard to ask you this, Am I wrong?*

C. True story ...

➤ Model the activity by talking about a problem that you have with a neighbor and what you have done or can do about it, for example, *The people who live in the apartment below us have their TV in the room below our bedroom. They watch TV until 1:00 or 2:00 in the morning, with the volume high . . .*

➤ Explain that students should read and answer each of the four questions included in the directions when they tell their stories to a partner. Have students also practice polite ways of speaking up about the problem.

➤ Do it yourself!

(For general suggestions, see *Introduction*, page Txiii.)

Procedure:

A. Write your <u>own</u> response ...

➤ Tell students to imagine that they are this woman's neighbor and respond to her complaint.

➤ Have students read the speech balloons. Ask *What's the problem?* (Your kids played music until after midnight and made a mess.) *What solution does the woman suggest?* (The kids should pick up the pizza boxes and soda cans.)

➤ After students complete the activity individually, review as a class. Read each speech balloon and elicit a variety of responses.

➤ Students read their conversations out loud with a partner and then change roles to practice both parts.

B. Culture talk ...

➤ Have students think about the problem they described in the *True story* activity. Ask *If you had this problem with a neighbor or co-worker in your country, what would you do?* Students discuss the answer to this question with classmates from different cultural backgrounds.

➤ Then read the question in the directions and have students discuss.

Tapescript
Conversation 1

[telephone rings]

Diane: Hello?

Mark: Diane? It's Mark downstairs. Have you got a minute?

Diane: Sure, Mark. Everything OK?

Mark: Absolutely. We're all fine. But I just wanted to make a request.

Diane: Sure. What's the problem?

Mark: Well, I hate to complain, but you know Maxine's mom is just home from the hospital, and . . .

Diane: Oh, I didn't realize she'd been sick. I'm sorry to hear that. Is she OK?

Mark: Yes, she'll be fine. She had some minor surgery, and she's supposed to just rest for a few days. And, well, your kids have been a little noisy when they get home from school.

Diane: Oh, I know. With all this rain, they haven't been able to go outside. I'm at my wits' end with their noise too. I'm sorry.

Mark: Do you think there's some way to keep the racket down a bit?

Diane: Hmm. I have an idea. Why don't I get them a couple of videos this afternoon?

Mark: Thanks so much. We really appreciate it.

Conversation 2

[buzzer sound] [door opens]

Wendy: Phil? Hi. What's up?

Phil: Wendy, hi. I've got to ask you a big favor.

Wendy: Sure.

Phil: Well, it's hard to ask you this, but do you think your sister could find another parking space?

(Tapescript is continued on page T94.)

🎧 **A.** Listening comprehension. **Listen to the conversations between neighbors.**

🎧 **B.** **Now listen to the conversations again and answer each question in your <u>own</u> words.**

Conversation 1

Students should mention:

1. What's the problem? Mark's mother-in-law had surgery and needs to rest. Diane's kids are noisy.

2. What's the solution? Mark asks Diane to keep the noise down. Diane will get videos for her kids.

Conversation 2

1. What's the problem? Wendy's sister parks in Phil's space.

2. What's the solution? Phil talks to Wendy about the problem. Wendy will ask her sister to park

somewhere else.

C. True story. **Do you have a problem with a neighbor or co-worker? What's the problem? What have you done about it? What can you do about it? Tell your story to a partner.**

➤ Do it yourself!

A. Write your <u>own</u> response. **Then read your conversation out loud with a partner.**

Hi. Have you got a minute? I hate to complain, but I've got to make a request.

YOU _____

Last night when you were out, your kids played music until after midnight.

YOU _____

And this morning, there are pizza boxes and soda cans all over the place. Would it be possible for them to pick up some of that stuff?

YOU _____

B. Culture talk. **In the country you come from, is it easy or difficult to ask other people to be more considerate? Compare cultures with your classmates.**

Awareness of community rules and laws

 A. Read and listen to the letters.

Ask Joan
Culture tips for newcomers

Dear Joan:

Every day I'm more surprised by my new country. Everything is against some rule or law!

I have a beautiful, friendly dog named Henry. It's difficult for a dog to live in a small apartment, and if he stays inside too much, he barks and bothers the neighbors. Henry loves to go to the park and run free. But yesterday a policeman gave me a ticket because he said I broke the leash law! Now I have to pay a $50 fine!

Joan, I don't think it's necessary to keep a dog on a leash all the time. Henry is a very friendly dog and he doesn't bother anyone. He always minds his own business.

Manuel in Manhattan

Dear Manuel:

I sympathize with you. It's hard to know all the rules and laws when you are a newcomer. Here are some things it's important to be aware of, no matter where you live:

• Most places have laws about animals. In most cities, you must have a license for a dog, you must keep the dog on a leash, and you must clean up any mess the dog leaves in the street.

• All states have laws that protect children from physical violence. And all states have laws about how old children must be to be left alone unsupervised at home.

• All states have laws about weapons, especially guns. Although laws differ from place to place, you must have a license for a gun, and there are laws about carrying guns and other weapons.

• All states have many laws about driving and parking, but the laws are often different in different places. For example, there are places where you may make a right turn after stopping at a red light and places where that is illegal.

Remember, above all: In this country, it is each person's responsibility to know what is legal and what is not legal. It's not acceptable to be unaware. So learn about the laws for the city and state where you live.

I'm sorry to hear that you got a ticket for the dog. But let the ticket be a lucky lesson and a warning to you to find out about the rules and the laws.

Joan

B. Check <u>True</u> or <u>False</u> for each statement.

	True	False
1. Laws are not the same everywhere.	☑	☐
2. Physical violence against children is illegal in this country.	☑	☐
3. It's illegal to have a gun anywhere in this country.	☐	☑
4. In some places it's OK to make a right turn at a red light.	☑	☐
5. If you don't know about a law, it's OK to break it.	☐	☑

Tapescript *(continued from page T93)*

Wendy: Another parking space? What do you mean?

Phil: Well, she takes the space I used to use. Ever since she moved in with you, I haven't been able to park in the driveway. There are two apartments in this building and only two spaces. I think each apartment ought to get *one* of the spaces. Am I wrong?

Wendy: No, actually, you're right. I hadn't realized she was taking your space. I get home early and take the one I always did. Don't worry. I'll talk to her. She'll park somewhere else from now on.

Phil: Thanks, Wendy. I appreciate it. Your sister probably doesn't even realize she's been taking my space.

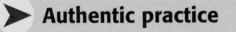

➤ Authentic practice

(For general suggestions, see *Introduction*, page Tx.)

Awareness of community rules and laws

Procedure:

🎧 A. Read and listen to the letters.

➤ Pause after the first letter and ask *What's the problem?* (Manuel let his dog off the leash and got a ticket.)

➤ After students read and listen to the second letter, say *Joan talks about four types of laws that newcomers should be aware of, or know about. What are they?* (laws about animals, laws that protect children, laws about weapons, laws about driving and parking)

➤ With a partner, have students read the four bulleted items in Joan's letter again. Draw a two-column chart on the board with the headings *It's usually required to . . .* and *It's illegal to . . .* Pairs copy and fill in the chart with the information from the four items. For example, students should write *have a license for a dog* in the first column and *leave young children at home alone* in the second column.

➤ Ask *Whose responsibility is it to know what is legal and what is not legal?* (each person's, mine)

Option: Have students underline in the letters all the instances of *It's* + an adjective and an infinitive. Students should find and underline *It's difficult for a dog to live, it's necessary to keep, It's hard to know, it's important to be aware, It's not acceptable to be unaware.*

B. Check <u>True</u> or <u>False</u> . . .

➤ After students complete the activity individually, review and discuss the answers as a class.

➤ Have students explain why items 3 and 5 are false. Say *Imagine that a friend or co-worker says, "It's illegal to have a gun anywhere in this country." What would you say in response?*

If your students are ready . . .

Culture / Civics note: An important principle in the legal systems of the United States and Canada is that ignorance of the law is no excuse. If you violate a law, you are held accountable, regardless of whether you were aware of the law. For this reason, it is important to find out the laws in your community. Traffic and parking regulations are usually clearly posted on signs, as are littering and dog clean-up rules. Government agencies provide brochures explaining regulations; these can be found at public libraries, government offices, and on the Internet. For example, the department of motor vehicles for each state or province publishes a driver's handbook that states traffic and parking regulations. Most community public works departments publish a guide to recycling regulations. People in your community, such as neighbors or building superintendents, are also good sources of information.

C. What's your advice ...

➤ Before doing this activity with your class, research your state's or community's laws about gun ownership and age requirements for baby-sitters. Resources you might use include the Internet, the community liaison at the local police department, and the reference desk at the local library.

➤ Have volunteers read the speech balloons. Then have students refer to page 87 to review ways to say they're not sure and how to suggest asking someone else.

➤ Point out the warning in the directions: *Ignorance of the law is no excuse.* Elicit or explain that *ignorance* is not knowing about something.

➤ Ask *How can you find out about the rules and laws in your community?* For each item, brainstorm community resources on the board. For example, to find out about local gun laws, you could ask a salesperson at a gun shop. To find out how old baby-sitters have to be, you could ask a teacher or administrator at your child's school.

➤ Have students work with a partner to complete the exercise. Then review as a class. Tell students what the gun law is in your state and what the age requirement for baby-sitters is. Tell students how you found out this information.

Challenge: Brainstorm and write on the board other questions students have about what is legal and what is not legal. Use the Internet or community resources to research the answers to the questions as a class.

➤ Do it yourself!

(For general suggestions, see *Introduction*, page Txiii.)

Procedure:

A. Pair work ...

➤ Have partners take turns reading the signs in the picture. Elicit or explain the meanings of *to gutter* and *littering*. If necessary, point to the gutter and explain that when a dog has to "go to the bathroom," the owner should move the dog to the area between the sidewalk and the street and then clean up after the dog. To explain *littering*, point to the boy near the trashcan and ask *What is he doing?*

➤ Have partners take turns talking about the people in the picture. For example, a student could point to the woman wearing a purple skirt and say *She's guttering her dog.*

➤ Have students find two laws that are being violated in the picture (The red car is parked between the "No parking" signs. The boy is littering.). Then ask *What do you think the penalty is for parking between the "No parking" signs?* (a ticket) Ask about other penalties, for example, *What is the fine for not cleaning up after your dog?* ($50) *What is the fine for not using your seatbelt?* ($100) Ask students what other laws are indicated in the picture, for example, *No U turn, No parking in bus stop.*

B. Discussion ...

➤ Have students read the ticket and answer the two questions. Then have students find the person in the picture who broke this law.

➤ As a class, read and discuss the meaning of each of the violations listed on the ticket. Ask which box would be checked on a ticket for the driver of the red car or for the boy who is throwing trash on the sidewalk.

Option: In groups, have students assign a fine amount for each of the four violations that aren't checked on the ticket. Then write the four violations as headings on the board. Under each heading, have groups write the fine amounts they agreed upon. Demonstrate how to calculate the average of all the fines assigned for the first violation. Have groups calculate the average fines assigned for the other violations. Review as a class. Discuss which violation was assigned the highest average fine and why the class feels this violation is the most serious.

Challenge: Have students calculate the fine after 30 days, after 60 days, and after 90 days ($50, $50.75, $51.51).

If your students are ready ...

Culture / Civics note: In the United States and Canada, a ticket is issued for many minor violations of the law such as illegal parking, littering, or failing to wear a helmet while riding a bicycle or motorcycle. These tickets are not paid to the police officer issuing the ticket. Information about the violation, how to contest the violation, the fine that you must pay, and instructions on how to pay are printed on the ticket. Generally, payment or notice that you plan to contest the violation must be made to the municipal office printed on the ticket, either by mail or by visiting the office in person. You must respond to tickets before the date stated on the ticket. Unpaid violations may result in further penalties such as an increased fine, and you may be prevented from renewing your motor vehicle registration.

C. What's your advice? Remember: Ignorance of the law is no excuse.

I want to buy a gun for protection. Do you know what the law is?

1. **YOU** _____

My neighbor asked my 10-year-old son to baby-sit. Isn't he too young? Do you know how old he has to be?

2. **YOU** _____

➤ Do it yourself!

A. Pair work. Talk about the signs. Talk about the people. Who is breaking the law? What are the penalties for the violations?

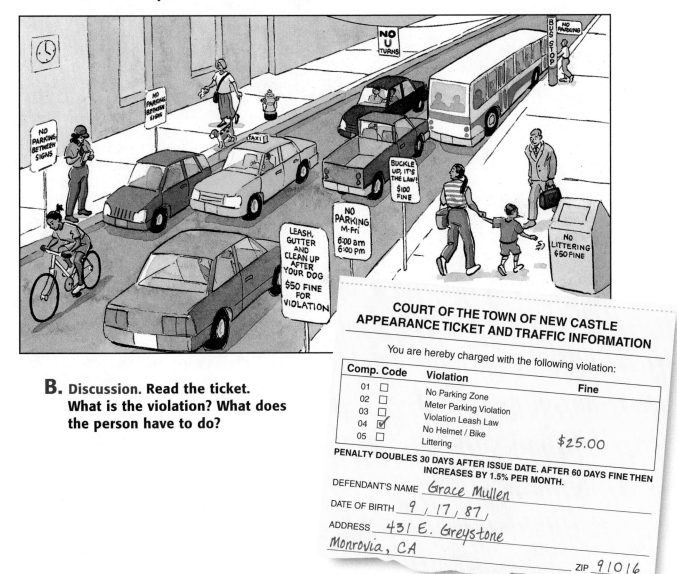

B. Discussion. Read the ticket. What is the violation? What does the person have to do?

COURT OF THE TOWN OF NEW CASTLE
APPEARANCE TICKET AND TRAFFIC INFORMATION

You are hereby charged with the following violation:

Comp. Code		Violation	Fine
01	☐	No Parking Zone	
02	☐	Meter Parking Violation	
03	☐	Violation Leash Law	
04	☑	No Helmet / Bike	
05	☐	Littering	$25.00

PENALTY DOUBLES 30 DAYS AFTER ISSUE DATE. AFTER 60 DAYS FINE THEN INCREASES BY 1.5% PER MONTH.

DEFENDANT'S NAME _Grace Mullen_

DATE OF BIRTH _9_ / _17_ / _87_ /

ADDRESS _431 E. Greystone_
Monrovia, CA

ZIP _91016_

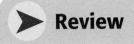

Review

(For general suggestions, see *Introduction*, page Txii.)

Procedure:

A. Pair work or group work.

➤ Make sure students know the word *hydrant*. Point out and have students label the fire hydrant in the picture.

Ask and answer questions.

➤ For each of the three pairs of people in the picture, have students ask and answer the questions *What is happening?* and *What is the problem?*

➤ Then ask the class *Who in the picture didn't understand or didn't follow the law?* (the man who is running to his car) *Who needs to ask someone to be more considerate?* (the woman with her hands over her ears) *Who is expressing sympathy?* (the woman sitting at the table)

Create conversations.

➤ Explain to students that they will create conversations for each of the three pairs of people in the picture. For each pair, partners decide who will play which role. Then have students look back through the unit for ideas.

➤ Explain that students will have one minute to role-play a conversation for each pair of people in the picture and that they should continue talking until you say *Stop*. Model the activity with a more advanced student. Point to the two women near the top of the page. Ask the student which role he or she would like to play. Ask a volunteer to time your conversation and to say *Stop* after one minute. If, for example, the student chooses to play the role of the woman wearing green, start the conversation by saying *Listen to that noise! It's rude to play music too loud.* The student responds, with help from the class if necessary. Keep the conversation going for one minute.

➤ For each pair of people in the picture, have one set of volunteers present their minute-long conversation.

Option: Have pairs draw an additional problem on the picture, such as a dog not on a leash, a person crossing in the middle of the street, a person throwing trash on the sidewalk, a car parked in front of the *Bus Stop* sign. Pairs create a conversation for the new problem. If possible, make a transparency of the picture on page 96. Pass the transparency around the classroom for students to draw their additional problems.

Tell a story.

Option: Create a character. Have students choose one person in the picture and tell about a recent happy or unhappy event in the person's life. Explain that students should make up the details surrounding the event. Model the activity. For example, point to the man walking his dog and say *He just got married. He's very happy. He and his wife live across from the flower shop. They just got a new dog . . .*

Challenge: Give a report. Put the transparency you made on the overhead. Then ask students to imagine that they are a police officer patrolling this neighborhood. They should tell a co-worker or their supervisor about their day, for example, *I had a busy day today. A man parked his car next to a fire hydrant. I wrote a ticket. Down the street someone was playing music too loud. The neighbor was upset. She asked me to help. I asked the man to turn down the music. A girl let her dog run free. I gave her a ticket. It's illegal to let a dog off the leash . . .*

🎧 B. Listen to the conversations...

➤ Tell students that they are going to listen to conversations between co-workers in an office building.

➤ After students listen to the conversation the first time, ask *What's the problem?* (Harold smokes in his cubicle. Nina has the cubicle next to his, and the smoke bothers her.) *What's the solution?* (Nina politely asks Harold to open the window or smoke in the break room.) *What does Nina do before she asks Harold to be more considerate about smoking?* (She introduces herself, congratulates him on his promotion, and welcomes him to the floor.)

➤ Students read the statements so that they know what to listen for and then listen to the conversation again. Play the cassette or read the tapescript as many times as necessary for students to complete the exercise.

Option: As a class, discuss laws and customs about smoking in your community. Ask *Where is it legal to smoke? Where is it against the rules? Is it considerate to smoke near people who don't smoke? Why or why not?* Ask students about smoking laws and customs in their countries.

C–E.

➤ Students work individually to complete the review exercises.

➤ Circulate to offer help as needed.

➤ Have students check answers with a partner. Review answers as a class.

➤ Identify any areas of difficulty that may require additional instruction and practice.

Option: For Exercise D, have students choose one of the three items and create an extended conversation.

Tapescript

Nina: I can't believe it's still legal in this day and age to smoke in an office building.

Woman: Who's smoking?

Nina: Harold—you know, that guy who just moved into the cubicle next to mine.

Woman: Oh, yeah, the guy who just got promoted. I met him at the meeting yesterday. He's not so bad.

Nina: Maybe not. But he sure is rude! If we had *real* offices with doors, I could close my door to keep the smoke out. But in a cubicle, there's no way to get away from it. What do you think I ought to do?

Woman: Well, why don't you start by introducing yourself? Congratulate him on his promotion. Welcome him to the floor. Then politely bring up the subject of the smoke.

Nina: I guess it's worth a try.

[pause]

Nina: Harold? Hi. I'm Nina. I sit in the next cubicle. I wanted to congratulate you on your promotion and welcome you to the floor.

Harold: Thanks, Nina. Nice to meet you. It's good to be here.

Nina: And I was wondering if I could ask you a big favor.

Harold: Sure. What is it?

Nina: Well, would it be possible for you to open the window when you smoke? Or even better, would you mind smoking in the break room down the hall? The smoke travels from your cube—it's not like an office with a door. And there's just that one window.

Harold: Oh, I'm sorry. I didn't realize the smoke was bothering you. No problem. I'll go to the break room to smoke. It might even help me smoke less!

Nina: Thanks, Harold. I really appreciate it.

B. Listen to the conversations between co-workers. Read the statements and listen again. Check _True_ or _False_.

		True	False
1.	Smoking is against the office rules.	☐	☑
2.	Harold smokes.	☑	☐
3.	Nina's office has a door.	☐	☑
4.	Nina asks Harold to smoke in the break room.	☑	☐

C. Complete each sentence.

1. In many towns you have to keep your dog on a _____leash_____.

2. Is it legal here to make a _____right turn_____ on red?

3. They just got _____engaged_____. They're going to get married in June.

4. Sam and Anne got _____separated_____. Now I hear they're getting a divorce.

5. She's upset because the factory closed and all the workers got _____laid off_____.

D. Write a response to each statement.

1. "I can't stand all that noise! It's after midnight!"

   _____

2. "How are things?"

   _____

3. "My daughter's getting a divorce."

   _____

E. Write sentences and questions from the cues.

1. legal / park in a bus stop? _Is it legal to park in a bus stop?_

   _____

2. impolite / bother your co-workers with a lot of noise _It's impolite to bother your_
   co-workers with a lot of noise.

3. important / be aware of the laws where you live _It's important to be aware of the laws_
   where you live.

4. OK / play music late at night in this apartment house? _Is it OK to play music late at_
   night in this apartment house?

F. Rewrite each sentence. Express the ideas in another way.

1. <u>Knowing the laws where you live</u> is essential. It's essential to know the laws where you live.

2. <u>Having a gun without a license</u> is illegal. It's illegal to have a gun without a license.

3. <u>Riding a bicycle without a helmet</u> is dangerous. It's dangerous to ride a bicycle without a helmet.

4. In this state, is <u>having a dog without a license legal</u>? In this state, is it legal to have a dog without a license?

G. Look at the ticket. Answer the questions.

1. What is the violation?

   No standing except trucks

2. What does the person have to do?

   pay a fine of $55

Permit Displayed: No ☐   Yes ☐
\#   Type   **Notice of Parking Violation**   Rev. 12/0
                                                              N/A=Not Availabl

PLATE	H	6	5	5	R	L			CD	DATE REGISTRATION EXPIRES

DATE REGISTRATION EXPIRES — MO. 05 DAY 11 YR. 05

STATE: NY 1☐ CT 2☐ PA 3☐ NJ 4☐ MA 5☐ FL 6☒ OTHER | P T Y P L E A T E 1 ☒ PAS 2 | SRF | COM | OTHER 3 | ☐ N/A

MAKE: 1 CEV ☐ 2 FORD ☒ 3 HONDA ☐ 4 DODGE ☐ 5 OLDS ☐ 6 BUICK ☐ 7 CADI ☐ 8 PONT ☐ 9 TOYT ☐ 0 NISSN ☐ OTHER | COLOR Gr. | Yr. of Veh. 98

BODY TYPE: 1 SEDAN ☐ 2 VAN ☐ 3 SUBN ☒ 4 DELV ☐ OTHER | ALTERNATE PLATE | STATE

THE OPERATOR AND OWNER OF THE ABOVE VEHICLE ARE CHARGED AS FOLLOWS:

AM ☐ Time 3:17 PM ☒ Date of Offense 8/18/03 Time 1st Obsv'd A.M.☐ : P.M.☐ Date 1st Obsy'd County

Front of ☒ 519 S. Winchester   Opposite ☐ Pct

Code	All Other Areas	Man. 96 St 7 So.	In Violation of Sect. 4/08 (subsect. below) of NYC Traffic Rules	Sign Restriction/ Other Information
14	☐ $55	☐ $55	No Standing (c)	
16	☐ $55	☒ $55	No Standing except trucks (k) (2)	Days in Effect ("ALL", unless otherwise stated):
17	☐ $55	☐ $55	No Standing except Auth. Vechicles (c) (4)	
18	☐ $55	☐ $55	No Standing Bus Stop (c) (3)	Hours in Effect ("ALL", unless otherwise stated):
20	☐ $50	☐ $55	No Parking (d)	Fr: 8 ☒ A.M. ☐ P.M.
21	☐ $35	☐ $55	No Parking, SCR (d) (1)	To: 6 ☐ A.M. ☒ P.M. Other Description/Rider

H. Composition. On a separate sheet of paper, write about the picture on page 96. Say as much as you can.

> **Now I can**
> ☐ ask about and understand rules and laws.
> ☐ ask someone to be more considerate.
> ☐ apologize for inconsiderate behavior.
> ☐ understand personal responsibility to know and obey rules and laws.
> ☐ make small talk.
> ☐ congratulate someone on good news.
> ☐ express sympathy and offer to help.
> ☐ _____.

F-G.

➤ Students work individually to complete the review exercises.

➤ Circulate to offer help as needed.

➤ Have students check answers with a partner. Review answers as a class.

➤ Identify any areas of difficulty that may require additional instruction and practice.

Challenge: For Exercise G, encourage students to infer meaning from context by having them work in groups to create a key to the abbreviations used on the ticket, for example, *MO. = month, NY = New York.*

H. Composition ...

➤ Provide students with concrete approaches to writing about the picture on page 96. Use one of the following options, give students a choice of options, or assign options based on students' levels of proficiency. Model what is expected of students for each option.

➤ Advise students to look back through the unit for help and ideas as they write.

➤ Circulate to offer help as needed.

Option: For each of the four situations in the picture on page 96, have students write a sentence expressing a judgment with *It's* + an adjective and an infinitive. Students might write *It's rude to play music too loud, It's right to have your dog on a leash, It's hard to talk about bad news, It's illegal to park next to a fire hydrant.*

Option: Have students write a sympathy note to the man in the picture on page 96 who had a death in his family. For example, *Dear Brian, I'm so sorry to hear about your mother. It's very hard to lose a family member. She was a great woman. Is there anything I can do? Please call me if you want to talk. I am home after 5:00 every night. Sincerely, Anna. P.S. Would you like to have coffee or go to a movie sometime?*

Challenge: Put the transparency from the *Challenge* activity on page 96 on the overhead. Ask students to imagine that they are the police officer patrolling this neighborhood and write up a report of what happened today, for example, *I had a busy day today. A man parked his car next to a fire hydrant. I wrote a ticket. Down the street someone was playing music too loud. The neighbor was upset. She asked me to help. I asked the man to turn down the music. A girl let her dog run free. I gave her a ticket. It's illegal to let a dog off the leash ...*

Now I can

➤ Read the first item in the box out loud, *Now I can ask about and determine rules and laws.* Elicit from the class an example of how to ask about or determine rules and laws, such as *Is it legal to make a right turn on red?*

➤ In pairs, have students take turns reading each item in the box and giving an example of what they have learned. When students can provide an example, they should check that objective. For the items students weren't able to check, they should look back through the unit for ideas.

➤ When students are finished reviewing with their partners, read each item out loud and elicit an example from the class.

Oral test (optional)

You may want to use the *Now I can* box as an informal evaluation. While students are working on the *Composition* activity, you can call them up individually and check their ability with two or three objectives.

UNIT 8

Health and safety

Note: Have students bring empty medication packages or containers to class for use on page 103.

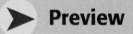 **Preview**

(For general suggestions, see *Introduction*, page Tviii.)

Warm up. What's the problem?

Procedure:

➤ Introduce the topic of sell-by dates by asking questions about the picture, such as *What three things are pictured here?* (a calendar, a receipt, a package of chicken) *What is the date today?* (August 14) *When was the chicken purchased?* (today, August 14) *What is the sell-by date on the package?* (August 12) *What's the problem? / Is this chicken still good?* (The chicken is not fresh; its sell-by date was two days ago.) *What should the customer who bought the chicken do?* (return the chicken to the supermarket) *What will the customer need to bring?* (the receipt)

➤ Have students use their own words to tell a partner what the problem is.

➤ To access students' prior experience, ask *What kinds of products have sell-by dates?* (meat, dairy products, medicines) *Why is it dangerous to buy food past its sell-by date?* (You can get sick.) *Why is it dangerous to buy medicine past its sell-by date?* (It may not be effective anymore.)

Option: Ask *What other information is on the package of chicken?* (price per pound, weight / number of pounds, package price) *What is the unit price of the chicken?* ($1.29 per pound) *How much would three pounds of chicken cost?* ($3.87)

If your students are ready . . .

Culture / Civics note: Perishable foods such as eggs, milk and other dairy products, meat, poultry, fish, baked goods, and baby food often have a calendar date stamped on the packaging. This date helps store managers determine how long food can be offered for sale and helps consumers judge a food's freshness. There are three commonly used types of food dating. The words "Best if used by" printed before the date indicate when the food is at its best quality. The words "Sell by" and date give the last day that the product can be sold, and the words "Use by" and date indicate the last day that the food should be consumed.

Unit 8 objectives

Procedure:

➤ Have students read the objectives. Ask *Where can you use what you're going to learn in this unit?* (at a supermarket, in a restaurant, at a pharmacy, in a kitchen) *Which objectives are related to food?* (the first, second, and fourth) *What are the other two objectives related to?* (medicines)

➤ To relate the content of the unit to students' prior experience, ask students if they have ever returned food to a supermarket or at a restaurant.

Health and safety

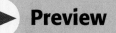

Preview

Warm up. What's the problem?

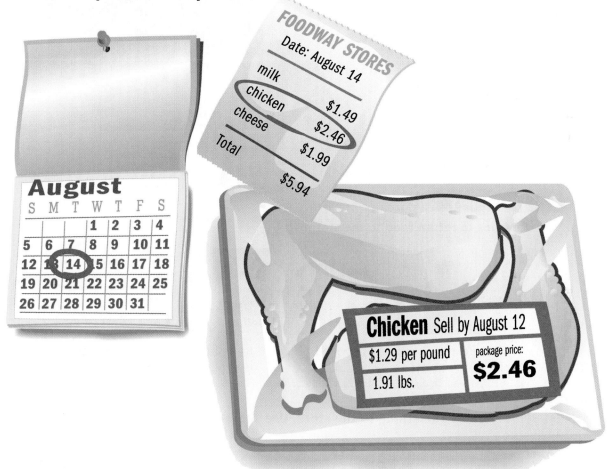

Unit 8 objectives

- Return food to a supermarket and explain why.
- Send food back in a restaurant and explain why.
- Give and understand directions for taking a medicine.
- Understand and apply food-safety techniques.
- Understand directions and warnings on medicines.

Practical conversations

Model 1   Return an item to the supermarket. Provide a justification.

A. Listen and read.

A: Excuse me.

B: Yes?

A: I bought this meat here today, and its sell-by date is expired.

B: Would you like to get another package?

A: No, thanks. I'll just take a refund.

B: Certainly. Can I see your receipt?

A: Here you go.

B. Listen again and repeat.

Vocabulary

Reasons to return food to the store

It's not fresh.

It's spoiled.

Its sell-by date is expired.

It's marked wrong.

C. Pair work. Return something to the store. Use these items or your **own** ideas.

a package

a carton

a container

a loaf

a bag

A: Excuse me.

B: ___1___?

A: I bought _____, and _____.

B: Would you like to get another _____?

A: ___2___.

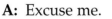

[1]How can I help you [2]Yes, Sure, OK, Can I get a refund instead?

➤ Practical conversations

(For general suggestions, see *Introduction*, page Tviii)

Model 1

Content: returning an item to the supermarket; providing a justification; the possessive adjectives *its* and *your*

Procedure:

🎧 A–B.

➤ Have students look at the photo and the picture of a calendar and a package of meat. Ask questions such as *What did the customer buy?* (a package of meat) *When did she buy it?* (January 8) *What is the sell-by date on the package?* (January 3) *How many days past its sell-by date is the meat?* (5 days) *What do you think the customer is saying?* (I want to return this meat . . .)

➤ After students listen to and read the conversation, ask *What does the customer say?* (I bought this meat here today, and its sell-by date is expired.) *What do you think "expired" means?* (past the time when it can be used or sold) *Does the customer get an exchange or a refund?* (a refund) *What does the cashier ask for?* (the customer's receipt)

➤ Review ways to make good on pages 47 and 53, such as *a replacement, a refund, an exchange, a store credit.*

🎧 Vocabulary

➤ After students listen to and repeat the vocabulary, point out that in the first three pictures the food is old. Explain that the vegetables are *not fresh* because they were picked too long ago and that the *spoiled* food has started to go bad and smells.

➤ Have students look at the last picture and ask *What's the problem?* (The package price is wrong.) Write on the board 3.45 pounds × $.49 per pound = and elicit the correct price from the class ($1.69).

➤ Brainstorm and write on the board other reasons to return food to the supermarket, such as *There's been a recall, The package is open, The package is damaged.*

C. Pair work . . .

➤ Point to each picture and elicit the name of the food from the class—*meat, orange juice,* and so on.

➤ Have students match the reasons to return something with the products. Point out that there is more than one possible reason to return each food item. Explain that *spoiled* is most appropriate with meat.

➤ Model the activity. Play the role of Student A and have the class play the role of Student B. Demonstrate using a food item and a time, such as *yesterday* or *this morning,* in Student A's first blank and a reason from the *Vocabulary* box in Student A's second blank. If necessary, prompt the class to give the way the item is sold—*package, carton, container,* and so on—in its second line. Point out that in the last line of the conversation, Student A can agree to an exchange or ask for a refund.

Option: Read the following story and have students draw an X over each picture in the *Vocabulary* box or in Exercise C as they hear the word or phrase.

I can't believe what a bad day I had at work. I work afternoons as a cashier at a supermarket, and today I had so many returns! Customers kept bringing back food they bought in the morning, before my shift even started. First a woman came in with a bag of chips that was marked wrong. She had been overcharged. Then a mother and daughter returned a container of ice cream. Its sell-by date was expired. Later, a man brought back a package of meat that was spoiled. He said that he bought it this morning, but he didn't have a receipt. I gave him a store credit. Another man returned a carton of juice that was open. I think the employees who stock the groceries in the morning should do a better job of checking the food they put on the shelves!

Ask students which reason to return food and which food item they did not cross out (It's not fresh, a loaf of bread).

Model 2

Content: sending food back in a restaurant; explaining why; making good on a complaint; the possessive pronouns *yours* and *mine*; ways to order meat

Procedure:

🎧 A–B.

➤ Ask questions about the photo, such as *Where are the people?* (in a restaurant) *Who is the man on the left?* (the waiter) *What are the customers eating?* (hamburgers) *What is the male customer doing?* (He's pointing to his hamburger.)

➤ After students listen to the conversation, check comprehension by asking questions such as *What's wrong with the man's hamburger?* (It's not well done.) *What's wrong with the woman's order?* (The milk's not fresh.) *What's the waiter going to do?* (take care of the problems) *How?* (take the hamburger back to cook it longer and bring fresh milk)

🎧 Ways to order meat

➤ After students listen to and repeat the vocabulary, elicit or explain that meat that is *rare* has been cooked for only a short time and is still red inside, while meat that is *medium* has been cooked longer and is pink. Meat that is *well done* has been cooked the longest. Write on the board *rare, medium, well done*. Point out other ways to order meat by drawing an arrow between *rare* and *medium* and writing *medium rare* and drawing an arrow between *medium* and *well done* and writing *medium well*.

➤ Ask students how they prefer their meat cooked. Take a class poll. Have students raise their hands for the way they order meat in restaurants.

C. Group work ...

➤ Write on the board *not rare, not medium, not well done, not good, not fresh*. Then brainstorm other reasons to send food back in a restaurant, such as *not what I ordered, not hot, has something (such as a hair) in it*.

➤ Model the activity. Read the role of Student A. Have half the class play the role of Student B and the other half play the role of Student C. For each line of the conversation with blank substitution lines, elicit a variety of ideas from the appropriate half of the class.

➤ Have students work in groups of three. Have groups practice the conversation three times so that each student plays the roles of Student A, Student B, and Student C.

➤ Do it yourself!

(For general suggestions, see *Introduction*, page Txiii.)

Procedure:

A. Personalization ...

➤ Give an example of something you returned at a supermarket or restaurant. Tell what you returned, what the problem was, and what the supermarket or restaurant did to make good. Draw the chart on the board and elicit the class's help in filling in the first row based on your example. Ask *What was the item I returned? What was the problem? What happened?*

➤ Students think of something they returned at a supermarket or restaurant and fill in the chart in their books.

➤ As a class, discuss students' experiences returning or sending back food. Add a couple of rows to the chart on the board. After a student talks about his or her experience, elicit the class's help in completing a row of the chart.

B. Pair work ...

➤ For each chart entry on the board, brainstorm a line a manager or waiter might say.

➤ Pairs choose either their own or their partner's example and create a conversation. If students have trouble, advise them to use the conversation on page 100 as a model if they're talking about an item returned to the supermarket and the conversation on page 101 if they're talking about an item sent back in a restaurant.

➤ Have volunteers role-play their conversations for the class.

A. Listen and read.

A: Is everything OK?

B: Actually, this hamburger is not well done.

A: Oh, I'm sorry. Let me take it back. What about yours?

C: Mine's OK, thanks. But this milk's not fresh.

A: Oh, I'm so sorry. I'll take care of that right away.

B. Listen again and repeat.

Ways to order meat

rare   medium   well done

C. Group work. Complain about food that's not good, not fresh, or not the way you ordered it. Use your own ideas.

A: Is everything OK?

B: Actually, this _____ is not _____.

A: Oh, I'm sorry. Let me take it back. What about yours?

C: Mine's _____. But _____.

A: _____.

➤ Do it yourself!

A. Personalization. Have you ever returned something at a supermarket or restaurant? Complete the chart. Explain the problem. What did the supermarket or restaurant do?

Item	Problem	What happened?
milk	carton was open	The supermarket gave me another carton.

B. Pair work. Choose one item and use it to role-play a conversation between a customer and a manager or waiter/waitress.

Practical conversations

Model 3   Pick up a prescription for another person.

A. Listen and read.

A: I'm here to pick up a prescription.

B: Sure, Mr. Martinez.... It's ready.

A: Thanks. Oh, by the way, are the instructions on the label?

B: Yes. And there's more information on this patient information sheet.

B. Listen again and repeat.

Patient Information Sheet

Directions: TAKE 2 CAPSULES NOW, THEN 1 CAPSULE 3 TIMES DAILY.

IMPORTANT NOTE: THE FOLLOWING INFORMATION IS INTENDED TO SUPPLEMENT, NOT SUBSTITUTE FOR, THE EXPERTISE AND JUDGMENT OF YOUR PHYSICIAN, PHARMACIST, OR OTHER HEALTHCARE PROFESSIONAL.

IT SHOULD NOT BE CONSTRUED TO INDICATE THAT USE OF THE DRUG IS SAFE, APPROPRIATE, OR EFFECTIVE FOR YOU.

CONSULT YOUR HEALTHCARE PROFESSIONAL BEFORE USING THIS DRUG.

Dr. Mila Ponti
625 First Ave.
South Orange, NJ 07081

Name: *Gloria Martinez*

R *For back pain,*
         Percotrol 250mg tid

Vocabulary

Important information about medications

Percotrol
Gloria Martinez
Take 3 x a day, expiration
date: 6/01/03 Dr. Mila Ponti
Refills: none

Percotrol
Patient Information

Instructions: This medication is for pain. Take exactly as your doctor orders.

Dosage: The normal dose is 250 mg. three times a day.

Warnings: Do not take this medication if you are pregnant or nursing a baby.

Adverse reactions: Two percent of patients using Percotrol report flu-like symptoms.

C. Pair work. Pick up a prescription. Ask for information.

A: I'm here to pick up a prescription.

B: _____1_____. . . . It's ready.

A: _____2_____. Oh, by the way, _____ the _____ on the label?

B: _____.

[1]OK, Certainly, No problem [2]Thanks so much

102   Unit 8

➤ Practical conversations

(For general suggestions, see *Introduction*, page Tviii.)

Model 3

Content: picking up a prescription for another person; discussing important information about medications

Procedure:

🎧 A–B.

➤ Ask questions about the photo, such as *What is the man on the left holding?* (a container of pills / medicine and a sheet of paper) *What is the man on the right wearing?* (a white coat) *What is his job?* (He's a pharmacist.)

➤ After students listen to the conversation, ask questions such as *What is Mr. Martinez doing?* (picking up a prescription) *Where are the instructions for taking the medication?* (on the label) *Where can Mr. Martinez find more information about the medication?* (on the patient information sheet)

➤ Talk about students' experiences with prescriptions. Ask *Have you had prescriptions filled in your home country? Have you had a prescription filled here? What pharmacy did you go to? How did you know how often to take the medication? What did you need to bring when you picked up your medication?*

➤ Have students read the patient information sheet individually. Then read it out loud. Ask questions such as *Who gave Mr. Martinez the patient information sheet?* (the pharmacist) *How many capsules, or pills, should the patient take now?* (two) *After that, how many times a day should the patient take the medication?* (three times a day) *How many capsules should the patient take each time?* (one) *Is it more important for patients to follow what their doctor or pharmacist says or what the patient information sheet says?* (what their doctor or pharmacist says)

➤ Have students look at the prescription. Ask questions such as *Who wrote the prescription?* (Dr. Mila Ponti) *Who is the patient?* (Gloria Martinez) *Who do you think Gloria Martinez is?* (Mr. Martinez's wife) *What medication is Mrs. Martinez taking?* (Percotrol) *What is Percotrol for?* (back pain)

🎧 Vocabulary

➤ Have students look at the label on the container of medication. Ask *What information can you find on the label?* (the name of the drug, the patient's name, the instructions, the expiration date, the doctor's name, how many refills the patient can get)

➤ Have students read the patient information sheet. Ask *What information can you find on the patient information sheet?* (instructions, dosage, warnings, adverse reactions) Elicit or explain the meaning of *dosage* as the amount of medicine that you should take at one time. Ask *Who should not take this medication?* (women who are pregnant or nursing a baby) Elicit or explain the meaning of *adverse* as bad. *What happens to some patients who take this medication?* (They feel as if they have the flu.)

Challenge: Record television commercials for prescription drugs. Have students watch each commercial and note the name of the drug, what it's for, possible adverse reactions or side effects, and warnings. Alternatively, have students make an effort to watch TV in English during one week and make a note of any prescription drug commercials they see. Discuss why drug companies advertise medications on TV that are available only with a doctor's prescription.

C. Pair work . . .

➤ Point out that in Student A's second line, students will use *is* or *are* in the second blank and information from either the label or the patient information sheet in the third blank, such as *expiration date, warnings, adverse reactions*. For the last line of the conversation, if the information asked about is not on the label, Student B can say *No. But that information is on the patient information sheet.*

If your students are ready . . .

Culture / Civics note: In North America, some medicines cannot be sold without a doctor's written orders, called a *prescription*. Generally, patients take the prescription to a pharmacy, where the medicine is prepared and sold. "Over-the-counter" medicine such as aspirin and cold medications can be bought without a prescription.

All prescription medicine is packaged with an identification label that contains the patient's name, the name of the medicine, instructions for taking the medicine, and the number of times the prescription can be refilled. The label may also contain an expiration date, which is the last day that the medicine can be safely used. In addition, a patient information sheet is included that contains more detailed information about the conditions that the medicine is used to treat and warnings about possible dangers or side effects.

Model 4

Content: giving directions for taking a medicine; clarifying the directions; the possessive adjective *your*

Procedure:

🎧 A–B.

➤ Ask questions about the photo, such as *Who is this man?* (Mr. Martinez) *Who is the woman he is talking to?* (Gloria Martinez) *What is she wearing?* (a robe) *Why?* (She isn't feeling well / has back pain.) *What is Mr. Martinez holding?* (a glass of water and the medication) *What is Mrs. Martinez doing?* (holding up three fingers) *Why?* (because she's asking about how often to take the medicine or how much medicine to take)

➤ After students listen to the conversation, ask *What is the dosage?* (one capsule three times a day) *What is another word for "instructions"?* (directions)

C. Pair work ...

➤ For each medicine pictured, have students ask and answer with a partner: *What's the name of the medication? What is it for? When do you take it?*

➤ Elicit from the class simple definitions based on the pictures for *rash, insomnia, nausea,* and *infection.*

➤ As a class, fill in the blanks in the conversation with the information from the container of *Clearox.* Read the conversation and elicit from the class the appropriate word or sentence for each blank substitution line.

➤ Students practice the conversation with a partner.

Option: Use the empty medication packages and containers that you and / or students have brought in. Draw the chart below on the board. Have groups copy the chart and use the medication packages to complete it. Groups should pass the packages to another group once they've found the information they need.

➤ Do it yourself!

(For general suggestions, see *Introduction,* page Txiii.)

Procedure:

A. Personalization ...

➤ Explain that an *ailment* is a sickness or illness that is not very serious. To make sure students understand the ailments listed, elicit the symptoms for each; for example, the symptoms of *the flu* are sore throat, difficulty breathing, fever, feeling tired. Brainstorm and write on the board other ailments for students to use in the last row of their charts, such as *cold, headache, ear infection.*

➤ Elicit or explain that a *home remedy* is something other than medicine that is used to treat an ailment and that it is usually suggested by a family member or friend, not by a healthcare professional.

➤ Discuss the example. Then brainstorm ideas for *pain* as a class. Have students complete as much of the chart as they can.

B. Discussion ...

➤ For each ailment, students tell their group the medicine and home remedy they listed and which of the two treatments they prefer.

Option: Assign each group a different ailment. On a sheet of paper, groups write their ailment as a heading and then list all the cultures represented in the class. Using its own members' charts and asking students from other groups, each group records as many different cultures' home remedies for their ailment as possible. Groups present their findings to the class.

Medication	What it's for	How much (dosage)	How often

A. Listen and read.

A: Here's the Percotrol for your back pain.
B: Thanks. What are the directions?
A: Take 1 capsule three times a day.
B: Three times a day?
A: That's right.

B. Listen again and repeat.

C. Pair work. Tell someone how to take medicine. Use the directions on these medications. Or use your own medications.

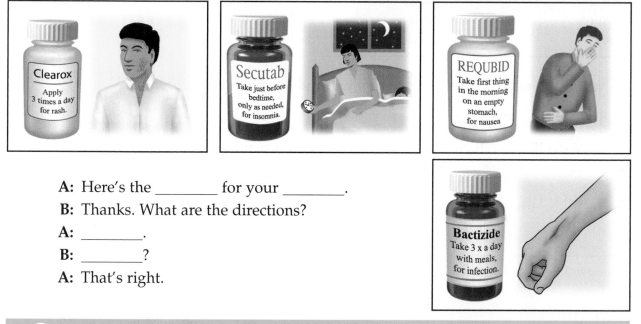

A: Here's the _____ for your _____.
B: Thanks. What are the directions?
A: _____.
B: _____?
A: That's right.

➤ Do it yourself!

A. Personalization. Complete the chart for medicines and other remedies you use.

Ailment	Medicine	Home remedy
the flu	aspirin	chicken soup
pain		
nausea		
rash		
other:		

B. Discussion. Compare medicines and remedies with a group.

Practical grammar

Possession

> **Review the possessive adjectives.**
>
> Evan takes **his** medicine before breakfast.
> Jane takes **her** medicine before dinner.
>
> | Subject pronouns | Possessive adjectives |
> |---|---|
> | I | my |
> | you | your |
> | he | his |
> | she | her |
> | it | its |
> | we | our |
> | you | your |
> | they | their |

A. Write the possessive adjective that corresponds to each subject pronoun.

1. They usually get _____their_____ food at the Magic Mart.

2. We'd like to return _____our_____ hamburgers. They're not well done.

3. She doesn't know if _____her_____ husband has any allergies.

4. Mr. Clark thinks _____his_____ daughter needs to go to the doctor.

5. You need to bring _____your_____ prescription with you.

> **Review the possessive nouns.**
>
> Lewis**'s** son is allergic to penicillin.   The pharmacy**'s** hours are 8 a.m. to midnight.
> The children**'s** doctor called the pharmacist.   The patients**'** appointments had to be changed.

B. Complete each sentence with a possessive noun.

1. __*Roberto's*__ doctor prescribed medication for his flu.
   Roberto

2. The _____doctor's_____ instructions are on the prescription.
   doctor

3. We don't know the _____medication's_____ side effects.
   medication

4. _____Joanna's_____ insomnia is better and she doesn't need medicine anymore.
   Joanna

5. The two _____brothers'_____ headaches are terrible.
   brothers

➤ Practical grammar

(For general suggestions, see *Introduction*, page Tix.)

Possession

Content: possessive adjectives, possessive nouns, and posessive pronouns

Procedure:

Review the possessive adjectives.

➤ Have students look at the grammar box. Say to the class *When I say the subject pronoun, you say the possessive adjective. For example, if I say I, you say my.* Call out subject pronouns in random order. Students respond with the corresponding possessive adjective.

➤ Point to yourself and say *I have my book*, stressing *I* and *my*. Then look at the class and say *You have your books*, stressing *you* and *your*. Point to a male student and elicit the sentence *He has his book.* Point to a female student and elicit the sentence *She has her book.* Point to two students and elicit the sentence *They have their books.* Use a gesture to indicate the entire class including you and elicit the sentence *We have our books.*

Challenge: In groups of three, students role-play a conversation. Say *Imagine that one of you has an ailment. A family member calls a nurse helpline for health-care advice.* Have students decide what the ailment is and who will play the roles of the patient, the caller, and the nurse. The patient describes his or her ailment, the caller relates the information to the nurse, and the nurse asks the caller about the patient's condition. Encourage students to use possessive adjectives. For example,

> **Nurse:** What is the problem?
> **Caller:** My brother has a rash on his arms.
> **Nurse:** Is the rash also on his legs?
> **Caller:** [to patient] Is the rash also on your legs?
> **Patient:** No, it's only on my arms.

Have volunteers role-play their conversations for the class.

A. Write the possessive adjective ...

➤ Have a volunteer read item 1. Ask *What is the subject pronoun?* (they) Have students underline *They*. Then ask *What possessive adjective corresponds to, or goes with, they?* (their) Have students write *their* on the line.

➤ Have students underline the subject pronoun in items 2 through 5. Then have them complete the sentences with the corresponding possessive adjectives.

Review the possessive nouns.

➤ Have students read the examples in the box. Write on the board the headings *Singular nouns* and *Plural nouns*. Under each, draw a t-chart with the headings *no -s* and *end in -s*. Have students look at the examples again and tell you where each possessive noun belongs on the charts; for example, *Lewis* is singular and ends in *-s*, so *Lewis's* belongs under *Singular nouns, end in -s*.

➤ Have students use the headings and examples on the board to infer the rules for making nouns possessive. For example, for *Singular nouns, no -s* and the example *pharmacy's*, elicit the rule *Add 's*.

➤ Point out that all nouns add *'s* to form the possessive except for plural nouns, ending in *-s*, which only add an apostrophe *(patients')*.

Option: Say a sentence beginning with *my*—for example, *My sister just got engaged*—and throw a ball or beanbag to a student. The student catches the ball and says what he or she just learned about you, *(Your name)'s sister just got engaged.* The student then says his or her own sentence beginning with *my*—such as *My apartment is on the second floor*—and throws the ball to another student.

B. Complete each sentence ...

➤ After students complete the exercise individually, review by asking the class. *How did you make the nouns possessive in items 1 through 4?* (by adding 's) *How did you make the noun possessive in item 5?* (by adding an apostrophe)

➤ Have students take turns reading the sentences with a partner.

Possessive pronouns

➤ Pick up an object on your desk and ask yourself *Is this my (pencil)?* Take a closer look and say *Yes, it's mine.* Pick up an object on a student's desk. Look at the student and ask *Is this your (book)?* Answer *Yes, it's yours.* Pick up an object on a male student's desk. Look at the class and ask *Is this his (pen)?* Answer *Yes, it's his.* Continue in a similar manner, demonstrating the use of the other possessive pronouns.

➤ Pick up the same objects and ask *Whose (pencil) is this?* Elicit the responses *It's yours, It's mine, It's his,* and so on.

➤ Have students read the examples and explanations in the grammar box. Point out that most of the possessive pronouns are formed by adding *-s* to the possessive adjective; *mine, his,* and *its* are exceptions.

C. Replace the words ...

➤ Do an oral exercise to prepare students for the written activity. Pool a few classroom possessions and then ask questions about ownership, for example, *Are these keys yours?* Elicit responses such as *No, those keys are hers* or *Yes, those keys are mine.*

➤ Students complete the exercise and check their answers by reading the sentences to a partner.

Option: Review the demonstratives *this, that, these,* and *those.* Remind students that *this* is for a single object close by, *that* is for a single object at a distance, *these* is for plural objects close by, and *those* is for plural objects at a distance.

Option: Write the headings *School, Work, Home* on the board. Brainstorm and write on the board belongings that might get confused in each place; for example, at home, you might not be sure who a *telephone message* is for or which *keys* belong to which family member. Students create new sentences similar to those in Exercise C, using the belongings they brainstormed, for example, *Those keys are mine.*

D. Complete each sentence.

➤ Read item 1 twice, filling in one of the answer choices each time. Ask students which sentence is correct and elicit the response *Ms. Elliot's pharmacist . . .*

➤ Students complete items 2 and 3 independently. Review the answers as a class.

Challenge: Have students create comparative questions similar to item 3 about their own and their partner's family members, belongings, or places they go, for example, *Whose daughter is older, mine or hers? Whose house is closer to the school, mine or hers?* Each pair of students joins another pair. Each student takes a turn reading his or her questions. Each pair of students guesses the answers to the other pair's questions, using *yours, his,* or *hers.*

➤ Do it yourself!

(For general suggestions, see *Introduction*, page Txiii.)

Procedure:

A. Pair work ...

➤ Have students label the men in the picture *A* and *B.* Write on the board *A:* and *B:* and create the first two lines of the conversation as a class, for example, *A: Is this coat yours or mine? B: I'm not sure. What size is your coat?*

➤ Students complete the conversation with a partner. Volunteers present their conversations to the class.

B. Discussion ...

➤ Model the activity by talking about something you took by mistake or something of yours that someone else took by mistake.

➤ In groups, students tell their own stories.

Challenge: Working in groups, have students compose an *Ask Joan* letter about a problem with something that was taken by mistake. In the letter, students ask Joan what to do about the item they took by mistake or the item of theirs that someone else took. Have each group read its letter to the class.

The yellow hard hat is **mine**. Is the blue one **yours**?

No, I think it's **his**.

Possessive pronouns

Possessive pronouns are not followed by nouns. They stand alone.

This isn't your hard hat. It's **mine**.

Subject pronouns	Possessive adjectives	Possessive pronouns
I	my	**mine**
you	your	**yours**
he	his	**his**
she	her	**hers**
it	its	**its**
we	our	**ours**
you	your	**yours**
they	their	**theirs**

C. **Replace the words in parentheses with a possessive pronoun.**

1. Those prescriptions are (my prescriptions). _Those prescriptions are mine._

2. That penicillin is (his penicillin). _That penicillin is his._

3. This rare hamburger is (your hamburger). _This rare hamburger is yours._

4. Is this patient information sheet (their patient information sheet)? _Is this patient information sheet theirs?_

D. **Complete each sentence.**

1. _____Ms. Elliot's_____ pharmacist can't fill this prescription right now.
   Ms. Elliot / Ms. Elliot's

2. I know _____his_____ dinner is OK. What about _____yours_____?
   he / his   your / yours

3. Whose pharmacy is closer, _____mine_____ or _____theirs_____?
   my / mine   their / theirs

➤ **Do it yourself!**

A. **Pair work. Create a conversation for the two men. Say as much as you can.**

B. **Discussion. Did you ever take something that belonged to someone else by mistake? Did anyone ever take anything of yours by mistake? Tell your story.**

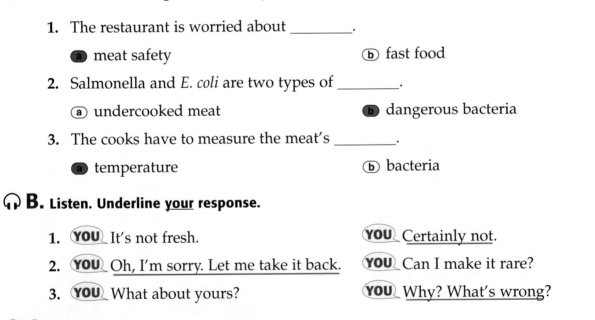

🎧 **A. Read and listen again. Then complete each statement. Fill in the ovals.**

1. The restaurant is worried about _____.

   ⓐ meat safety   ⓑ fast food

2. Salmonella and *E. coli* are two types of _____.

   ⓐ undercooked meat   **ⓑ** dangerous bacteria

3. The cooks have to measure the meat's _____.

   ⓐ temperature   ⓑ bacteria

🎧 **B. Listen. Underline your response.**

1. **YOU** It's not fresh.   **YOU** <u>Certainly not.</u>

2. **YOU** <u>Oh, I'm sorry. Let me take it back.</u>   **YOU** Can I make it rare?

3. **YOU** What about yours?   **YOU** <u>Why? What's wrong?</u>

🎧 **C. Listen again. Read your response out loud.**

Authentic practice

(For general suggestions, see *Introduction*, page Tx.)

Procedure:

🎧

Note: The procedure for the picture story is different in this unit. Students use their own words to re-create the conversation, which contains receptive-level language.

➤ Divide the class into two groups, *transmitters* and *receivers*. Explain that, as with a radio, for any communication to take place, someone has to transmit the message and someone has to receive it.

➤ Ask the receivers to leave the room. The transmitters read and listen to the picture story. Then they close their books.

➤ Ask the receivers to return and pair each one with a transmitter. The transmitters tell the receivers as much of the conversation as they can remember. The receivers take notes.

➤ The receivers stay in the room, and the transmitters take their books and step outside. The receivers choose two volunteers to role-play the conversation. Allow the receivers five minutes to compare notes and try to re-create the conversation. While the transmitters are outside the classroom, they find partners and practice reading the conversation.

➤ The transmitters return to the classroom. The two volunteers present the conversation, with coaching from the rest of the receivers group.

➤ All students open their books. Play the cassette or read the conversation again. This time the entire class reads and listens to the picture story. As a class, discuss the differences between the actual picture story and the version presented by the receivers.

Option: Have students create a *Meat Safety Rules* sign to post in this kitchen. One rule on the sign might be *After you cut raw chicken, wash the knife, the cutting board, and your hands.*

Option: Brainstorm other precautions to follow when preparing food, such as *Wash hands after you use the restroom, Keep counters clean, Wash and dry raw meat, Don't leave food sitting out too long, Don't serve food that contains raw eggs.*

Challenge: In pairs, have students write more polite suggestions that the woman wearing the yellow scarf could use to point out what her co-worker needs to do. For example, instead of *I don't believe what you're doing!* she could say *You probably didn't realize, but it's dangerous to slice tomatoes . . .*

🎧 A. Read and listen again . . .

➤ After students read and listen to the conversation again, ask comprehension questions such as *Where are the two women?* (at work in a kitchen) *What two things does the woman wearing the green scarf do wrong?* (She uses the same cutting board to cut raw chicken and tomatoes. She doesn't cook the hamburger long enough.) *What bacteria can raw chicken have?* (salmonella) *What bacteria do you think rare beef can have?* (E. coli) *What do salmonella and E. coli cause?* (food poisoning)

➤ Students complete Exercise A. Have them check answers with a partner. Then review as a class.

🎧 B–C.

➤ Allow students to listen to the items as many times as necessary to complete the activity. Have students check answers with a partner before reading their responses out loud in Exercise C.

Tapescript

1. You're not going to slice that bread on *that* cutting board, are you?
2. You know we don't serve rare meat here. That's the policy.
3. I don't believe what you're doing!

If your students are ready . . .

Culture / Civics note: In the United States and Canada, government regulations ensure that the food served in restaurants and other food businesses is safe to eat. Food-service workers are required by law to understand and follow safe food-handling practices such as maintaining personal cleanliness; washing hands with soap and water; using disposable gloves; storing raw and cooked food properly; and sanitizing cooking equipment, utensils, tableware.

T106

Warm-weather food safety

Procedure:

🎧 A. Listening comprehension ...

➤ Tell students that they are going to listen to a public service announcement on the radio. Ask what a *public service announcement* is. Elicit or explain that it is a special message on television or radio, giving information about an important subject. Ask students if they have seen or heard any public service announcements and what they gave information about.

➤ After students listen to the announcement, ask *What is the announcement about?* (safe food handling in warm weather) *Why is this information being given on the radio?* (so that people won't get food poisoning) Students work with a partner to answer the question in Exercise A. Make sure students understand *purpose* as the goal of or reason for the announcement. Have volunteers read their answers to the class.

Option: Record public service announcements broadcast on television. Show them to the class and have students identify and discuss the purpose of each one.

🎧 B. Listen again ...

➤ Have volunteers read items 1 through 5 out loud. Encourage students to use context to determine the meaning of *thaw*. Say *If you leave frozen food on the counter it thaws, so what does "thaw" mean?* (to let frozen food unfreeze and soften until it is ready to cook)

Option: In groups, have students write the title *Safe food handling in warm weather* on a sheet of paper. Then have them draw a two-column chart with the headings *Do* and *Don't*. Students write the five sentences from Exercise B in the appropriate columns on their charts. Then students talk about what they remember from the announcement and add other do's and don'ts to their charts; for example, under *Do*, students can write *Put food in the refrigerator as soon as possible, Keep your refrigerator at 40°F.* Then play the cassette or read the announcement again so that students can add anything they missed.

C. True story ...

➤ Model the activity by telling a story about yourself or someone you know who has had food poisoning. Provide as many details as possible, including the cause, where the person got the food poisoning, symptoms the person had, and if a supermarket or restaurant was responsible, what was done to make good. Then ask the class

What should managers, cooks, and individuals do to prevent food poisoning?

➤ In groups, students tell their own stories. After each story, groups discuss what can be done to prevent food poisoning in the future. Have each group choose the most interesting story from their group to tell the class.

➤ Do it yourself!

(For general suggestions, see *Introduction*, page Txiii.)

Procedure:

A. Write your <u>own</u> response ...

➤ Have students refer to Exercise B under *Warm-weather food safety*, or to the chart they made, as they write their responses.

➤ Have volunteers read the speech balloons. Then ask *What's the weather like?* (hot) *What are the problems?* (thawing meat on the counter, leaving chicken in the car) Explain that students should give the man in the photo advice about safe food handling in warm weather.

➤ After students complete the activity individually, read each speech balloon and elicit a variety of responses from the class. Then have students read their conversations with a partner.

B. Culture talk ...

➤ Each student in a group answers the question and group members compare practices.

Challenge: Students work in groups with classmates from the same cultural background. They brainstorm a list of travel tips regarding food and water safety for tourists traveling to their country or region and then present a two-minute talk to the class or create a pamphlet.

Tapescript

Good afternoon, consumers! Welcome to another in our series of daily tips for safe food handling. Today's topic is safe food handling in warm weather. Have you ever had food poisoning? It's no laughing matter. Every year, more than 7 million Americans suffer from food-borne illnesses. The main cause of food-borne illness is bacteria. You can't see, smell, or taste most bacteria, but at warmer temperatures, bacteria multiply very fast. And when bacteria become numerous, they can cause illness. The good news is that most food-borne illnesses can be avoided by proper food handling.

(Tapescript is continued on page T108.)

⌒ A. **Listening comprehension. Listen to the public service announcement on the radio. Then answer the question in your own words.**

What's the purpose of the announcement? <u>Students should mention: to prevent food poisoning,</u>

<u>to give information about safe food handling</u>

⌒ B. **Listen again. Listen for <u>Do's</u> and <u>Don'ts</u>. Check the boxes according to the advice.**

	Do	Don't
1. Be aware of the danger of bacteria in warm weather.	☑	☐
2. Leave food in the car.	☐	☑
3. Wash hands after using the bathroom.	☑	☐
4. Replace kitchen towels and sponges frequently.	☑	☐
5. Thaw frozen food on the kitchen counter.	☐	☑

C. **True story. Do you know anyone who has had food poisoning? What was the cause? How can you prevent food poisoning? Tell your partner or your group.**

➤ Do it yourself!

A. **Write your <u>own</u> response. Give advice about food safety. Then read your conversation out loud with a partner.**

> Hi. I'm running late. Could you please take the meat out of the freezer?

YOU _____

> Please put the meat on the counter near the window. It's hot today, so it will defrost fast.

YOU _____

> I already bought the chicken. I'll just keep it in the car while I pick up my prescription. Do you think that's OK?

YOU _____

B. **Culture talk. In the country you come from, how do you keep foods safe in warm weather? Compare cultures with your classmates.**

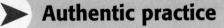
Over-the-counter (OTC) medications

A. Read the article about over-the-counter medications.

Pocket Digest

Educate yourself about OTCs

by Bonnie Crain, M.D.

Who's never had a cold? Where's the baby who hasn't suffered from teething woes, or the adult who hasn't had sore muscles or a headache, or an itchy rash from a food allergy?

No one gets through life without a little pain and suffering, not bad or serious enough to visit the doctor, but bad enough to seek relief on the pharmacy shelf.

What are OTCs?

Over-the-counter medicines, referred to as "OTCs," are medicines you can purchase without a doctor's prescription, simply by going to the nearest drugstore and choosing them yourself. Many of us make our choices based on word of mouth, advertisements, or by reading medicine package labels. Thousands of drugs are available over the counter, and it's important to be careful when choosing or taking them. Here are some important facts about OTCs:

1. OTCs are drugs. Just because they are available without a prescription doesn't mean they're harmless.
2. Many OTCs have side effects.
3. Mixing medications may be dangerous. Many OTCs can interact or interfere with the effects of your prescription drugs or with other OTCs.

How to use OTCs safely

Read package labels carefully. Be sure you understand warnings. Don't exceed the recommended dosage. When in doubt, ask the pharmacist or your doctor for advice. It's your responsibility, but the druggist and the doctor can help.

B. Answer the questions about over-the-counter drugs. Fill in the ovals.

1. What are OTCs?

   (a) medicines you buy without a prescription   (b) side effects

2. Where do you get OTCs?

   (a) at the drugstore   (b) from advertisements

3. What do OTCs do?

   (a) warn us   (b) treat ailments

4. What is a possible danger in using OTCs?

   (a) drug interactions   (b) lack of information

For extra practice, go to pages 159 and 160.

- After you go shopping, put food into the refrigerator as soon as possible. Don't leave food in a hot car. Bacteria multiply fast in a warm environment.

- Keep your refrigerator as cold as possible without freezing your lettuce! Refrigerators should run at 40 degrees Fahrenheit.

- Freeze fresh meat, poultry, and fish if you can't use it before the use-by date.

- Wash your hands in hot soapy water *before* preparing food and *after* using the bathroom, changing diapers, or handling pets.

- Bacteria live in kitchen towels and sponges. Wash them and replace them often.

- Keep raw meat, raw poultry, and raw fish away from other food. Wash your hands, the cutting board, and the knife in hot soapy water *after* cutting up chicken or meat and *before* cutting up salad ingredients.

- Thaw food in the microwave or refrigerator, not on the kitchen counter, because bacteria can grow on the outside of the food before the inside thaws.

If you follow these simple commonsense rules, you'll enjoy the summer season more than ever. Tune in every day at this time for more health tips for everyone. For more information, log on to our Web site at foodsafe.com.

[Information adapted from the USDA Food Safety and Inspection Service.]

➤ Authentic practice

(For general suggestions, see *Introduction*, page Tx.)

Over-the-counter (OTC) medications

Procedure:

A. Read the article ...

➤ Have students look at the article. Ask *Who wrote the article?* (Bonnie Crain, M.D.) *What do you think "M.D." stands for?* (Doctor of Medicine)

➤ Students read the article individually. As they read, have students underline answers to the two boldface heads.

➤ After students read, ask *What does OTC stand for?* (over-the-counter) *What are OTCs?* (medicines that you can buy without a doctor's prescription) *Where can you buy OTCs?* (at a drugstore, at a

supermarket) *What kinds of ailments can be treated with OTCs?* (cold, teething pain, sore muscles, headache, rash) *What are the recommendations for using OTCs safely?* (Read package labels carefully. Be sure you understand warnings. Don't take more than the recommended dosage.)

➤ Have volunteers read the three important facts about OTCs out loud. Ask *How can OTCs be harmful or dangerous?* (They can have side effects. They can interact or interfere with other medicines you are taking.) Elicit or explain the meaning of a *side effect* as an effect that a drug has on your body in addition to curing pain or illness. Give an example, such as *If you take medication to cure a rash and it gives you a headache, the headache is a "side effect."*

Option: Have students create a Venn diagram comparing OTCs and prescription medications. For example,

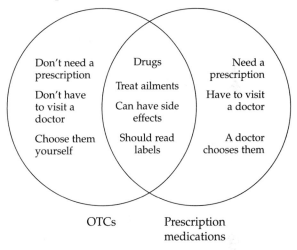

OTCs   Prescription medications

Challenge: Working in groups, ask students to write a one-sentence summary of the article. Explain that the sentence should tell the main idea of the article, or the point the author is trying to make, for example, *It's important to be careful when using over-the-counter medicines.* Have each group write its sentence on the board. Each group reads the sentences on the board and chooses the one it thinks is the best. Review each sentence with the whole class, asking if any group thought it was the sentence that summarized the article best. Keep a tally on the board. Read the sentence that most groups thought was best and discuss as a class what makes it a good summary of the article.

B. Answer the questions ...

➤ Students complete the activity individually and then check answers with a partner.

➤ Review the answers as a class. For each answer, ask *How do you know?* and have students find information in the article that supports their answer.

Directions and warnings on medicines

Procedure:

➤ Have students read the labels. Then have them find and underline in the text the words *antihistamine, overdose, indications, persists, consult.* In groups, have students read what comes right before and after these words and use the context to figure out the meanings. Students collaborate to write a definition for each word, for example, *antihistamine = a medicine for relief of allergy symptoms.* If dictionaries are available, have students check their definitions, or review as a class.

➤ For each medication, ask the class *What is the name of the OTC? What is it for? What is the dosage for adults? Who should not take this medicine?*

➤ Review ways to give advice. If helpful, have students refer to page 20 to review the use of imperatives to give instructions or warnings and the use of *Why don't . . . ?* to make suggestions. Also review *Maybe you'd better . . .* and verbs followed by infinitives, such as *be sure* and *need.* Elicit other ways to give advice, such as *should, could.*

➤ Students complete items 1 through 5 individually. Review as a class. Read each item individually and elicit a variety of responses from the class. Then have students take turns reading the questions and their answers with a partner.

Option: Discuss the importance of keeping drugs out of the reach of children. Ask students where they keep medications in their homes.

Option: If possible, request free brochures from a poison control center in your community. Have students read the brochures and ask and answer questions with a partner about the information given, or have students find specific information in the brochure.

Field project: Find out about a health fair in your community. They are often held at hospitals, schools, or parks. If possible, take your students to a health fair and have them pick up information about food safety, prescription drugs, OTCs, poison control, and / or any other information that is of interest to them.

➤ Do it yourself!

(For general suggestions, see *Introduction,* page Txiii.)

Procedure:

➤ Model the activity and review topics discussed in this unit by talking about customs and laws for medications in the United States. Explain that only doctors can write prescriptions and that medications for less serious ailments are available over the counter. Point out that drug companies are required to provide information about side effects or adverse reactions and warnings about possible dangers in using the medication. You may wish to refer to the *Culture / Civics note* on page T102.

➤ In diverse groups, students answer the two questions and talk about other customs and laws for medications in their home countries. Suggest that students talk about what types of medicines are available over the counter and what medications require a prescription.

What's your advice? Read the package labels. Then tell each person what to do.

Alledrine
Antihistamine

For relief of the stuffy nose
and itchy eyes of seasonal allergies

Uses: Alleviates symptoms of seasonal allergies.
Directions: *See chart.*

Dosage	Age	First Dose	Next Dose	Maximum per day
Adults	12 and over	2 tablets	1 tablet	4 tablets

NOT RECOMMENDED FOR CHILDREN UNDER 12 YRS. CONSULT DOCTOR.

Warnings:
Do not use if you have a high fever (over 101°F).
Do not use if you are pregnant or nursing.
KEEP THIS AND ALL DRUGS OUT OF THE REACH OF CHILDREN.
In case of accidental overdose, seek professional assistance or call a poison control center immediately.

24 tablets   NEW

 **NEW**   Lemon / Mint
ThroatEze

Extra Strength
With Kryptocaine

Anesthetic—for temporary relief of the pain of sore throat due to colds and voice overuse.
Indications: For temporary relief of occasional throat pain.
Directions: Adults and children over 2 years of age. Allow disk to melt slowly in mouth. May be repeated every 2 hours as needed or as directed by a physician.
Warnings: If condition is severe, persists for more than 2 days, or is accompanied by fever, vomiting, or rash, consult doctor promptly.

KEEP OUT OF THE REACH OF CHILDREN

Active ingredient: Each disk contains Kryptocaine Hydrochloride 2.0 mg.

Made in USA.

24 sore throat disks

1. "My ten-year-old daughter has a stuffy nose and a high fever. Should I buy her Alledrine?" _____

2. "I have allergies every fall. I feel terrible. Do you think Alledrine will help?" _____

3. "Oh, my gosh. I read the package wrong. I took eight Alledrine tablets today. What should I do?" _____

4. "My throat is so sore I can hardly talk. Do you know anything that will help?" _____

5. "I've been taking ThroatEze for a week, but now I have a fever and a sore throat. Should I keep taking ThroatEze?" _____

➤ Do it yourself!

Discussion. In your home country, are prescriptions necessary for all medications? Who can write a prescription? Discuss other customs and laws for medications.

> **Review**
>
> **A. Pair work or group work.**
>
> • Where are the people?
> • What are their problems?
>
> Ask and answer questions.
> Create conversations.
> Tell a story.
> Say as much as you can.

➤ Review

(For general suggestions, see *Introduction*, page Txii.)

Procedure:

A. Pair work or group work.

➤ Have students match each of the objectives on page 99 with a pair of people in the conversation; for example, *Return food to a supermarket and explain why* can be matched with the man and woman standing in front of the produce stand. Explain that one objective will not be used. Review as a class and ask which objective students did not find a match for in the picture (Understand and apply food-safety techniques).

Ask and answer questions.

➤ Partners take turns pointing to different pairs or groups in the picture and asking *Where are they? What is the problem?*

Create conversations.

➤ Have students create a conversation for at least one pair of people in the picture. Encourage them to look back through the unit for ideas.

Option: Circulate and, as you pass each student, point to one of the people in the picture who has a speech balloon. The student writes a line of conversation for the person you pointed out. Each student reads his or her line. The rest of the class guesses who in the picture is speaking. For example, if a student reads the line *Actually, this steak is not rare,* the class should guess the man sitting at a table on the left side of the picture, talking to the waitress. When a student guesses, ask *How can you tell?*

Tell a story.

Option: Describe an illness. Have students imagine that the woman with the leg brace is a friend of theirs. Students tell the story of how she got food poisoning. Students can talk about where she got the food poisoning, what food caused the illness, her symptoms, whether she reported it to the restaurant, what was done to make good, and what the restaurant can do to prevent other cases of food poisoning.

Option: Whose coat is it? Have students tell the story of the two men who took each other's coats by mistake from the perspective of the man on the left, for example, *After I ate lunch at Brenda's Café today, I picked up the wrong coat. I thought it was my coat, but another man said it was his . . .*

Option: Talk about your day. Have students imagine that they are the waitress in the picture and talk about their day. Students should talk about the problems at each table.

Option: Create a commercial. Have students tell what symptoms Cold-B-Gone cold tablets treat and make up warnings and adverse reactions / side effects. They can use this information to create a TV commercial for the medication.

🎧 B. Listen to the conversations...

➤ Tell students that they are going to listen to three separate conversations. Then play the cassette or read the conversations from the tapescript.

➤ Have students read the statements individually and then listen again and complete the exercise.

➤ To review, play the cassette or read the conversations a third time. Pause between each conversation and ask the class what it was about.

➤ For items 1 and 3, have students write a true sentence that tells what the conversation is about.

C–E.

➤ Students work individually to complete the review exercises.

➤ Circulate to offer help as needed.

➤ Have students check answers with a partner. Review answers as a class.

➤ Identify any areas of difficulty that may require additional instruction and practice.

Option: Write the three ailments from Exercise C on the board and then brainstorm other ailments such as *headache, back pain, sore muscles*. Mime one of the ailments and call on students to guess which ailment you are suffering from. The student who guesses correctly stands up and mimes a different ailment. Continue until most of the ailments have been used.

Option: For Exercise D, have students write a third line of the conversation for each item. For example, for item 1, if the response was *No, thanks. I'll just take a refund*, the next line of the conversation could be *Manager: No problem. So long as you have your receipt.*

Tapescript

Conversation 1

Man: You're not going to take that capsule on an empty stomach, are you?
Woman: Why not? The label says to take it before breakfast, doesn't it?

Conversation 2

Woman: Let's give Katie a couple of those tablets. That should help.
Man: We'd better not. The patient information sheet says, "Not for children under the age of six."

Conversation 3

Man: Look at this milk. It says sell by April twelfth. I got it this morning.
Woman: Take it back. Today's the fifteenth!

		True	False
1.	**Conversation 1.** They're talking about what to eat for breakfast.	☐	☑
2.	**Conversation 2.** They're discussing a sick child.	☑	☐
3.	**Conversation 3.** They're returning milk in a restaurant.	☐	☑

C. Look at the pictures of the ailments. Write the name of each ailment.

1. _____rash_____	2. _____sore throat_____	3. _____insomnia_____

D. Write a response to each statement or question.

1. **Manager:** Would you like to get another package?

   _____

2. **Waiter:** Is everything OK?

   _____

3. **Pharmacist:** Take one tablet three times a day.

   _____

4. **Co-worker:** I don't believe what you're doing!

   _____

5. **Boss:** They told you the policy, didn't they?

   _____

E. Complete each sentence with a possessive noun.

1. This is _____Edwin's_____ prescription. Don't take it.
   Edwin

2. My _____neighbor's_____ daughter ate a rare hamburger and got food poisoning.
   neighbor

3. The _____medicine's_____ label is missing, and I don't know how much to take.
   medicine

4. The _____patients'_____ appointments all had to be rescheduled.
   patients

5. Dr. _____Klein's_____ office is closed today.
   Klein

F. **Replace the words in parentheses with a possessive pronoun.**

1. That prescription for Bactizide is (my husband's prescription). <u>That prescription for</u>
<u>Bactizide is his.</u>

2. My hamburger is perfect. How's (your hamburger)? <u>My hamburger is perfect.</u>
<u>How's yours?</u>

3. These are his tablets. Where are (our tablets)? <u>These are his tablets. Where are ours?</u>
_____

4. My rash is better. What about (their rash)? <u>My rash is better. What about theirs?</u>
_____

G. **Complete each sentence.**

1. <u>My</u> husband never takes Alledrine for his allergies.
    My / Mine

2. My appointment was rescheduled for tomorrow. What about <u>yours</u>?
                                                  your / yours

3. Whose prescription is this, yours or <u>theirs</u>?
                                        their / theirs

H. **Write two rules for safe food handling.**

1. _____
2. _____

I. **Composition. On a separate sheet of paper, write about the picture on page 110. Say as much as you can.**

> **Now I can**
> ❑ return food to a supermarket and explain why.
> ❑ send food back in a restaurant and explain why.
> ❑ give and understand directions for taking a medicine.
> ❑ understand and apply food-safety techniques.
> ❑ understand directions and warnings on medicines.
> ❑ _____.

F–H.

➤ Students work individually to complete the review exercises.

➤ Circulate to offer help as needed.

➤ Have students check answers with a partner. Review answers as a class.

➤ Identify any areas of difficulty that may require additional instruction and practice.

Option: For Exercise H, have students work with a partner or small group and brainstorm as many rules for safe food handling as they can remember.

I. Composition ...

➤ Provide students with concrete approaches to writing about the picture on page 110. Use one of the following options, give students a choice of options, or assign options based on students' levels of proficiency. Model what is expected of students for each option.

➤ Advise students to look back through the unit for help and ideas as they write.

➤ Circulate to offer help as needed.

Option: Have students choose one person from each pair on page 110 and write a sentence. For example, for the woman at the produce stand, students might write *She is returning the tomatoes because they're not fresh*, or for the man pointing to his plate, *His steak is not well done*.

Option: Have students write a letter of complaint to Brenda's Café from the man who has a problem with the meat he ordered or from the woman who was served milk that wasn't fresh. The letter should include when the customer ate at the restaurant, what he or she ordered, what the problem was, whether the customer tried to send the food back, and how the waitress responded. You may wish to review business-letter format on page T4.

Challenge: Have students write a public service announcement with the purpose of encouraging people to be careful when choosing or taking OTCs such as Cold-B-Gone cold tablets. Have students include several do's and don'ts for using OTCs safely.

Now I can

➤ Read the first item in the box out loud, *Now I can return food to a supermarket and explain why*. Elicit from the class an example of how to give a reason for returning food to the store, such as *I bought this milk here today, and its sell-by date is expired*.

➤ In pairs, have students take turns reading each item in the box and giving an example of what they have learned. When students can provide an example, they should check that objective. For the items students weren't able to check, they should look back through the unit for ideas.

➤ When students are finished reviewing with their partners, read each item out loud and elicit an example from the class.

Oral test (optional)

You may want to use the *Now I can* box as an informal evaluation. While students are working on the *Composition* activity, you can call them up individually and check their ability with two or three objectives.

T112

Money

Note: For the *Do it yourself!* activity on page 117, students will need to use the Yellow Pages. Have students bring to class credit card offers they receive in the mail for use on page 121.

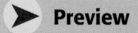 Preview

(For general suggestions, see *Introduction*, page Tviii.)

Warm up. What's the problem?

Procedure:

➤ Have students read the credit card statement. Then ask questions about it, such as *What is the name of the credit card company?* (Credit Express) *Who is the account holder?* (Roseanne Calderon) *What is her account number?* (7819 622 4700) *How much does Ms. Calderon owe?* ($157.18) *How can she make the payment?* (by check or money order) *What is the problem?* (Her account is 30 days past due.) *When does she need to pay by?* (May 18, 2003) *What happens if she doesn't pay by May 18?* (A delinquency charge will be added to the amount of the bill.)

➤ Elicit or explain the meaning of *delinquency charge* as a fine or fee for not paying a bill on time.

➤ To draw on students' own experiences, ask *Who has a credit card? How much time do you have to make a payment? Have you ever been late with the payment? How much was the delinquency charge, or late fee?*

Challenge: In pairs, students create a phone conversation between a customer service representative for Credit Express and Roseanne Calderon. Explain that she can't find her statement and wants to know how much she owes and when the payment is due. For example,

> **Customer service representative:** Credit Express, how can I help you?
>
> **Ms. Calderon:** Hello, my name is Roseanne Calderon. I would like to pay my bill, but I can't find my statement.
>
> **Customer service representative:** Do you know your account number?
>
> **Ms. Calderon:** Yes, it's 7819 622 4700 . . .

Unit 9 objectives

Procedure:

➤ Have students close their books. In groups, have students brainstorm what they think they will learn to do in this unit, based on the *Warm up* activity. Ask groups to write three possible objectives, for example, *Use credit cards, Understand bills, Talk about owing money, Call a credit card company to ask questions about a bill.* To prompt students, write on the board ways students can begin their objectives—such as *Discuss, Talk about, Understand, Ask, Ask for, Read, Express.*

➤ Students open their books and look at the objectives. Read the first objective out loud. Elicit or explain the meaning of *debt* as money that you owe. Ask *Do any groups have an objective similar to this?* Elicit similar examples from students. Continue reading each objective, explaining unfamiliar words and eliciting similar objectives from the class.

Money

▶ **Preview**

Warm up. What's the problem?

Statement of Personal Card Account

Payable upon receipt in U.S. Dollars with a check drawn on a bank located in the U.S., or a money order.
Please enter Personal Account Number on all checks and correspondence.

Credit Express

```
        YOUR ACCOUNT IS 30 DAYS PAST DUE.
    PAY BY 05/18/03 TO AVOID DELINQUENCY CHARGE
```

Personal Account Number
7819 622 4700

Statement Closing Date
04–26–03

Total Amount Due
$157.18

Roseanne Calderon
420 W. 95th St.
New York, NY 10025

Mail payment to:
Credit Express
P.O. Box 6700
Newark, NJ 07101–1270

```
8525924869 00097318000092257B
```

Detach here and return upper portion with check or money order. Do not staple or fold.

Unit 9 objectives

- Discuss problems with debt.
- Find the appropriate person for financial information.
- Offer good and bad financial news.
- Complain about banking services.
- Express satisfaction and dissatisfaction.
- Get consumer advice for problems with debt.

Practical conversations

A. Listen and read.

A: I'd like some information on mortgages. Are you the right person?

B: Yes, I am. How can I help you?

A: Can you tell me the current interest rate?

B: Sure. It's 9.5%. Would you like a brochure?

A: You know, on second thought, I think I'll shop around.

B: Of course. But as long as you're here, why don't you take this along?

MORTGAGE

15 years $80,000
Interest 8%

B. Listen again and repeat.

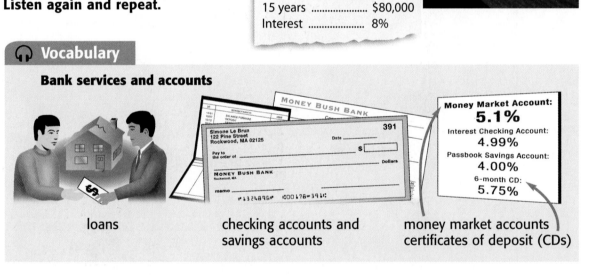

Vocabulary

Bank services and accounts

Money Market Account:
5.1%

Interest Checking Account:
4.99%

Passbook Savings Account:
4.00%

6-month CD:
5.75%

loans

checking accounts and
savings accounts

money market accounts
certificates of deposit (CDs)

C. Pair work. **Ask for information on interest rates. Decline an offer.**

A: I'd like some information on _____. Are you the right person?

B: Yes, I am. _____?

A: Can you tell me the current interest rate?

B: ___1___. It's _____%. Would you like a brochure?

A: You know, on second thought, I think I'll shop around.

B: ___2___. But as long as you're here, why don't you take this along?

[1]Of course, I'd be glad to, Absolutely   [2]OK, No problem, Certainly

2%

10%

7.5%

3.75%

➤ Practical conversations

(For general suggestions, see *Introduction*, page Tviii.)

Model 1

Content: finding the appropriate person for information; discussing interest rates for bank services and accounts; declining an offer

Procedure:

🎧 A–B.

➤ Ask questions about the photo, such as *What is the man thinking about?* (moving, buying a house) *How can people get enough money to buy a house?* (They can borrow money from a bank.) *In your home country, how do most people get money to buy a house?*

➤ After students listen to the conversation, ask questions such as *What does the man ask for information on?* (mortgages) *At first, does he know who to ask?* (no) *What does he say?* (Are you the right person?) *What specific question does he have about mortgages?* (the current interest rate) *Does he think 9.5% is a good interest rate?* (probably not, because he says he'll shop around)

➤ Check students' understanding of *on second thought, shop around,* and *as long as* by having them rephrase in their own words the last two speakers' lines in the conversation. For example, students might begin with *Actually, I've changed my mind. I think I'll check some other banks.* If necessary, provide simple definitions.

➤ Have students look at the mortgage information at the bottom left of the photo. Elicit or explain that a *mortgage* is a legal arrangement in which you borrow money from a bank to buy a house and pay back the money over a period of years. Ask *How much is being borrowed?* ($80,000) *How long does the borrower have to pay back the money?* (15 years) *How much does it cost to borrow the money?* (8% per year)

🎧 Vocabulary

➤ Have students look at the interest rates for the different types of accounts listed in the last illustration. Ask *Which types of account have higher interest rates?* (CDs and money market accounts) Explain that CDs and money market accounts usually have higher interest rates than checking and regular savings accounts because there are rules about when or how often you can withdraw money from your account.

C. Pair work ...

➤ Say out loud each of the interest rates listed and have students repeat. Point out that if there is more than one digit after the decimal point, each digit is pronounced separately, for example, *three point seven five percent.* After students repeat, have them say each interest rate in the *Vocabulary* box.

➤ Ask students which interest rates are more appropriate for: mortgages and loans (10%, 7.5%), CDs and money market accounts (3.75%), checking and savings accounts (2%).

Note: Free, step-by-step home-buying guides are available in nine languages from the Fannie Mae Foundation. Information on how to obtain these guides can be found online at www.homebuyingguide.org.

Field project: If appropriate, have students go to a bank and ask about the current interest rate for one of the following: mortgages, loans, interest-bearing checking accounts, savings accounts, money market accounts, CDs. Students should first rehearse with a partner what they will say. Alternatively, students can visit an online bank's Web site and search for the same information.

If your students are ready ...

Culture / Civics note: *Interest* is the fee that the lender, such as a bank, charges when you borrow money. Interest can also be the money that a bank pays you when you keep money in an account. Interest is often expressed as a percentage amount called *an interest rate.* This is a percentage of the amount of money being loaned or being kept in an account. Interest rates vary from bank to bank, so it is important to shop around for the best rate.

A money market account usually pays a higher interest rate than a standard interest-bearing checking or savings account, and it offers limited check-writing privileges as well. However, typically a minimum balance must be maintained to avoid a monthly fee, and there are restrictions on the number of withdrawals that can be made per month.

A certificate of deposit, or *CD,* is a type of deposit account that generally offers the highest rate of interest. With a CD, you deposit a fixed amount of money and agree not to withdraw it for a specific amount of time ranging from three months to five years or more. In return, you receive a fixed amount of interest; the longer the amount of time, the higher the rate. Withdrawing the money before the end of the fixed time results in a penalty.

Model 2

Content: offering good and bad financial news

Procedure:

🎧 A–B.

➤ Ask questions about the photo, such as *Where is the couple?* (in their kitchen) *Where are they looking at?* (the mail) *Who is just coming home?* (the woman) *Why do you think so?* (She is carrying her bag.)

➤ After students listen to the conversation, ask questions, such as *What is the good financial news?* (The bank approved their loan application.) *What is the bad financial news?* (The couple bounced three checks.)

➤ Have students look at the three checks below the photo. Have a volunteer read what is stamped in red on all the checks. Ask *What does "insufficient funds" mean?* (not enough money) *So what does "bounce a check" mean?* (The bank will not make payment on the check because there is not enough money in the account of the person who wrote it.) *What does the bank charge for bouncing a check?* ($36 per check) If helpful, explain or demonstrate that when a check *bounces*, like a ball it comes back to you.

➤ Ask whether any students know what fee their bank charges for bouncing a check.

🎧 Vocabulary

➤ After students listen to and repeat the vocabulary, ask *Do you want the good news or the bad news first?* Elicit a response from the class and discuss those phrases first.

➤ Encourage students to use context to figure out the meaning of unfamiliar words; for example, say *"Approved" is under good news. So if the bank approves your loan application, do they say "yes" or "no" to loaning you the money?* (yes) With *penalty* and *finance charges*, students will probably figure out that they are types of fees charged by a bank. Explain *penalty* more specifically as a fee you are charged if you withdraw money from a CD before the specified time and *finance charges* as interest that a bank or credit card company charges on money you borrow; for example, if you don't pay the entire amount due on your credit card bill each month, you have to pay a finance charge.

➤ To prepare students for the *Pair work* activity, have them make sentences with the phrases under *Financial bad news*, for example, *I bounced a check, We are behind on our mortgage payments.* Make sure students use the correct possessive form with *mortgage payments.*

C. Pair work …

➤ Model the activity with a more advanced student. Play the role of Student B. Point out that Student A can ask for the good or the bad news first. Demonstrate responding accordingly with a sentence about financial bad news or good news. As a class, brainstorm a variety of ways for Student A to fill in the first blank in his or her last line.

➤ Students practice the conversation with a partner, taking turns playing the roles of Student A and Student B.

➤ Do it yourself!

(For general suggestions, see *Introduction*, page Txiii.)

Procedure:

➤ Model the activity by talking about a bank account you have and what you like and don't like about the account, for example, *I have a checking account. I like that I earn interest on my checking account. I don't like that my bank charges me if I use an ATM at another bank.*

➤ In groups, students talk about whether or not they have a bank account and what type it is. Students discuss what they like about their account and what they don't like.

➤ Say each type of account—*checking, savings, money market, CD*—and have students who have this type of account raise their hands. Write on the board the name of the most common type of account in class. Draw a two-column chart with the headings *Advantages* and *Disadvantages*. Elicit information to fill in the chart from the class.

A. Listen and read.

A: Hi, Fred. How was your day?

B: Well, do you want the good news or the bad news?

A: Let's take the good news first.

B: Well, they approved our loan application.

A: That's good. So, what's the bad news?

B: We bounced three checks.

B. Listen again and repeat.

Vocabulary

Financial bad news	Financial good news
bounce a check	They approved our
be behind on your mortgage payments	loan application
have to pay a late fee	mortgage
have to pay a penalty	credit card application
have to pay finance charges	

C. Pair work. Talk about good and bad financial news.

A: Hi, _____. How was your day?

B: Well, do you want the good news or the bad news?

A: Let's take the _____ news first.

B: Well, _____.

A: That's ___1___. So, what's the _____ news?

B: _____.

¹great, fantastic, terrible, awful, a shame, too bad

▶ Do it yourself!

Discussion. **What kinds of accounts do you have at the bank? What are the advantages and disadvantages of each kind of account?**

Model 3   Put yourself in another's shoes. Discuss debt. Suggest the Yellow Pages.

A. Listen and read.

A: I'm behind on my car payments.

B: How far behind?

A: Three months. And now they might repossess my car.

B: Oh, no! How did that happen?

A: Well, to tell you the truth, I got in over my head.

B: If I were you, I'd check the Yellow Pages under "Credit Counseling." They help people get out of debt.

B. Listen again and repeat.

Vocabulary

Consequences of debt

I'm behind on my mortgage payments. They might foreclose on my house.

I'm behind on my rent. They might evict me.

I'm behind on my car payments. They might repossess my car.

I'm behind on my credit card payments. They might cancel my card.

C. Pair work. A friend is in debt. Suggest checking the Yellow Pages or calling one of the counseling services below. Or make your _own_ suggestion.

A: I'm behind on my _____.

B: How far behind?

A: _____. And now they might _____.

B: Oh, no! How did that happen?

A: Well, to tell you the truth, I got in over my head.

B: If I were you, I'd _____.

CREDIT AND DEBT COUNSELING SVCES.

In debt? Need Help?
Help is a phone call away.
Call **1-800-NO-DEBTS**
Stop those harassing calls.
Consolidate your bills into
one affordable monthly payment.

Drowning in debt? In over your head?
Creditors calling?
Call **1-800-555-HELP** or
Log on to overmyhead.com

➤ Practical conversations

(For general suggestions, see *Introduction*, page Tviii.)

Model 3

Content: discussing debt and its consequences; putting yourself in another's shoes; suggesting the Yellow Pages; conditional sentences

Procedure:

🎧 A–B.

➤ Have students look at the body language of the people in the photo. Ask *What is the man doing?* (He has his hand on his hips.) *What does this suggest?* (He is upset or has a problem.) *What is the woman doing?* (pointing to herself)

➤ After students listen to and read the conversation, ask questions such as *What is the problem?* (He's behind on his car payments.) *What might happen?* (They might repossess his car.) *What does the woman suggest?* (to check the Yellow Pages under "Credit Counseling") *What does she say before she makes the suggestion?* (If I were you, . . .)

➤ Discuss the meaning of *repossess*. Elicit or point out that *re-* means again and *possess* is to own or have something; so when they repossess the car, they take ownership again, or take it back. Ask *Who is "they"?* (the bank)

➤ To explain *in over my head*, draw on the board a stick figure under water. Say *He can't swim. He is in a serious situation. The man from the conversation is in a serious situation because he doesn't have the money to make his car payments.* Ask students if they have ever felt *in over their heads*. Ask what the situation was. Ask *Who do people owe money to?* (credit card companies, car dealers, banks, utility companies, friends, relatives)

➤ Say *When the woman says "If I were you," she puts herself in the man's shoes.* Explain that to *put yourself in another's shoes* is to imagine what you would do if you were in someone else's situation.

Option: Elicit from the class examples of idioms used in students' first languages to talk about debt.

🎧 Vocabulary

➤ After students listen to and repeat the vocabulary, have students underline in the speech balloons *repossess, foreclose, cancel, evict*. With a partner, students read the speech balloons again and write a simple definition for each word, for example, *foreclose = The bank takes away your house because you can't make the mortgage payments.* Review as a class.

C. Pair work . . .

➤ Have students read the ads. Discuss what a credit counselor does for people. Explain that a credit counselor can combine all your debts so that you pay only one monthly bill that is an amount you can afford.

➤ Model the conversation with a more advanced student. Play the role of Student A. Demonstrate completing the sentences in Student A's first and second lines with a problem and a consequence from one of the speech balloons in the *Vocabulary* box. For Student B's last line, elicit a variety of suggestions from the class, for example, *call 1-800-555-HELP, ask for more time to make the payments, get a second job, check the Yellow Pages for a counseling service.*

Note: You may wish to point out that in the sentence *If I were you, I'd check . . . , 'd* is a contraction of *would*, not a contraction of *had*.

If your students are ready . . .

Language note: Several idioms use the image of water, especially deep water, to refer to being in debt or in other overwhelming circumstances. In addition to *in over my head*, we also say *drowning in debt, in too deep, going under, knee-deep in debt,* and *in hot water.*

Culture / Civics note: An important resource for locating the address and telephone number of a local business or service is the Yellow Pages section of the telephone directory. Named for the yellow paper that it is printed on, the Yellow Pages section contains the names, addresses, and telephone numbers of local businesses and organizations organized by categories such as painters, restaurants, and credit counseling.

Model 4

Content: complaining about bank services; expressing dissatisfaction and satisfaction; giving advice; putting yourself in another's shoes; use of *keep* and a gerund

Procedure:

🎧 A–B.

➤ After students listen to and read the conversation, ask *What does the woman on the left complain about?* (her bank) *What's the problem?* (They keep raising fees.) *Where does Marie bank?* (at Green Tree) *How does she feel about the service there?* (She's satisfied.)

➤ Encourage students to use context to figure out the meaning of *raising*. Ask *Is the bank making the fees more or less expensive?* (more expensive)

🎧 Dissatisfaction

➤ Point out that the prefix *dis-* means "not"; so, if someone is *dissatisfied*, they are not satisfied, or not happy.

➤ After students listen to and repeat the phrases, ask *When would you use these expressions? When do you feel unhappy or frustrated?* Elicit responses such as *when my computer freezes, when my neighbor plays loud music.*

🎧 Satisfaction

➤ Have students use the words to create original sentences expressing satisfaction with something, for example, *I'm pretty happy with my car.*

🎧 Vocabulary

➤ After students listen to and repeat the vocabulary, have them read the information in each illustration. For each illustration, ask questions that make the meaning of the vocabulary item clear. For example, for *raise fees*, ask *By how much will fees go up?* (by 2%) For *lower interest rates*, ask *How much interest did customers earn on checking accounts before?* (4.5%) *How much interest will customers earn now?* (3.8%)

➤ Review by asking *What word means "go up"?* (raise) *What words mean "go down"?* (lower, reduce)

➤ Ask *What does your bank do that makes you feel dissatisfied?* (raise fees, close early, charge you to use the ATM, charge you for bounced checks) *How do customers find out about new charges and changes in interest rates, fees, and services?* (The bank sends letters or posts signs.)

C. Pair work . . .

➤ Brainstorm on the board names of local banks for students to use in the conversation.

➤ Have students write the gerund, or *–ing*, form of each verb in the *Vocabulary* box. Make sure students drop the *-e* in *raising, reducing,* and *closing.*

➤ Do it yourself!

(For general suggestions, see *Introduction,* page Txiii.)

Procedure:

A. Look up . . .

➤ Read the example out loud. Ask *What is the name of the organization that provides credit counseling?* (Credit Counseling of Hudson Valley) *Why is the information that comes after their name in quotation marks?* (because these are the exact words the service uses in its ad)

➤ To model the activity, use the first ad on page 116 to create a chart entry as a class. Ask *What is the name of the service?* (Credit and Debt Counseling Services) *What does the service "say" it can do for you?* ("Stop those harassing calls. Consolidate your bills . . .") Write the entry on the board. Be sure to include quotation marks.

➤ If the Yellow Pages are not available, students can complete the activity outside class or use the online Yellow Pages.

B. Discussion . . .

➤ Have students read the example again. Discuss the meaning of *red* and *black* as they relate to financial situations. Explain that *to be in the red* means to owe more money than you have and *to be in the black* means to have more money than you owe.

➤ In groups, students read their chart entries and talk about what each service *says* it can do.

➤ When groups have finished discussing, ask if there were any claims that they did not understand. Write them on the board and discuss their meanings as a class.

Note: The concept of credit and debt counseling services is expanded in the *Authentic practice* on page 122. The information presented advises caution in choosing a counseling service.

Model 4 Complain about bank services. Give advice.

A. Listen and read.

A: Marie, I want to change banks.

B: How come?

A: Well, my bank keeps raising fees. I've had enough! Where do you bank?

B: At Green Tree. I'm satisfied with the service there. If I were you, I'd change to Green Tree.

B. Listen again and repeat.

Dissatisfaction

I've had enough!
I'm fed up!
I've had it!

Satisfaction

satisfied
pretty happy
pleased

Vocabulary

Complaints about bank services

MONEY BUSH BANK

Dear Client:
We're sorry to inform you that as of April 1, fees on all accounts will go up 2%. We take this measure in order to

Interest Checking **3.8%**
Interest Checking **4.5%**

MONEY BUSH BANK

Dear Client:
Effective immediately, we no longer offer free checking or free traveler's checks. We are sorry for this inconvenience

Jones Street Branch closed. Please use Smith Street Branch.

raise fees   lower interest rates   reduce services   close branch offices

C. Pair work. Express dissatisfaction with your bank. Advise your partner.

A: _____, I want to change banks.

B: ___1___?

A: Well, my bank keeps _____. I _____! Where do you bank?

B: At _____. I'm _____ there. If I were you, I'd change to _____.

¹What's the matter, Is there anything wrong

➤ Do it yourself!

A. Look up "Credit and Debt Counseling Services" in the Yellow Pages. Write the names of two services. What does each service <u>say</u> it can do for you?

Credit Counseling of Hudson Valley: "Tired of seeing red? Get in the black."
1.
2.

B. Discussion. Talk about the claims each service makes. Explain what it means.

Conditional sentences

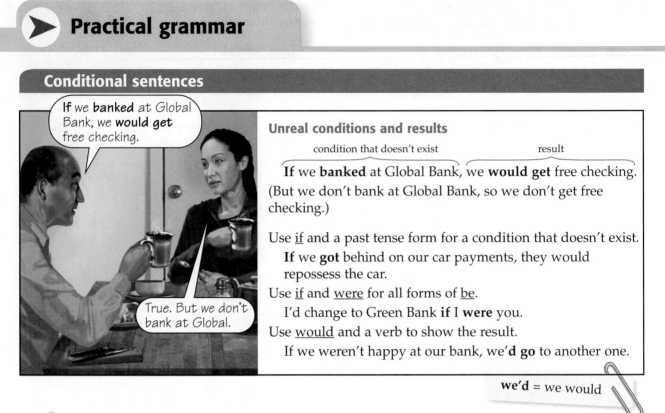

Unreal conditions and results

      condition that doesn't exist   result

If we **banked** at Global Bank, we **would get** free checking.
(But we don't bank at Global Bank, so we don't get free checking.)

Use <u>if</u> and a past tense form for a condition that doesn't exist.
    If we **got** behind on our car payments, they would repossess the car.
Use <u>if</u> and <u>were</u> for all forms of <u>be</u>.
    I'd change to Green Bank **if** I **were** you.
Use <u>would</u> and a verb to show the result.
    If we weren't happy at our bank, we'**d go** to another one.

we'd = we would

A. Check the statements that describe conditions that don't exist.

1. ☐   We banked at Global Bank last year, and we got a higher interest rate.

2. ☑   If we banked at Global Bank, we'd get a higher interest rate.

3. ☐   When we applied for a mortgage, they asked us how much money we needed.

4. ☑   If I were you, I would complain.

B. Complete each unreal conditional sentence.

1. If we ____<u>were</u>____ in debt, we'<u>d call</u>____ a credit counseling service.
               be   call

2. What ____<u>would</u>____ you ____<u>do</u>____ if your boss ____<u>didn't pay</u>____ you?
                          do   not pay

3. If people ____<u>were</u>____ more careful, they ____<u>wouldn't get</u>____ in over their heads.
               be   not get

4. If I ____<u>needed</u>____ a loan, I'd____<u>ask</u>____ about the interest rate.
            need   ask

5. We ____<u>wouldn't have</u>____ a joint checking account if we ____<u>weren't</u>____ married.
           not have   not be

6. If I ____<u>didn't have</u>____ a good job, I ____<u>wouldn't buy</u>____ that car.
          not have   not buy

➤ Practical grammar

(For general suggestions, see *Introduction*, page Tix.)

Conditional sentences

Procedure:

➤ Have two volunteers read the speech balloons out loud. Then write other conditional sentences on the board, and for each, ask whether or not the condition is true. For example, write on the board *If I got a promotion, I would put more money into my savings account.* Then ask *But did I get a promotion?* (no)

➤ Read and discuss the explanations and examples in the grammar box. Write on the board

Condition that doesn't exist	Result
<u>If</u> + past tense	<u>would</u> + verb
<u>If</u> I g<u>o</u>t a promotion	I <u>would put</u> more money . . .

➤ Point out that *were* is the past tense form for *am*, *is*, and *are*. Provide some examples, such as *If you were at work right now, you would be earning money.*

➤ To help students internalize the structure, write on the board several conditions that don't exist for students, for example, *If I had a million dollars, If I were mayor of this city, If I had a plane ticket to anywhere in the world.* Model the activity by completing the sentences yourself. Then students use *would* and a verb to tell a partner the result for each condition.

➤ Point out that when conditional sentences are written, a comma follows the condition, for example, *If we banked at Global Bank, we would get free checking.* Explain that when the condition comes at the end of a sentence, no comma is necessary, for example, *I'd change to Green Bank if I were you.*

Option: Write several conditional sentences on the board, some with the condition at the beginning and some with the condition at the end of the sentence. Omit the commas. Have students copy the sentences, adding commas where appropriate. When students are finished, have volunteers add the commas to the sentences on the board.

Option: Have students rewrite the examples on the board, inverting the order of the *if* clauses.

Option: Draw on the board a two-column chart with the headings *Situation I don't like* and *If the situation were different.* Model writing sentences about situations you don't like in the first column, for example, *It's raining today, I don't have a computer, I have to work on the weekend.* Students copy the chart and write their own sentences. Then model how to write sentences about what you would do if the situation were different. For example: *If it weren't raining, I would go for a walk after class; If I had a computer, I would shop online; If I didn't have to work on the weekend, I would go to the movies.* In the second column on their charts, students write sentences about what they would do if the situations they described were different.

We'd

➤ Write on the board *I would, you would, he would, she would, it would, we would, they would.* Have students look at the yellow language note. Ask what the contraction is for *we would* (we'd). Then elicit from the class and write on the board the contractions *I'd, you'd, he'd, she'd, it'd, they'd.*

A. Check the statements . . .

➤ In each item, have students underline the first part of the sentence, up to the comma. Read item 1. Then read the underlined portion of the sentence, *We banked at Global Bank last year.* Ask *Did they bank at Global Bank last year?* (yes) For items 2 through 4, advise students to ask themselves if the first part of each sentence is true; students should check the box only if the answer is *no*.

B. Complete each . . .

➤ Have students circle *if* in each item. Point out that the verb after *if* should be written in the past tense and that the other verb is used with *would*. Remind student to use *were* for the past tense of *be* after *if*.

➤ To check answers, have students read the sentences to a partner. Then review as a class.

T118

Keep and gerund

Content: describing continuing actions with *keep* and a gerund

Procedure:

➤ Use *keep* and a gerund to share some recurring complaints that you have, for example, *My neighbor keeps parking in my space, My credit card company keeps charging me late fees.* Rephrase each complaint to demonstrate that *keep* and a gerund are used to describe actions that continue and might not stop, for example, *Every night when I come home from work, my neighbor is in my parking space.*

➤ Have volunteers read the speech balloons. Ask *Has Money Bush raised the fees on checking accounts once or many times?* (many times) Read the explanation and example in the grammar box out loud. Explain that Sven often buys things he can't afford. Write on the board *keep + a gerund (-ing verb).*

➤ Have students think about frustrating situations at work or at home that happen over and over again. Elicit several examples using *keep* and a gerund from students.

Option: Write on the board *Why don't you like John?* Then write *because he keeps calling me.* Call on students and ask similar questions, such as *Why are they switching banks? Why did the woman fire her secretary? Why should we bring an umbrella?* Explain that students should make up answers using *keep* and a gerund, modeling their answers after the example on the board.

C. Complete the sentences ...

➤ Write item 1 on the board. Elicit the correct answer from the class. Then students complete items 2 through 6 individually.

➤ To check answers, have students read the sentences with a partner. Then review as a class. Make sure students drop the *-e* in *bouncing* and double the *-t* in *getting.* Refer students to page 150 for help with how to spell gerunds.

➤ Do it yourself!

(For general suggestions, see *Introduction,* page Txiii.)

Procedure:

A. Pair work ...

➤ Ask your own *What would you do if ...?* question and elicit several responses from students.

➤ Students work with a partner to create three questions. Remind students to use a past tense verb.

B. Discussion ...

➤ Have each pair of students join another pair to ask and answer each other's questions. Each group decides on its most interesting question and answer to share with the class.

Option: Have students write five sentences using group members' responses to their questions. For example, if a student asked Dmitri *What would you do if you won the lottery?* and Dmitri replied *I would buy a new house for my mother,* the student would write *Dmitri would buy a new house for his mother if he won the lottery.*

Challenge: Pass around several transparencies, and have each student write on a transparency one of his or her sentences from the optional activity above. Have volunteers read the sentences on the overhead projector out loud. Elicit the class's help in making any necessary corrections. Then turn off the overhead projector. Ask questions about the sentences, for example, *What would Dmitri do if he won the lottery?* Groups take turns answering the questions, and each correct answer earns the group a point. The group with the most points wins the game.

Keep and gerund

Again! Money Bush **keeps raising** the fees on checking accounts. I've had enough.

Let's change to Green Tree.

Use <u>keep</u> and a gerund to describe an action that continues and might not stop.

> Sven **keeps buying** things he can't afford. He needs to get out of debt.

C. **Complete the sentences about continuing actions with <u>keep</u> and gerunds.**

1. John and Elena _____keep bouncing_____ checks. They have to pay a penalty too.
   bounce

2. They _____keep paying_____ the rent late, so they always pay a late fee.
   pay

3. We _____keep banking_____ at Money Bush, but the service is terrible.
   bank

4. Why do they _____keep complaining_____ about the service? They should just change banks.
   complain

5. She _____keeps spending_____ her whole paycheck, so she doesn't save any money.
   spend

6. It's bad to _____keep getting_____ in debt. We shouldn't buy that new car.
   get

➤ Do it yourself!

A. **Pair work. Write three questions to ask your classmates.**

1. What would you do if _____?

2. What would you do if _____?

3. What would you do if _____?

B. **Discussion. Talk about the most interesting answers.**

Authentic practice

A. Read and listen again. Then choose the sentence closer in meaning. Fill in the ovals.

1. "It keeps you from spending more than you have."

   ⓐ It makes you keep spending, no matter how much money you have.

   ● It prevents you from getting in over your head.

2. "Credit cards are an invitation to live beyond your means."

   ● Credit cards encourage you to spend more than you have.

   ⓑ Credit cards help you stay out of debt.

3. "If I were in your shoes, I'd get myself a debit card."

   ⓐ I'd buy those shoes for myself if I had a debit card.

   ● If I were you, I would use a debit card too.

B. Listen. Underline your response.

1. **YOU** <u>If you had a debit card, you wouldn't spend more than you had.</u>   **YOU** Oh, good. I don't want to get in over my head.

2. **YOU** <u>Well, you can really get into debt.</u>   **YOU** Let's take the good news first.

3. **YOU** What's the bad news?   **YOU** <u>So don't keep using that credit card.</u>

C. Listen again. Read your response out loud.

➤ Authentic practice

(For general suggestions, see *Introduction*, page Tx.)

Procedure:

🎧

➤ Before students open their books to this page, ask *What does the cashier at the supermarket ask you when you pay for your groceries?* (if you have the store's savings club card, if you are using coupons, whether you want paper or plastic bags, how you are going to pay)

➤ After students read and listen to the picture story, ask questions such as *What does the cashier ask the customer?* (whether she wants paper or plastic bags, whether she is using a credit card or a debit card to pay) *How is a debit card different from a credit card?* (With a debit card, the amount of your purchase is automatically deducted from your bank account.) *What's the advantage of a debit card over a credit card?* (With a debit card, you can't spend more money than you have.) *What's another advantage of a debit card?* (no finance charges)

Option: *Paper or plastic?* is a reduced form of the question *Would you like paper or plastic bags?* The intonation is what conveys that it is a question. In questions offering a choice, native speakers' voices rise on and pause after the first choice. As a class, brainstorm several complete questions offering a choice, for example, *Do you want coffee or tea?* In pairs, have students reduce the questions, *Coffee or tea?* Model the intonation for questions offering a choice, and then have students practice asking their partners the complete and the reduced questions.

🎧 A. Read and listen again . . .

➤ Read each item. Have students find and underline the sentence in the picture story. Have students read the picture story again and try to figure out the meanings of the sentences from the context.

➤ If students have trouble, suggest that they read only the answer choices and decide which one makes more sense based on what they understand from the picture story. Model this strategy. Read the two answer choices for item 1 and ask *Do debit cards make you keep spending, no matter how much money you have, or do they prevent you from getting in over your head?* If necessary, review the meaning of *in over your head.*

➤ After reviewing the answers to the exercise, have students use the correct answers to create simple definitions for *keeps you from, live beyond your*

means, and *if I were in your shoes*; for example, *keeps you from* = prevent.

➤ Discuss the expression *if I were in your shoes*, meaning if I were you. Ask *Why does the expression refer to shoes?* (If you put yourself in someone else's place, or imagine what you would do if you were that person, it's like wearing his or her shoes, or being that person.)

Challenge: Have students create original sentences using *keeps you from* and a gerund to mean prevent, for example, *Shopping around keeps you from wasting money.*

🎧 B–C.

➤ Make sure students understand that a *risk* is a chance you take that something bad may happen and that *killing* can mean hurting or making life difficult for someone.

Tapescript

1. I've had some problems *myself* with living beyond my means.
2. This might be a silly question, but what's the risk in using a credit card?
3. The finance charges are killing me.

If your students are ready . . .

Language note: The structure *keep (somebody) from* + a gerund means to prevent someone from doing something. For example, *It keeps you from spending* means that it prevents you from spending.

Culture / Civics note: Although many cultures prefer to conduct business in cash, in North America credit cards are a very popular method of payment. However, credit card debt is a growing problem, as many people find it difficult to resist using credit cards to pay for goods that they cannot afford. With most credit cards, not paying the total balance of a bill results in a substantial finance charge. This additional charge, which averages 18% of the total balance, can quickly add up, making the balance much more difficult and expensive to pay off.

Debit cards have become an increasingly popular alternative to credit cards. Unlike the "buy now, pay later" credit card payment plan, purchases made with a debit card are immediately deducted from the user's deposit account. Since debit card users can only buy something if they actually have the money in their account, using a debit card instead of a credit card can help them live within their means.

Reading the fine print

Procedure:

🎧 A. Listening comprehension . . .

➤ Tell students that they are going to listen to two separate conversations about credit.

➤ Students read the questions before listening to the conversation a second time. Read question 2 out loud. Explain that in both conversations, students will hear four reasons why the first speaker thinks the offer is good. Tell students that they should try to write down two of the reasons.

➤ Review the answers as a class. For each conversation, elicit and write on the board the four reasons why the first speaker thinks the offer is good. Discuss the meaning of each reason.

➤ Ask *What is "fine print"?* Elicit or explain that it is a part of a contract or other document that has important information that you may not notice, often deliberately written in smaller letters than the rest of the document. For each offer, ask *What does the fine print say?* (For the first offer, the 3% interest is charged every month. For the second offer, no annual fee is charged only if you spend more than $20,000 per year; no interest is charged the first year only if you live in Arizona, Oklahoma, or Alaska.) If necessary, play the cassette or read the tapescript again and have students listen specifically for this information.

B. True story . . .

➤ Discuss the meaning of the last line of each conversation in Exercise A: *You know, when things sound too good to be true, they usually are!* Provide an example, such as *I was shopping in my favorite store. I found a sweater I really liked, and there was a sign on the table that said 50% off. But when I went to pay, the salesperson rang up the regular price. I said, "But the sign says 50% off." She explained that only the orange sweaters were 50% off.*

➤ Prompt students to think of an experience they can relate by asking *Do you ever receive credit card offers in the mail? Do you ever get sales calls at home? What kinds of advertisements do you look at? Have you ever tried to buy something you thought was on sale and then found out it wasn't?*

Challenge: If students have brought in credit card offers they've received in the mail, groups of students can look at these offers and / or the offer on page 161 and evaluate whether they're *too good to be true*. Students draw a two-column chart with the headings *Too good to be true* and *Fine print*. For each offer, students look at the fine print and find a stipulation that makes a claim in the offer too good to be

true. For example, for one offer, students might write *0% interest for the first year* under *Too good to be true* and *Annual fee of $75* under *Fine print*.

➤ Do it yourself!

(For general suggestions, see *Introduction*, page Txiii.)

Procedure:

A. Write your <u>own</u> response . . .

➤ Advise students to look back at the picture story on page 120 for help in writing their responses.

B. Culture talk . . .

➤ In diverse groups, students answer the question and discuss similarities and differences among their cultures in how people get out of debt. Prompt discussion by asking *Is it acceptable to be in debt in your culture? Do many people have credit cards? Do people get bank loans to buy houses and cars? Who do people borrow money from? Who do people turn to for help when they get in over their head?* If helpful, write the questions on the board for students to refer to as they discuss.

Tapescript
Conversation 1

[newspaper rattling]

Woman: Look at this great offer. "Beautiful suite of solid oak bedroom furniture. Only thirty-nine hundred dollars."

Man: Thirty-nine hundred dollars for bedroom furniture? That's not *that* cheap. And we're already carrying a pretty big debt. We can't keep living beyond our means.

Woman: I know. But this is such a great deal. No money down. No payments until after Christmas. Low monthly payments after that. Only 3% interest.

Man: Oh, come on. What's in the fine print? If I were you, I'd look at the bottom of the ad for the fine print.

[pause] [newspaper rattling]

Woman: Oh, my goodness. You're right. The 3% is *every* month. On second thought, I think our bedroom set will be OK for a while.

Man: Good idea. You know, when things sound too good to be true, they usually are!

(Tapescript is continued on page T122.)

🎧 **A.** **Listening comprehension. Listen to the conversations about credit. Then read the questions and listen again. Answer the questions.**

Conversation 1

1. What's the offer for? <u>bedroom furniture</u>

2. What are some reasons she thinks it's a good offer? <u>no money down, no payments until after Christmas, low monthly payments after Christmas, only 3% interest</u>

3. Why should you always read the fine print? <u>because when things sound too good to be true, they usually are</u>

Conversation 2

1. What's the offer for? <u>a Platinum Laser Card, a credit card</u>

2. What are some reasons he thinks it's a good offer? <u>no annual fee, no late fees, no credit limit, no interest on unpaid balances for the first year</u>

3. Why should you always read the fine print? <u>because when things sound too good to be true, they usually are</u>

B. **True story. Did you ever see an offer that was too good to be true? What was it for? Where did you see it? *Was* it too good to be true? Tell your partner or your group.**

For extra practice, go to page 161.

➤ **Do it yourself!**

A. **Write your <u>own</u> response. Then read your conversation out loud with a partner.**

> I'm already in debt, but these new cards sound better than the one I use. What do you think?

YOU _____

> Someone told me to get a debit card. This might be a silly question, but what is that exactly?

YOU _____

> What would you do if you were in my shoes?

YOU _____

B. **Culture talk. In the country you come from, how do you get help when you're in debt? Compare cultures with your classmates.**

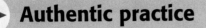

Authentic practice

Consumer advice for problems with debt

A. Read this information about debt from the U.S. Federal Trade Commission's Web site.

Consumer Information

Address: @ http://www.consumerinformation   › go

Knee-Deep in Debt

Having trouble paying your bills? Are you worried about losing your home or your car? You're not alone. Many people face financial crises at some time in their lives. Whether the crisis is caused by personal or family illness, the loss of a job, or simple overspending, it can seem overwhelming, but often it can be overcome.

Self Help

Contacting Your Creditors: Contact your creditors immediately if you are having trouble making ends meet. Tell them why it's difficult for you, and try to work out a modified payment plan that reduces your payments. Don't wait until your accounts have been turned over to a debt collector.

Dealing with Debt Collectors: Federal law dictates how and when a debt collector may contact you. A debt collector may not call you before 8 a.m., after 9 p.m., or at work if the collector knows that your employer doesn't approve of the calls.

Credit Counseling

If you can't work out a repayment plan with your creditors, consider contacting a credit counseling service. Be cautious.
- Find out what services the business provides and what they cost.
- Don't rely on oral promises. Get everything in writing.
- Check out any company with the Better Business Bureau. They may be able to tell you whether other consumers have registered complaints about the business.

For More Information

The Federal Trade Commission (FTC) works for the consumer to prevent fraudulent, deceptive, and unfair business practices. To file a complaint or to get information, call toll-free **1-877-FTC-HELP** (1-877-382-4357), or use the online complaint form at www.ftc.gov

Web zone

B. Complete each sentence with the phrase closer in meaning to the underlined word or phrase. Fill in the ovals.

1. Whether the crisis is caused by personal or family illness, the loss of a job, or simple <u>overspending</u>, it can seem overwhelming, but often can be overcome.

   ● a spending more money than you have   ○ b spending less money than you have

2. Contact your creditors immediately if you are having trouble <u>making ends meet</u>.

   ● a living within your means   ○ b getting in over your head

Tapescript *(continued from page T121)*

Conversation 2

[paper tearing, as an envelope]

Man: Hey, honey. Look at this. A Platinum Laser Card.

Woman: Oh, no. Not one of *those* offers again. Just because they keep sending them is no reason to keep opening them. If I were you, I'd just throw that out. Sight unseen. Those offers are as phony as a $3 bill.

Man: Now hold on a minute. Listen to this: "No annual fee. No late fees. No credit limit. No interest on unpaid balances for the first year."

Woman: Yeah, right! Turn it over and read the fine print.

[pause] [paper rattling]

Man: You're right. No annual fee if you spend over $20,000 a year. No interest on unpaid balances for the first year . . . as long as you live in Arizona, Oklahoma, or Alaska!

Woman: You know, honey, when things sound too good to be true, they usually are!

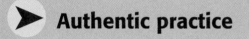

Authentic practice

(For general suggestions, see *Introduction,* page Tx.)

Consumer advice for problems with debt

Procedure:

A. Read this information . . .

➤ Put students in groups of five. Groups assign each member one paragraph of the reading. Give students about one minute to read their sections and think about how to retell the information in their own words.

➤ Ask students to close their books. Students tell their group members what they understood and can remember about the section they read.

➤ Give a quiz that includes one question from each section of the article. Questions should not be too difficult or require students to remember very specific information. They should assess students' general understanding of what they read. Quiz items might include *Name one cause of people's financial problems* (personal or family illness, loss of a job, overspending). *Who should you contact right away if you are having trouble paying your bills?* (your creditors, the people you owe money to) *Can debt collectors call you whenever they want?* (no) *If you contact a credit counseling service, what is one of the things you should do?* (get everything in writing, check out the company) *What does the Federal Trade Commission do?* (helps consumers, prevents unfair business practices)

➤ Review the answers to the quiz questions as a class, discussing the meaning of each section of the article as you review. Have groups correct each other's quizzes. See which group does best on the quiz.

Option: Have a volunteer draw on the board a cartoon illustrating the expression *knee-deep in debt.*

Option: Have students practice reading words in meaningful units. Have students underline in the first paragraph of the article the following phrases: *paying your bills, losing your home, some time in their lives, the loss of a job.* Say each phrase out loud—joining the words together and pronouncing them as a group rather than focusing on the individual words—and have students repeat. Then have students practice reading out loud to a partner the first paragraph of the article and focusing on pronouncing the underlined phrases as "chunks," or units.

Option: If students have access to computers, have them look at the Web sites of the Better Business Bureau (www.bbb.org) and the Federal Trade Commission (www.ftc.gov). Have students locate a local Better Business Bureau and write down its address and telephone number. On the Better Business Bureau site, students can click on *Check Out a Company.* Have them type in the name of a local business or the name of the company they work for. Students can click on *Consumer Information* and then *Money* and read about debit cards or a topic of their / your choice. On the Federal Trade Commission site, have students click on *Consumer Protection* and read about debt relief or a topic of their / your choice. Have students practice filling out (but not submitting) the online complaint form. Write *Better Business Bureau* and *Federal Trade Commission* on two different areas of the board. Each pair writes on the board one thing they learned from each site. As a class, read and discuss what students have written on the board.

B. Complete each sentence . . .

➤ After students complete the exercise individually, review the meaning of the prefix *over-* in *overspending.* Elicit or explain that it means too much, too many, or to too great a degree. (Be careful of generalizing too much, as the prefix *over-* in *overcome* has a meaning more similar to surmount or go over.)

➤ Ask *If you're having trouble making ends meet, what can you not do?* (pay your bills) Say *So if you're having trouble paying your bills, you're having trouble . . .* and elicit the correct answer.

C. Answer the questions ...

➤ If students have trouble answering item 1, have them look at the article on page 122 again. Read the title and ask what the article is about. If necessary, explain that *debt* is money that you owe. Students should also use the information on page 122 to identify solutions to debt.

If your students are ready ...

Language note: *Debt* and *owe* are not used only to talk about financial matters. For example, if you do something nice for someone else, he or she might say *I am in your debt* or, more informally, *I owe you one.*

Credit card bills

Procedure:

A. Read the credit card bill ...

➤ Have students read the bill and then ask and answer questions about the bill with a partner. Students can ask each other questions such as *What is the account number? How much did the customer spend at Game City?* Model the activity by asking a more advanced student a question about the bill and then having the student ask you a question.

➤ Ask the class *How much does the customer owe?* ($487.65) *How much does the customer have to pay?* ($20) *What will happen if the customer pays less than $487.65?* (A finance charge will be added to the customer's next bill.) *What's a finance charge?* (interest on the unpaid balance)

➤ Students complete the check as if the bill were theirs. Draw a check on the board and have volunteers fill in different parts of it. As a class, make any necessary corrections. For example, you may need to demonstrate how to write out the check amount or point out that students should sign, not print, their names on the check.

➤ Have students write the account number on the check.

Option: Ask *How is the available credit line determined?* (by subtracting the balance from the total credit line) Write the following balances on the board: *$1,237.50, $9,042.00, $13.25, $350.00, $2,569.73.* Ask students to calculate the available credit line ($8,762.50, $958, $9,986.75, $9,650). You may wish to explain rounding off to students.

B. Answer the questions.

➤ After students complete item 1, have them make sure that the date they wrote on the check in Exercise A is at least two days prior to 11/20/03.

➤ Do it yourself!

(For general suggestions, see *Introduction*, page Txiii.)

Procedure:

➤ In groups, students talk about how much they wrote their checks for and why.

➤ Lead a whole-class discussion. Ask *Who wrote their check for $487.65? Why? Who wrote their check for less? How much did you write it for? Why? What did you consider before you wrote the check?* Elicit or point out that, in addition to wanting to avoid a finance charge, it's important to consider how much money you have in your checking account, how much debt you already have, and how much debt you feel comfortable carrying.

C. Answer the questions in your <u>own</u> words.

1. What is debt? _____

2. What are some solutions to debt? _____
_____

Credit card bills

A. Read the credit card bill. If this were your bill, how much would you pay? Write a check.

Globalbank Expresscard

Account Number   6788 0001 9345 9011
Payment must be received by 1:00 p.m. local time on 11/20/03 to avoid penalties or fees.

Closing Date	Total Credit Line	Cash Advance Limit	New Balance	Available Credit Line
10/24/2003	$10,000	$4000	$487.65	$9512

Sale Date	Post Date	Reference Number	Activity Since Last Statement	Amount
	10/06	42131300	Payment THANK YOU	$200.66
9/26	9/27	HBX8943	MISSISSIPPI.COM 800-555-3222	146.23
9/29	9/29	QF90755	GREAT UNION MESA CA	87.65
10/02	10/02	35MD460	GAME CITY STA MARTA CA	119.76
10/04	10/07	9TCOX59	FLYING FOOT ELMSFORD CA	134.01

Account Summary							Amount Due	
Previous Balance	(+)Purchases & Advances	Payments	(-) Credits	(+)Finance Charge	(+) Late Charges	(=)New Balance	Minimum Due	**20.00**
$200.66	$487.65	$200.66				$487.65	Fees	
Make check payable to the order of Globalbank Expresscard							Past Due	

		1024
	Date _____	

PAY TO THE ORDER OF ___ Globalbank Expresscard ___ | $ [____]

THE SUM OF _____ Dollars

GLOBALBANK
16 Main Street
Santa Marta, CA 95020

MEMO _____

021000021ʌʌ:507000327685"∎   1024

B. Answer the questions.

1. When does Globalbank have to receive the check so that the client doesn't have to pay a late fee? <u>by 1:00 p.m. on 11/20/03</u>

2. Did the client pay last month's bill in full? <u>yes</u>

➤ Do it yourself!

Discussion. How much did you pay? Was that the full amount? Why? Explain the reason for your decision.

 Review

(For general suggestions, see *Introduction,* page Txii.)

Procedure:

A. Pair work or group work.

Ask and answer questions.

➤ Ask the class *Where are the people?* (at home in their kitchen) *Who are the people?* (a husband / father, a wife / mother, a son)

➤ Have students take turns pointing to the people in the picture and asking *What is he / she doing?* Review as a class. Make sure students understand that the husband is coming home from work and has good and bad news to tell and that the wife is looking at the family's bank statement and offers for credit cards that came in the mail. Also, the wife or the son has been shopping online.

➤ Write on the board *What problem does this family have?* and have students discuss. Review as a class. If necessary, point out that the family might be in over their heads or living beyond their means. Ask students how they can tell that this family may be overspending and in debt (the bounced check, the checks and bills on the table, the credit card offers the wife has been looking at, the online shopping Web site on the computer screen, the credit card used to pay for groceries). Have students discuss what advice they would give the family.

Create conversations.

➤ With a partner, students create a conversation between the husband and the wife. Have students look back at pages 115 and 121 for ideas. Have volunteers role-play their conversations for the class.

Option: Assign half the class the role of the wife and half the role of the husband. Allow students some time to look back through the unit for ideas. Then students stand up and form two concentric circles, with the students on the inside playing the role of the wife and the students on the outside playing the role of the husband. Students face each other, pair up, and have a conversation. After about a minute, the "husbands" walk to their right, pairing up with the "wife" who is two students down from their previous partner. These two students have a conversation. After a minute, instruct the students in the outside circle to walk to the right again and have a conversation with a new partner. Repeat until students have had an opportunity to practice the conversation with several partners.

Option: Have students imagine that they are friends with a member of this family. Students create a conversation between themselves and either the mother, the father, or the son. Students should put themselves in the family member's shoes and give advice about how to get help when you're in debt and / or how to avoid living beyond your means. Refer students to pages 116, 120, and 121 for ideas.

Tell a story.

Option: Put yourself in another's shoes. Have students tell what they would do if they were the husband, wife, and / or son. For example, *If I were the wife, I would get a debit card and throw all the credit card offers in the trash.*

Option: Create a character. Have students choose one person in the picture and tell what he or she is doing and thinking at the moment and how his or her day was. Encourage students to provide as many details about the family member's day as possible.

Option: Solve financial problems. Have students tell how the family gets their finances in order. For example, *The wife calls Green Tree bank and applies for a debit card. She asks her bank to recommend a credit counselor. She and her husband meet with the credit counselor . . .*

⌒ B. Listen to the conversation . . .

➤ Tell students that they are going to listen to a conversation about checking accounts at Express Bank.

➤ After students listen to the conversation the first time, have them open their books and look at the directions. Ask *Are you going to listen for the good news or the bad news?* (the good news) Read the items out loud so that students will know what to listen for. Allow students to listen to the conversation as many times as necessary to complete the activity.

Option: After reviewing the answers, have students write the heading *Bad news* over items 5, 6, and 7. Play the cassette or read the tapescript again and have students make changes to items 5, 6, and 7 so that the right-hand column provides the bad news from the fine print on the brochure. Students should change items 5, 6, and 7 to read *minimum balance of $10,000, no interest on balance, valid only at the Main Street branch.*

C–E.

➤ Students work individually to complete the review exercises.

➤ Circulate to offer help as needed.

➤ Have students check answers with a partner. Review answers as a class.

➤ Identify any areas of difficulty that may require additional instruction and practice.

Note: For Exercise D, make sure students realize that they need to either use *if* + the past tense of a verb in the box or *would* + a verb in the box, depending on the location of the blank.

Tapescript

Man: Hey, honey—good news!

Woman: M-hmm?

Man: I'm changing banks. I just stopped by Express Bank and picked up a brochure. They've got a great deal on checking.

Woman: Yeah?

Man: Yeah. If you open an account this week, you get a free microwave oven. And . . . you get free checks. Not the regular kind—the beautiful ones with the scenes of the national parks on them. And . . . there are no fees for the first year. And . . . We can get no-bounce checking . . . And . . .

Woman: Hold on, hold on. That sounds too good to be true. What's the catch?

Man: No catch. It says it all right here. You're such a doubting Thomas.

Woman: Check the fine print. There's got to be some bad news.

Man: [pause] Uh-oh. Yeah. There *is* bad news: Minimum balance $10,000. No interest on balances. Offer only valid at the Main Street Branch. That's miles from here.

Woman: When something sounds too good to be true . . .

Man: . . . It usually is!

🎧 **B.** Listen to the conversation. Listen again and check the good news about checking accounts at Express Bank.

1. ☑ free microwave oven
2. ☐ free trips to national parks
3. ☑ no fees for the first year
4. ☑ no-bounce checking
5. ☐ no minimum balance
6. ☐ high interest on balance
7. ☐ valid at branches nearby

C. Write your <u>own</u> response.

1. "I'm behind on my credit card payments." _____

2. "I was living beyond my means and I got in over my head." _____

3. "This might be a silly question, but what's the difference between a credit card and a debit card?" _____

D. Complete each unreal conditional sentence with the appropriate words. Choose verbs from the box.

> forget   evict   get   cancel

1. If I got behind on my rent, they _____would evict_____ me.
2. If I didn't pay my credit card bill, they _____would cancel_____ my card.
3. If I _____forgot_____ to send in my car payments for a couple of months, they'd repossess my car.
4. If I _____got_____ behind on my mortgage payments, they'd foreclose on my house.

E. Complete the sentences about continuing actions with <u>keep</u> and gerunds.

1. They _____keep sending_____ me these bills. What should I do?
   (send)

2. Don't _____keep using_____ this credit card, or you'll get in over your head.
   (use)

3. Elsa _____keeps telling_____ me to read the fine print. She's right.
   (tell)

4. My bank _____keeps raising_____ fees and lowering interest rates!
   (raise)

Unit 9   125

F. Read the credit card bill. Write a check for the full amount.

HANDICard

Account Summary							Amount Due
Previous Balance	(+)Purchases & Advances	Payments	(–)Credits	(+)Finance Charge	(+)Late Charges	(=)New Balance	Minimum Due **20.00** Fees Past Due
166.32	340.97	166.32				340.97	

Make check payable to the order of HandiCard

| | | 890 |
| | Date _____ |

PAY TO THE ORDER OF   HandiCard

THE SUM OF ___three hundred and forty and $\frac{97}{100}$___ $ | 340.97 |

Second National Bank
270 Beltway
Mountainview, NY 10549   Dollars

MEMO _____

021000021^^:4535*/"∎890

G. Composition. On a separate sheet of paper, write about the picture on page 124. Say as much as you can.

Now I can
- ❑ discuss problems with debt.
- ❑ find the appropriate person for financial information.
- ❑ offer good and bad financial news.
- ❑ complain about banking services.
- ❑ express satisfaction and dissatisfaction.
- ❑ get consumer advice for problems with debt.
- ❑ _____.

F. Read the credit card bill...

➤ Make sure students realize that they do not need to make a decision about how much to pay. They write the check for the full amount, $340.97. Have students use today's date.

G. Composition...

➤ Provide students with concrete approaches to writing about the picture on page 124. Use one of the following options, give students a choice of options, or assign options based on students' levels of proficiency. Model what is expected of students for each option.

➤ Advise students to look back through the unit for help and ideas as they write.

➤ Circulate to offer help as needed.

Option: Have students create the receipt for the groceries the son is putting away. Students list the items and prices, for example, *a carton of milk—$1.89*. They then calculate the total amount spent.

Option: Have students use *keep* and a gerund to write sentences describing each family member's continuing actions that are causing the family to be in debt, for example, *The wife keeps paying only the minimum balance on their credit card bills.*

Option: Students write the conversation between the husband and the wife. Have them use the same format as the model conversations on pages 114 through 117.

Challenge: Have students write an *Ask Joan* letter describing the family's financial problems. The letter should be from the husband, wife, or son and ask for Joan's advice on how to deal with the family's overspending.

Now I can

➤ Read the first item in the box out loud, *Now I can discuss problems with debt*. Elicit from the class an example of how to discuss problems with debt, such as *I'm behind on my rent. They might evict me.*

➤ In pairs, have students take turns reading each item in the box and giving an example of what they have learned. When students can provide an example, they should check that objective. For the items students weren't able to check, they should look back through the unit for ideas.

➤ When students are finished reviewing with their partners, read each item out loud and elicit an example from the class.

Oral test (optional)

You may want to use the *Now I can* box as an informal evaluation. While students are working on the *Composition* activity, you can call them up individually and check their ability with two or three objectives.

Your career

Note: Have students bring job ads from the local newspaper to class for use on pages 128, 133, and 137.

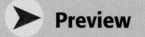 **Preview**

(For general suggestions, see *Introduction*, page Tviii.)

Warm up. What do you have to do to apply for these jobs? Talk with a partner.

Procedure:

➤ Have students look at the newspaper clippings. Ask *What are these?* (classified / want ads, ads for jobs) Brainstorm and write on the board questions students can ask each other about the ads, such as *What job is the ad for? Where is the job? Do you need to have experience? What skills are required? How do you apply for the job?* Students take turns asking and answering questions about the ads with a partner.

➤ When students are finished talking with their partners, elicit answers to the questions on the board for each ad. Then ask *What is a "medical biller"?* (a person who prepares and sends out bills for a doctor's office) *What is a "manicurist"?* (a person who cuts and polishes fingernails)

➤ Discuss the steps to take to apply for the medical biller position. Ask *What do you fax to Human Resources?* (a letter describing your qualifications and interest in the position, a list of your work experience) Have pairs discuss what to do before calling or sending a fax in response to the ad for a manicurist. Review as a class. Point out that even if you're calling, not faxing a letter, it's a good idea to first prepare a list of the jobs you've had with dates, pay, and supervisors' names and telephone numbers.

➤ Have pairs brainstorm questions to ask when contacting Mary about the manicurist position, such as *Is the position full-time or part-time? What are the hours? What is the pay? How do I apply for the job?*

➤ Ask students to tell their partner how they got the job they now have. Then ask volunteers to share with the class.

➤ Summarize and check comprehension by reading the *Warm up* question and eliciting an answer from one or more students.

Option: Have students create a key to the abbreviations used in the ads. For example, *NJ = New Jersey, ATTN = attention*. Students can include abbreviations used in the uncircled ads as well.

If your students are ready . . .

Culture note: In many countries, jobs are obtained through friends, family, or other connections. While networking is a very effective method of getting a job in the United States, most job seekers use a variety of methods. Advertise-ments for jobs are commonly found in the classified section of local newspapers, in store windows, on Internet sites, and on community bulletin boards. Job seekers should also check out their public libraries, which are excellent sources of free resources such as resume and interviewing workshops and computers with word-processing and resume-writing programs, printers, and Internet access.

Unit 10 objectives

Procedure:

➤ Have students read the objectives. Discuss the meaning of each objective and then have students who have had that experience raise their hands. For each objective, ask for a couple of volunteers to talk about their experiences. If necessary, prompt volunteers by asking questions such as *Where did you see the ad? What job was it for?*

➤ Have students circle the objective that they are most interested in being able to do.

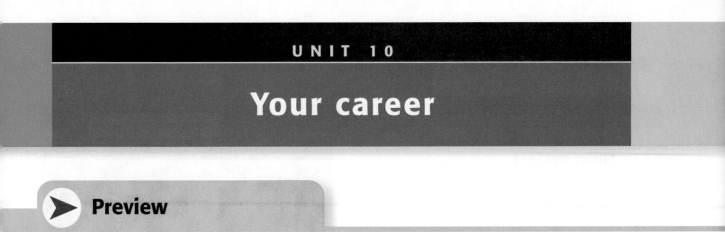

> ## Preview

Warm up. What do you have to do to apply for these jobs? Talk with a partner.

Unit 10 objectives

- Respond to a classified job ad.
- Call for an interview.
- Talk about job history and references at an interview.
- Move to a first-name basis.
- Accept and respond to feedback on the job.

Model 1   Call for an interview.

🎧 **A.** **Listen and read.**

> **A:** Hello. My name is Angela Andrade. I'm calling about the ad for a purchaser in today's paper.
> **B:** Yes, Ms. Andrade. Could you fax me your job history and salary requirements?
> **A:** Sure.
> **B:** Please send it to my attention. I'm Roseanne Leon.

🎧 **B.** **Listen again and repeat.**

PURCHASER
CALL Roseanne Leon
at 723-2000 or
FAX 723-2100.

C. **Pair work.** **Call for an interview for one of these jobs. Or find an ad in your newspaper and role-play a call. Use your _own_ names.**

IMMEDIATE
OPENING
MEDICAL BILLER
Wanted for busy NJ office.
Must have experience in
Windows-based system.
Fax 222 6745
ATTN: Human Resources

★ **CHEF MANAGER** ★
Exp'd, limited nites. Good
pay. Private club.
Call 685 9800

> **A:** Hello. My name is _____. I'm calling about the ad for _____ in today's paper.
> **B:** Yes, _____. Could you fax me your job history and salary requirements?
> **A:** ____1____.
> **B:** Please send it to my attention. I'm _____.

[1]Of course, I'd be glad to, Absolutely

➤ Practical conversations

(For general suggestions, see *Introduction*, page Tviii.)

Model 1

Content: responding to a classified job ad; calling for an interview

Procedure:

🎧 A–B.

➤ To set the scene for the conversation, ask questions about the photo and ad, such as *Where is the woman on the left?* (at home) *Where is the woman on the right?* (at work, in an office) *Which woman is interested in the job as a purchaser?* (the woman on the left) *Which woman is Roseanne Leon?* (the woman on the right) Elicit or explain the meaning of *purchaser* as a person who buys products for a company to sell.

➤ After students listen to the conversation, check comprehension by asking questions such as *What is the name of the woman on the left?* (Angela Andrade) *What does she need to do to apply for the purchaser job?* (fax her job history and salary requirements to Roseanne Leon) *What are "salary requirements"?* (the amount of money she needs to earn) *What does she need to write on the fax?* (ATTN: Roseanne Leon)

➤ Discuss the meaning of *job history*. If necessary, explain that a job history is a list of all the jobs you've had. As a class, brainstorm a list of what information about each job to include on a job history, for example, *position / job title, dates of employment, supervisor's name, address and telephone number of the business, a job description.* Have students copy the list and provide the information for their current job. Model the activity by writing on the board the information about your current job, for example, *Job title: Teacher . . .*

Challenge: Have students prepare their own job histories. First students list the jobs they've had in reverse chronological order, beginning with their current job. For each job, students write down the information they know from the list on the board—job title, dates of employment, and so on. Students research any missing information outside of class. Advise students that for positions held in their home countries, they can list the location (*São Paulo, Brazil*) and not provide a more specific address and telephone number. If possible, take students to the computer lab to type and print out their job histories.

C. Pair work . . .

➤ Point out that students must use *a* or *an* in front of the position title in Student A's second blank.

➤ Have two more advanced students model the conversation for the class. Allow them to solicit help from the class, if necessary.

➤ In pairs, students use the two ads on this page to practice calling for an interview.

Option: If you or students have brought in want ads from the local newspaper, have students look for jobs they are interested in and use these ads to practice calling for an interview.

Field project: If possible, locate a fax machine at the site where your class is held. Demonstrate how to use the fax machine and have students take notes. Then, if students actually want to inquire about or apply for a job, they will be able to fax a job history, response letter, or application.

If your students are ready . . .

Culture / Civics note: Filling out *an application form* is often the first step in applying for a job in North America. Typically, you provide your name, address, phone number, the position and salary that you are seeking, and your education and work history. Employers may also request the names and telephone numbers of several *references*, people such as former supervisors or teachers who can provide information about your skills and work history.

Many employers may also requre a *resume*, a short written summary of your education, work experience, and skills. Resumes should be submitted with *a cover letter*, in which you introduce yourself, state your reason for sending your resume, and highlight the special features of your education and experience that qualify you for the job.

Model 2

Content: talking about job history and references; giving reasons for changing jobs or leaving a job; *for* with an amount of time

Procedure:

🎧 A–B.

➤ Ask questions about the photo, such as *Where are the two men?* (in an office) *What are they wearing?* (office clothes) *What does the man on the right have in front of him?* (a folder or envelope)

➤ After students listen to the conversation, ask questions such as *What four questions did the interviewer ask?* (Who was your last employer? Why did you leave that job? Do you have a reference? May we contact them?) *Where did Mr. Chavez work before?* (at Carmody Cleaners) *How long did he work there?* (for two years) *Why did he leave that job?* (They closed the shop.) *What do you think Mr. Chavez has in the folder?* (a list of references, a job history)

➤ Have students turn to page 4. Review what a *reference* is. Elicit that it is someone who can talk about your work and skills, usually a previous employer.

Option: Have students create a list of at least three references. For each reference, students provide the person's name, position, relationship to them, how long the person has known them, and phone number and address.

🎧 Vocabulary

➤ Discuss the meaning of *opportunities to advance.* Ask *When you advance, how does your job change?* (You have more responsibility. Your work is more difficult or requires more skill. You make more money.) Give an example. Say *The chance to be promoted from salesperson to manager is an opportunity to advance.*

➤ Elicit or explain the meaning of *personality conflict* as a situation in which two people cannot work together because their personalities are very different. Ask students if they have ever had a *personality conflict* with a co-worker or supervisor. Ask them to describe the situation. Point out that, if a personality conflict is given as a reason for leaving a previous job, the applicant should be prepared to explain how he or she tried to overcome the problem in a positive way.

➤ Brainstorm and write on the board other reasons to change jobs or leave a job, such as *I moved / relocated, I got laid off, I needed to make more money, I didn't have benefits.*

➤ Have students ask three nearby classmates *So, why did you leave your last job?*

C. Pair work ...

➤ Model the conversation with a more advanced student. Play the more difficult role of Student B. Demonstrate citing your own last employer, choosing a reason for leaving from the *Vocabulary* box or from the board, and offering one or more references. Prompt Student A to choose from *them, him,* or *her* to complete Student A's last line.

If your students are ready ...

Culture / Civics note: In North America, interviews are one of the most important steps of the hiring process. Interviews offer employers and job applicants a chance to meet and evaluate each other. For job applicants, interviews are an important opportunity to highlight their skills, experience, and personal qualities. In addition, by asking questions, applicants can learn about the available position and decide if the job is right for them.

Interviewers value applicants who demonstrate a positive attitude. Criticizing former employers or co-workers implies that you have a poor attitude and are hard to get along with. If you were fired from a previous job or left because of a personality conflict, briefly explain the situation honestly, without sounding bitter or defensive. Highlight what you learned from the experience and mention the steps you have taken to improve your work performance or relationships.

➤ Do it yourself!

(For general suggestions, see *Introduction*, page Txiii.)

Procedure:

➤ As a class, brainstorm questions the interviewer could ask, such as *Who was your last employer? Why did you leave your last job? Do you have a reference? Do you have a job history? What are your skills?* Then brainstorm questions the applicant can ask, such as *What are the hours? Are there opportunities for me to advance?*

➤ Have students practice the interview twice, with each partner taking a turn as the interviewer and the applicant. When playing the role of the applicant, students can answer the interviewer's questions using information about their own work history, skills, and so on.

🎧 **A. Listen and read.**

A: So, Mr. Chavez, who was your last employer?

B: I worked at Carmody Cleaners for two years.

A: And why did you leave that job?

B: Actually, they closed the shop.

A: Do you have a reference?

B: Yes, Mr. White. I can give you a list.

A: May we contact them?

B: Of course.

🎧 **B. Listen again and repeat.**

🎧 **Vocabulary**

Reasons to change jobs or to leave a job

So, why did you leave your last job?

They closed.

They moved to a new location.

There were no opportunities for me to advance.

The hours were not good for me.

I needed full-time / part-time employment.

I had a personality conflict with my _____.

C. Pair work. Explain why you left your last job. Provide references.

A: So, _____, who was your last employer?

B: I worked _____.

A: And why did you leave that job?

B: Actually, _____.

A: Do you have a reference?

B: Yes, _____.

A: May we contact _____?

B: ____1____.

[1]Sure, Certainly, Absolutely

> **Do it yourself!**

Pair work. Create an interview for the two people in the picture.

Model 3   Accept positive feedback. Move to a first-name basis.

🎧 **A. Listen and read.**

A: Have you got a minute?

B: Sure.

A: I've been meaning to tell you, Dan. You're doing a great job.

B: Really? Thanks, Mr. Meland. I'm happy to hear that.

A: Thank *you*. By the way, please call me Jerry.

🎧 **B. Listen again and repeat.**

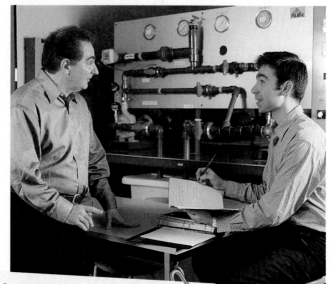

🎧 **Ways to move to a first-name basis**

Please call me Jerry.
Why don't you call me Jerry?
I think it's time you called me Jerry.
Just call me Jerry.

🎧 **Vocabulary**

Ways to accept positive feedback at work

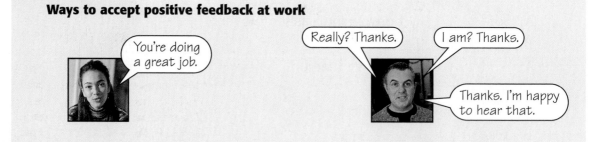

You're doing a great job.

Really? Thanks.

I am? Thanks.

Thanks. I'm happy to hear that.

C. Pair work. Accept a compliment on your work. Use your <u>own</u> names. Move to a first-name basis.

A: Have you got a minute?

B: ___1___.

A: I've been meaning to tell you, _____. You're doing a ___2___ job.

B: _____. I'm happy to hear that.

A: Thank *you*. By the way, _____.

¹Yes, Of course, Absolutely   ²good, nice, fantastic

➤ Practical conversations

(For general suggestions, see *Introduction*, page Tviii.)

Model 3

Content: giving and accepting positive feedback at work; moving to a first-name basis

Procedure:

🎧 A–B.

➤ Point to the man on the right in the photo. Have students look at his expression. Ask *How is he feeling?* (happy, pleased, excited)

➤ After students read and listen to the conversation, ask questions such as *What is the name of the man on the right?* (Dan) *What is the relationship between the two men?* (supervisor and employee) *Why do you think so?* (At first, the man on the left calls Dan by his first name, but Dan calls him Mr. Meland. The man on the left compliments the other man's work.)

➤ Ask *What does Dan's supervisor tell him?* (that he's doing a great job) *Is this positive feedback or negative feedback?* (positive feedback) *What is "feedback"?* Elicit or explain that *feedback* is information on your performance, or how well you are doing at something.

➤ Have students read the *Model 3* bar. Have them circle *Accept positive feedback* and underline *Move to a first-name basis*. Then students circle in the conversation the line in which Dan accepts the positive feedback from his boss and underline the line in which the supervisor gives Dan permission to call him by his first name. Students should circle *Really? Thanks, Mr. Meland. I'm happy to hear that* and underline *Thank you. By the way, please call me Jerry.*

🎧 Ways to move to a first-name basis

➤ After students listen to and repeat the phrases, point out that *I think it's time you called me (Jerry)* is appropriate when someone has known you for a while and has been calling you by a title and your last name, such as Mr. Meland.

➤ Approach different students and greet them using a title and their last names. For example, say *Hello, Ms. Kamara* or *Good afternoon, Mr. Espinoza.* Elicit from each student one of the responses from the yellow language note, for example, *Please call me Melissa.*

Option: Have students make a list of people they are on a first-name basis with and of people they call by a title and their last name. Students should note the relationship with each person on their lists, for example, *Julia—friend at work, Jack—young neighbor, Mr. Harris—supervisor, Mrs. Decker—older neighbor.*

Option: Have students compare the use of first names, last names, and titles in the countries they come from. In groups, students can discuss answers to these questions: *In the country you come from, who do you call by their first name? Who do you call by a title and their last name? Do bosses give their employees permission to call them by their first name?*

🎧 Vocabulary

➤ After students listen to and repeat the vocabulary, ask *Have you ever received positive feedback at work? What did your boss or a co-worker say to you? How did you respond?* Write other ways to accept positive feedback on the board. For example, students might say *Thanks so much, I appreciate it,* or *I'm really happy to hear that.*

➤ Approach different students and give them positive feedback on their performance in your class. For example, say *Your participation in class is excellent, Your English is really improving, You're doing a fantastic job.* Elicit from each student a way to accept positive feedback from the *Vocabulary* box or from the board.

C. Pair work . . .

➤ Brainstorm and write on the board other adjectives Student A can use to compliment Student B's work.

➤ Model the conversation with a more advanced student. Play the role of Student A, the supervisor. If necessary, prompt Student B to include a title and your last name when he or she accepts your positive feedback in Student B's second line.

Model 4

Content: giving and accepting feedback in a performance review; discussing career goals and ways to advance on the job

Procedure:

🎧 A–B.

➤ After students listen to and read the conversation, ask comprehension questions such as *What is the employee's name?* (Phil) *Did he receive positive or negative feedback in his review?* (positive feedback) *Is Phil on a first-name basis with his boss?* (yes) *What is Phil's goal?* (to be a supervisor) *What does Phil need to become a supervisor?* (training)

➤ Have students look at the Performance Review below the photo. Ask *How often is Phil reviewed?* (each year) Then ask students if they have ever had a performance review. As a class, brainstorm and write on the board what might be evaluated on a performance review, for example, whether an employee *arrives at work on time, does good work, follows safety rules, takes care of personal business on his or her own time, works well with co-workers.*

Option: Have students copy from the board the performance review items that are appropriate for their job. Have students evaluate their own performance by writing *excellent*, *good*, or *needs to improve* next to each item. Model the activity by evaluating your own job performance for a couple of the items on the board. For each item, explain why you chose excellent, good, or needs to improve.

🎧 Vocabulary

➤ For each way to advance on the job, elicit from the class something specific that Phil from the model conversation could do. For example, for *training*, Phil could go to a class to learn more about some part of his job; for *on-the-job training*, Phil could shadow a supervisor for the day to see first-hand what he or she does.

Note: On-the-job training is sometimes abbreviated as *OJT*.

C. Pair work . . .

➤ Ask students what their career goals are. Write several on the board. Write them so that they can be used in Student B's last line in the conversation, for example, *I'm interested in being . . . : a manager, promoted to lead assembler, transferred to office work.*

➤ Model the activity with a more advanced student. Play the role of Student B. Demonstrate responding affirmatively in Student B's first line and using a way to accept positive feedback from page 130 in Student B's second line. If necessary, allow Student A to solicit help from the class.

Note: If a negative response is given in Student B's first line, Student A / the supervisor can preface his next remark with *well*, for example, *Well, you've had a really good first year with us, Phil.*

➤ Do it yourself!

(For general suggestions, see *Introduction*, page Txiii.)

Procedure:

A. Personalization . . .

➤ To complete the performance review form, students can use the expression *I'm interested in . . .* with *being* or another gerund, or they can use infinitives to note their goals, for example, *to be a manager, to earn more money, to work more hours.*

B. Discussion . . .

➤ Remind students of verbs followed by infinitives that they can use to talk about their goals, for example, *plan, want, expect, would like.* If helpful, refer students to page 149 for other verbs followed by infinitives.

Challenge: In their groups, students can come up with advice to help each group member reach his or her goals. For example, if a student wants to be promoted from a dishwasher to a waiter, the group could suggest that the student *talk to the restaurant manager about opportunities, ask other servers how they got their jobs, learn more English, look at the want ads for restaurants hiring servers with your experience.*

Field project: If your program has access to a career center, have students visit the center on a field trip or as an out-of-class assignment. Most career centers have a handout or worksheet about setting long-term goals. If your center has a goal-setting worksheet, have your students complete one with your assistance.

T131

🎧 **A.** **Listen and read.**

> **A:** Have you had a chance to read your review yet?
>
> **B:** Yes, I have.
>
> **A:** You've had a really good first year with us, Phil.
>
> **B:** Thanks, Rob.
>
> **A:** Where do you see yourself in two years?
>
> **B:** Well, I'm interested in being a supervisor.
>
> **A:** Great. Let's see if we can get you some training.

🎧 **B.** **Listen again and repeat.**

PERFORMANCE REVIEW

BUSINESS UNIT:	Brimstone Tire, Tulsa
EMPLOYEE NAME:	Philip Lee
REVIEW PERIOD:	2003

🎧 **Vocabulary**

Ways to advance on the job

training

hands-on experience

extra experience

on-the-job training

C. **Pair work.** **Discuss career goals. Use your <u>own</u> goal and names.**

> **A:** Have you had a chance to read your review yet?
>
> **B:** _____.
>
> **A:** You've had a really good _____ with us, _____.
>
> **B:** ___1___.
>
> **A:** Where do you see yourself _____?
>
> **B:** Well, I'm interested in being _____.
>
> **A:** ___2___. Let's see if we can get you some _____.

[1]Really? Thanks; Thanks, I'm happy to hear that   [2]OK, Good, Fantastic

➤ Do it yourself!

A. **Personalization.** **Where do you see yourself in the future? Complete the bottom of the performance review form.**

B. **Discussion.** **Discuss career goals with a partner or a group.**

Evaluation: _Excellent work._____

What are your career goals for the next five years?

_____

_____

_____

Practical grammar

Talking about the present: Review

Use the simple present tense for general statements and to describe habitual actions.
   The office **opens** at 9:00.
   He **goes** to work at 7:30.
Use the simple present tense with frequency adverbs.
   I usually **get** to work on time.
Use the simple present tense with <u>have</u>, <u>want</u>, <u>need</u>, and <u>like</u>.
   She **doesn't like** her job.

Use the present continuous for actions in progress. Don't use it with frequency adverbs. Don't use it with <u>have</u>, <u>want</u>, <u>need</u>, or <u>like</u>.
   She's **talking** to the interviewer right now, but she doesn't need a job.

A. **Choose the simple present tense or the present continuous.**

1. I can't talk to you right now. I _____ am reading _____ my performance review.
    read / am reading

2. I _____ have _____ a few important questions to ask at the interview.
    have / am having

3. Usually I work at an office, but today I _____ am working _____ at home.
    work / am working

4. Ivan _____ talks _____ to his supervisor once a week.
    talks / is talking

5. It always _____ rains _____ when I have a day off!
    rains / is raining

B. **Complete each sentence with the simple present tense or the present continuous.**

1. They always _____ ask _____ job applicants for references.
    ask

2. He _____ doesn't like _____ his supervisor.
    not like

3. Look at Nan fixing that copier. She _____ is doing _____ a great job! Let's go tell her.
    do

4. That interviewer never _____ ends _____ the interview on time.
    end

5. I _____ need _____ to fax a letter to them. What's their fax number?
    need

➤ Practical grammar

(For general suggestions, see *Introduction*, page Tix.)

Talking about the present: Review

Content: the simple present tense compared with the present continuous; the present perfect and the present perfect continuous with *for* and *since*

Procedure:

➤ Read the explanations and examples for the simple present tense out loud. Provide opportunities for students to practice using the simple present tense in each case.

➤ Say *Tell me about this class. What do we do in this class?* to elicit general statements from students, such as *It starts at 6:30. It ends at 8:00. We listen to conversations. We talk to our classmates.*

➤ Prompt students to talk about habitual actions by having them tell a partner what they do every day, for example, *I wake up at 6:00 a.m., I make coffee, I take a shower.* Circulate to make sure students are using the simple present tense.

➤ Write *usually* on the board, and then brainstorm other frequency adverbs, such as *always, sometimes, never.* For each frequency adverb on the board, elicit an original sentence from a volunteer, for example, *I always arrive at work on time.*

➤ With their partners, have students say what they *like, want, need,* and *have*—and what they *don't like, don't want, don't need,* and *don't have,* for example, *I want to be promoted to supervisor.*

➤ Read the explanation and example for the present continuous out loud. Then mime reading the newspaper and ask *What am I doing right now?* Elicit the response *You are reading the newspaper.* Then have volunteers mime activities and the class guess what they are doing right now.

➤ Draw on the board a two-column chart with the headings *Simple present* and *Present continuous.* As a class, brainstorm words that indicate which tense to use. For example, under *Simple present,* you might write *usually, always, sometimes,* and *never* and *like, want, need,* and *have.* Under *Present continuous,* write words like *right now, today,* and *at the moment.*

A. Choose …

➤ Write item 1 on the board. Elicit the correct answer from the class. Then ask *How do you know the answer is "am reading"?* (because of "right now") Have students fill in the correct answer and write *right now* to the right of item 1. Students complete items 2 through 5 individually, writing the word or phrase that prompted them to choose their answer to the right of each item.

➤ Have students check answers with a partner. Then review as a class. To the right of items 2 through 5, students should write *have, today, once a week,* and *always.*

B. Complete each sentence …

➤ Again, have students write the word or phrase that prompts them to choose their answer to the right of each item. For item 3, ask *When is Nan fixing the copier?* Explain that if we can look at her, she must be doing it right now. Have students write *right now* next to item 3. For items 1, 2, 4, and 5 students should write *always, like, never,* and *need.*

Actions that started in the past and continue in the present

➤ Have students write down where they work, where they live, a sport they play, and a TV show they watch or a radio station they listen to regularly. Then ask students when they started doing each thing and have them write *since* and a point in time next to each activity, for example, *work at Perillo Plumbing—since 2000*. Next ask students how long they have been doing each thing and have them write *for* and a period or amount of time next to each activity, for example, *work at Perillo Plumbing—since 2000, for 2 years*.

➤ Have students read the explanations and examples in the grammar box. Then have them use the information they wrote down to create sentences about their own actions that started in the past and continue in the present. Point out that for each activity they wrote about, there are four possible sentences. For example, for *work at Perillo Plumbing—since 2000, for 2 years*, any one of the following four sentences can be created: *I've worked at Perillo Plumbing since 2000, I've worked at Perillo Plumbing for two years, I've been working at Perillo Plumbing since 2000, I've been working at Perillo Plumbing for two years*. If helpful, write on the board *I am working at Perillo Plumbing since 2000* and draw a large X through it.

C. Matt Joong is applying for a job ...

➤ Have students underline in the letter the words and phrases that suggest what tense to use. Point out that in addition to the words and phrases they looked for on page 132, students should also underline *for* + an amount of time and *since* + a specific day, month, year, time, or date. In the letter, students should underline *today's, Currently, since May 1999, always, never*, and *for the last month*.

➤ After students complete the exercise individually, have them check answers by reading the letter to a partner. Each student in a pair should take a turn reading the letter.

➤ Point out that *Attachments* at the bottom of the letter refers to the job history and list of references that Matt Joong is faxing with the letter.

Challenge: Have students look at the want ads they brought in and choose a job they are interested in. Students write a response letter expressing their interest in the job. They use Matt Joong's letter as a model and substitute their own information and reason for wanting to leave their current job. If necessary, refer students to page 129 to review reasons to leave a job.

➤ Do it yourself!

(For general suggestions, see *Introduction*, page Txiii.)

Procedure:

A. Pair work ...

➤ Read the first speech balloon and then ask the class *What would you ask next?* (How long have you worked there?) Read the second speech balloon and ask *What question would you have asked before this one?* (Where do you live?) Students practice asking and answering these four questions with a partner.

B. Discussion ...

➤ Have each student tell a new partner about their first partner's job history and residence. For example, *Faraz works at the Cineplex. He's been working there for six months. He lives on Telegraph Road. He's lived there for a year.*

Option: Have students write sentences about their partner's job history and residence.

Option: Have students ask several classmates about their job history and residence and record their classmates' responses on a chart like this one.

Name of student	Where do you work?	How long have you worked there?	Where do you live?	How long have you lived there?
Marta	Discount Drugs	7 months	Apple St.	18 months

Actions that started in the past and continue in the present

Use the present perfect or the present perfect continuous with <u>for</u> and <u>since</u> to talk about actions that started in the past and continue in the present. For this purpose the two forms mean almost the same thing.

I've **worked** here **since** August, 2000. (present perfect)

She's **been talking** to the interviewer **for** an hour. (present perfect continuous)

Remember: <u>for</u> + amounts of time.

Remember: <u>since</u> + a specific day, month, year, time, or date.

Be careful! Don't use the present continuous with <u>for</u> and <u>since</u>.

C. **Matt Joong is applying for a job. Complete the response letter he faxed.**

Sir or Madam: April 4, 2003

_____I'm writing_____ to respond to the ad _____you have_____ for an
  1. I write / I'm writing   2. you have / you have had

electronics technician in today's *Journal News*. Currently _____I work_____
                                                         3. I work / I have been working

at Sparky's Computer Repair. _____I've been working_____ there since May 1999. At
                              4. I'm working / I've been working

Sparky's _____I repair_____ computers. Sparky's always _____treats_____
          5. I'm repairing / I repair   6. treats / is treating

me well. But, unfortunately, Sparky's _____has_____ no opportunities for
                                       7. has / is having

advancement, and the management never _____provides_____ on-the-job training.
                                       8. provides / is providing

For that reason, for the last month, _____I've been studying_____ electronics at the
                                      9. I study / I've been studying

Claremont Technical School.

If you would like me to come in for an interview, you can reach me at 322-2121 any day after 5:30. I'm enclosing a job history and a list of references. I look forward to hearing from you.

Sincerely,

Matt Joong

Matt Joong
Attachments

➤ Do it yourself!

A. **Pair work. Ask questions about your partner's job history or residence.**

Where are you currently employed?

How long have you lived at that address?

B. **Discussion. Talk about the job and housing history of your classmates.**

🎧 **A. Read and listen again. Answer the questions in your <u>own</u> words. Then discuss with a partner or a group.**

Students should mention:

1. Has Sam done a good job this quarter? <u>yes, but he needs to work on his "people skills"</u>

2. What is Jerry's opinion of Sam's work? <u>Jerry is pleased / happy with Sam's work.</u>

3. What should Sam do to improve his "people skills"? <u>check in with his workers, ask how</u>

   <u>they're doing, praise them</u>

4. Why do you think it is important to show appreciation? _____

   _____

🎧 **B. Listen. Underline <u>your</u> response.**

1. **YOU** <u>Really? I'm happy to hear that.</u>   **YOU** I can give you a list.

2. **YOU** <u>Has there been a problem?</u>   **YOU** Can I fax you my resume?

3. **YOU** I'll send it to your attention.   **YOU** <u>That's good advice. Thanks.</u>

🎧 **C. Listen again. Read <u>your</u> response out loud.**

➤ Authentic practice

(For general suggestions, see *Introduction,* page Tx.)

Procedure:

🎧
➤ Have students look at the facial expression of the man wearing the yellow hard hat. Ask *Which picture is he happiest in?* (picture 1)

➤ After students read and listen to the picture story, check comprehension by asking questions such as *What is the name of the man in the yellow hard hat?* (Sam) *What is Sam's supervisor's name?* (Jerry) *Is Sam on a first-name basis with his boss?* (yes) *Why is Sam smiling in picture 1?* (His boss gives him positive feedback / compliments him on his work.) *How does Sam respond to the positive feedback?* (He says, "Thanks, Jerry. I've been working at it.") *What less positive feedback does Jerry give Sam?* (Some of his workers don't feel appreciated enough.) *What suggestion does Jerry make?* (Sam should ask his workers how they're doing and praise them.)

➤ Elicit or explain the meaning of *praise* as positive feedback. Ask *How does Sam feel when his boss praises him?* (happy) *Have you ever received praise at work? How did it make you feel? How do you think Sam's workers will feel if he praises them?* (happy, appreciated) *Do you think praising his workers will have any effect on their productivity / on how hard they work?* (They may work harder if they know they're appreciated.)

Challenge: Discuss how to accept negative feedback. Have students underline in the picture story how Sam responds to his boss's suggestions about how to improve his people skills. Students should underline *I'll try that. Thanks for the input, Jerry.* On the board, write two or three examples of negative feedback that a supervisor could give an employee, for example, *I noticed that you've been late three times this week, Customers have been complaining that they can't get any help because you're busy talking to friends on the phone.* Have groups brainstorm positive responses to the negative feedback.

🎧 **A. Read and listen again . . .**
➤ Students answer the questions individually. Then have students read and discuss their answers to each question in a group.

➤ Ask *What does someone with good "people skills" do?* Brainstorm and write on the board a list of behaviors such as *smiles, says hello, asks people how they're doing, makes small talk, asks people "What's wrong?" when they look upset, tells people when they're doing a good job, makes people feel appreciated, gives compliments before negative feedback.*

Option: Have students copy the list from the board and evaluate their own people skills by writing *always, sometimes,* or *never* next to each behavior.

🎧 **B–C.**
➤ Have students find and circle in picture 4 *all the difference in the world* and *input.* Ask students to think of a different word or phrase to replace each of these. For example, instead of *all the difference in the world,* you could say *a lot of difference* or *a big difference* and instead of *input, advice* or *feedback.*

➤ Have students check their answers to Exercise B with a partner before reading their responses out loud in Exercise C.

Tapescript

1. I've been hearing some really good things about you.
2. But I've been meaning to give you some input on your people skills.
3. A little praise'll make all the difference in the world.

How to present yourself at a job interview

Procedure:

🎧 A. Listening comprehension ...

➤ Tell students that they are going to listen to job tips on the radio. Elicit or explain the meaning of *tips* in this context as advice.

➤ After students listen to the announcement the first time, ask *What are today's job tips about?* (how to impress a potential employer in a job interview)

🎧 B. Read the following job tips ...

➤ Have students read the job tips so that they know what to listen for. Then play the cassette or read the tapescript again. Allow students to listen to the announcement as many times as necessary to complete the exercise.

Note: In item 2, the tip is *Call the interviewer by his or her last name.* Remind students that when we use a last name we also use a title such as *Mr., Ms.,* or *Dr.*

Option: Have students listen to the announcement again and write down as many additional job tips as they can. Then, in pairs, have students choose a job tip to act out. Each pair presents their role-play and the class guesses the job tip.

C. True story ...

➤ Each student in a group should answer all three questions. If students have never had a job interview, ask them to anticipate questions an interviewer would ask and to think of questions they might want to ask.

If your students are ready ...

Language note: Chronological or sequential connectors are used to present a list or series of items. Connectors organize ideas for the speaker and for listeners and help to keep listeners' attention. In the radio announcement, the following connectors are used: *first of all, second, three, four, five, next, finally, one more thing.* Ordinal numbers are most commonly used, but cardinal numbers may be used, especially with a long list. Ways to conclude a list include *finally, last, last of all,* and *last but not least.*

➤ Do it yourself!

(For general suggestions, see *Introduction,* page Txiii.)

Procedure:

A. Write your <u>own</u> response ...

➤ Brainstorm ways to hear about job openings, such as in newspaper ads, from announcements on bulletin boards, at the school's career center or an employment agency, and from a friend or neighbor. Ask students how they found out about their current jobs.

➤ Explain that students should imagine that this woman is interviewing them for a job and respond to her inquiries. Students write their responses individually.

➤ When students are finished, read each speech balloon and elicit a variety of appropriate responses from the class. Then have students read their interviews out loud with a partner.

B. Culture talk ...

➤ Ask *What negative feedback did you receive at jobs you had in your home country? How did you respond?* In groups, have students compare their answers with those of their classmates.

➤ Remind students of Sam's response to negative feedback from his boss in the picture story on page 134. Have students compare their responses with Sam's.

Tapescript

[music]

Welcome to "Job Tips," your radio guide to getting a good job, holding on to it, and moving up and out when you're ready. Today's tips will help you impress a potential employer at that all-important job interview. First of all, be sure to be on time for your interview. In fact, it's a good idea to plan to be a few minutes early, just in case you run into unexpected traffic or are otherwise delayed. Second, shake hands firmly, but not painfully! Be friendly, but not too familiar. Don't call the interviewer by his or her first name unless you're invited to do so. Three: Break the ice with a little small talk, but not about yourself. It's always safe to comment on the weather or the traffic, but don't go on and on. Making small talk says you feel open, relaxed, and friendly—a good image to project. Look the interviewer in the eye. Four: Expect the interviewer to lead the discussion. Answer his or her questions thoughtfully and fully and as honestly as

(Tapescript is continued on page T136.)

A. Listening comprehension. **Listen to the job tips.**

B. Read the following job tips. Listen again and check the tips the speaker advises.

1. ☐ Wear nice clothes to the interview.
2. ☑ Call the interviewer by his or her last name.
3. ☑ Make small talk about the weather.
4. ☐ Don't look relaxed.
5. ☐ Don't ask questions about the company or the job.
6. ☐ Be sure to ask about company benefits before the interviewer mentions them.

C. True story. **Have you ever had a job interview? What questions did the interviewer ask? What questions did you ask about the company or job? Tell your partner or your group.**

➤ Do it yourself!

A. Write your <u>own</u> response. Then read your interview out loud with a partner.

How did you hear about this position?

YOU _____

Please tell me something about your current job or work history.

YOU _____

What would you like to ask me?

YOU _____

B. Culture talk. **In the country you come from, how do you accept and respond to negative feedback from a supervisor? Compare cultures with your classmates.**

Friendliness and familiarity with an employer

🎧 **A.** Read and listen to the letters.

 # Ask Joan
Culture tips for newcomers

Dear Joan:
I have been working in this country since last year, and I've had a job in a fast-food restaurant for about three months. Yesterday I had my first performance review with my boss. He said, "Andy, you're doing a great job. We're very happy with you. We're looking forward to having you work with us for a long time!" I went home feeling great about my new country.

Then today something terrible happened. I was cleaning up the grill at about 5 after 5. My boss saw me and said, "Andy! Go home. Get out of here!"

What happened? What is wrong with the people in this country? I'll never understand. Maybe I should just go home to my country.

Andy in Anaheim

Dear Andy:
Stop worrying! When your boss told you to go home, he was letting you know that he recognized that you're willing to work long hours for him. He wanted to let you know how much he appreciates your effort. He wanted you to know that you had worked enough for one day.

Sometimes it's easier for people to say something in the

joking way your boss did than to tell you directly. Your boss wanted to let you know that your relationship has become more friendly and less formal.

In the culture of this country, this is normal and good! The next time this happens, smile and say, "Thanks! I'll just finish the grill and then leave." This will let your boss know you understand the "message."

Congratulations on the good review. And best of luck for continued success in the job.

Joan

B. Mark each statement <u>True</u> or <u>False</u>.

	True	False
1. Andy has worked at the fast-food restaurant for a year.	❑	❑
2. Andy's boss is satisfied with Andy's work.	❑	❑
3. Andy thinks his boss is angry at him.	❑	❑
4. Andy's boss *was* angry.	❑	❑
5. Andy's boss wants him to return home to his country.	❑	❑

you can. Five: Express interest in the company and the job. Don't be afraid to ask questions to clarify anything you don't understand. Next, be sure to know something about the com-pany. It creates the impression of a person who is interested. Prepare at least one question about the company, its future, or the job. Employers are looking for people who take an interest. And finally, it's OK to ask about company benefits, but it's generally a good idea to wait for the interviewer to bring up the subject of salary and other compensa-tion in this first meeting. Oh, and one more thing. The interviewer may tell you to expect a phone call or a letter. It's very unusual for an interviewer to offer you a job on the spot. That's it for today. Thanks for listening to "Job Tips."

[music]

Authentic practice

(For general suggestions, see *Introduction*, page Tx.)

Friendliness and familiarity with an employer

Procedure:

🎧 A. Read and listen to the letters.

➤ Play the cassette or read the letters. Pause after the first letter and ask comprehension questions such as *How long has Andy been working in this country?* (since last year) *How long has he had a job in a fast-food restaurant?* (for about three months) *Why was Andy happy yesterday?* (His boss gave him positive feedback on his performance review.) *Why is he upset today?* (His boss said, "Andy! Go home. Get out of here!")

➤ After students listen to Joan's response, ask *Was Andy's boss really angry with him?* (no) *What did he mean when he told Andy to go home?* (He realizes that Andy works long hours, and he appreciates Andy's hard work.) *What should Andy do next time the boss tells him to go home?* (smile and say, "Thanks! I'll just finish the grill and then leave")

➤ Ask *Have you ever misunderstood something your boss said to you? What did your boss say? What did you think your boss meant?* Ask a couple of volunteers to describe their experiences to the class.

B. Mark each statement...

➤ After students complete Exercise B individually, have them check answers with a partner.

➤ Have pairs change the false answers to make them true.

C. Discussion...

➤ Students write answers to the questions individually and then read and discuss their answers in groups.

➤ For item 3, prompt students to provide more information by asking *Have you ever misunderstood when someone was joking with you? What did they say? What did you think they meant? How did you feel? How did you clear up the misunderstanding?*

Letters of response to job ads

Procedure:

A. Read the job ad...

➤ Have students look at the job ad. Ask *What do you have to do to apply for this job?* (fax your resume or a letter) Elicit or explain that a resume is similar to a job history but also includes information about your education and skills.

➤ Have students read Rebecca Malone's letter of response to the job ad. Then ask questions such as *Where has she been working?* (in a stationery store) *For how long?* (for the last year and a half) *Why is she changing jobs?* (because she is relocating) *What has she been doing in the stationery store?* (framing pictures and documents)

➤ Ask *What type of job is Rebecca Malone applying for?* (a job in production at a picture framing company) *What skills / experience does she have?* (framing pictures and documents) *Is she qualified for the job described in the ad?* (yes)

➤ Have students read the letter out loud to a partner.

B. Role play...

➤ In groups, have students brainstorm questions that Mr. Page could ask and questions that Ms. Malone could ask.

➤ Have students pair up within their groups and rehearse a conversation between Ms. Malone and Mr. Page.

➤ Pairs present their role-plays to their groups. The group listens to make sure each pair discusses skills, experience, and references, and then the group provides feedback. If necessary, pairs can revise their conversations based on the group's feedback.

➤ Do it yourself!

(For general suggestions, see *Introduction*, page Txiii.)

Procedure:

➤ Have students read the job ads. For each ad, ask *What do you have to do to apply for this job?* (call or fax) *Which job are you more interested in or qualified for?*

➤ Once students have chosen an ad, have them note their qualifications for the job, for example, *I have been working on cars since I was sixteen years old.* Students who don't have relevant experience should note what they can do to become qualified for the job, for example, by getting *on-the-job training* or *hands-on experience.* Have these students review the vocabulary on page 131.

➤ Explain that students should use Rebecca Malone's letter as a model in writing their own response letters. Have students look at her letter again and lightly cross out all the information they need to change to their own. Students can then use what is left as a frame for their letter, substituting their own information for the words that are crossed out.

➤ As students are writing, circulate and note recurring errors. When students finish, have them exchange letters with a partner. Point out two or three errors that you noticed the class making. Have students check their partners' letters for these errors and make any necessary corrections. Students return letters to their partners. You may want to have students rewrite their letters, incorporating the corrections.

Option: Have students choose a job they are interested in and qualified for from the want ads in the local newspaper and then write a response letter.

Option: If possible, bring in fax cover sheets for students to practice filling out. Have students use fax numbers and contact names from the job ads on this page or from the job ads students brought in.

Challenge: In groups, have students read several response letters to the same job ad. Each group chooses two applicants to interview for the job. Groups then create at least five interview questions. Groups interview the students whose letters they chose and then discuss who to offer the job to and why.

C. Discussion. First write answers. Then discuss with your classmates.

1. What's Andy worried about? <u>His boss told him to go home.</u>
2. What's Joan's explanation? <u>Andy's boss was letting him know that he appreciated Andy's effort and long hours.</u>
3. Has anyone ever said anything to you that caused a misunderstanding like Andy's? Explain. _____

Letters of response to job ads

A. Read the job ad and the response letter.

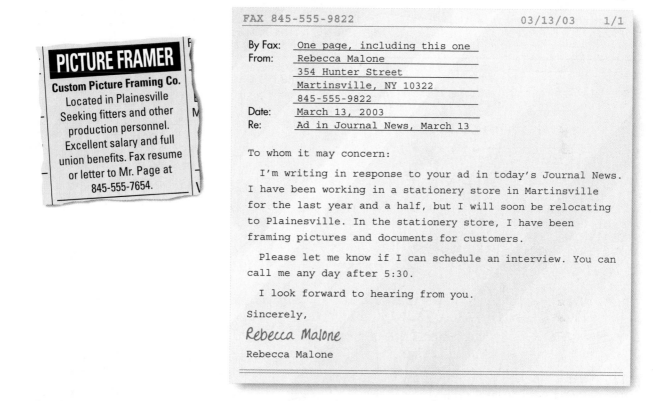

PICTURE FRAMER

Custom Picture Framing Co.
Located in Plainesville
Seeking fitters and other
production personnel.
Excellent salary and full
union benefits. Fax resume
or letter to Mr. Page at
845-555-7654.

```
FAX 845-555-9822                        03/13/03    1/1

By Fax:   One page, including this one
From:     Rebecca Malone
          354 Hunter Street
          Martinsville, NY 10322
          845-555-9822
Date:     March 13, 2003
Re:       Ad in Journal News, March 13

To whom it may concern:

   I'm writing in response to your ad in today's Journal News.
I have been working in a stationery store in Martinsville
for the last year and a half, but I will soon be relocating
to Plainesville. In the stationery store, I have been
framing pictures and documents for customers.

   Please let me know if I can schedule an interview. You can
call me any day after 5:30.

   I look forward to hearing from you.

Sincerely,

Rebecca Malone

Rebecca Malone
```

B. Role play. Role-play a telephone conversation between Ms. Malone and Mr. Page. Discuss skills, experience, and references.

➤ Do it yourself!

Read the ads. Then write a letter in response to one of the jobs. Use a separate sheet of paper.

★ MANICURIST ★

Exp'd manicurists at Galleria
of White Plains. Perform all
nail services. Must speak
fluent English. Contact Mary
at 602-555-7899 or FAX 602-
555-7890

Help Wanted

**Automotive Manager
OIL CHANGE**
$30K+
A new 4-bay lube facility
opening in Brewster is looking for a key person with
auto exp. Call Mr. George at
415-555-6432 or fax 415-555-
6400, Mon-Fri, 9-5.

For extra practice, go to page 162.

Review

(For general suggestions, see *Introduction*, page Txii.)

Procedure:

A. Pair work or group work.

Ask and answer questions.

➤ On a separate sheet of paper, have groups write as many questions as they can about each picture, for example, for picture 1, *Who are the people?* (a husband and wife) *Where did they live before?* (in Chicago) *Where do they live now?* (in Corona, Illinois) On their papers, groups should indicate which picture each question is about. Collect the questions and then give each group another group's questions to answer. Students take turns reading the questions, and the group discusses the answers.

Create conversations.

➤ Assign each pair of students a picture. Assign picture 1 to more advanced students. Students create a conversation between the two people in their picture. If students need help or ideas, refer them to appropriate pages in this unit: for picture 2, refer students to page 128; for picture 3, page 129; for picture 4, pages 130 and 131.

➤ For each picture, have one pair role-play their conversation for the class. Have these pairs present their conversations in order so that the conversations create a picture story.

Tell a story.

➤ First have pairs use the present continuous to describe what is happening in each picture. For example, in picture 1, *The husband and wife are looking at the job ads in the newspaper*; in picture 2, *The wife is calling for an interview.*

➤ Then have students use the simple present tense to tell the complete story of the wife's job. Remind students to use ordinal numbers, or other sequential connectors, such as *next* or *finally*, when they tell the story. For example, *First, a husband and wife move from Chicago to Corona, Illinois. She needs to find a job, so they look at the classified ads in the local newspaper. She sees an ad for an accountant position. Next, she calls about the ad . . .*

➤ As a class, tell the complete story of the wife's job. Have different volunteers tell each part of the story.

Challenge: Game. Give groups about two minutes to study the pictures and remember everything they can about them. Advise them to pay attention to details, such as times, dates, and names. While they are studying the picture, draw on the board the following game board.

TIME	NAMES	EVENTS	WORDS
100	100	100	100
200	200	200	200
300	300	300	300
400	400	400	400
500	500	500	500

Each group / team takes a turn selecting a category and an amount, for example, *Names for 100.* The higher the amount, the more difficult the question. If the team answers the question correctly, it earns the number of points indicated. Once a question has been asked for an amount in a category, cross this box off. Each team should have the same number of opportunities to answer a question. Use the following questions or create your own. They are in order from least to most difficult (from 100 to 500 points).

TIME: *When does the wife interview for the job?* (April 22) *When does the wife have her performance review?* (one year later) *At what time are the man and woman looking at the paper?* (8:20) *What time does the wife call about the ad?* (9:15) *What is the date on the newspaper?* (April 16)

NAMES: *What is the name of the state where the husband and wife live?* (Illinois) *What is the wife's name?* (Vanessa Chow) *What is the name of the newspaper?* (Corona Register) *What is the husband's name?* (Ronald Chow) *What is the interviewer's name?* (Boris Zakowsky)

EVENTS: *What happens first?* (The husband and wife look at the newspaper.) *What happens last?* (The wife has a performance review.) *What happens second?* (The wife calls about the ad.) *What happens third?* (The wife has an interview.) *What happened before the first picture?* (The husband and wife moved.)

WORDS: *What job is the wife interested in?* (accountant) *What section of the newspaper do the husband and wife read?* (classifieds) *In picture 3, what's on the desk in front of the wife?* (application) *What's in one of the moving boxes?* (pots and pans, dishes, or toaster) *What's in the box with the purple label?* (dishes)

⌒ B. Listen to the job interview ...

➤ Tell students they are going to listen to a job interview.

➤ After students listen to the conversation the first time, ask *Who is being interviewed?* (Ms. Chung) *Do you think Ms. Chung will get the job?* (no) *Why not?* (She asks to call the interviewer by his first name, she says she has a personality conflict with her current supervisor, and so on.)

➤ Have students open their books and read items 1 though 5. Tell students to listen for and check the mistakes Ms. Chung makes.

➤ Review and discuss the answers as a class.

Option: Have pairs come up with interview tips for Ms. Chung.

C. Complete the letter ...

➤ Students complete the letter individually. If students have trouble, suggest that they circle the words or phrases in the letter that indicate which tense to use, such as *for a while, never, for about three weeks.*

➤ Circulate to offer help as needed.

➤ Have students check answers by reading the letter to a partner. Review answers as a class.

Tapescript

Jim: Thank you for being on time, Ms. Chung. We appreciate punctuality here. So I see from your resume that you're working at Johnson Laboratories.

Ms. Chung: Yes, that's right, . . . uh. May I call you Jim?

Jim: Uh, well, yes . . . sure.

Ms. Chung: But I'm going to quit. I have a personality conflict with my supervisor. He doesn't like my clothes. And he expects me to do all the work. Plus, he's not reasonable about punctuality.

Jim: What do you mean?

Ms. Chung: Well, last week I had to take my dog to the vet. I got stuck in traffic, and so I was even later than I usually am. Well, you won't believe what happened.

Jim: What happened?

Ms. Chung: My supervisor said I should take care of personal business on my own time! And I'm supposed to call if I'm going to be late. Anyway, I think I should get another job. How much is this job paying?

Jim: Excuse me?

Ms. Chung: What's the salary? And does it have good benefits? I really need a good dental plan.

Jim: Well, actually, we can discuss the benefits and the salary at another time. Is there anything you'd like to know about the company?

Ms. Chung: No, not really. It seems like a nice place.

Jim: Well, I have a few other candidates coming in for an interview. I'll be in touch with you.

Ms. Chung: Thanks, Jim.

B. Listen to the job interview. Read the statements and listen again. Check the mistakes Ms. Chung made.

1. ☐ She was late.

2. ☑ She was too familiar with the interviewer.

3. ☑ She talked too much about herself.

4. ☑ She asked about the salary too soon.

5. ☑ She didn't ask a question about the company.

C. Complete the letter about Mark's recent activities.

Hi, Frank,

Well, I'm sorry I _____haven't written_____ for a while. I am very
  1. haven't written / am not writing

busy and I never _____have_____ any time anymore. Let
  2. have / have had

me bring you up to date. I ___'ve been living___ in this new
  3. am living / 've been living

apartment for about three weeks, and I _____like_____ it
  4. like / am liking

very much. I _____need_____ new furniture and a new
  5. need / have been needing

refrigerator, but that's nothing. What I really _____want_____
  6. am wanting / want

is a new job. I ___'ve been working___ at the local supermarket
  7. 've been working / 'm working

for about six months, and that's six months too long! The manager

never _____notices_____ anything good that I do. I don't
  8. is noticing / notices

feel appreciated, and I'm fed up! Tonight I _____have_____
  9. am having / have

an interview for a new job, and I'll let you know how it goes.

In a hurry!

Mark

D. Read each statement or question. Write your __own__ response.

    1. "Why did you leave your last job?" _____

        _____

    2. "I've been meaning to tell you — we're very satisfied with your work." _____

        _____

    3. "Where do you see yourself in a year?" _____

        _____

    4. "I think it's time we moved to a first-name basis." _____

        _____

E. Composition. **On a separate sheet of paper, write about the picture on page 138. Say as much as you can.**

Now I can
- ❏ respond to a classified job ad.
- ❏ call for an interview.
- ❏ talk about job history and references at an interview.
- ❏ move to a first-name basis.
- ❏ accept and respond to feedback on the job.
- ❏ _____.

D. Read each statement or question ...

➤ Students complete the exercise individually. If they have trouble, advise them to look back through the unit for ideas.

➤ Circulate to offer help as needed.

➤ Have students take turns reading the items and their responses with a partner. Then read each item and elicit a variety of appropriate responses from the class.

E. Composition ...

➤ Provide students with concrete approaches to writing about the picture on page 138. Use one of the options that follow, give students a choice of options, or assign options based on students' levels of proficiency. Model what is expected of students for each option.

➤ Advise students to look back through the unit for help and ideas as they write.

➤ Circulate to offer help as needed.

Option: Have students write the complete story of the wife's job on page 138 using the simple present tense. Remind students to use ordinal numbers or other sequential connectors, such as *next* or *finally*, when they write the story.

Option: Have students write a response letter to the ad for an accountant. Students write the letter as if they were Vanessa Chow. Students should use the response letter on page 137 as a model.

Option: Have students write a letter from Vanessa Chow to a friend in Chicago. In the letter, Vanessa describes her recent activities. Students should use the letter on page 139 as a model.

Now I can

➤ Read the first item in the box out loud, *Now I can respond to a classified job ad*. Elicit from the class an example of how to respond to a classified job ad, such as *Hello. My name is _____ . I'm calling about the ad for a baby-sitter in today's paper.*

➤ In pairs, have students take turns reading each item in the box and giving an example of what they have learned. When students can provide an example, they should check that objective. For the items students weren't able to check, they should look back through the unit for ideas.

➤ When students are finished reviewing with their partners, read each item out loud and elicit an example from the class.

Oral test (optional)

You may want to use the *Now I can* box as an informal evaluation. While students are working on the *Composition* activity, you can call them up individually and check their ability with two or three objectives.

This is an alphabetical list of all active vocabulary in *Ready to Go 3*. The numbers refer to the page on which the word first appears. When a word has two meanings (a new <u>brush</u> OR <u>Brush</u> your hair), both are in the list.

A

about 3
absolutely 47
across 18
actually 5
ad 128
advance 129
adverse 102
after 60
afternoon 19
ago 30
air conditioner 46
aisle 45
allergic 86
always 31
amazing 3
anymore 45
application 11
apply 4
appointment 60
appreciate 4
approval 115
approve 115
around [about] 19
as 49
as long as 114
ask 20
ask (someone) for help 31
assistant 59
attendant 59
attention 128
auto part 73
awful 2

B

baby-sitter 4
back 45
bag 100
bank *n.* 18
bank *v.* 118
bank teller 4
bargain 72
basement 17
be down 33
be sure 62
beautician 59

beautiful 2
before 60
behind on (a payment) 115
believe 32
below 44
below standard 44
between 18
bill 123
board 58
bounce (a check) 115
box 72
branch office 117
brand 45
break *n.* 59
break *v.* 31
break time 61
bring in 47
brochure 114
broken *adj.* 31
brother-in-law 89
bus 18
buyer 44
by mail 81
by phone 73
by the hour 58
by the job 58
by the way 102

C

can *n.* 72
can *v.* 16
cancel 116
capsule 103
car seat 47
carry 45
carton 100
cent 72
certainly 100
certificate of deposit (CD) 114
change 117
check 33
checking account 114
chef 128
chef manager 128
cigarette 86
clean 32
client 59

clogged *adj.* 32
close 86
closing time 61
clothes 73
coffee 19
coffee shop 19
cold 86
community 94
companion 58
complain 44
complaint 53
compliment 130
computer 5
computer malfunctions 33
conflict 129
congratulations 88
consequence 116
consideration 66
consumer 53
consumer complaint 53
contact 129
container 72
convenient 46
cook 5
cookie 44
copier 32
corner 18
could 4
counseling 116
coupon 72
crashed *adj.* 33
credit 47
credit card 115
crib 47
current 114
customer 44

D

dealer 44
death 89
debt 116
decide 62
defective 44
dentist 60
depressed 89
directions 18
discontinued *adj.* 46

This is a unit-by-unit list of all the social language from the practical conversations in *Ready to Go 3*.

Unit 1

Model 1

Nice weather today.
You know, I don't think we've met.
Nice to meet you.
Nice to meet you too.
By the way, . . .
You do?
Thanks!

Model 2

That's incredible!
That's amazing!
You're kidding!
Wow! It's a small world.

Model 3

Could you do me a favor?
Of course.
I need a reference.
Would you mind _____ing . . . ?
Not at all.
I'd be glad to.
Thanks so much.
I appreciate it.

Model 4

Tell me something about yourself.
I'm pretty good / not very good at that.
Actually, . . .

Unit 2

Model 1

Excuse me.
Can you tell me how to get to _____?
Sure.
Go straight.
Turn right / left.
Make a right / left.
Make your (second) left / right.
Go down the hall.
Go to the end of the hall.

Go up / down the stairs.
Take the escalator / the elevator.

Model 2

Hold the elevator, please!
Going up?
There you go.

Model 3

Hello. (to answer the phone)
Could you please tell me how to get there?
I'm taking the bus / train / subway.
At the corner of _____ and _____.
Take the number _____ to _____ and transfer
    there to the _____.
OK.
It's right on the corner.
You can't miss it.

Model 4

I was wondering, . . .
Would you like to _____ sometime?
We'd love to.
That would be nice.
Sounds great.
Yes. Let's do that!
When would be good?
How about _____?
Around _____ o'clock?
That's fine.
Why don't we _____?

Unit 3

Model 1

I wonder if this _____ is still under warranty.
No problem.

Model 2

Uh-oh.
I'm going to get in trouble.
What do you mean?
Don't worry.
It's always better to speak up.

Model 3

Can you believe it?

That's ridiculous.

What a waste of time!

You can say that again!

Model 4

What's the matter?

My computer is down / is frozen / crashed.

But that didn't help.

Unit 4

Model 1

Could you have a look at _____?

Well, no wonder.

They're not up to code / not too good / below standard.

Model 2

Do you carry _____?

That's a shame.

Really?

Would you like to have a look?

Model 3

I'm sorry, those were discontinued / didn't meet EPA rules.

That's too bad.

Model 4

How can I help you?

I heard there's been a recall.

Please bring it in and we'll give you a replacement.

Can I get a credit instead?

Absolutely. So long as you have your receipt.

Unit 5

Model 1

Tell me, what are you doing these days?

I'm working as _____.

That's great!

How are you paid?

By the hour / job / week / trip.

By the hour, plus room and board / plus tips.

Model 2

What are the hours?

We pay minimum wage / time and a half for overtime / double time.

Could you repeat that, please? I'd like to make a note of it.

Model 3

I'm sorry, but I have to reschedule.

How's _____?

Actually, that won't work.

Yeah. That's good for me.

Model 4

Is that a problem / an emergency?

No, not really.

Why don't you do that at lunch time / at break time / after closing time?

Unit 6

Model 1

What a bargain!

That must be a mistake.

Model 2

Can I make a suggestion?

Call _____ or log on to _____.

Hey, why didn't *I* think of that?

Unit 7

Model 1

Would it be possible for you to _____?

It's after _____ o'clock.

Oh, I'm sorry. I didn't realize that.

You're welcome.

Model 2

Is it legal to _____?

Well, to tell you the truth, I'm not sure / not positive / I have no idea.

As far as I know, it is.

Model 3

How are things?

How's it going?

How're you doing?

How are you?

What's up?
What's new?
Pretty good.
How about you?
Great, actually.
Congratulations.
I'm really happy to hear that.

Model 4

You look upset.
Is there anything wrong?
Well, actually, _____.
Oh, I'm so sorry to hear that.
Is there anything I can do?
Thanks for offering.

Unit 8

Model 1

Yes?
No, thanks.
I'll just take a refund.
Certainly.
Can I see your receipt?
Here you go.

Model 2

Is everything OK?
Actually, this _____ is not _____.
Let me take it back.
Oh, I'm so sorry. I'll take care of that right
   away.

Model 3

I'm here to _____.
Oh, by the way, _____?

Model 4

Here's _____.
That's right.

Unit 9

Model 1

I'd like some information on _____.
Are you the right person?
Can you tell me the _____?
You know, on second thought, I think I'll shop
   around.
Of course.

But as long as you're here, why don't you
   _____?

Model 2

How was your day?
Do you want the good news or the bad news?
Let's take the good news first.
That's good.
So, what's the bad news?

Model 3

Be behind on _____.
Oh, no! How did that happen?
I got in over my head.
If I were you, I'd _____.

Model 4

How come?
I've had enough!
I'm fed up!
I've had it!
I'm pretty happy.

Unit 10

Model 1

I'm calling about the ad for _____ in today's
   paper.
Could you fax me _____?
Please send it to my attention.

Model 3

Have you got a minute?
I've been meaning to tell you, . . .
You're doing a great job.
Really? Thanks.
I am? Thanks.
Thanks. I'm happy to hear that.
Thank *you*.
By the way, please call me _____.
Why don't you call me _____?
I think it's time you called me _____.
Just call me _____.

Model 4

Have you had a chance to _____?
You've had a really good _____ with us.
Where do you see yourself in (two) years?
Well, I'm interested in being _____.
Let's see if we can get you some _____.

The following verbs from *Ready to Go 3* have irregular past-tense forms.

Base form	Past-tense form	Past participle
be	was / were	been
begin	began	begun
break	broke	broken
bring	brought	brought
buy	bought	bought
can	could	been able to
choose	chose	chosen
come	came	come
do	did	done
drink	drank	drunk
drive	drove	driven
eat	ate	eaten
fall	fell	fallen
fight	fought	fought
find	found	found
forget	forgot	forgotten
get	got	gotten
give	gave	given
go	went	gone
have	had	had
hear	heard	heard
hurt	hurt	hurt
know	knew	known
leave	left	left
let	let	let
lose	lost	lost
make	made	made
mean	meant	meant
meet	met	met
pay	paid	paid
put	put	put
read	read	read
ring	rang	rung
run	ran	run
say	said	said
see	saw	seen
sell	sold	sold
send	sent	sent
speak	spoke	spoken
take	took	taken
tell	told	told
think	thought	thought
understand	understood	understood
wear	wore	worn
withdraw	withdrew	withdrawn
write	wrote	written

Irregular comparative and superlative forms of adjectives

Adjective	Comparative	Superlative
bad	worse	worst
far	farther	farthest
good	better	best
little	less	least
many/a lot of	more	most
much/a lot of	more	most

Verbs followed by gerunds

appreciate	enjoy	postpone
avoid	explain	practice
can't help	feel like	prevent
consider	finish	quit
delay	imagine	recommend
detest	keep	risk
discuss	mind	suggest
dislike	miss	understand

Verbs followed by infinitives

afford	decide	offer
agree	expect	plan
appear	help	prepare
ask	hope	promise
arrange	hurry	request
be sure	intend	seem
can't afford	learn	want
can't wait	manage	wish
choose	need	would like

Verbs followed by gerunds or infinitives

begin	hate	remember
can't stand	like	start
continue	love	try
forget	prefer	

Verbs followed by objects and infinitives

advise	force	promise *
allow	help *	remind
ask *	hire	require
cause	invite	teach
choose *	need *	tell
convince	order	want *
encourage	pay *	warn
expect *	permit	would like *

* Words with a star can also be followed by an infinitive without an object.

How to spell the gerund and the present participle

Add -ing to the base form of the verb.
      speak   speaking

If the base form ends in -e, drop the -e and add -ing.
      have   having

In verbs of one syllable, if the last three letters are a consonant-vowel-consonant (C-V-C) series, double the last consonant and then add -ing.

      C V C
      ↓ ↓ ↓
      s i t   sitting

Exception: Don't double the last consonant in words that end in -w, -x, or -y.
      fix   fixing

In verbs of more than one syllable that end in a consonant-vowel-consonant series, double the last consonant only if the stress is on the last syllable.
      permít   permitting
but not   órder   ordering

AN EQUAL OPPORTUNITY EMPLOYER

Please complete all requested information. Use ink and print.

GENERAL INFORMATION

TODAY'S DATE	DATE AVAILABLE FOR WORK:

NAME: LAST   FIRST   MIDDLE

SOCIAL SECURITY NUMBER

STREET ADDRESS

CITY   STATE   ZIP

TELEPHONE (HOME):   TELEPHONE (WORK):

IF YOU HAVE WORKED FOR OUR COMPANY BEFORE, STATE WHERE, WHEN, FINAL POSITION AND REASON FOR LEAVING:

HAVE YOU EVER APPLIED TO OUR COMPANY BEFORE? _____ YES _____ NO

IF YES, WHERE:

HAVE YOU EVER BEEN CONVICTED OF A CRIME BY A CIVILIAN OR MILITARY COURT: _____ YES _____ NO

POSITION DESIRED: SALARY DESIRED:

FULL TIME _____ 35+ HRS PER WK   PART TIME _____ LESS THAN 35 HRS

AGE (IF YOU ARE UNDER 18 YOU MAY HAVE TO PROVIDE A WORK PERMIT BEFORE STARTING WORK)

ARE YOU AT LEAST 18 YRS OLD? _____ YES _____ NO

ARE YOU AT LEAST 16 YRS OLD? _____ YES _____ NO

PLEASE INDICATE THE HOURS (BOTH DAY AND EVENING YOU ARE AVAILABLE TO WORK:

SUN _____ MON _____ TUES _____ WED _____

THURS _____ FRI _____ SAT _____

NOTE: ALTHOUGH EVERY EFFORT TO ACCOMMODATE INDIVIDUAL PREFERENCES WILL BE MADE, BUSINESS NEEDS MAY REQUIRE ANY OR ALL OF THE FOLLOWING: EXTENSION OF HOURS, A ROTATING WORK SCHEDULE, SATURDAY AND/OR SUNDAY HOURS, OVERTIME

DO YOU HAVE ANY RELATIVES EMPLOYED BY OUR COMPANY? _____ YES _____ NO
IF YES, IDENTIFY BY NAME AND LOCATION

WORK EXPERIENCE (START WITH CURRENT EMPLOYER AND CONTINUE WITH FORMER EMPLOYERS

EMPLOYER #1

ADDRESS	CITY	STATE	ZIP
PHONE	SUPERVISOR	TITLE	
POSITION	FINAL SALARY	REASON FOR LEAVING	

DATES ON EMPLOYMENT:
     FROM: TO:

EMPLOYER #2

ADDRESS	CITY	STATE	ZIP
PHONE	SUPERVISOR	TITLE	
POSITION	FINAL SALARY	REASON FOR LEAVING	

DATES ON EMPLOYMENT:
     FROM: TO:

EMPLOYER #3

ADDRESS	CITY	STATE	ZIP
PHONE	SUPERVISOR	TITLE	
POSITION	FINAL SALARY	REASON FOR LEAVING	

DATES ON EMPLOYMENT:
     FROM: TO:

EMPLOYER #4

ADDRESS	CITY	STATE	ZIP
PHONE	SUPERVISOR	TITLE	
POSITION	FINAL SALARY	REASON FOR LEAVING	

DATES ON EMPLOYMENT:
     FROM: TO:

PROFESSIONAL REFERENCES - LIST PERSONS FAMILIAR WITH YOUR WORK ABILITY (EXCLUDE RELATIVES)

NAME	PHONE NUMBER	HOW ACQUAINTED	HOW LONG
NAME	PHONE NUMBER	HOW ACQUAINTED	HOW LONG
NAME	PHONE NUMBER	HOW ACQUAINTED	HOW LONG

EMERGENCY CONTACT

IN CASE OF EMERGENCY, CONTACT (NAME):	(PHONE NUMBER):

DO NOT WRITE BELOW THIS LINE.

(HIRING PERSONNEL: COMPLETE THIS SECTION ONLY AFTER AN OFFER OF EMPLOYMENT IS MADE.)

JOB TITLE	T (TEMP OR R (REG)	FT OR PT	STORE #	MALE OR FEMALE	START DATE
DATE OF BIRTH	HOURLY OR COEFF. MGR. OR SALARIED (PAY TYPE: CIRCLE ONE)	RATE: (ONLY IF HOURLY): _____ PER HOUR		NEXT REVIEW DATE	
RACE (CIRCLE ONE) WHITE - BLACK - HISPANIC - ASIAN/PACIFIC ISLAND - AMERICAN INDIAN		SIGNATURE OF HIRING INDIVIDUAL:		YES OR NO REQUEST BACKGROUND: CIRCLE ONE	

(Continued on page 152.)

(Continued from page 151.)

EDUCATION AND TRAINING

SCHOOL	PLEASE PRINT NAME, STREET, CITY, & ZIP FOR EACH SCHOOL	NUMBER OF YEARS COMPLETED	TYPE OF COURSE/MAJOR
COLLEGE			
HIGH SCHOOL			
ADDITIONAL TRAINING			

INDICATE THE JOB SKILLS WHICH YOU HAVE PERFORMED:
_____ TYPING (_____) WPM   _____ COMPUTER SOFTWARE (LIST: _____)   _____ OTHER

ADDITIONAL INQUIRES

HAVE YOU EVER BEEN DISMISSED OR ASKED TO RESIGN FROM ANY EMPLOYER? _____ YES _____ NO

IF YES, PLEASE EXPLAIN: _____

IF EMPLOYMENT IS OFFERED, CAN YOU PROVIDE VERIFICATION OF YOUR LEGAL RIGHT TO WORK IN THE U.S.? _____ YES _____ NO

WHY ARE YOU INTERESTED IN WORKING FOR OUR COMPANY? _____
_____

WHAT DIDN'T YOU LIKE ABOUT YOUR PREVIOUS JOBS? _____

PROVIDE INFORMATION ABOUT COMMUNITY ACTIVITIES, PROFESSIONAL TRADE OR SERVICE ORGANIZATIONS TO WHICH YOU BELONG WHICH YOU BELIEVE MAY DEMONSTRATE YOUR JOB RELATED ABILITIES (YOU MAY EXCLUDE THOSE WHICH INDICATE RACE, COLOR, RELIGION, SEX, NATIONAL ORIGIN, AGE, HANDICAP.)
_____
_____

REFERRAL SOURCE

_____ WALK-IN APPLICANT	_____ AGENCY	_____ EMPLOYEE REFERRAL	_____ NEWSPAPER	_____ OTHER
	NAME OF AGENCY:	NAME OF EMPLOYEE:		PLEASE LIST:

IF HIRED, I AGREE TO ABIDE BY THE RULES AND REGULATIONS OF THE COMPANY. I UNDERSTAND THAT MY EMPLOYMENT IS AT-WILL. THIS MEANS THAT I DO NOT HAVE A CONTRACT OF EMPLOYMENT FOR ANY PARTICULAR DURATION OR LIMITING THE GROUNDS FOR MY TERMINATION IN ANY WAY. I AM FREE TO RESIGN AT ANY TIME. SIMILARLY, THE COMPANY IS FREE TO TERMINATE OR CHANGE THE TERMS AND/OR CONDITIONS OF MY EMPLOYMENT AT ANY TIME FOR ANY REASON OR NO REASON. THE ONLY TIME MY AT-WILL STATUS COULD BE CHANGED IS IF I WERE TO ENTER INTO A WRITTEN CONTRACT WITH THE COMPANY EXPLICITLY PROMISING ME JOB SECURITY.

ALL OF THE INFORMATION I HAVE SUPPLIED IN THIS APPLICATION IS A TRUE AND COMPLETE STATEMENT OF THE FACTS, AN IF EMPLOYED, ANY OMISSIONS OR FALSE OF MISLEADING STATEMENTS ON THIS APPLICATION OR DURING THE INTERVIEW PROCESS COULD RESULT IN IMMEDIATE DISMISSAL REGARDLESS OF WHEN SUCH INFORMATION IS DISCOVERED. I FURTHER AUTHORIZE ALL COURTS, PROBATION DEPARTMENTS, PROSECUTOR'S OFFICES, BOARDS, EMPLOYERS, EDUCATIONAL AND CREDIT COMPANIES, OTHER INSTITUTIONS AND AGENCIES, WITHOUT EXCEPTION, TO FURNISH THE COMPANY OR ITS REPRESENTATIVES ANY INFORMATION ANY OF THEM HAVE CONCERNING ME. THIS WAIVER DOES NOT PERMIT THE RELEASE OR USE OF DISABILITY-RELATED OR MEDICAL INFORMATION IN A MANNER PROHIBITED BY THE AMERICANS WITH DISABILITIES ACT (ADA) AND OTHER RELEVANT FEDERAL AND STATE LAWS. I FURTHER AUTHORIZE A CHECK BY ANY CONSUMER AGENCY OF MY EMPLOYMENT HISTORY AS WELL AS ANY INCIDENTS OF EMPLOYMENT DISHONESTY, RETAIL THEFT OR CRIMINAL ACTIVITY. I UNDERSTAND THAT MY EMPLOYMENT AND/OR RETENTION MAY BE AFFECTED IN WHOLE OR IN PART BY A REPORT RECEIVED FROM THIS AGENCY. I HEREBY DISCHARGE AND EXONERATE THE COMPANY, ITS AGENTS AND REPRESENTATIVES, OR ANY PERSON SO FURNISHING INFORMATION, FROM ANY LIABILITY AND ALL LIABILITY OF EVERY NATURE AND KIND ARISING OUT OF THE FURNISHING, INSPECTION OR COLLECTION OF SUCH DOCUMENTS, RECORDS, AND OTHER INFORMATION OR THE INVESTIGATION MADE BY THE COMPANY. A PHOTOSTATIC COPY OF THIS AUTHORIZATION WILL BE CONSIDERED AS EFFECTIVE AND VALID AS THE ORIGINAL (WHEREVER LEGALLY REQUIRED, A COPY OF ANY CREDIT REPORT AN OTHER INFORMATION WILL BE AVAILABLE UPON MY REQUEST.)

I AGREE TO PROTECT THE COMPANY'S CONFIDENTIAL INFORMATION, TRADE SECRETS, AND OTHER PROPRIETARY INFORMATION AND WILL NOT REVEAL SUCH INFORMATION TO ANYONE AT ANY TIME DURING OR AFTER CESSATION OF MY EMPLOYMENT.

I FURTHER UNDERSTAND THAT THE COMPANY WILL NOT EMPLOY PERSONS WHO USE ILLEGAL DRUGS OR ENGAGE IN SUBSTANCE ABUSE, AND THAT THE COMPANY RETAINS THE RIGHT TO SCREEN FROM EMPLOYMENT SUCH INDIVIDUALS.

IF HIRED, I UNDERSTAND THAT THE FIRST 90 DAYS OF EMPLOYMENT ARE CONSIDERED A PROBATIONARY PERIOD, DURING WHICH TIME I WILL NOT BE CONSIDERED A REGULAR EMPLOYEE. I WILL BE CONSIDERED A REGULAR EMPLOYEE AFTER I HAVE SUCCESSFULLY COMPLETED THIS PROBATIONARY PERIOD.

_____   _____
SIGNATURE OF APPLICANT   DATE

(THIS APPLICATION WILL ONLY BE CONSIDERED FOR 3 MONTHS. AFTER THAT TIME, YOU MUST COMPLETE A NEW APPLICATION FOR FURTHER CONSIDERATION.)

CITYMALL FLOOR PLAN

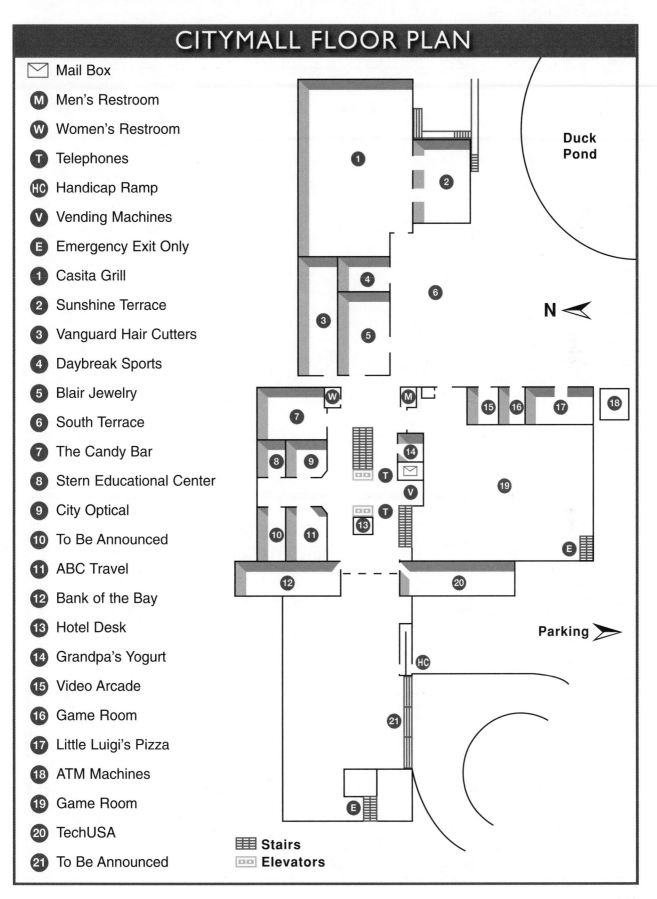

✉ Mail Box

Ⓜ Men's Restroom

Ⓦ Women's Restroom

Ⓣ Telephones

(HC) Handicap Ramp

Ⓥ Vending Machines

Ⓔ Emergency Exit Only

① Casita Grill

② Sunshine Terrace

③ Vanguard Hair Cutters

④ Daybreak Sports

⑤ Blair Jewelry

⑥ South Terrace

⑦ The Candy Bar

⑧ Stern Educational Center

⑨ City Optical

⑩ To Be Announced

⑪ ABC Travel

⑫ Bank of the Bay

⑬ Hotel Desk

⑭ Grandpa's Yogurt

⑮ Video Arcade

⑯ Game Room

⑰ Little Luigi's Pizza

⑱ ATM Machines

⑲ Game Room

⑳ TechUSA

㉑ To Be Announced

Duck Pond

N ◄

Parking ►

▦ Stairs

▱ Elevators

http://www.hi-tekbikes.com/support/warranty.htm

Hi-Tek BIKES

Products | Tips & Tutorials | Customer Support | Site Map | About Us

Index
Dealer Locator
Sonar FAQ
GPS FAQ
Mapping FAQ
Software FAQ
Registration
Warranty
Repair
Contact Us

Hi-Tek Warranty and Service Program (U.S. Only)

With Hi-Tek, you can enjoy the peace of mind that comes with knowing your purchase is backed by the number one warranty and service program in the industry. First, there's our famous Full One-Year Warranty. Then, we make sure any repairs you might need will be handled quickly and completely — without surprises.

Full One-Year Warranty

The best warranty in the business. In the unlikely event your unit malfunctions or fails to conform to the product's written specifications due to a defect in materials or workmanship, we will repair it absolutely free for one year from the date of your original purchase. (Some limitations do apply, so please read the complete warranty and service details carefully in the Hi-Tek warranty statement enclosed with each Hi-Tek product.)

To receive repair service you must obtain a Return Authorization number from our Customer Service Department. You may contact the Customer Service Department via email or call toll free at 1-800-555-2166.

Please see our Non-Warranty Repair information for out-of-warranty repairs.

© 1998-2002 Hi-Tek Bikes | Blandford, Texas USA

Products | Tips and Tutorials | Customer Support | About Us | Site Map | Contact Us

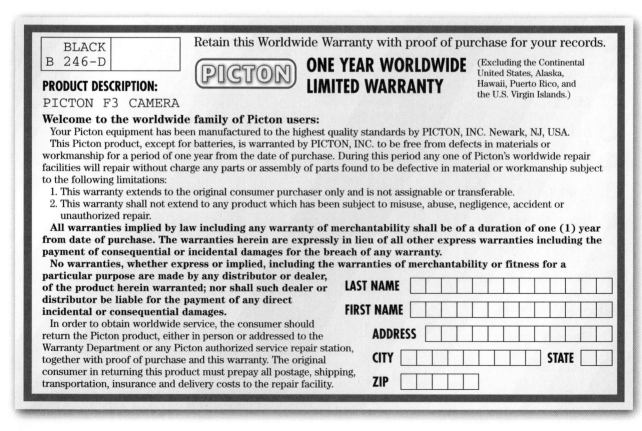

BLACK
B 246-D

PRODUCT DESCRIPTION:
PICTON F3 CAMERA

Retain this Worldwide Warranty with proof of purchase for your records.

PICTON

ONE YEAR WORLDWIDE LIMITED WARRANTY

(Excluding the Continental United States, Alaska, Hawaii, Puerto Rico, and the U.S. Virgin Islands.)

Welcome to the worldwide family of Picton users:

Your Picton equipment has been manufactured to the highest quality standards by PICTON, INC. Newark, NJ, USA.

This Picton product, except for batteries, is warranted by PICTON, INC. to be free from defects in materials or workmanship for a period of one year from the date of purchase. During this period any one of Picton's worldwide repair facilities will repair without charge any parts or assembly of parts found to be defective in material or workmanship subject to the following limitations:

1. This warranty extends to the original consumer purchaser only and is not assignable or transferable.
2. This warranty shall not extend to any product which has been subject to misuse, abuse, negligence, accident or unauthorized repair.

All warranties implied by law including any warranty of merchantability shall be of a duration of one (1) year from date of purchase. The warranties herein are expressly in lieu of all other express warranties including the payment of consequential or incidental damages for the breach of any warranty.

No warranties, whether express or implied, including the warranties of merchantability or fitness for a particular purpose are made by any distributor or dealer, **of the product herein warranted; nor shall such dealer or distributor be liable for the payment of any direct incidental or consequential damages.**

In order to obtain worldwide service, the consumer should return the Picton product, either in person or addressed to the Warranty Department or any Picton authorized service repair station, together with proof of purchase and this warranty. The original consumer in returning this product must prepay all postage, shipping, transportation, insurance and delivery costs to the repair facility.

LAST NAME
FIRST NAME
ADDRESS
CITY   **STATE**
ZIP

JetBus Bus Company
Post Office Box 36201
San Antonio, Texas 78205
210-555-1450   www.jetfast.com

>>

July 2, 2003

Ms. Clarita Guzman
202 East Pine Street, #8A
Kingston, IL 60026

Dear Ms. Guzman:

I was very sorry to learn about your disappointing experience with JetBus and apologize for our delay in responding.

We know that your time is valuable and realize that this must have been frustrating. I regret the inconvenience and can promise you that we are working very hard to prevent schedule irregularities and to improve our overall on-time performance.

We want to encourage you to ride with us again soon and hope that you will have the opportunity to use the enclosed toward the purchase of future JetBus travel.

Please accept our apology and give us the opportunity to regain your confidence.

Sincerely,

Mike McKenna

Michael McKenna
Manager
Consumer Affairs

MTM:mrx

Enclosure

>>

Employment Standards Administration Wage and Hour Division

General Information on The Fair Labor Standards Act

Child Labor: An employee must be at least **16** years old to work in most non-farm jobs and at least **18** to work in non-farm jobs declared hazardous by the Secretary of Labor. Youths **14** and **15** years old may work outside school hours in various non-manufacturing, non-mining, non-hazardous jobs under the following conditions:

No more than –
> **3** hours on a school day or **18** hours in a school week;
> **8** hours on a non-school day or **40** hours in a non-school week.

Also, work may not begin before 7 a.m. or end after 7 p.m., except from June 1 through Labor Day, when evening hours are extended to 9 p.m. Different rules apply in agricultural employment.

ENFORCEMENT: The Department of Labor may recover back wages, either administratively or through court action, for the employees that have been underpaid in violation of the law. Violations may result in civil or criminal action.

Fines of up to $10,000 per violation may be assessed against employers who violate the child labor provisions of the law and up to $1,000 per violation against employers who willfully or repeatedly violate the minimum wage or overtime pay provisions. The law prohibits discriminating against or discharging workers who file a complaint or participate in any proceedings under the Act.

Note:
• Certain occupations and establishments are exempt from the minimum wage and/or overtime pay provisions.
• Special provisions apply to workers in American Samoa.
• Where state law requires a higher minimum wage, the higher standard applies.

FOR ADDITIONAL INFORMATION, contact the nearest Wage and Hour Division office — listed in most telephone directories under United States Government, Labor Department.

Five-Star Uniforms

P.O. Box 306, San Miguel, NM 87503
Phone:(505) 555-9860 Fax: (505) 555-9861

Date: _____

Firm: _____

ATTN: _____

Address: _____

City, State, Zip: _____

Phone: _____ Fax: _____

Qty.	Item #	Color	Size	Description	Unit Price	Total

Item #	Color	Price Sizes 36–46 Short, Reg & Tall	Price Sizes 48 Short, Reg & Tall; 50 Reg & Tall	Price Sizes 52 Reg & Tall; 54–56 Reg
3399NV	Navy Coveralls	$23.50	$30.00	$33.50
3399KH	Khaki Coveralls	$23.50	$30.00	$33.50
3399GY	Gray Coveralls	$23.50	$30.00	Not Available
3399MB	Medium Blue Coveralls	$23.50	$30.00	Not Available
3399RD	Crimson Red Coveralls	$23.50	$30.00 (no 48 short)	Not Available

Turnaround delivery time 10–14 business days.
Only UPS Ground freight available.

With your help, it's all falling into place.

Corrugated Cardboard

Newspapers

Magazines & Catalogs

Phone Books

Paper & Envelopes

Smooth Cardboard

Cardboard Tubes

EMPTY PIZZA BOX

Pizza Boxes (No Food Scraps)

Cardboard Boxes (Remove Inside Wrappers)

SOAP

CEREAL

Computer Paper

Paper Bags

Paper/Cardboard Egg Cartons (No Styrofoam)

Corrugated Cardboard (Flattened Boxes)

Use Green bins, clear bags or any bin with this Green decal.

Milk & Juice Cartons

Aluminum Products

Metal Cans

COFFEE

Glass Jars

Wire Hangers

Detergent, Shampoo & Lotion Bottles

Plastic Jugs

Household Metal

Empty Aerosol Cans

EMPTY

Plastic & Glass Bottles

Paint Cans (Dried Out/Lid Removed)

Use Blue bins, Blue translucent bags or any bin with this Blue decal.

Empty and rinse all containers; remove caps and lids. Labels are OK.

Caps & Lids

Soiled Paper Cups & Plates

Plastic Rings

Plastic Wrap

Styrofoam

Deli & Salad Bar Containers

Plastic Bags

I ♥ NY

Chinese Take-Out Containers

Batteries

Plastic & Wood Hangers

Paper Towels & Napkins

Light Bulbs

Ceramics & Glassware

Mirrors

Plastic Toys

Yogurt Containers

Non-recyclables/trash

Don't Litter.
City of New York, Rudolph W. Giuliani, Mayor
Department of Sanitation, Kevin P. Farrell, Commissioner
4/01

For more information: (212) 219-8090
www.nyc.gov/sanitation
Printed on recycled paper, of course.

NEW YORK CITY
NYC
RRR
RECYCLES

FOR YOUR HEALTH

Patient: MAYER, PETER   Dr.   JOHNSON, LEON

Medication: MOBIC 7.5 MG TABLET B-I   Pharmacy Phone: (973) 555-1234

Directions: TAKE 1 TABLET DAILY   Rx NO.   382-812X

WHY AM I TAKING THIS DRUG?

For arthritic conditions, pain, inflammation, fever.

HOW DO I STORE THIS?

Store at room temperature away from moisture and sunlight. Do not store in the bathroom.

HOW SHOULD I TAKE IT?

Take with food/antacid as directed. Tell MD of other drugs you use/diseases you have, allergies or if pregnant. Limit alcohol intake.

IF I SHOULD MISS A DOSE?

Take missed dose as soon as remembered but not if it is almost time for the the next dose. Do not "double-up" the doses.

ARE THERE ANY SIDE EFFECTS?

Dizziness, drowsiness. Report eye/ear problems, urine color change, black stools, difficulty breathing, mental changes, sun sensitivity, stomach pain.

Refill Your Prescription On-Line at WWW.FORYOURHEALTH.COM

This information is an educational service and does not address all possible uses, actions, precautions, interactions, or side effects of this medicine. If you desire any additional prescriptions counseling, please ask your pharmacist or your doctor.

FOR YOUR HEALTH

Over-the-Counter Medications are Drugs, Too

Literally thousands of drugs are available for purchase "over-the-counter" (OTC), which means that a person does not need a prescription to purchase them. Just because these drugs can be purchased without a doctor's prescription does not mean they are harmless. Many of these drugs have side effects, which must be listed on the package. Especially for older adults who also may be on prescription medications, taking OTCs may alter the effect of the prescribed medicine. Always check with a pharmacist or physician about possible drug interactions before adding any medication.

A directory of common OTC ingredients, categorized by ailment, is listed below. Only the actual, active ingredients are given. Compare these ingredients with the ingredients listed on the outside of the packages.

Allergies, Coughs, and Colds

Most OTCs for colds or allergies contain a "shotgun" of ingredients aimed at multiple symptoms. Often, a person can take only one ingredient instead of the combinations offered and can then avoid the side effects from the medications they do not need. It does not make sense to take more medication than necessary to relieve symptoms. Remember, these medications will not cure a cold — they only relieve symptoms.

Decongestants: Phenylephrine, ephedrine, phenylpropanolamine (PPA), or other words ending with "-ephrine" or "-edrine."

Antihistamine: Chlorpheniramine or pyrilamine, or often words ending with "-amine."

Expectorants: Glyceryl guaiacolate and potassium iodide. The effectiveness of expectorants is unproved.

Cough suppressant: Dextromethorphan hydrobromide.

Constipation

More than 700 OTC laxative products are available to the American public, making us a "super bowel-conscious" society. Only the most popular types are listed below. As one noted authority pointed out, "It's sometimes better to flush laxatives directly down the toilet without first passing them through the human body."

Bisacodyl, phenolphthalein, castor oil: Stimulant/irritant type of laxatives (the ones which are least desirable).

Epsom salt (magnesium sulfate), magnesium hydroxide, magnesium citrate: Saline cathartics, which remain in the intestines.

Mineral oil, dioctyl sodium sulfosuccinate, dioctyl calcium sulfo-succinate: Fecal softeners which make elimination easier.

Psyllium seed, methylcellulose, sodium carboxymethyl-cellulose, and tragacanth: Bulk forming laxatives, which form a soft bolus of material which promotes bowel movement.

Upset Stomach

Effervescent antacids: Contain sodium bicarbonate (baking soda), potassium bicarbonate, and citric acid. Should be used sparingly and occasionally.

Aluminum hydroxide: An effective antacid that will not cause stomach acid rebound.

Magnesium hydroxide: Often combined with aluminum hydroxide, because this product is a known laxative and antacid.

Simethicone: Also called polydimethylsiloxane. The FDA has ruled this product to be ineffective in relieving gas.

Pain, Fever, and Headache

Aspirin: Probably one of the most important OTC drugs. Americans consume almost 19 billion aspirin tablets per year. Aspirin is effective in reducing fever, pain, and inflammation. Aspirin, however, is associated with increased stomach irritation, bleeding time, and "ringing in the ears."

Acetaminophen: Usually no side effects. Does not cause gastrointestinal bleeding sometimes associated with aspirin. However, taken in large doses or for extended periods, it can cause liver damage.

Ibuprofen: Although touted to be easier on the stomach than aspirin, the prescription formula of this product advises that it be taken with food.

Diarrhea

Although many OTC ingredients are purported to alleviate the symptoms of diarrhea, the FDA has stated that none effectively relieve diarrhea symptoms. Alumina powder, attapulgite, belladonna alkaloids, bismuth salts, calcium carbonate, calcium hydroxide, sodium carboxymethylcellulose, charcoal, kaolin, pectin, salol, and zinc phenolsulfonate are among the most commonly used ingredients in antidiarrheal medication. Most bouts of diarrhea will spontaneously clear. Consult physician if high fever accompanies the diarrhea or if the diarrhea lasts for more than two days.

Apply today for the Adventure Diamond Card

Adventure Diamond offers you these superior benefits:

- **0% introductory APR† on purchases**
- **No annual fee**
- **Up to 2% Moneyback Bonus**
- **Internet Account access and bill payment**
- **Superior 24-hour customer service**
- **$500,000 travel accidental death insurance‡**
- **$25,000 auto rental coverage‡**
- **Plus many more privileges**

Adventure Diamond

6011 0145 7054 1938

J L WEBB

No other card rewards you like the no-annual-fee Adventure Diamond Card. You'll enjoy an unbeatable 0% introductory APR† on purchases! So apply for your Card right away and enjoy no interest on purchases for the next 5 billing periods†.

Plus, you'll receive up to a 2% Moneyback Bonus award*. You will earn a Moneyback Bonus award of up to 1%, paid yearly, based on your annual level and type of purchases. Then exchange your award check for certificates worth double your award amount from select partners (see back).

You'll also enjoy great discounts at our Internet site, superior 24-hour Cardmember service and much more. So apply for your Adventure Diamond today. It's the only Card you'll need!

APPLY TODAY!

There's always something more to Adventure Diamond

†See Important Information Section.
*Certain restrictions apply.
See reverse side for details.

▲ Detach here ▲

Adventure Diamond Card Application

IMPORTANT: PLEASE PRINT USING CAPITAL LETTERS AND COMPLETE ALL INFORMATION.

Step 1 Please tell us about yourself

FIRST   MIDDLE   LAST NAME

DATE OF BIRTH (MO., DAY, YR.) M M D D Y Y

HOME ADDRESS   APT. NO   CITY   STATE   ZIP CODE

HOME TELEPHONE*   WORK TELEPHONE   SOCIAL SECURITY NUMBER*

DO YOU ☐ OWN ☐ RENT   HOUSING PAYMENT* (per month) $ LENGTH OF TIME AT PRESENT ADDRESS   YEARS Y Y Y Y   MONTHS M M
☐ OTHER

ARE YOU A U.S. CITIZEN OR PERMANENT U.S. RESIDENT?   MOTHER'S MAIDEN NAME (for security purposes)
☐ YES ☐ NO

Step 2 Please tell us about your household finances

EMPLOYER

OCCUPATION   HOW LONG?

EMPLOYER'S CITY/STATE/ZIP

DO YOU HAVE A
☐ SAVINGS ACCOUNT
☐ CHECKING ACCOUNT

YOUR ANNUAL SALARY $ ___
PLUS BONUS + $ ___
OTHER HOUSEHOLD INCOME†
TOTAL HOUSEHOLD INCOME† $ |__|,|__|__|__|,|__|__|__|

* This information is required to complete this application.

† Alimony, child support, spouse's income or separate maintenance income need not be disclosed if you do not wish to have it considered as a basis for paying this obligation. Minimum Annual Household Income of $15,000 required for any Adventure Card Account. If you are relying on the income of another person to qualify for an Account and would like to apply with co-applicant, see Important Information section. For highest credit line, please include all sources of Annual Household income.

Step 3 Please sign below

I understand that my credit line will be set after you have reviewed my financial information. I have read and agree to the Important Information on the back. I certify that I am 18 years of age or older and that the information provided is accurate.

Free additional Card (Complete below)
Yes, please send me an additional Card at no extra cost for:

PRINT NAME OF AUTHORIZED USER (FIRST, MIDDLE INITIAL, LAST NAME)

X _____ / ___
SIGNATURE   DATE

Send in your application online at Adventurecard.com today.

Pasadena Classified
Line Advertising Coupon

Yes!

*Run My Pre-Paid Line Classified Ad
In The Next Issue $10.00 For 20 Words
20¢ For Each Additional Word*

Office Use Only	
Operator	# Weeks

Category _____

Name _____

Address _____

Telephone _____

Cost per week _____

Number of weeks _____

Total amount _____

My payment of $ _____ enclosed

Please charge my Visa/MC

Card # _____

Expiration date _____

Mail to: Pasadena Classifieds, P.O. Box 950, Monrovia, CA 91016 • Classified Deadline Tuesday 11:00 am

Workbook Answer Key

Note: In communicative exercises where several answers are possible, this answer key contains some examples of correct answers, not all possible answers. Any valid answer in this type of exercise should be accepted.

UNIT 1

Exercise 1

1. awful   2. gorgeous   3. amazing   4. beautiful
5. horrible   6. incredible   7. You're
New word: weather

Exercise 2

2. Yes, it certainly is. Just awful.   3. You know, I don't think we've met. I'm Tina Roche. I live in 3B. 4. Nice to meet you, Tina. I'm Amy Kwan. I live in 5J.   5. Nice to meet you too, Amy. How long have you been living here?   6. My husband and I moved here about a year ago.   7. Where did you live before that?   8. In Austin, Texas.

Exercise 3

1. c   2. f   3. e   4. b   5. d   6. a

Exercise 4

Conversations will vary. Following is one example of what students may write.

1. A: Hi, Boris. What are you doing?

    B: I'm filling out this job application.

    A: How long have you been looking for a job?

    B: _For two months_. This application is for a full-time job as _a mechanic_.

    A: Wow! That's great. Do you like _fixing cars_?

    B: Yes, I do. And I'm pretty good at _working with my hands_. But I need a favor. Would you mind writing me a letter of recommendation?

    A: _Not at all_. I'd be glad to.

    B: _Thanks so much. I appreciate it_.

Exercise 5

2. have been driving   3. has, been working
4. have been living   5. have, been looking
6. have been taking   7. has been talking

Exercise 6

1. for   2. since   3. since   4. for   5. since   6. for
7. for   8. since

Exercise 7

2. How long has Alan been driving a pickup truck?
3. How long have you been shopping at the international supermarket?   4. How long have the technicians been repairing computers?   5. How long has Tatiana been making her own clothes?
6. How long has your back been hurting?

Exercise 8

2. living   3. doing   4. studying   5. making
6. working

Exercise 9

Answers will vary.

Exercise 10

1. a   2. b   3. b   4. a   5. a   6. b

Exercise 11

1. f   2. d   3. a   4. e   5. c   6. g   7. b

Exercise 12

Answers will vary.

Exercise 13

Answers will vary.

Exercise 14

1. Not OK   2. Not OK   3. OK   4. Not OK   5. OK
6. Not OK   7. OK   8. Not OK   9. Not OK   10. OK

Exercise 15

Answers will vary.

Exercise 16

1. True   2. False   3. False   4. False   5. True

Exercise 17

Answers will vary.

<hr>

UNIT 2

Exercise 1

1. e   2. c   3. d   4. f   5. b   6. h   7. a   8. g

Exercise 2

2. end   3. elevator   4. hall   5. second   6. right
7. in

Exercise 3

1. between   2. at the corner of   3. across from
4. next to   5. at the corner of   6. on, across from

Exercise 4

Answers will vary.

Exercise 5

Following are possible answers. Your students may
write other answers that are also acceptable.

2. Don't walk   3. Let's not drive   4. Call   5. Take
6. Please go   7. Why don't, go out to eat   8. Please
tell

Exercise 6

1. Let's ask the mechanic for directions.   2. Let's
not go out to eat tonight.   3. Take the stairs to the
basement.   4. Please join us for coffee after the
meeting.   5. Why don't we walk to the mall after
class?

Exercise 7

Answers will vary.

Exercise 8

Following are possible answers. Your students may
write other answers that are also acceptable.

1. Tell, to take   2. Ask, to come   3. Tell, to go up
4. Ask, to cook   5. Tell, to ask

Exercise 9

1. b   2. b   3. a   4. a   5. a

Exercise 10

1. e   2. a   3. d   4. b   5. f   6. c

Exercise 11

2. a   3. c   4. c   5. c   6. a

Exercise 12

Answers will vary.

Exercise 13

Marvin Street, Grant Street

Exercise 14

Answers will vary. Following is one example of
what students may write.

Go south on Truman Street. Walk two blocks to
Prospect Street. Take the number 3 bus going east.
Get off at Taylor Street. Walk north on Taylor two
blocks. My house is at the corner of Taylor Street
and Pike Street.

See you on Sunday at two o'clock.

Exercise 15

1. Marian   2. dinner   3. May 11   4. 6:30
5. 35 Grove Street   6. RSVP   7. call   8. 929-3430

Exercise 16

Answers will vary.

<hr>

UNIT 3

Exercise 1

1. a fryer   2. a power saw   3. a drill   4. a printer
5. a freezer   6. a floor polisher   7. a sewing
machine   8. a fax machine

Exercise 2

1. trouble   2. printer   3. jammed   4. call   5. fault
6. speak up   7. under   8. purchased   9. warranty

Exercise 3

1. c   2. a   3. e   4. b   5. d

Exercise 4

Conversations will vary. Following is one example of what students may write.

1. A: I can't believe it!

   B: What's the matter?

   A: The _copier_ is _jammed_.

   B: Again? That's the third time this week!

   A: I know. And it was just _serviced_ last month.

   B: Well, we'd better _write up a repair or replace order_.

2. A: Can you help me?

   B: Sure. _What's the matter_?

   A: Well, my computer _is frozen_ and I have to _check stock_.

   B: Did you try _calling the help line_?

   A: No, I didn't. I'll do that right now.

Exercise 5

2. bought   3. broken   4. fixed   5. sent   6. cleaned
7. serviced   8. written, repaired

Exercise 6

1. was checked   2. are cleaned / 're cleaned
3. was taken   4. was serviced   5. were repaired
6. were made   7. was purchased

Exercise 7

2. Why was this computer serviced?   3. Where was the sander repaired?   4. When were these sewing machines cleaned?   5. When were those pictures taken?   6. Where was your camera made?
7. How was the letter sent?

Exercise 8

Answers will vary.

Exercise 9

1. b   2. a   3. a   4. a   5. b

Exercise 10

Item: Kenisco Deep Fryer 5000		
Date	Repair	Under Warranty?
March 4, 2003	Basket replaced	(Y) N
(Dates will vary.)	_temperature control fixed_	(Y) N

Exercise 11

1. False   2. True   3. False   4. True   5. False
6. True   7. False

Exercise 12

Answers will vary. Following is one example of what students may write.

Lisa: Oh, no! I can't believe what I just did!

YOU _What did you do?_

Lisa: I was trying to fix this machine, and I broke the handle. This is the second time I've done that this month. What should I do?

YOU _Maybe you'd better tell someone._

Lisa: I don't know. Maybe I should just forget about it. I don't want anyone to know I broke it.

YOU _Don't worry. It's always good to speak up._

Exercise 13

1. purchase   2. replace   3. free   4. purchaser
5. parts   6. magnetron tube   7. Microtastic
8. labor

Exercise 14

2. When did you purchase this item?   3. Where was this food processor purchased?   4. Was this product received as a gift?   5. Where will this food processor be used?   6. How many other food processors have you owned?   7. What was the price paid for this food processor?   8. What made you decide to purchase a Kitchenelle Food Processor?

UNIT 4

Exercise 1

2. convenient   3. a cookie   4. zippers   5. below standard   6. complaints

Exercise 2

1. carry   2. anymore   3. complained   4. defective
5. shame   6. great   7. in the back   8. have a look

Exercise 3

Answers will vary.

Exercise 4

Conversations will vary. Following is one example of what students may write.

1. A: Can I help you?

   B: Yes, please. I bought this _air conditioner_ yesterday and it's not working. I think it's _defective_.

   A: I'm sorry. Would you like to get a _replacement_?

   B: No, thanks. I'd rather have a _refund_. Is that OK?

   A: _Absolutely_. I'll just need to see your receipt.

2. A: Have the Quality brand _shower heads_ been discontinued?

   B: Yes, they have.

   A: Why?

   B: _They're not up to code_.

   A: That's _a shame_. They were _great_.

   B: That's what everyone said. Can I show you something else?

   A: _OK_.

Exercise 5

2. He used to take the bus to work. Now he drives his own car to work.   3. He used to live with three friends. Now he lives with his wife and baby.
4. He used to spend all his money. Now he saves his money in the bank.   5. He used to speak only Spanish. Now he speaks Spanish and English.

Exercise 6

Answers will vary.

Exercise 7

1. b   2. b   3. a

Exercise 8

2. as expensive as High-Tech tools   3. as safe as Infant World cribs   4. as exciting as the city
5. as effective as Bug-Dead

Exercise 9

Answers will vary.

Exercise 10

1. a   2. a   3. a   4. b   5. b

Exercise 11

1. attendant   2. customer   3. attendant
4. attendant   5. customer   6. attendant
7. attendant   8. customer   9. customer

Exercise 12

1. recalling   2. 70,000   3. defective   4. dealer
5. repair

Exercise 13

Answers will vary. Following is one example of what students may write.

1. He has a 2000 Hurricane.   2. There is a recall.
3. He needs to bring his car to any Worldwide Motors dealer.

Exercise 14

1. False   2. True   3. False   4. False   5. True

Exercise 15

Answers will vary. Following is one example of what students may write.

1. Let the cans dry and dispose of with household trash.   2. Take them to a local scrap metal dealer or auto repair shop.   3. Take them to a Household Chemical Clean-up Day location.

Exercise 16

Letters will vary.

UNIT 5

Exercise 1

1. tips   2. time, half   3. room, board   4. trip
5. minimum wage   6. double time

Exercise 2

Answers will vary.

Exercise 3

2. You did? That's terrific! What kind of job is it?

3. I'll be a mover for Hercules Moving Company.

4. They're a great company. Is it full-time or part-time?

5. Full-time. Nine to five.

6. And how will you be paid?

7. By the hour.

8. Plus tips?

Exercise 4

1. e   2. f   3. a   4. c   5. b   6. g   7. d

Exercise 5

Conversations will vary. Following is one example of what students may write.

1. A: _Dan_? Hi, it's _Tina_. I'm sorry, but I have to reschedule our _lunch meeting_. I _need to run an errand_.

   B: _That's OK_. When do you want to reschedule?

   A: Will _tomorrow afternoon at 12:30_ work?

   B: _Sure_. That's great for me. I'll see you _tomorrow afternoon_.

   A: Thanks, _Dan_.

2. A: Excuse me. Do you know if it's OK to _speak to my friend_?

   B: Well, unless it's an emergency, the supervisors expect you to do that _on your own time_.

   A: And what if I need to _make a phone call_?

   B: It's also not a good idea to do that on company time. Why don't you do that _at break time_?

Exercise 6

2. remember to ask   3. Be sure to let   4. plan to be
5. want to work   6. don't forget to have

Exercise 7

2. Why did Jisela decide to take the job?   3. What did you forget to ask Mr. Kwon about?   4. Where do you need to go at break time?   5. What do they want to do tonight?

Exercise 8

Answers will vary.

Exercise 9

Answers will vary. Following is one example of what students may write.

2. her to eat   3. us to make   4. me to reschedule
5. him to ask   6. them to finish

Exercise 10

2. Pablo's boss reminds him to reschedule the meeting.   3. His co-worker, Barry, tells him to take lots of pictures.   4. Pablo asks Marcia to open his mail while he's gone.   5. His co-worker, Hanna, wants him to bring her a Mexican blanket.

Exercise 11

1. b   2. b   3. b   4. b   5. a

Exercise 12

1. OK   2. Not OK   3. OK   4. Not OK   5. OK
6. Not OK   7. OK

Exercise 13

1. minimum wage   2. exempt   3. tipped   4. tips, make up   5. overtime

Exercise 14

1. no   2. yes   3. no

Exercise 15

2. number   3. hour   4. full-time   5. plus
6. overtime   7. double time   8. years   9. time and a half   10. week

Exercise 16

1. baby-sitter   2. office assistant   3. parking attendant

Exercise 17

Position	regular pay	time and a half	double time
medical billing assistant	$5.20	_$7.80_	_$10.40_
busboy (before tips)	_$4.10_	_$6.15_	$8.20
school custodian	_$7.50_	$11.25	_$15.00_

Exercise 18

Answers will vary. Following is one example of what students may write.

Heather: Which job are you interested in?

(YOU) _I'm interested in the mechanic job._

Heather: OK. What would you like to know about the job?

(YOU) _What are the hours?_

Heather: It's full-time. Monday through Friday. The job starts at 7 a.m. and ends at 3 p.m. You might have to work later on some days. If you do, you'll get overtime pay.

(YOU) _And could you please tell me what the pay is?_

Heather: We pay minimum wage to start, with raises for good performance. When would you like to come in for an interview?

(YOU) _How's tomorrow morning at 10:00?_

Heather: That's good for me. I'll see you then.

(YOU) _OK. Thanks._

UNIT 6

Exercise 1

1. coupon   2. jars   3. container   4. mistake   5. bag
6. bargain   7. bottle   New word: package

Exercise 2

Answers will vary.

Exercise 3

1. loaf   2. crackers   3. boxes   4. two   5. mistake
6. each   7. ounce   8. bargain   9. coupon   10. sale price

Exercise 4

Conversations will vary. Following is one example of what students may write.

A: I really need to buy _office supplies_ but I don't have time to _go shopping_.

B: Can I make a suggestion? Why don't you _order them by phone or online_?

A: How do I do that?

B: Call _1-800-office1_. Or you can log on to _office1.com_.

A: That's a great idea. Thanks!

Exercise 5

Answers will vary.

Exercise 6

2. must not eat   3. must like   4. must love   5. must have

Exercise 7

Sentences will vary. Following are examples of what students may write.

2. He must not have a car.   3. He must be sick.
4. They must get tips.   5. She must get great bargains.

Exercise 8

Sentences will vary. Following are examples of what students may write.

2. He must be unemployed. / He must need a job.
3. It must not be working.

Exercise 9

1. What a terrible warranty!   2. What expensive shower heads!   3. What a delicious dinner!
4. What a gigantic house!   5. What a nice letter of recommendation.

Exercise 10

Answers will vary. Following is one example of what students may write.

2. What a gorgeous dress!   3. What a bargain!
4. What a great meal!   5. What awful weather!
6. What an incredible selection!

Exercise 11

1. a   2. b   3. b   4. a   5. b

Exercise 12

1. e   2. f   3. d   4. a   5. b   6. c

Exercise 13

1. b   2. a   3. e   4. c   5. d

Exercise 14

1. a   2. a   3. b   4. b   5. a   6. a

Exercise 15

2. 10 cents per ounce   3. 3 dollars per pound
4. 30 cents per pad   5. 25 cents per ounce
6. 60 cents per battery

Exercise 16

Answers will vary.

Exercise 17

1. f   2. a   3. e   4. c   5. d   6. b

Exercise 18

Submitted by	(Answers will vary.)		
Company name	State Bank		
Billing address	1440 Commerce Street, Cleveland, Ohio		

ITEM NUMBER	QTY	UM	DESCRIPTION
425BP	3	DZ	medium blue ballpoint pens
671BB	2	IN	2" black vinyl binders
593ST	2	RL	tape
180IC	4	PK	4" X 6" index cards
247JC	3	BX	jumbo paper clips

UNIT 7

Exercise 1

1. park in the managers' lot   2. bring a dog to the park   3. turn down the TV   4. put the trash cans here   5. turn right on red   6. move your car

Exercise 2

Answers will vary.

Exercise 3

1. c   2. e   3. b   4. a   5. d

Exercise 4

Conversations will vary. Following is one example of what students may write.

1. A: Hi, _Carmen_. How _are you_?

    B: _Not bad_. What's new with you?

    A: Well, _I just got a promotion_!

    B: Wow! _Congratulations_! That _is_ big news.

2. A: What's wrong? You look really _depressed_.

    B: Actually, _I lost my job_.

    A: _Oh, I'm so sorry to hear that_. Can I do anything to help you?

    B: _Not really. But thanks for offering_.

Exercise 5

Answers will vary.

Exercise 6

2. It's illegal to smoke in the building.   3. It's wonderful to get married outdoors in spring.
4. It's not / It isn't always easy to meet new people.
5. It's impolite to talk loudly on the phone.   6. It's really convenient to buy clothes online.

Exercise 7

Answers will vary.

Exercise 8

Answers will vary.

Exercise 9

1. a   2. b   3. b   4. a   5. a

Exercise 10

1. d   2. e   3. a   4. b   5. c

Exercise 11

2. b   3. a   4. c   5. b   6. a

Exercise 12

1. c   2. g   3. a   4. e   5. d   6. b   7. f

Exercise 13

1. a   2. b   3. b   4. b   5. a

Exercise 14

Sentences can be written in any order.

2. It's illegal to park between the signs.   3. It's illegal to litter.   4. It's illegal to not wear a seat belt.
5. It's illegal to park Monday to Friday, 6 a.m. to 6 p.m.   6. It's illegal not to leash, gutter, and clean up after your dog.

UNIT 8

Exercise 1

2. f   3. a   4. e   5. b   6. c

Exercise 2

1. fish   2. spoiled   3. sell-by date   4. return
5. receipt   6. rare   7. medium   8. fresh
9. take it back

Exercise 3

1. dosage   2. label   3. sheet   4. instructions
5. warnings   6. prescription   7. expires   8. capsule

Exercise 4

1. c   2. d   3. a   4. b

Exercise 5

Conversations will vary. Following is one example of what students may write.

A: I picked up the prescription for your _rash_.

B: Great, thanks. I really need it. What are the directions?

A: _Apply twice a day_.

B: _Twice a day_?

A: That's right.

B: Are there any other instructions?

A: Yes, they're on _the patient information sheet_.

Exercise 6

2. his   3. your   4. my   5. our   6. her

Exercise 7

2. Is Mrs. Singh's prescription ready?   3. This bag's sell-by date was three weeks ago.   4. The pharmacists' uniforms are white and blue.
5. These customers' complaints were taken care of by Piotr. / Piotr took care of these customers' complaints.

Exercise 8

2. The high chair is hers.   3. The shower heads are theirs.   4. The moving van is his.   5. The cash register is hers.

Exercise 9

1. our   2. Your   3. My, hers   4. her   5. yours
6. mine, theirs

Exercise 10

1. Tony   2. Lauren   3. Henry   4. Mindy   5. Tristen
6. Tasha

Exercise 11

1. a   2. a   3. b   4. a   5. a

Exercise 12

1. True   2. False   3. True   4. False

Exercise 13

2. before, after   3. cooked   5. color   6. refrigerator
8. hot   9. red   10. clean   13. bag   14. sponges

Exercise 14

Answers will vary.

Exercise 15

1. False   2. True   3. True   4. False   5. True
6. True

Exercise 16

1. d   2. f   3. b   4. e   5. a   6. c

Exercise 17

Answers will vary.

Exercise 18

_8 a.m._: 1 Aplex, _10 a.m._: 1 Prilex, 1 Epicillin;
noon: 2 Mednizone; _2 p.m._: 1 Prilex;
_6 p.m._: 2 Mednizone; _8 p.m._: 1 Prilex, 1 Epicillin;
_10 p.m._: 1 Nox

UNIT 9

Exercise 1

1. Good news   2. Bad news   3. Bad news   4. Good news   5. Bad news   6. Good news   7. Bad news
8. Good news

Exercise 2

1. right   2. buy   3. interest rate   4. application
5. around   6. brochure

Exercise 3

1. c   2. e   3. g   4. f   5. b   6. d   7. a

Exercise 4

Conversations will vary. Following is one example of what students may write.

1. A: I got some _good_ news today.

   B: Really? What is it?

   A: The bank _approved our loan application_.

   B: _That's fantastic_.

2. A: Have you ever been behind on your _credit card payments_?

B: Yes, once. Why? What happened?

A: Oh, I got in over my head, and now they might _cancel my card_.

B: I'm sorry to hear that. How far behind are you?

A: _Three months_.

B: Well, if I were you, I'd _call a credit counseling service_.

A: Maybe you're right.

Exercise 5

2. 'd buy / would buy, could   3. closed, 'd have to / would have to   4. wouldn't be / would not be, didn't have / did not have   5. were, would, put   6. got, 'd get / would get

Exercise 6

2. If I had children, I'd buy the larger package. 3. If we used a credit card, we'd be in debt.   4. If our bank raised its fees, we'd go to another bank. 5. If they owned a house, they'd have a mortgage.

Exercise 7

Following are possible answers. Your students may write other answers that are also acceptable.

2. he'd walk to work   3. he'd get a full-time job 4. he'd make more money   5. they'd start having children

Exercise 8

2. keep getting   3. keep forgetting   4. keeps lowering   5. keeps calling   6. keeps spoiling 7. keep closing   8. keep spending

Exercise 9

1. b   2. a   3. a   4. b   5. b

Exercise 10

1. True   2. I don't know   3. False   4. False   5. True

Exercise 11

1. b   2. c   3. c   4. b

Exercise 12

Answers will vary.

Exercise 13

Answers will vary.

Exercise 14

1. It's Roseanne Calderon's.   2. She's one month behind.   3. $157.18   4. By May 18, 2003.   5. With a check or money order.

Exercise 15

Roseanne Calderon 420 W. 95th St. New York, NY 10025	DATE _5 / 11 / 03_	**304**
PAY TO THE ORDER OF ___ _Credit Express_ ___		$ 157.18
One hundred and fifty-seven and ¹⁸⁄₁₀₀ ___		DOLLARS
Money Tree Bank 512 E. 44 st. New York, NY 10017		
MEMO _ACCT # 7819 622 4700_	_Roseanne Calderon_	
1 : 041000689 : 1 60660668' 304		

UNIT 10

Exercise 1

1. moved   2. leave   3. hands-on   4. references 5. opportunities   6. conflict   7. salary   8. call

Exercise 2

1. b   2. d   3. e   4. a   5. c

Exercise 3

Answers will vary.

Exercise 4

Conversations will vary. Following is one example of what students may write.

A: Well, _Maria_, you've had a _good first year_ with us. You're really doing a _great_ job.

B: Thank you, Ms. _Cezus_. I'm _happy to hear that_.

A: _Please_ call me _Joan_. Everyone else does.

B: _OK_.

A: Now, I've been meaning to ask you about where you see yourself in _two years_.

B: Well, I think I'd like to be _a supervisor_, but I'm not sure. Are there any opportunities for _training_?

A: Absolutely.

Exercise 5

Answers will vary.

Exercise 6

2. 'm leaving   3. want   4. fax   5. are, doing
6. don't call   7. have   8. 's talking

Exercise 7

Answers will vary.

Exercise 8

Note: For questions 1–3, the number of years will vary depending on current date.

1. has lived / has been living, [four years]
2. has worked / has been working [2 years]
3. has lived / has been living [three years]
4. has studied / has been studying, September 1998
5. has worked / has been working, May 2002

Exercise 9

Answers will vary.

Exercise 10

1. a   2. b   3. a   4. a   5. b

Exercise 11

1. He is telling Lisa about his performance review.
2. Fred's workers are unhappy because they don't feel like Fred appreciates them.   3. Fred's boss suggests that he praise them more often.

Exercise 12

1. c   2. a   3. b   4. b   5. b

Exercise 13

1. False   2. True   3. True   4. False   5. False
6. True

Exercise 14

1. a   2. b   3. b   4. b   5. (Answers will vary.)

Exercise 15

Answers will vary.

Skills for test taking